YOGA & PILATES FOR EVERYONE

YOGA & PILATES FOR EVERYONE

FRANÇOISE BARBIRA FREEDMAN, BEL GIBBS,
DORIEL HALL, EMILY KELLY,
JONATHAN MONKS, JUDY SMITH

HERMES HOUSE

This edition is published by Hermes House

Hermes House is an imprint of Anness Publishing Ltd
Hermes House, 88–89 Blackfriars Road, London SE1 8HA
tel. 020 7401 2077; fax 020 7633 9499
info@anness.com

A CIP catalogue record for this book is available from the British Library.

Publisher Joanna Lorenz
Editorial Directors Judith Simons and Helen Sudell
Senior Editor Sarah Ainley
Project Editors Katy Bevan, Simona Hill, Ann Kay, Debra Mayhew and Catherine Stewart
Designers Ruth Hope, Adelle Morris, Ann Samuel, Anita Schnable and Lisa Tai
Photography John Freeman, Christine Hanscomb, Alistair Hughes, Michelle Garrett, Clare Park and Stephen Swain
Additional Photography Bonieventure Bagalue
Photographer's Assistants Alex Dow and Lisa Shalet
Photography Stylist Sue Duckworth
Illustrators David Cook (Linden Artists), Sam Elmhurst and Lucy Grossmith
Production Controller Pedro Nelson

Previously published in four separate volumes: **Meditation**, **Pilates and Yoga**, **The Complete Guide to Yoga** and **Yoga for Pregnancy and to Get Back Into Shape**

10 9 8 7 6 5 4 3 2 1

Contents

Introduction 6

IYENGAR YOGA 10
Iyengar Basics 14
Standing Asanas 24
Seated Asanas 46
Twists 62
Inverted Asanas 70
Supine and Prone Asanas 78
Routine Practice 92
Yoga Therapy 110

PILATES 144
Warming Up and Mobility Exercises 158
Abdominal and Back Exercises 166
Upper and Lower Body Exercises 178
Stretches 190
Making Pilates a Part of Your Life 200

YOGA-PILATES 228
Core Strength 232
Standing Postures 258
Twisted Postures 282
Balanced Postures 294
Seated Postures 308
Sequences 330

YOGA FOR PREGNANCY AND AFTER 348
Yoga for Conception and Early Pregnancy 352
Yoga for Mid-term Pregnancy 364
Yoga For Late Pregnancy and Birth 374
Postnatal Yoga 384

YOGA FOR CHILDREN 394
What's it All About? 398
Animal Parade 420
Putting it All Together 448
Quiet Time 464

MEDITATION 478
The Practice of Meditation 482

Societies and Useful Addresses 506
Acknowledgements 508
Index 509

Introduction

More and more of us are looking for fitness programmes that address not just the body but the mind, too. We are turning to holistic forms of exercise that aim to develop the whole person. Yoga and Pilates are the two leading forms of mind-body fitness taught in the West. Practised regularly, they can benefit every aspect of our lives, from our posture to our moods, and our physical well-being to our sense of happiness and peace.

Yoga and Pilates have evolved as they have been taught and studied, and as our understanding of the body has developed. They continue to be refined as people seek new ways of maintaining their well-being despite busy lifestyles. Yoga-Pilates – featured in one of the sections of this book – is the latest incarnation of mind-body exercise: a practice that draws on both systems to create a dynamic and fully integrated workout.

This book gives you all you need to establish a holistic exercise programme for yourself, or for your family, at any stage of your lives. There are six separate sections:
Iyengar Yoga
Pilates
Yoga-Pilates
Yoga for Pregnancy and After
Yoga for Children
Meditation

Each section has been written by respected practitioners in that particular field. Each can be used to help you develop and deepen your understanding of the practice.

The benefits of yoga

Yoga is the best possible exercise there is for improving suppleness. However, yoga postures are more than physical poses; they work on the mind and spirit, and promote increased awareness, vitality and inner peace.

There are many forms of yoga: astanga, for example, is flowing and dynamic, while Shivananda is very gentle. Iyengar yoga, covered in the first section of this book, is the most precise method. It was developed in the 1960s by an advanced practitioner, B.K.S. Iyengar, who wanted to

below left and right A student of Iyengar yoga practises a standing posture (left); a Pilates exercise for toning the triceps (right).
opposite Namaste is the traditional greeting among yogis.

integrate modern thinking about the body with the ancient system he had studied for many years. Iyengar emphasizes the importance of correct alignment at all times.

In the Iyengar section of this book, as in the other sections, step-by-step photographs show clearly how to approach each posture and provide a useful reference for practice at home. There are also suggestions for ways of modifying the movements for beginners and those who are less flexible – all the Iyengar poses can be modified. Equipment, such as blocks and straps, is used to help practitioners get into postures without straining joints or overstretching muscles. This attention to detail makes Iyengar yoga very safe, provided that it is always practised with care and with respect to the body's limitations.

The classical postures of Iyengar yoga slow and deepen the breathing, allow energy to flow freely and bring a "feel-good" factor to the body, while also relaxing and resting the mind. They are designed to promote strength, balance, flexibility and relaxation. When you begin to practise them regularly, you will be amazed at how quickly your body begins to shed the tightness and tension that have been restricting it, leading to a wonderful sense of release and well-being.

It's important to make sure that you are achieving the right alignments when you first take up yoga, so there is no substitute for attending a class where your movements can be observed and checked by a qualified teacher. This book is designed for use in conjunction with regular classes.

What is Pilates?

Pilates is a very focused form of exercise that helps to strengthen and tone the body without automatically adding muscle bulk. Over time, it helps to develop a sculpted, streamlined physique.

Put at its simplest, Pilates is based on the idea that bad habits or injuries lead to various imbalances and weaknesses in the body. Controlled, repetitive actions are used to realign and re-educate the body. Mental focus and breathing techniques are also very important to Pilates practice, used to encourage graceful movements and improved awareness.

The Pilates system was created by Joseph Pilates in the early 20th century. Pilates developed an interest in fitness during a childhood dogged by sickness in Germany. He studied many forms of exercise, including yoga, gymnastics and body-building, in order to improve his health. Eventually, Pilates used his knowledge and understanding of how the body works to create his own exercise method, which he said could either rehabilitate an injured body or strengthen a healthy one.

Pilates exercises have been modified over the years, but teachers hold true to the fundamental ideas of Joseph Pilates. They emphasize the importance of "core strength" – a stable centre – as well as good alignment and posture. Concentration and controlled breathing help to make Pilates an effective method of relaxation as well as physical fitness.

Yoga-Pilates: an integrated system

You can combine yoga and Pilates to create a fitness programme tailored to your individual needs. Yoga and Pilates naturally share many features. For example, certain Pilates exercises are based on yoga poses, and both practices emphasize the importance of good breathing, awareness, and of working within your own abilities.

Yoga-Pilates aims to take the best from both methods, combining the core strength that is the fundamental idea of Pilates with the flexibility and versatility of yoga.

In a sense, you can use Pilates to form a firm foundation on which to build with yoga. In practice, this might mean warming up with Pilates, then moving on to a series of yoga postures in one session. The book provides several sequences that you can use and adapt as you become more aware of your body's needs and strengths.

You don't need to know yoga or Pilates in order to do yoga-Pilates; however, if you are already a student of one or the other, yoga-Pilates can show you new ways of working your mind and body. For example, practising Pilates may bring extra strength and stability to your yoga, while incorporating yoga into your Pilates workout can help with relaxation and breathing.

For the expectant mother

This book also includes yoga sequences and exercises designed specifically for women hoping to conceive and for those who already have. Yoga can bring enormous benefits at every stage of conception, pregnancy, birth and parenthood. The gentle movements of yoga will help your

above This gentle, well-supported yoga pose is part of an exercise that has been designed to ease the back pain and strain that so often accompany pregnancy – especially in the later stages when the weight of the growing baby really makes itself felt.

pregnant body to "open out" to accommodate your growing baby. Your abdominal muscles and pelvic floor muscles will become very elastic, so that the baby can be born. All the emphasis in prenatal yoga practice is upon facilitating this opening and elasticity. After birth, the situation is reversed. It is time to "close up" your body while maintaining and developing the physical suppleness and the openness of heart and mind that birth brought. This is a gradual process, but by about nine months after the birth you can expect to feel better than you felt before.

The yoga-for-pregnancy approach featured in this book enables women to "birth lightly", increasing the body's suppleness and making use of the breath to increase the efficacy of uterine contractions in labour. This allows you to release fear and tension while your baby is born. Yoga breathing exercises develop inner strength, stamina and serenity, by acting on the nervous system. As you gradually develop the habit of deep, slow breathing, you encourage your nervous system to make you feel good about yourself and your life.

The prenatal yoga sequences featured here focus on opening the body to let energy flow freely, to nurture your growing baby. Gentle stretches, working with your deepening breath, foster the fluidity and flexibility of your changing body, while developing strong supportive muscles and a healthy cardiovascular system. You will also find sequences aimed at opening up the body in preparation for conception and also for getting your body back in shape after the birth.

Remember that, with yoga, Pilates and yoga-Pilates, as with any form of exercise, certain poses are unsafe if you are pregnant, or at a certain stage of pregnancy. Always seek medical advice and a teacher qualified in instructing pregnant women.

above Lying stretched out on the floor, on your back, is the perfect preparation for meditation. In this position you can relax fully and focus your attention on the movement of the breath within your body. Meditation will greatly enhance the practice of disciplines such as yoga and Pilates.

Starting young

Yoga is indeed a way of life, and it's never too soon to begin. If you have children, you can involve them in your practice too – in doing so you will be bestowing a gift whose benefits will last them all their lives. The penultimate section of the book shows how to capture young imaginations with adaptations of the asanas, creating easy animal postures, group activities and games that everyone can join in.

Mind as well as body

Making yoga part of your daily routine will bring a clearer mind and a more open-hearted acceptance of life, opening the way to the state of meditation. A brief introduction to meditative practice is included at the close of this book to help you approach this expansion of consciousness.

The meditative section in this book is based on the work of the ancient Indian sage Patanjali, said by many to have authored a set of texts on yoga meditation called the *Yoga Sutras*, on which most of the yoga taught today is based. Patanjali is thought to have lived around 300BC (although it is certain that yoga itself is far older than this) and the writings attributed to him fuse the many yogic traditions that existed in his time to create a coherent philosophical system. The Sutras were then handed down orally from teachers to students for generations, before being written down in Sanskrit.

right In yoga, attention to detail is needed to perfect your alignment. Pilates and Yoga-Pilates may help to bring added strength to your practice, and enable you to target specific areas of weakness.

Stay motivated

Almost everyone who exercises admits that it can be difficult to keep motivated. This book aims to give you the greatest possible choice and flexibility, so that you can develop exactly the right exercise programme for you. Once you have developed an understanding of your body, you'll be able to take elements from the different disciplines, and create workouts to meet your needs perfectly and even to suit your mood.

Iyengar Yoga

Here are classic yoga postures that are suitable for all levels of fitness and flexibility, as well as different age groups. The benefits include a calmer mind and supple body.

Judy Smith

What is Yoga?

Yoga is a practical philosophy, not a religion, and requires no allegiance to any particular system of belief. The word "yoga" comes from the Sanskrit word "yug", meaning to join, yoke or unite. It is a traditional Indian philosophy that involves the integration of the physical and spiritual in order to achieve a sense of well-being. This synthesis and inseparability of the body and mind leads to a greater connection to one's consciousness.

In the practice of yoga, the body is linked to the movement, mind and breath to bring about a feeling of balance, relaxation and harmony. The practitioner uses the physical self to refine the mind. Through this thorough training of the body and thought, one is taught to awaken every cell of one's self and one's soul.

The practice of physical postures (asanas) improves a variety of ailments, strengthens and tones muscles and develops flexibility. Various movements in the postures result in blood saturating, nourishing and cleansing the remotest parts of the body. Psychologically, yoga increases concentration, stills the mind and promotes a feeling of balance, tranquillity and contentment.

There is a difference between yoga and other physical exercises. Yoga asanas are psycho-physiological, while physical jerks are purely external. Asanas develop body awareness, muscles and flexibility, as well as generating internal awareness and stabilizing the mind. In physical exercises, body movements may be done with external precision, whereas in yoga, together with the precision, a deeper awareness is awakened, which brings about balance in body and spirit.

Mr B.K.S. Iyengar has systematized over 200 classical yoga asanas, the result of which is Iyengar yoga. This version of yoga practice is methodical and progressive, and emphasizes precision, detailed correctness and absolute safety. The postures have been structured and categorized to allow students of all levels of fitness and ability to progress surely and safely from basic to more challenging postures and, by so doing, to gain flexibility, strength and sensitivity in mind, body and spirit.

Iyengar yoga, with its attention to detail, challenges both the head and the physical frame, and enables those who practise it to exercise control and discipline in all aspects of life. It is advisable to practise every day, but it is easy to tailor the routines suggested in this section to suit the amount of time available. It is best to set aside a similar time each morning or evening to practise and to make this part of your daily routine. Not only will your posture and flexibility improve, but you will became physically stronger, calmer and a more balanced and centred human being.

above Regular yoga practice benefits all aspects of your being, strengthening your body, renewing your energy, calming your mind and brightening your spirit.

If you have not practised yoga before, the advice in this section should be used in conjunction with the expert guidance of a trained teacher. Joining a class is a motivating and enjoyable way to learn the postures and ensures that you are practising correctly.

Everyone can be helped by yoga, from the elderly and children to people with minor complaints and various problems, both physical and mental. When they begin, their

right When first learning the more challenging postures, it is a great support to have an attentive teacher.
below The constant practice of yoga brings flexibility, freedom from tension and peace of mind.

bodies and minds may be stiff and unyielding, but they will walk out of the class taller and with their entire beings radiating serenity and peace.

Practising the asanas and pranayama (breathing) with honesty and diligence, intelligence and awareness, will bring about clarity, energy and serenity in all aspects of your life. The asanas and programmes offered in this section are suitable for both beginners and more experienced practitioners and should be repeated and practised as often as circumstances allow, anything from an hour a week to several hours a day. Practised regularly, Iyengar yoga will bring you joy, light and happiness as you travel along your path to enlightenment.

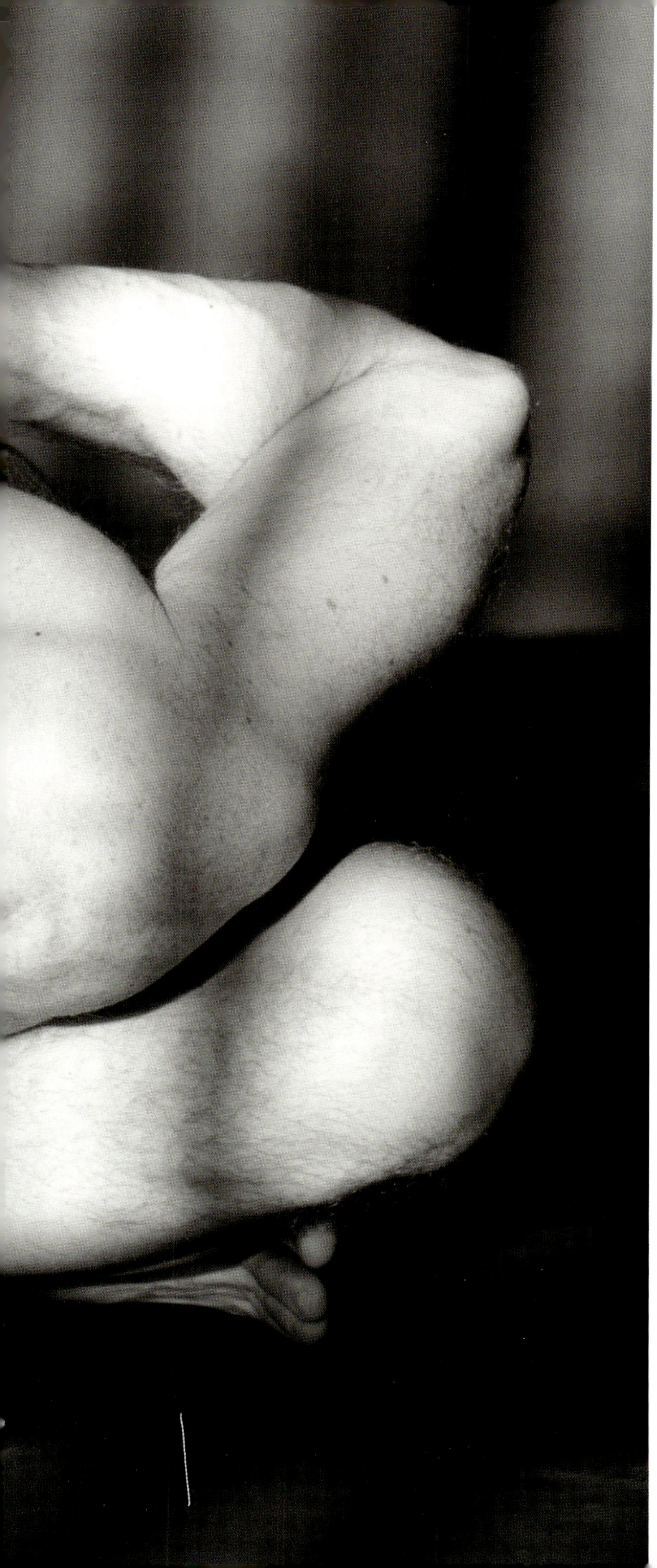

Iyengar basics

"Yoga is a practical philosophy. It shows, from moment to moment, the way to face the world and at the same time to follow a spiritual path. Yoga strikes a balance between the happiness of the world, that is self-centred happiness, and the happiness which extends beyond one's own self." B.K.S. Iyengar

History and Philosophy

Iyengar yoga focuses on correct alignment of the body so that it can develop harmoniously and anatomically perfect. If the student practises with intelligence and awareness, there is little chance of injury or pain. As all bodies are different and people have specific weaknesses and difficulties, Iyengar yoga makes use of props to help students achieve the best possible poses within their limited capacity.

The Iyengar method, which is renowned for its precision and attention to detail, involves the practice of asanas (postures) and pranayama (breathing). Because of the intense concentration required to position parts of the body, both skeletally and muscularly, the mind becomes focused and sharp, and this results in a form of "meditation in motion". Practitioners strive for this state of total physical awareness, mental clarity and ultimate serenity.

A vital aspect of Iyengar yoga is the sequencing of postures. There is a cumulative effect when poses are practised in a particular order, and when this is adhered to there is less chance of injury and incorrect practice. Iyengar yoga can also be used therapeutically to treat a variety of ailments.

There are numerous styles of yoga, of which Iyengar is one. It was developed by Yogacharya B.K.S. Iyengar, one of the world's most respected experts on yoga. As a child he suffered from various illnesses, and at the age of 16 was introduced to yoga by his sister's husband, Sri T. Krishnamacharya, who was a teacher in Mysore. Iyengar began practising yoga to regain his health and strength, and in 1936 his guru sent him to Pune for six months to teach.

The precision and perfection in his practice was reflected in his teaching, and the number of students grew. He became recognized and respected as a yoga teacher, and in 1952 he met Yehudi Menuhin. This encounter was instrumental in introducing yoga and Mr Iyengar to the Western world. Menuhin was a dedicated student and invited Mr Iyengar to England to teach him. Many people joined in these classes, and soon a large number of Westerners became his students and invited him back the following year.

Back in Pune, he decided that he wanted the masses to experience yoga but was restricted by the size of the rooms and halls in which he taught. In 1975 he opened his own institute, the Ramamani Iyengar Memorial Yoga Institute, named in memory of his wife, who died just before his dream was realized. Students from all over the world regularly visit Pune and spend a month being taught by his daughter, Geeta, and son, Prashant, with their father keeping a watchful eye on everybody. Mr Iyengar is in his mid-80s, and to see him carry out some of the asanas is a real inspiration to his devoted followers. There are hundreds of Iyengar yoga institutes training students in his method of yoga around the world, including Europe, America, Japan, Israel, Australia, New Zealand, South Africa and Canada, as well as Bombay, Bangalore, Delhi, Madras and Rishikesh.

Mr Iyengar's comprehensive book *Light on Yoga* was published in 1966. This work has been acknowledged as the Bible of yoga and has been widely translated. Other books written by Mr Iyengar are *Light on Pranayama*; *The Art of Yoga*; *The Tree of Yoga* and *Light on Yoga Sutras of Patanjali.*

left The founders of yoga and gurus past and present are venerated and admired.
opposite It is through the dedication and hard work of B.K.S. Iyengar himself that Iyengar yoga has become such a popular form of yoga.

The Yoga Sutras

The philosophy followed by B.K.S. Iyengar is that of Patanjali, a sage who lived in India around 300BC. Patanjali is depicted as a statue with a man's torso and the coiled tail and seven-headed crown of a serpent. In the traditional symbolism of ancient India, this represents infinity. Two of his hands are folded in prayer, representing a meditative state, while the other two hands are holding a conch and discus of light. The conch reminds us of our yoga practice and the discus represents the wheel of time or the law of cause and effect. One half of his face is smiling, the other is serious.

Patanjali is known as the founder of yoga and he codified a set of 196 aphorisms called the Yoga Sutras. This work systematizes the principles and practices of yoga by bringing together all the various strands of the theory and practice, and presenting them in one concise, comprehensive text. These aphorisms cover all aspects of life, beginning with a code of conduct and ending with man's vision of his true self. Patanjali shows how, through the practice of yoga, we can transform ourselves, gain control over the mind and emotions, overcome obstacles hindering our spiritual enlightenment and attain the goal of yoga.

The eight limbs of yoga

According to Patanjali, yoga consists of eight limbs. Each of these limbs has its own separate identity, but all form part of a whole, and when they are integrated, the eight stages become true yoga. The eight aspects of yoga are:

1 **Yama** (Social discipline)
These five universal laws include: non-violence; truthfulness; non-stealing; sexual restraint; and freedom from desire. As codes of ethical behaviour, they should be followed in everyday life to promote harmony and understanding in society.

2 **Niyama** (Individual discipline)
These five principles of personal conduct are cleanliness; contentment; austerity; study of one's own self; and devotion to God. While the yamas apply to universal morals, the niyamas are rules of behaviour that apply to one's physical and mental discipline.

3 **Asana** (Postures)
According to Patanjali's Sutras, "Postures bring about stability of the body and poise of the mind." Practising asanas improves flexibility, vitality and health, and activates the organs (heart, lungs, kidneys, liver, spleen and pancreas). However, the true importance of postures is the connection between body and mind, so the two become interwoven, initiating the path from physical to spiritual awareness.

4 **Pranayama** (Breath control)
Patanjali states that pranayama should be practised only after a firm foundation in asana has been established. Practising pranayama releases tension in the body, calms the nervous system and keeps the mind tranquil.

5 **Pratyahara** (Withdrawal and control of the senses)
This withdrawal of the senses from objects of desire is the link between the first four limbs and the last three. After following the rules for universal and personal ethics (yama and niyama) and practising asanas and pranayama, one can turn one's senses inwards and achieve complete tranquillity.

left Simple cross legs position, or Sukhasana, is a comfortable pose in which to meditate. Choose a posture you will be able to stay in for a long time.

6 **Dharana** (Concentration)
After work on the body in asanas, refinement of the mind though pranayama and internalization of the senses of perception in pratyahara, the sixth stage, dharana, is reached. Here the mind is in a state of total absorption and is concentrated on a single point or task in which it is totally engrossed. The longer the mind remains in this state of focus, the more powerful it becomes.

7 **Dhyana** (Meditation)
When the practitioner maintains uninterrupted focus of attention in dharana, it becomes dhyana. In this state of deep concentration and undisturbed meditation, the mind, body and breath become one and merge into a single state of being.

8 **Samadhi** (Self-realization)
This is the culmination of yogic achievement – a true sense of communion and peace. This settling of the mind is the essence of yoga, where one has risen above the senses as a result of the complete refinement of both body and mind. The body and senses are at rest as if asleep, the mind and reason are alert as if awake, yet everything has gone beyond consciousness.

The first five limbs (yama, niyama, asana, pranayama and pratyahara) are known as the disciplines of yoga. They prepare the body and clear the mind and senses in readiness for the next three limbs (dharana, dhyana and samadhi), which are known as the attainments of yoga. Patanjali says, "The study of the eight limbs of yoga leads to the purification of the body, the mind and the intellect; the flame of knowledge is kept burning and discrimination is aroused."

The demands of modern life can bring about stress, which leads to illness as well as mental anguish. Good health is the harmony between body, mind and soul. It is a result of a balanced diet, exercise and a mind that is stress-free. In yoga, the asanas revitalize the body and pranayama brings about a sense of calmness. This helps to free the mind of negative thoughts caused by the fast pace of today's world. It is encouraging to know that in this age of pressure, there are well-established techniques in yoga to restore health and help contribute to a life of happiness and harmony.

top This is a statuette representing Patanjali, the ancient Indian sage acknowledged as the founder of yoga. His sutras, or writings, have been translated from Sanskrit and interpreted by many.
bottom Here on the right is Patanjali as the serpent god, and one of a trinity of devotees witnessing the dance of the god Natajara at his temple in Chidambaram. The other figures are Vyaghrapada, a rishi or sage, with the feet of a tiger, and Simhavarman, an early king.

How to Practise the Asanas

The first part of this book presents a basic introduction to Iyengar yoga. It offers a selection of postures from each of the asana groups – standing postures for vitality; seated postures for serenity; twists, which are cleansing; inverted poses for developing mental strength; supine poses, which are restful; and prone poses, which are energizing. There are also sequences on relaxation and pranayama (breathing).

Generally, the asana groups and the individual postures within each group are listed in the order in which they should be learned and practised as outlined in the system devised by Mr Iyengar.

Instructions are given for each posture, and photographs show the final posture, as well as the various stages leading to it. Students who already have some experience of yoga practice will find the sequences of photographs useful reminders, while the instructions are clear enough for beginners to follow. There are also tips on how to improve the posture and how props can help less flexible students. (See overleaf for details of props and how to use them.)

The Routine Practice chapter provides over 20 suggested programmes that vary in degree of difficulty and duration. Students should begin with Sequence 1 and proceed at their own pace, remembering to consolidate and not be in too much of a hurry to get to the last routine. It is not about how fast you work, but about the quality, understanding and proficiency of your practice.

The Yoga Therapy chapter provides programmes and advice for students with minor medical conditions. Props are used in most of these sequences to help less able students attain the best pose possible within their personal physical constraints.

Approaching yoga practice

"An asana is not a posture which you assume mechanically. It involves thought, at the end of which a balance is achieved between movement and resistance." B.K.S. Iyengar

Practice is essential for improving both physical and mental discipline. There are no rules for when, how often or how long you should do this, but obviously the more regular the practice, the greater the benefit to the practitioner. Practice must be adapted to suit one's circumstances, and the intensity and level of each session should reflect this. For example, if you feel tired after a long day at the office, practise restful/calming postures; if you feel stiff and lethargic, practise standing poses. Listed below are some general guidelines for practice:

above Baddhakonasana, a seated posture. Practising yoga in company, or in an organized class with a qualified teacher, is a motivating way to begin, and continue, to learn.

- This book should be used in conjunction with, not instead of, attending classes. It is important to be instructed and corrected by a teacher.
- Wear light, loose, comfortable clothing that allows free and uninhibited movement.
- Practise with bare feet on a non-slip mat or floor. A carpet is not good as the feet slide and cannot grip the surface.

- The best time to practise is on an empty stomach. If possible, wait at least 4–5 hours after a heavy meal and 2–3 hours after a snack.
- Practise in a warm, airy room out of direct sunlight.
- Remove hard contact lenses.
- In each group of asanas, first practise the easier version before attempting the more difficult one. It is advisable to gain proficiency in the simpler version over a period of a few days before progressing to the final pose.
- Practise with full concentration and awareness of the parts of the body involved in each asana. The postures should be done slowly, smoothly and with full understanding.
- Pay attention to accuracy and alignment. When the body is correctly aligned, the flow of energy is uninterrupted.
- It is important to breathe while in the postures. Where no specific instructions are given, breathe normally. Generally you should inhale on upward movements, where the chest and abdomen are expanded and broad, and exhale on downward/forward movements, where the chest and abdomen may be compressed.
- Maintain the pose for as long as is possible without causing any physical or mental strain. Keep the eyes, mouth, throat and abdomen relaxed throughout.
- The eyes should be kept open and the mouth shut in all postures, unless otherwise instructed.
- If adverse physical or mental effects are felt during or after practice, seek the advice of a qualified Iyengar teacher.
- Each practice session should be followed by 5 minutes relaxation in Corpse pose (Savasana).

above right One of the five basic forward bending postures, Trianga Mukhaikapada Pascimottanasana.
right Finger to Toe pose, or Padangusthasana, strengthens the legs and makes the spine more flexible. Both standing and sitting forward bends aid digestion and tone the abdominal organs.

Equipment

Historically, yogis used logs of wood, stones and ropes to help them practise asanas effectively. Mr Iyengar has invented a variety of props that allow the postures to be held easily and for longer, without strain. The use of props makes the asanas more accessible to all yoga students, whether they are stiff or flexible, young or old, weak or strong, beginners or advanced. Props may also be used by those who wish to conserve their energy because of fatigue or injury. They allow muscular extension to take place while the brain remains passive. Mr Iyengar refers to this as practising "with effortless effort".

Non-slip mats These prevent the feet from sliding during standing poses. It is helpful to draw or fold a line down the centre of the mat to assist with alignment.

Chair A chair is used for easy twisting postures, e.g. Chair pose (Bharadvajasana), or as a support for the body in Chair Sarvangasana and Ardha Halasana.

Wooden blocks These are used when stiffer students find that they cannot reach the floor with their hands. In sitting and standing postures, they can be used to support the legs or hands and to help with twisting poses.

Foam blocks Many students find it difficult to lift the spine in seated poses. Sitting on one or two foam blocks helps to achieve this spinal lift. Blocks are used to support the neck and shoulders in Salamba Sarvangasana, and in restorative poses the blocks are used to support the student's head.

Bolsters Used mainly in restorative and recuperative postures, bolsters support the head or the spine. A couple of cushions or rolled-up blankets can be substituted.

Eyebags These are small bean bags used to calm the eyes in recuperative poses. Also used is the traditional crêpe bandage, that should be lightly wrapped around the head and eyes, helping to release tension around the eye area.

Straps Use straps around the feet in straight-legged postures where the hands cannot catch the toes or foot. The strap is used in Salamba Sarvangasana to prevent the arms sliding apart, and in Supta Baddhakonasana to secure the feet together, close to the pelvis.

opposite A selection of props used to help students. Furniture and other objects in the home can be adapted and used as props, or they can be purchased from yoga centres.
right Bolsters and blankets are useful. You may already have similar items at home.
far right Blocks are made of wood, cork or foam.

above Halasana stools come in different heights for all shapes of body. Bandages and bean bags are useful aids to calm the eyes and keep the mind quiet.

Halasana stool This stool is used to support the thighs in Ardha Halasana. In standing twists, the raised foot is supported on a stool or chair. The head may be supported on the Halasana stool in restorative poses.

Blankets Folded blankets may be used instead of foam blocks. They are used to support the head in Savasana, pranayama and restorative postures. They give additional lift to the spine in seated and twisting asanas. A rolled-up blanket can be used to support the feet in Virasana. On a practical note, in Savasana the body temperature is lowered, so cover up and use the blanket for warmth.

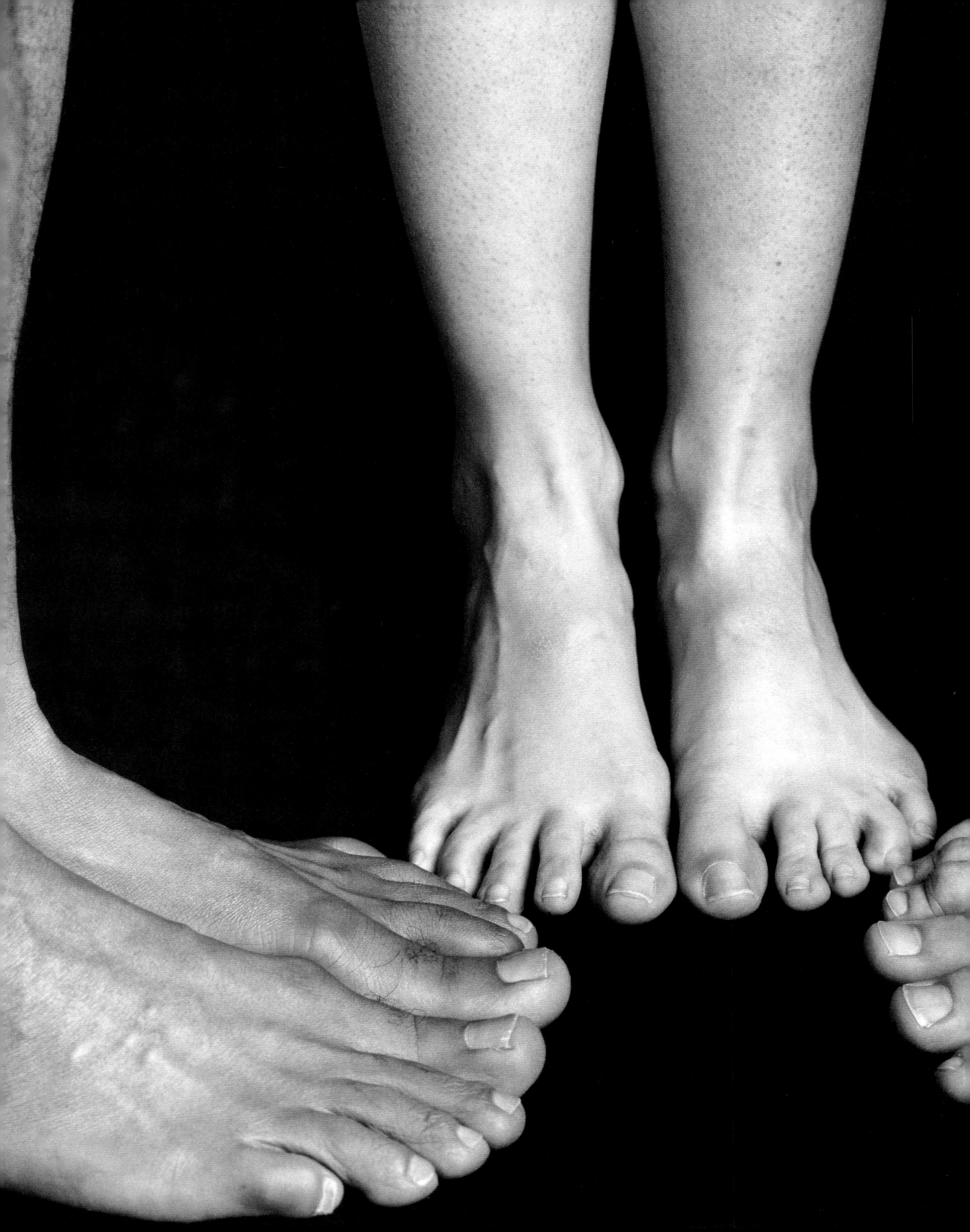

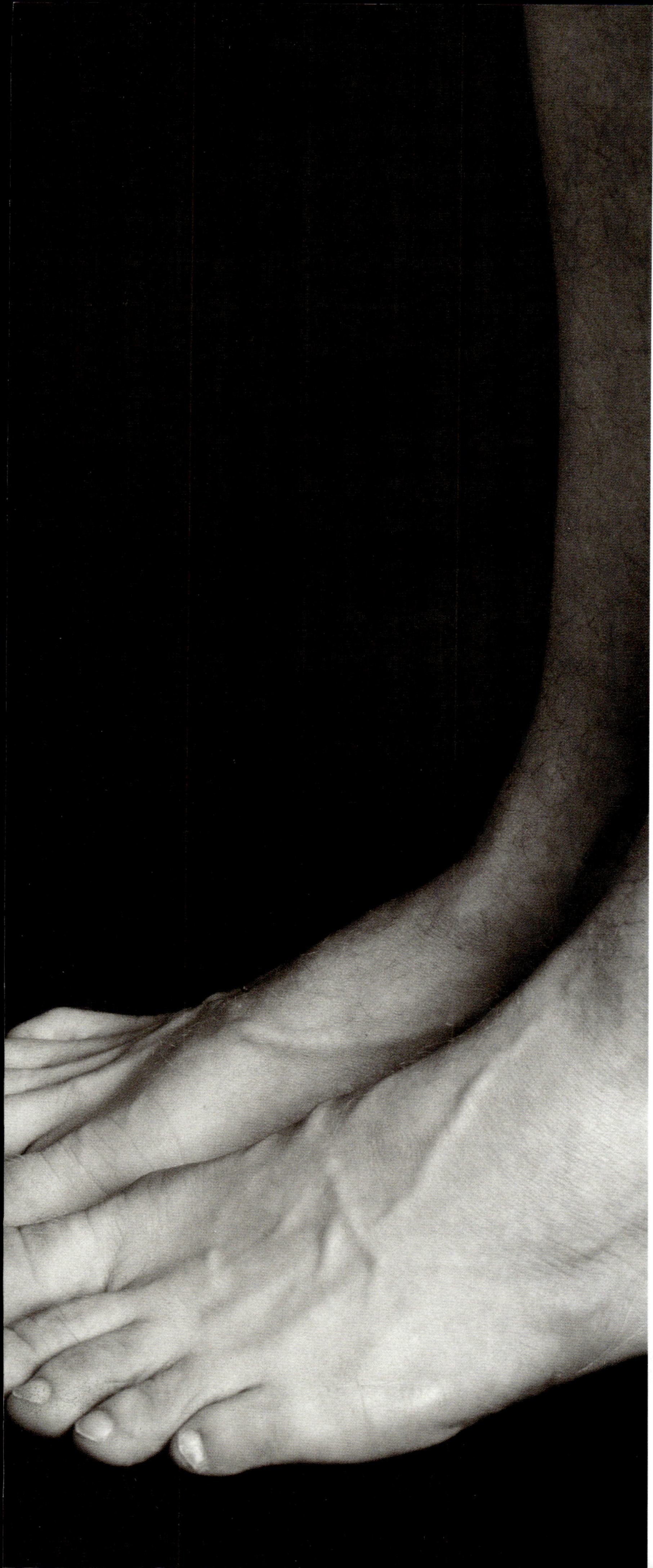

standing Asanas

Standing postures are dynamic and energizing and form the basis of all other postures. Through them practitioners become familiar with various parts of the skeletal and muscular body and learn to use their intelligence to bring action and awareness to these parts. Standing postures develop strength, stamina and determination.

Mountain Pose

TADASANA

This pose teaches you how to stand correctly. It brings attention to posture and makes you aware of how the legs and feet have to work in order to stand up straight. All standing poses begin and end with Tadasana.

1 Stand with the feet together – big toes, inner ankles and inner heels touching. Spread the body weight evenly over the feet, keeping the inside edges of the feet parallel.

Tighten/lift the kneecaps and pull up the thigh muscles so the legs stretch strongly. Feel the spine extending upwards and the lift in the front of the body. Roll the shoulders back and take the shoulder blades into the body to open the chest.

Focus on Tadasana

- Although relatively simple, this posture is crucial as it teaches awareness of the body and the recognition of any postural difficulties. Try to perfect this posture before moving on to the next pose.
- Press the feet firmly into the floor and extend the crown of the head towards the ceiling.
- Extend the sides and back of the neck, balancing the head on the top of the spine.
- Feel the front body "opening" from pubis to chin.
- Project the breastbone towards the front of the chest.
- Ensure that the body is stretching evenly on all sides – front, back, left and right. Strain is caused to the body by leaning habitually to one side or the other.

2 Allow the arms to hang down the sides of the body with the palms facing the legs.

Extend the neck up, relax the face and look straight ahead. Hold for 30–60 seconds.

Focus on feet

- It is important to keep the inside edges of the feet parallel, and the big toes and ankle bones together Weight should be evenly spread over the heels and soles of the feet.

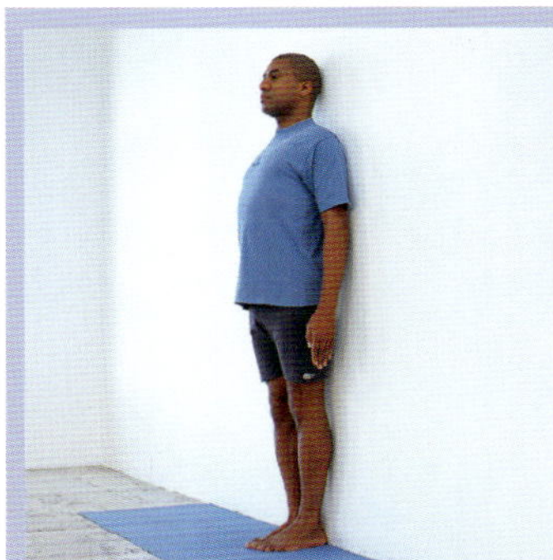

Modification

- If you find it hard to balance, try Tadasana standing against a wall. This is also helpful to ensure that you are standing straight, and not leaning forwards or backwards.

Tree Pose

VRKSASANA

This posture tones and stretches the leg muscles and teaches balance. Consistent practice of the balancing postures will improve your concentration and increase muscle tone and general poise.

1 Stand in Tadasana – feet together, eyes still.

2 Bend the right knee to the side (without disturbing the left leg). Hold the ankle and place the sole of the right foot high on the left inner thigh with the toes pointing towards the floor. Keep the bent (right) knee back in line with the left leg and keep the left leg steady.

3 Inhale and stretch the arms over the head with palms facing one another. Straighten the elbows and extend the arms and trunk up.

Join the palms if you can do so without bending the elbows, otherwise keep them apart. Hold for 30–60 seconds. Exhale, then lower the arms and the right leg and repeat on the other side.

Focus

- To help maintain balance, try to focus the eyes on an object in the middle distance. Balancing poses such as Vrksasana can contribute to improving concentration in the long term.

Modification

- To help with balance, use the wall for support and hold the foot up with a strap.
- Keep the grounded foot pressing firmly into the floor.
- Don't allow the left leg to bow to the side.

Extended Triangle Pose

UTTHITA TRIKONASANA

This pose strengthens the legs, makes the hips more flexible and relieves backache. In this posture, when turning the feet, it is important not to turn the hips as well. Start on the right side, then repeat the posture to the left.

1 Stand in Tadasana.

2 Inhale deeply, jump or step* your feet 1–1.2m/3–4ft apart and extend the arms out to the side, keeping the palms facing the floor (* students with back problems should step their feet apart).

Ensure that both feet are level with one another, legs extended and straight, knees lifted.

3 Turn your left foot out about 90 degrees (so that it is parallel to the side of your mat), and turn your right foot slightly inwards (about 15 degrees). The left heel should be in line with the instep of the right foot. As you turn the right foot in, rotate the right leg outwards, and as you turn the left foot outwards, rotate the whole leg to the left, so that the legs are rotating away from one another. Keep the left knee pulled up and facing in the same direction as the left foot.

Modification

- The final aim is to reach the floor, with the palm face down. If you cannot reach, place the hand on the ankle. If you need more help, use a brick standing on its end under the left hand to get more extension in the spine and to allow the chest to turn towards the ceiling.
- Students who are less flexible can do this posture with the back against the wall to aid balance. In this case, place the brick next to the wall to keep it steady, or try the posture with the back foot against the wall.
- If the neck aches when turning the head, either look straight ahead or look towards the left foot.

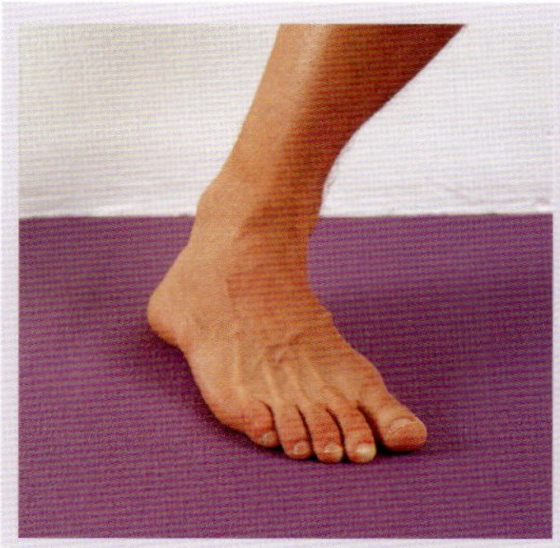

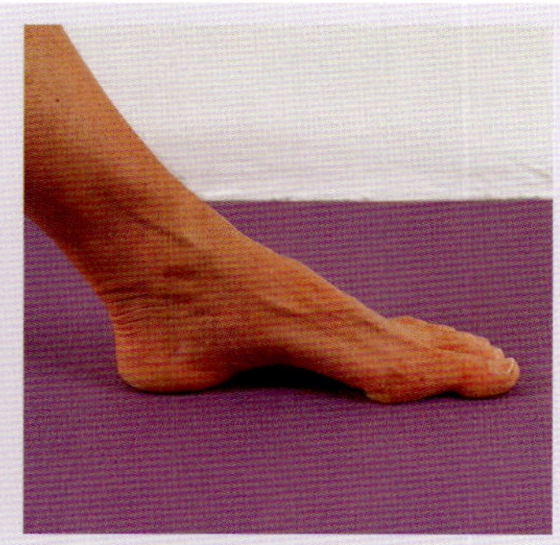

Focus

- Turn the back foot in 15 degrees. Press the corners of both feet into the floor and lift the instep.
- Stretch the toes forwards and the heels back to lengthen the soles of the feet.

4 Lift the trunk, extend the arms further and then exhale and stretch the trunk sideways to the left. Hold the left ankle with the left hand.

Extend the right arm upwards, keeping the palm facing forwards and keeping it in line with the left arm. Turn the head and look towards the right thumb.

Extend both legs strongly and rotate the navel forwards and upwards.

Hold for 30–40 seconds, inhale and come up, then turn the right foot out and the left foot inwards and repeat on the other side. After doing both sides, come back to the centre of the mat in Tadasana.

Extended Lateral Angle Pose

UTTHITA PARSVAKONASANA

This posture strengthens legs and spine, and helps to open the chest. The full lunge twists the body, stimulating the organs inside the body and aiding digestion and the elimination of toxins.

1 Stand in Tadasana.

2 Inhale deeply, jump or step your feet 1.3m/4.5ft apart and extend the arms out to the sides, keeping the palms facing the floor. Next, turn the right foot inwards 15 degrees and the left foot outwards 90 degrees. Broaden the palms and extend the whole of each arm from the top of the shoulder to the fingertips. Move the shoulders away from the ears.

3 Keep the right leg firm and straight, and bend the left knee to 90 degrees – keeping the shin perpendicular and the thigh parallel to the floor. Exhale and extend the trunk sideways, placing the fingertips of the left hand on the floor by the outer edge of the left foot. Keep the right leg stretched and firm – to do this press the outer edge of the right foot into the floor.

Focus

- As with all directional postures, begin with the right side, then continue with the left for balance.
- If the neck is uncomfortable, look straight ahead, not towards the ceiling.
- Move the buttock of the left (bent) leg forwards towards the left inner thigh and, at the same time, keep the left knee moving back slightly, thus keeping the groin open.
- Keep the top arm pointing towards the ceiling, as this will help to keep the chest open and lifted.
- Make sure that the back foot is turned in by 15 degrees and the instep is in line with the heel of the front foot.

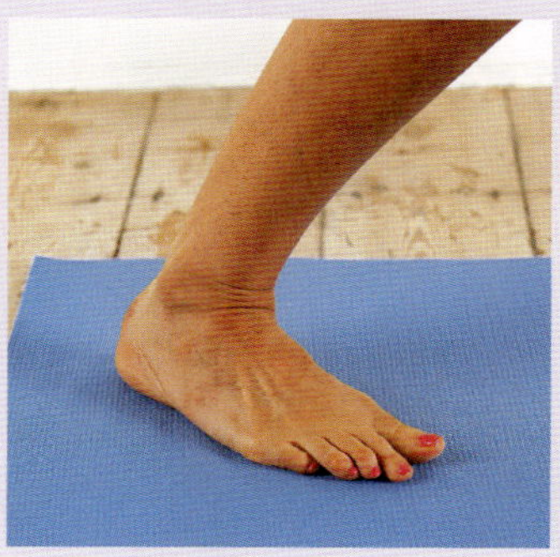

Modification

- Use a wooden block under the left hand to open the chest more.
- Do the posture with the back against the wall to improve the alignment.
- This posture can be done at right angles to the wall, with the back foot against the wall for support.

4 Turn the right arm towards the head and extend this arm over the head with the palm facing the floor. Turn the head to look towards the ceiling.

Fully extend the right leg and arm and turn the navel towards the ceiling.

Breathe normally and hold for 30–40 seconds. Inhale and come up, turn both feet forwards, rest hands on hips and then repeat the posture on the right side.

After finishing both sides, come back to Tadasana in the centre of your mat.

Warrior Pose II

VIRABHADRASANA II

This pose strengthens the legs, brings flexibility to the spinal muscles and tones the abdominal muscles. Although this is called the second posture it is practised first as it is less challenging.

1 Stand in Tadasana.

2 Inhale deeply, jump or step your feet 1–1.2m/3–4ft apart and extend the arms out to the side, palms facing the floor.

3 Turn the right foot out and the left foot in 15 degrees.

4 Extend the trunk up from the hips and, as you exhale, bend the right leg to 90 degrees, keeping the left leg firm and straight. Extend the arms strongly to the right and left with the palms facing the floor, stretch the trunk upwards, open the chest, turn the head and look along the right arm.

Extend the left arm more to the left so that the trunk doesn't lean towards the right. The crown of the head should be extending straight up towards the ceiling.

Open the chest, relax the face and breathe normally. Hold for 30–40 seconds, inhale and come up. Turn the feet forwards and repeat on the other side.

After completing both sides, come back into Tadasana.

Focus

- Make sure that the back foot is turned in 15 degrees.
- Firmly press the outer edge and the heel of the back foot into the floor to create strength and stability in the back leg.

Modification

- Lean the back of the body against the wall for better alignment.
- Alternatively, place the back heel against the wall, with the fingertips of the back hand touching the wall.

Warrior Pose I

VIRABHADRASANA I

This is a challenging pose in which the chest is well expanded, which in turn improves breathing. It also helps with stiffness in the shoulders, back and neck.

1 Stand in Tadasana, inhale deeply, jump or step the feet 1–1.2m/3–4ft apart and raise the arms to shoulder level.

2 Turn the palms upwards and extend the arms towards the ceiling, keeping the elbows straight and the palms facing one another. If your lower back aches when taking the arms up, then keep your hands on your hips.

3 Turn the right foot and leg in deeply, about 40 degrees, and the left foot out 90 degrees. Simultaneously turn the hips, trunk and shoulders to the left.

Both sides of the trunk should be parallel – so bring the right hip forwards, while taking the left hip slightly back, to keep them even.

4 Exhale and bend the left leg to form a 90-degree angle. Extend the trunk upwards, as if it were being lifted out of the hips. Move the shoulder blades into the body to open the chest. Extend the chin towards the ceiling and look up. Maintain the full extension on the back leg and keep the hips, shoulders and trunk rotating to the left. Hold for 20–30 seconds, inhale, come up and lower the arms. Repeat on the other side, coming back to Tadasana.

Focus

- Don't strain or hold the breath in this posture. Breath is energy, so breathe evenly.
- If the lower back is uncomfortable in this pose, do it with the hands on the hips.

Modification

- If difficulty is experienced in turning the back foot inwards, either work with the back heel against a wall, or support the back heel with a foam block used as a raise.

Half Moon Pose
ARDHA CHANDRASANA

This pose strengthens the legs and helps improve balance. Regular practice will improve concentration and co-ordination. Because of the strong extension of the spine, it helps correct alignment and makes the back supple.

1 Start in Tadasana, then move into the full pose for Utthita Trikonasana.

2 Bend the left knee and place the left hand about 30cm/1ft beyond the outer edge of the left foot. Bring the weight of the body on to this foot, using the hand to maintain balance.

3 Exhale and draw the right foot slightly in towards the left leg. Straighten the left leg and the right leg will lift up.

Focus

- Keep the top hip (the one facing the ceiling) directly above the bottom hip (of the standing leg).
- If the neck is stiff, look ahead, not towards the top hand and the ceiling.

Modification

- If balancing is difficult, do the posture with the back of the body against the wall.
- Use a wooden block as support for the left hand.
- Alternatively, rest the foot of the lifted leg on a ledge or stool, using blocks to achieve the correct height.

4 Raise and extend the right leg – keeping it parallel to the floor. Keep the left leg firm and pulled up and ensure that it is perpendicular to the floor.

If you are confident with the balance, extend the right arm up towards the ceiling, keeping it in line with the left arm.

Slowly turn the head to look at the right hand and open the chest, lifting the ribs upwards by twisting the waist.

Hold for 20–30 seconds, breathing normally, then come up and repeat on the second side. After finishing both sides, come back to Tadasana.

Extended Leg Raises

UTTHITA HASTA PADANGUSTHASANA I & II

This pose tones the muscles of the lower spine and strengthens the legs. It is done by standing on one leg, extending the other leg, to the front or the side, and catching the big toe with the fingers.

1 Stand in Tadasana.

2 Bend the right knee and clutch the big toe with the first and second finger of the right hand.

3 Utthita Hasta Padangusthasana I – Straighten the right leg forwards. Keep the knee of the extended leg pointing upwards, and the standing leg vertical.

Focus

- As the right leg is raised and straightened, ensure that the left foot (on the floor) does not turn out. Keep the toes on this foot pointing forwards.
- Keep the trunk upright, not leaning towards the raised leg. If you lean, support the lifted foot on a ledge.
- Balancing poses improve concentration and poise.

4 Utthita Hasta Padangusthasansa II – Sideways Extended Leg Raise – keep the left foot pointing forwards and bend the right knee to the side. Hold the big toe with the fingers of the right hand. Stretch the right leg out to the side. Ensure that the right knee faces the ceiling. Straighten the right arm. Extend the spine upwards. Stretch the left arm out to the side. Look ahead, breathing normally, and hold for 20–30 seconds. Stretch the trunk up, open the chest, moving the shoulder blades into the back, keep the left leg firm and straight.

Modification

Initially holding the toes may prove to be too challenging, especially if you have tight hamstrings, so using a strap around the foot or resting the foot on a chair is recommended.

Warrior Pose III
VIRABHADRASANA III

This posture is an intensified continuation of Virabhadrasana I. It tones the abdominal organs, strengthens the legs, makes the spine more flexible and improves balance. It gives the practitioner agility in both body and mind.

1 Follow the instructions for Virabhadrasana I.

2 Exhale and extend the trunk and arms forwards over the left thigh.

Keep the hips level by pulling the right hip forwards if necessary.

3 Extend the trunk more, straighten the left leg and lift the right leg up so that it is parallel to the floor. With the right leg, trunk, head and arms parallel to the floor, extend the fingertips away from the head and extend the right inner heel away from the head. Hold this position for 20–30 seconds.

Come down by bending the left leg, lowering the right foot to the floor and raising the trunk up – this is Virabhadrasana I. Repeat on the other side, and then come back to Tadasana.

If the lower back is painful, support the lifted leg on a ledge and the hands on a chair. Do not strain or compress the back of the neck.

Modification
- The fingertips of the extended hands can press into the wall, or rest on a chair or ledge to extend the spine more.
- The hips must be level and the raised leg straight.

Reverse Triangle Pose

PARIVRTTA TRIKONASANA

This pose increases the flow of blood to the lower back region and therefore improves the flexibility of the spine. It also strengthens the legs and hips and invigorates the abdominal organs.

1 Stand in Tadasana, inhale and spread feet and arms apart.

2 Turn the right foot out 90 degrees and the left foot in 45 degrees. Exhale and rotate the trunk and head to the right.

3 Extend the left arm over the right leg and place the fingertips of the left hand on the outside of the right foot.

Focus

- Keep the right hip pointing upwards, so it does not collapse down into the body.
- Keep the head in line with the tailbone when looking up, maintaining a straightness in the spine.

4 Turn the trunk towards the right and extend the right arm strongly upwards in line with the right shoulder. Extend the spine and open the chest. Keep the head in alignment with the tailbone. Hold for 30–40 seconds. Inhale, rotate the trunk back to its original position and come up. Repeat on the other side and then come back to Tadasana.

Modification

- Less-flexible students can do this posture with the back against the wall.
- Use a wooden block under the right hand to get more extension in the spine and to allow the chest to turn towards the ceiling.
- Do the posture with the back foot against the wall.
- Put a foam block under the right heel to allow the chest to rotate farther.

Revolving Lateral Angle Pose

PARIVRTTA PARSVAKONASANA

This posture is a more intense version of Parivrtta Trikonasana and therefore the effects are greater. The abdominal organs are more constricted, thus aiding digestion and helping to eliminate toxins from the colon.

1 Begin in Virabhadrasana II, with the right leg bent and the arms extended out to the sides, keeping the palms facing the floor.

2 Rotate the trunk, pelvis, abdomen and chest towards the bent right leg. Take the left side of the trunk over the right thigh, bend the left elbow and hook it over the right thigh.

3 Rotate the trunk and chest more, and place the fingertips of the left hand on the floor on the outside of the right foot. Extend the right arm up towards the ceiling.

Focus

- Throughout this posture, make sure the back (left) leg is straight.
- Keep the right shin perpendicular to the floor.

4 Turn the right palm towards the head, extending the arm over the head in line with the ear. Keep the left leg strong and straight. Turn the chest towards the ceiling more and, if possible, look up.

Hold for 20–30 seconds, then inhale, lift the left hand from the floor, raise the trunk, and come up. Repeat on the other side, and then come back to Tadasana.

Modification

- Work parallel to the wall, supporting the lower hand on a block and the back heel on a raise.
- Work with the back heel against the wall. The heel is lifted on the wall while the toes are on the floor.
- This is a strenuous postition, so if it is too much, try keeping the top hand resting on the waist.
- Assistance in stretching the arm fully can help.

Intense Side Chest Stretch

PARSVOTTANASANA

This helps to maintain mobility in the neck, shoulders, elbows and wrists, and strengthen the abdominal muscles. It improves flexibility in the spine and hips and, once the head is down, calms the brain.

1 Stand in Tadasana, and join the hands behind in Namaste. Inhale and jump or step the feet 1–1.2m/3–4ft apart.

2 Turn the right foot out 90 degrees and the left foot in 45 degrees. Turn the hips, trunk and shoulders to the right.

3 Extend the spine forwards. Lift the chin towards the ceiling and look up to make the back concave.

Focus

- Keep the palms flat together behind the back. This will increase flexibility in the wrists and shoulders. If the hands cannot go into Namaste, however, hold the elbows behind the back.

4 Exhale and extend the trunk over the right leg, taking the head towards the right foot. Keep both legs poker straight, the hips level and the weight evenly distributed between both feet. Hold for 30–40 seconds, raise the trunk, turn the feet forwards, release the hands and repeat on the other side. Come back to Tadasana.

Modification

- Until stability is learned, do the posture with the hands on the waist and, after coming forwards, place the hands on the floor on either side of the front foot.
- Don't allow all the weight to collapse on to the front leg. Press both feet equally into the floor.
- If the back is painful, place each hand on a wooden block after coming forwards, and then extend down.

Forward Extension Legs Wide Apart

PRASARITA PADOTTANASANA

This pose is usually practised towards the end of the standing poses. Increased blood flows to the trunk and head, quietening the body and mind and promoting a feeling of tranquillity and serenity.

1 Stand in Tadasana.

2 Inhale and jump or step the feet 1.2–1.5m/4–5ft apart. Make sure the toes of each foot are level and the feet are parallel.

3 Straighten the legs by pulling up the knees and thigh muscles. Exhale and extend the trunk forwards from the hips, stretching the spine.

Place the fingertips on the floor, shoulder-width apart, directly under the shoulders.

Straighten the arms, stretch the legs and extend the trunk forwards, making the back concave and extending the front of the body from the pubis to the chin. Look up.

4 Bend the elbows back, extend the trunk to the floor and place the crown of the head on the floor. Lift the shoulders to release the head nearer to the floor, breathe normally and hold for 20–30 seconds. Inhale, lift the head and trunk and make the back concave. Place the hands on the hips and come back to Tadasana.

Focus

- Move the inner thigh muscles away from each other, i.e. inner thighs move towards outer thighs.
- Press the outer edges of both feet into the floor without letting the outer ankle bones bulge down.
- Even though the trunk moves forwards and then down, keep both legs stretching up towards the ceiling.
- This pose stretches the hamstring muscles.

Modification

- If the hands don't reach the floor, support each hand with a wooden block.
- If the head doesn't reach the floor, support the crown of the head with foam or wooden blocks.

Forward Extension

UTTANASANA I

In this pose the spine is given an intense stretch. The abdominal organs are toned and, because the head is down, the increased flow of blood soothes the brain cells. It also relieves fatigue.

1 Stand in Tadasana with the feet 30cm/1ft apart. The inner edges of the feet should be parallel to one another and the toes level. Keep the legs and knees straight.

2 Fold the arms, catching the left elbow with the right hand and the right elbow with the left hand. Inhale and extend the folded arms above the head in line with the ears. Lift and extend the entire body upwards.

3 Exhale and extend the trunk forwards.

Focus

• This is a relaxing forward bend, although the legs remain strong, with the knees lifted. Allow gravity to do the rest of the work for you.

4 Extend the trunk down to the floor, keeping the legs straight, and extend the trunk and arms nearer to the floor. Inhale, lift the trunk, release the elbows and come back to Tadasana.

Modification

• For students with a stiff or painful back and tight hamstring muscles, do supported Uttanasana I – put the hands on a support at hip level, and extend the spine forwards. An alternative is to rest the head on a support, such as a Halasana stool softened with a blanket.

• If the back is uncomfortable in the final posture, take the feet wider apart and turn the toes slightly inwards.

• Keep the legs extending strongly upwards to elongate the spine and to protect the lower back.

Finger to Toe Pose

PADANGUSTHASANA

This posture strengthens the legs, makes the spine more flexible and also activates and tones the abdominal organs, improving digestion. Students who cannot catch their toes can hold their ankles.

1 Stand in Tadasana with the feet 30cm/1ft apart. Bend the trunk forwards and down, then catch the big toes with the thumbs, index and middle fingers. Stretch the legs up and extend the trunk forwards. Straighten the arms, inhale, make the back concave, lift the chest and look up.

2 Exhale, bend the elbows out and extend the trunk down.

3 On the next exhalation, bend down farther by pulling on the toes, and take the head towards the feet.

Hold for 20–30 seconds, inhale and come up into Tadasana.

Modification

- If you are unable to reach the feet, use two straps wrapped around the toes, or rest the hands on blocks.
- If the back hurts, take the feet slightly wider apart and turn the toes inwards.

Focus

- Use the first two fingers on each hand to wrap firmly around the big toe so you can use the leverage to pull your top half down. Move further into the posture with each exhalation.

Eagle Pose
GARUDASANA

This is a balancing posture that keeps both ankles and shoulders flexible and is recommended for preventing cramps in the calf muscles. Concentration and balance are also improved.

1 Stand in Tadasana. Exhale and slightly bend the right knee and cross the left thigh and knee over the right thigh. Take the left shin behind the right calf, and hook the left foot behind the right calf muscle.

Balance on the right foot, spreading out the foot, with the weight evenly distributed between the toes and heel. Ensure that both hips are level and face forwards. If the knees are painful, practise the pose with the legs in Tadasana and intertwine the arms only.

When first learning this posture, it is necessary to separate out the hand and foot movements, but eventually these will become one flowing movement.

Focus
- Cross the right arm over the left, and touch palms.
- If you find it hard to balance, it may help to keep the eyes still, focusing on an object or a spot in the distance in front of you.

2 Bend the elbows and lift them to shoulder level with the thumbs towards the face. Cross the right elbow over the left, intertwining the forearms, placing the palms together.

Hold for 15–20 seconds, release the arms and legs, come back to Tadasana and repeat on the other side, crossing right thigh over left and left elbow over right.

Modification
- To help with balance, do the posture with the back against the wall.
- To practise the leg work only, push the fingertips against a wall to hold you upright.
- In full posture, keep both knees facing forwards and extend the trunk upwards.

Fierce Pose
UTKATASANA

This pose is like sitting on an imaginary chair. It makes the shoulders and ankles more flexible and strengthens the legs. The abdominal organs and spine are toned and the chest is fully expanded.

1 Stand in Tadasana – feet together, chest lifted, shoulders relaxed and down.

2 Inhale and extend the arms up towards the ceiling with the palms facing one another. Straighten the elbows and extend the palms and fingers up.

3 Exhale, bend the knees and lower the trunk down – as if you were going to sit on a chair.

Bend strongly in the ankle joints, press the heels down, bend in the knees, bend in the hips and stretch the arms strongly up. Keep the chest as far back as possible. If the elbows are straight, then join the palms.

Focus
- Bend more at the ankle and knee joints.
- Move the thighs down towards the floor while lifting the hips and trunk away from the legs.
- Although the trunk leans forwards, try to draw it back towards the vertical.

Modification
- It may be easier, at first, to rest against the wall to help with balance. Regular practice will help with stiff shoulders and ankles, strengthening the legs and activating the spine.

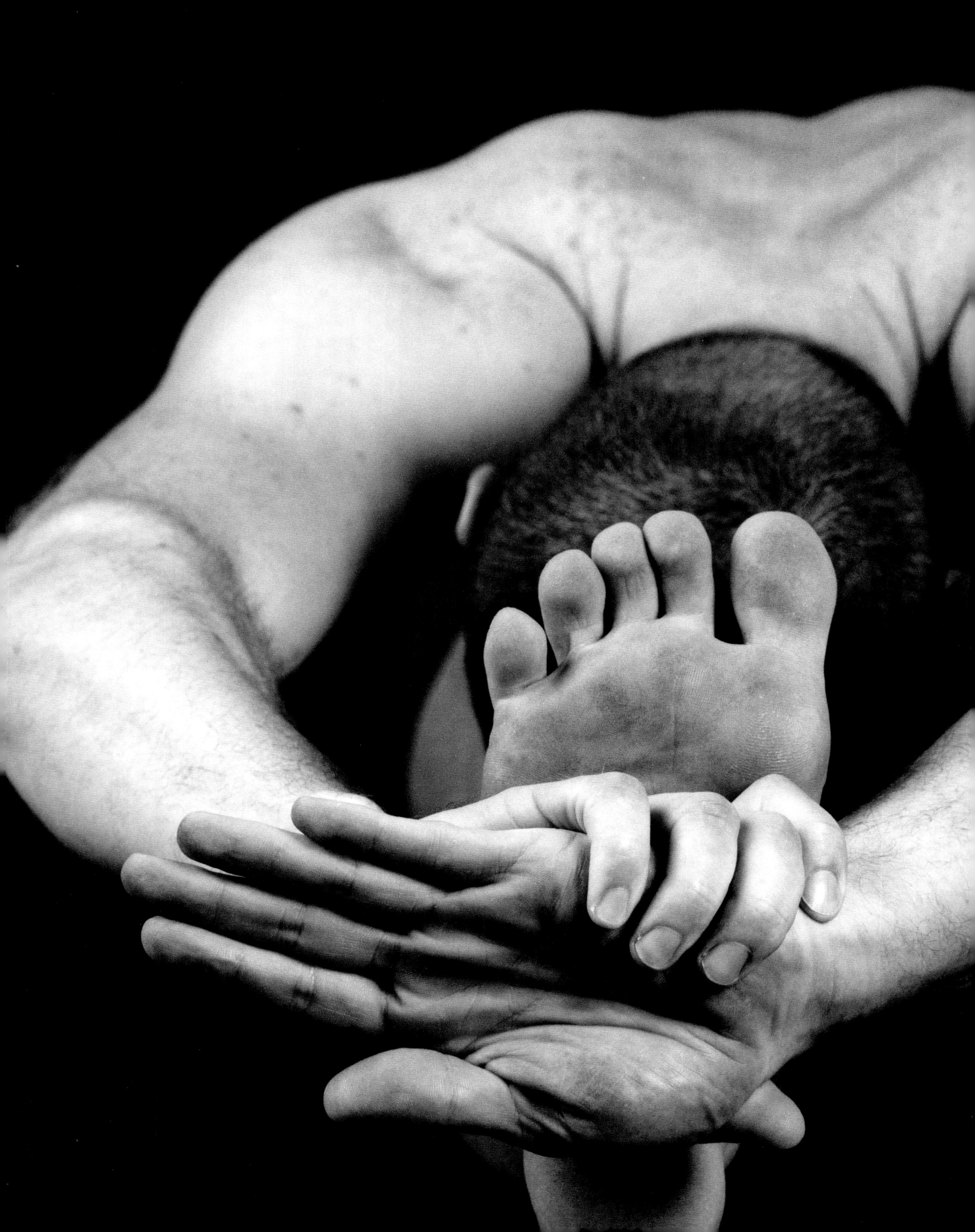

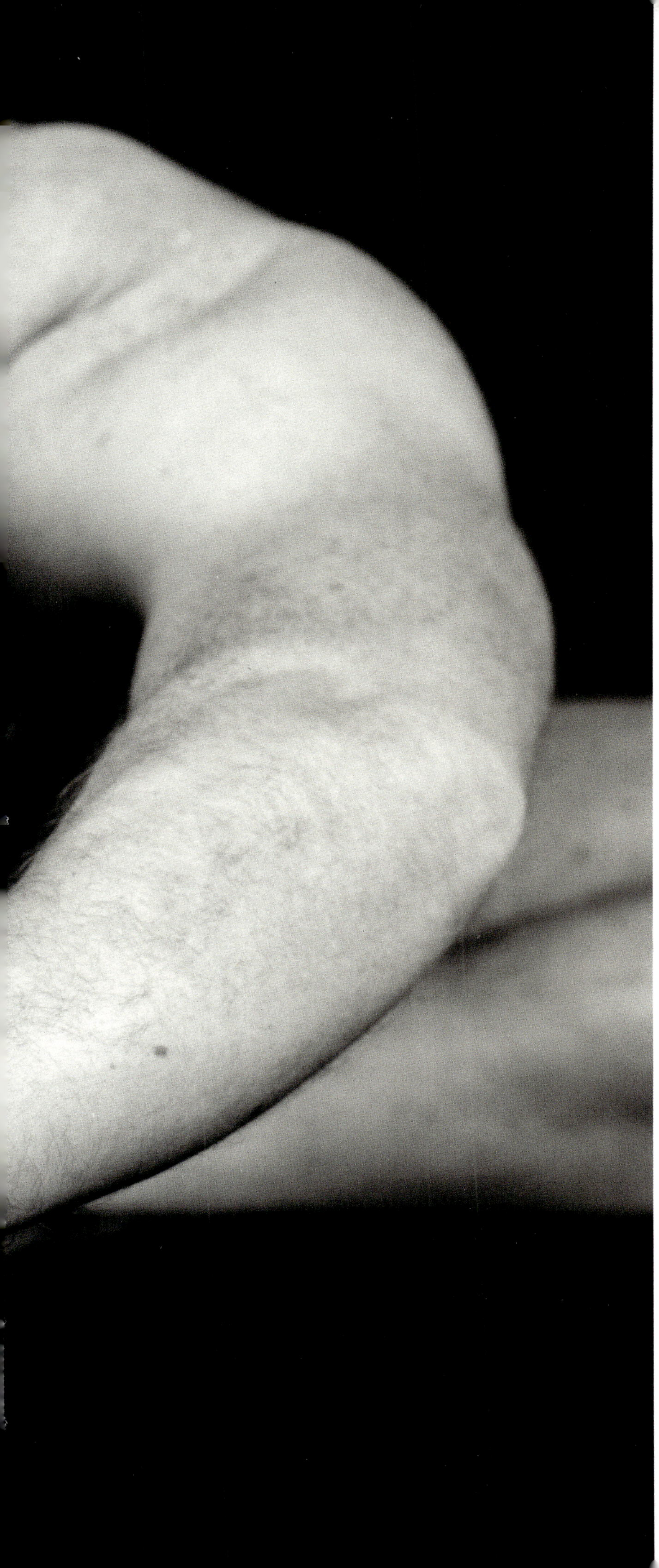

seated Asanas

All seated postures improve flexibility to the hips, knees and ankles. They reduce tension in the diaphragm and throat, making breathing smoother and easier. They keep the spine firm, pacify the brain and stretch the muscles of the heart.

Simple Cross Legs

SUKHASANA

This posture keeps the knees and ankles flexible and nourishes the abdominal organs by encouraging blood circulation. Since the spine is erect in this pose, the mind stays alert and attentive.

1 Sit on a foam block and cross the legs – place the left foot under the right thigh. Press the fingertips into the floor in order to lift the trunk.

2 Extend the spine up, take the shoulders back and open the chest. Maintain the extension of the spine and put the hands on the knees.

3 Hold for 30–60 seconds. Change the crossover of the legs – so that the other shin-bone is in front – and repeat, extending the spine and then placing the hands on the knees again.

Soften the groin area so that the knees release down towards the floor. Note which shin-bone is in front. Cross at the shins, not the ankles, and ensure the shin-bones cross in line with the centre of the body.

Focus

- Sukhasana can be done with the back against the wall, extending the spine up the wall.
- Broaden the base of the posture by spreading the buttocks to the sides.

Hero Pose

VIRASANA

This pose stretches the tops of the feet, ankles and knees. It helps to relieve leg cramps and is a good remedy for indigestion. It also helps to correct flat feet and reduces discomfort in the legs.

1 Kneel on a blanket or yoga mat with the knees together, the feet hip-width apart and the toes pointing straight back behind you.

2 Sit between the feet, using the fingers to move the calf muscles away. If you cannot reach the floor comfortably, use a foam block or rolled-up blanket to raise you up.

3 Put the palms of the hands on the soles of the feet (fingers pointing towards the toes) and stretch the trunk up. Take the shoulder blades into the body, lift the chest and extend the spine up.

Hold for 1–2 minutes, come out of the pose and straighten the legs.

Modification

- Sit on the edge of a foam block, or two, using as much support as is needed to alleviate knee pain.
- If the tops of the feet are painful, put them on a rolled-up blanket.
- If the knees are uncomfortable, put a rolled-up blanket between the calf and back thigh muscles.

Hero Pose with Extended Arms

VIRASANA WITH PARVATASANA

This pose can also be done sitting in Sukhasana. It creates movement in the shoulder joints and develops the muscles of the chest. The abdominal organs are drawn in and the chest lifts and opens.

1 Sit in Virasana and interlock the fingers with the right index finger over the left.

Turn the palms away from you, stretch the arms forwards and straighten the elbows.

2 Extend the arms up with the elbows straight. The upper arms are in line with the ears and the palms are facing the ceiling.

Don't overarch in the lower back – extend the trunk and arms strongly upwards. Hold for 30–60 seconds, lower the arms, change the interlock of the fingers (i.e. left index finger over right) and repeat.

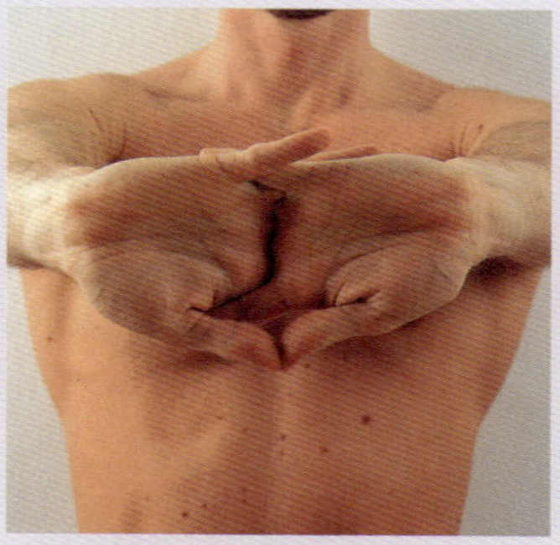

Focus

- Clasp the hands at the root of the fingers and, when extending the arms up, don't allow the fingers to slide apart.
- Change the interlock of the fingers halfway through this pose.

Modification

- If there is difficulty clasping the hands together due to stiffness in the shoulders, then use a strap. Practising this pose will help to relieve the problem.
- If the tops of the feet are painful, put them on a rolled-up blanket.

Hero Pose Forward Bend

ADHO MUKHA VIRASANA

This posture helps to soothe and calm the brain, as well as allowing the body to rest. It relieves fatigue and headaches, stretches and tones the spine and relieves back and neck pain.

1 Kneel on a blanket with the big toes together and the knees hip-width apart. Sit on the heels with the buttocks, and if they don't reach the heels, put a folded blanket on the heels.

Once the buttocks are down, extend the trunk forwards and put the forehead on the floor. Stretch both arms and the sides of the trunk forwards, and put the palms on the floor. Don't take the knees too far apart.

Modification

- The tailbone end of the spine must be supported on the heels. If this cannot be done, put a foam block between the buttocks and the heels.
- If the forehead cannot reach the floor, rest it on a foam block or a folded blanket.

Staff Pose

DANDASANA

This is the basic posture for seated poses and forward bends. It teaches how to sit up straight and extend the spine up.

1 Sit on a raise with the legs stretched out in front. Keep the legs and feet together. Tighten the thigh muscles and knees, extend the heels forwards and extend the toes up towards the ceiling. Place the fingertips on the floor behind the hips, press into the floor and extend the trunk up. Don't overarch the lumbar spine. Roll the shoulders back, open the chest. Look straight ahead and relax the eyes. Move the shoulders away from the ears and the shoulder blades towards the front of the body.

Focus

- Balance the head on the spine centrally.
- Open the ribcage.
- Press the backs of the legs into the floor. Extend the inner heels away from the body, keeping feet upright.

Head of Cow Pose

GOMUKHASANA (ARMS ONLY)

Gomukhasana expands the chest and gives flexibility to the shoulders. As the spine extends strongly upwards, the shoulder joints become less restricted. This pose also makes the wrists more flexible.

1 Sit in Sukhasana or Virasana and extend the right arm.

2 Bend the right arm behind the back and take the forearm up the back with the palm facing outwards.

3 Use the left hand to bring the right elbow closer to the trunk, so that the right hand moves farther up the back.

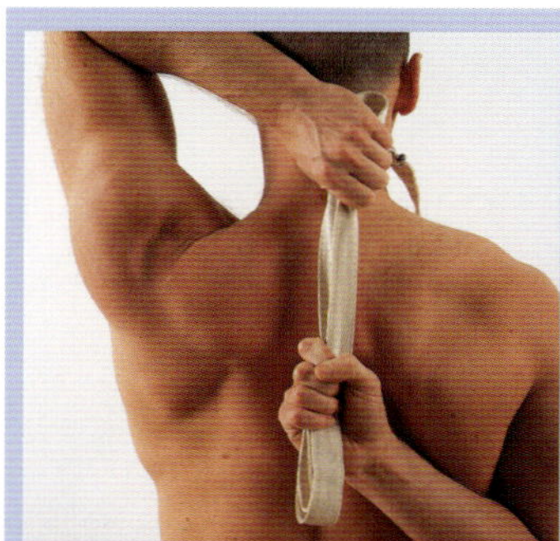

Modification

- Use a strap if the hands cannot grasp one another.
- Keep both sides of the trunk at an equal length and keep the head straight and the eyes level. Don't overarch the lower back.

4 Extend the left arm up, turn the palm forwards, bend the elbow, put the palm of the hand below the nape of the neck and clasp the right hand.

5 Roll the right shoulder back and stretch the left elbow towards the ceiling. Keep the trunk upright and look straight ahead. Hold for 30–60 seconds and repeat on the other side.

Cobbler Pose

BADDHAKONASANA

This pose keeps the knees and hips flexible. It stimulates the pelvis, abdomen and lower back and keeps the kidneys and prostate healthy. It strengthens the bladder and uterus and helps to reduce sciatic pain.

1 Sit in Dandasana on a folded blanket or foam block.

2 Taking the knees out to the side, bend the legs, and use the hands to bring the heels towards the groin.

3 With the fingertips on the floor beside the hips, lift up the trunk, take the shoulders back and open the chest.

Modification

- If you cannot hold the ankles, use a strap.
- If it is difficult to sit up straight, sit with the back supported against a wall.
- Place a support under the knees to relieve the groin.

4 Keep the spine lifted, the chest open and hold the ankles, pressing the soles of the feet together.

Roll the shoulders back and down towards the floor, without overarching the lower back.

Hold for 30–60 seconds, release the ankles and come back to Dandasana.

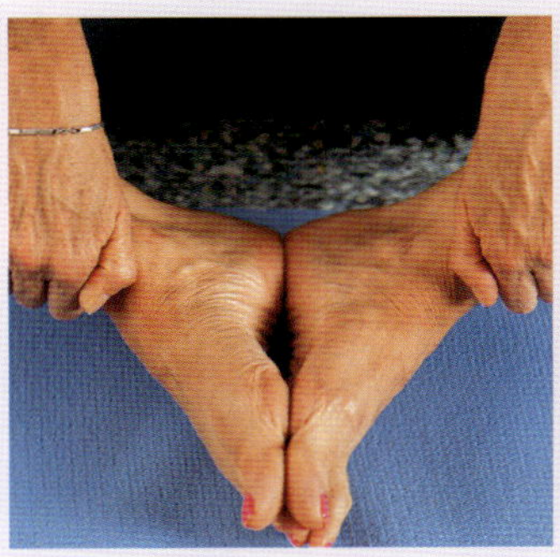

Focus

- Pull the feet in towards the groin as far as you can.
- In the final pose, hold the toes with the hands and lift from the base of the spine.

Seated Angle Pose

UPAVISTAKONASANA

This posture stretches the hamstrings and helps blood circulate in the pelvic region. It strengthens the muscles that support the bladder and uterus, relieves stiffness in the hip joints and alleviates sciatica.

1 Sit in Dandasana on a blanket or mat with no support.

2 Take one leg out to the side, then the other, and widen the distance between the legs. Ensure that the centre of each knee, thigh and foot faces the ceiling. Put the fingertips on the floor behind the hips, press down and extend the spine and trunk upwards.

3 Keeping the spine erect, catch the big toes with the first two fingers of each hand and pull on them. Alternatively, put a strap around each foot. Hold the straps as close to the feet as possible.

Extend the spine, keeping the back concave and opening the chest. Look up.

4 Exhale, bend forwards and, keeping the spine stretched, extend the trunk along the floor, trying to get the chest as close to the floor as possible, breathing normally.

Hold for 30–60 seconds and come back to Dandasana.

Modification
- Sit against the wall to support the back.
- Sit on a foam block positioned by the wall for further support.
- Hold the feet with straps if it is difficult to reach.

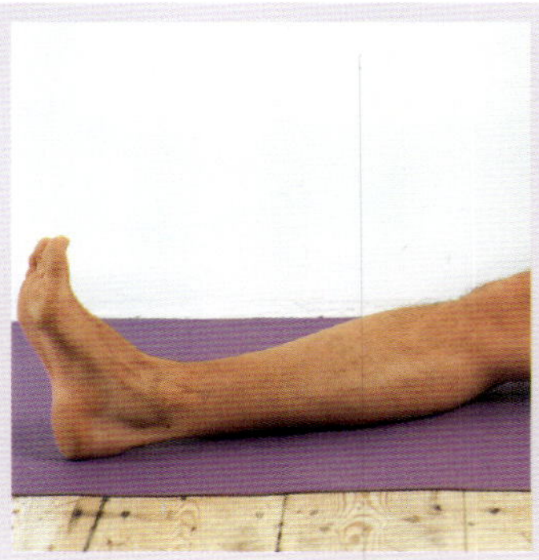

Focus
- Don't allow the feet to roll out. Keep the toes up.
- Extend the inner heels away from the body.
- Press the backs of the legs into the floor and keep the knees facing up.

Boat Pose

PARIPURNA NAVASANA

This pose increases the circulation in the abdomen and tones the abdominal muscles. It improves digestion and relieves lower backache by strengthening the spinal muscles. It also stimulates the thyroid gland.

1 Sit in Dandasana on a blanket or mat with no support. Place the hands on the floor beside the hips.

2 Take the trunk slightly back, bend the knees and raise the bent legs, stretching them forwards.

3 Keep both legs very straight (knees and thighs pulled up) and balance on the buttock bones. Raise the feet to 60 degrees, so that they are higher than the head.

Focus

- The abdominal and leg muscles are used to maintain the balance, not the back muscles.
- Don't collapse the lower back – move it into the body and upwards.
- Stretch the backs of the legs strongly.

4 Stretch both arms forwards, keeping them parallel to the floor with palms facing one another.

Keep stretching the spine and take it into the body so that the trunk doesn't collapse and the chest remains open.

Look straight ahead and make sure there is no tension or strain in the head and neck. There is a tendency to hold the breath in this pose, which causes tension in the eyes, so breathe normally throughout.

Hold for 30–60 seconds, exhale and come back to Dandasana.

Modification

- If balancing on the buttock bones is difficult, keep the hands on the floor, or put the raised feet against the wall.
- If the back is painful, do the posture with bent knees.

Half Boat Pose

ARDHA NAVASANA

The difference between this pose and Paripurna Navasana is the height to which the legs are lifted. Keeping the legs lower tones the liver, gall bladder and spleen. It also strengthens the spinal muscles.

1 Sit in Dandasana on a blanket or mat with no support. Place the hands on the floor beside the hips.

Interlock the fingers and put the hands behind the head just above the neck. Bring the elbows slightly in so that the arms form a semi-circle.

2 Exhale, simultaneously taking the trunk slightly back and raising the legs from the floor to 30 degrees. Keep the knees and thighs pulled up, extend the backs of the legs towards the heels and keep the feet level with the head.

The body rests on the buttock bones and no part of the spine should touch the floor. Look towards the feet.

Breathe normally and keep the eyes soft. Don't strain the neck by pulling the head forwards with the clasped hands – the palms should touch the back of the head and the head should rest lightly on the palms.

Hold for 30–60 seconds, remembering to breathe normally.

Focus

- The difference between Paripurna Navasana and Ardha Navasana is that here the legs are raised to only 30 degrees, not to 60 degrees, and the body is not lowered.
- Interlock the fingers at the back of the head just above the neck.

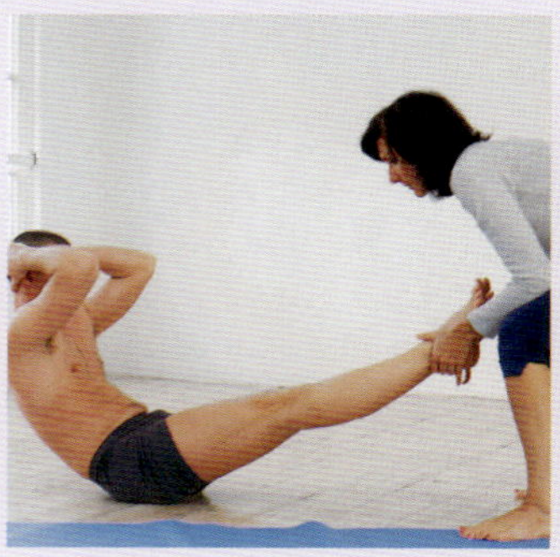

Modification

- If there is a problem with balance, position the raised feet flat against the wall. To hold this position for any length of time requires very strong abdominal muscles, so help may be required.

Head to Knee Pose

JANUSIRSASANA

Janusirsasana stimulates the digestive system, tones the abdominal muscles and brings the brain and heart into a restful state. Forward bends are beneficial for a good night's sleep.

1 Sit in Dandasana on a support, bend the left knee to the side and place the left foot so that the big toe touches the inside of the right thigh.

2 Inhale and extend both arms straight up to the ceiling, moving the shoulder blades into the body. The upper arms are beside the ears. Stretch the spine upwards.

3 Exhale, bend forwards and catch the sides of the right foot with both hands. Make the spine concave and look up. If the lower back aches, do not proceed any further.

Focus

- Keep the right leg straight with the toes pointing up. Press the back of the right leg down on to the floor.

4 Exhale, widen the elbows out to the side, extend the trunk further forwards and take the head down.

Hold for 30–60 seconds, inhale, release the foot, come up and repeat on the other side.

Modification

- If you can't reach the right foot, use a strap around the foot, holding it in a "V" shape with both hands.
- If you are able to catch the foot, hold it around the sides of the foot, not the toes.
- If the lower back is painful, rest the forehead on a stool or bolster.
- Sit on a foam block and support the bent knee on a foam block if it is uncomfortable.

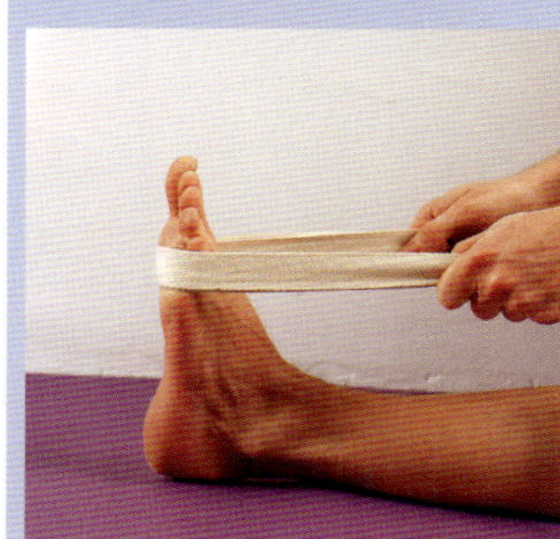

Forward Bend with One Leg Bent Back

TRIANGA MUKHAIKAPADA PASCIMOTTANASANA

This posture improves flexibility of the ankles and knees. It also helps to tone the abdominal muscles and organs.

1 Sit in Dandasana on a support. Bend the left leg back and place the foot beside the left hip.

2 Inhale and extend the arms up, palms facing and upper arms beside the ears. Extend the spine and trunk.

3 Exhale, extend the trunk forwards and clasp the right foot.

Modification

- An easy version is to rest the head on a bolster or rolled-up blanket.
- It may also help to sit on a raise – a folded blanket or a foam block are both good for this.

4 Inhale, lengthen the spine upwards, make the back concave and look up. Exhale, extend the trunk forwards, elongating the spine and taking the head towards the right leg. Widen the elbows out to the side.

Hold for 1–2 minutes, inhale, release the foot, raise the head and come up. Repeat on the other side.

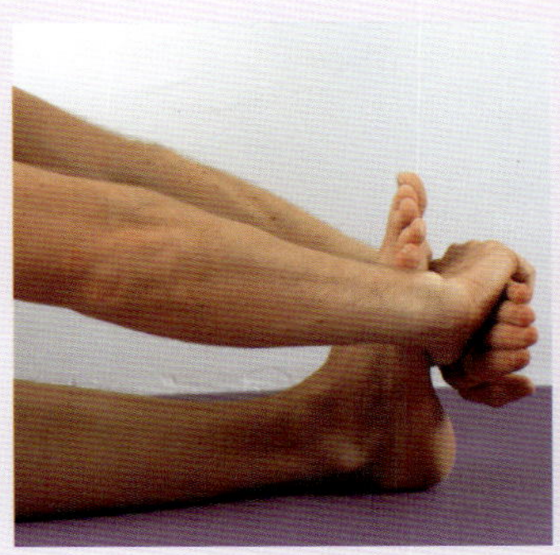

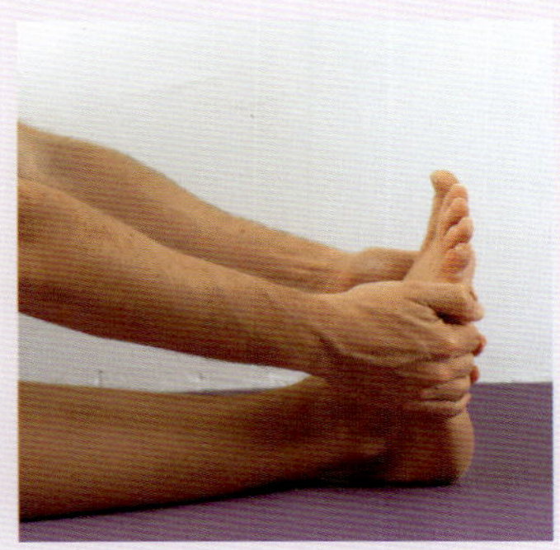

Focus

- Try to catch the hands around the foot. If you can't manage this at first, then use a strap, or clutch the foot on either side, but not the toes.
- Press both buttocks down towards the floor. Pull on the foot (or strap) to lengthen the spine and open the chest.
- Move the shoulders away from the ears and relax the neck and head.

Full Forward Bend

PASCIMOTTANASANA

This posture tones and activates the abdominal organs, aids digestion and rejuvenates the spine. As the body is in a horizontal position in forward bend poses, there is less strain on the heart.

1 Sit in Dandasana on a support.

2 Inhale, extend the arms up (palms facing), keeping the upper arms besides the ears.

3 Exhale, extend the trunk forwards, clasp the sides of both feet with the hands (or use a strap). Inhale and extend forwards, make the back concave, lift the chest and look up.

Focus

- Press the backs of the legs down into the floor to extend the spine more.
- Extend the inner heels away, with toes stretching towards the ceiling.
- Pull on the feet or the strap to lengthen the trunk.

4 Exhale, continue extending the spine/trunk forwards over the legs and catch the hands around the foot (or reach further with the strap). Bend the elbows out to the side.

Fully extend the front of the body and the sides of the trunk. Take the head down. If the back aches, rest the head on a bolster or stool. Hold for 30–60 seconds, inhale and come up.

Modification

- If the backs of the knees are painful when pressed into the floor, place a rolled-up blanket under the knees
- If the forehead cannot reach the floor, rest it on a foam block or a folded blanket.
- In cases of extreme stiffness, or pain in the back, rest the head on a stool covered with a blanket.

Garland Pose
MALASANA

In this pose the arms hang from the neck like a garland. It relieves lower back pain and reduces stiffness in the knees and ankles. It also activates and nourishes the abdominal organs.

1 Sit in Dandasana on a support.

2 Bend the knees and come up into a squatting position.

3 Keep the feet together and support the heels by pulling the support forwards underneath the heels. Separate the thighs and knees and extend the trunk forwards between the legs.

Focus
- If the heels come off the support, add another support. The heels must press on to something.
- The inner thighs lightly grip the sides of the trunk.
- Extend the spine and lengthen the side ribs.
- Round the back when taking the head down.

4 Stretch the arms forwards, pressing the palms into the floor, extend the spine towards the head and look up. Wrap the arms around the legs.

5 Exhale, bend forwards and take the head down towards the floor. Hold the ankles with the hands. Hold for 30–60 seconds and then come up.

Lotus
PADMASANA

Exercise extreme caution when attempting this posture. If the knees are painful, stop immediately and practise Sukhasana as a preparation for Padmasana.

1 Sit in Simple Cross Legs pose (Sukhasana), with the right shin-bone crossed in front.

2 Bring the right foot forwards, supporting it on a foam block if necessary.

3 Carefully lift the right foot and place it as high up on the left thigh as possible.

Bring the left foot forwards and support it on a block on the other side.

Lift the left foot on to the right thigh. If there is pain in the knees, sit in half-Padmasana, i.e. first leg in Padmasana and second leg in Sukhasana.

4 Press the fingertips into the floor beside the hips to extend the spine up. Continue to lift from the base of the spine upwards through the neck to the top of the head.

Hold for 30–60 seconds. Release the legs, and repeat with the left shin-bone crossed in front of the right.

Many people will find they lack the flexibility in the knees to do this posture at first, but in time suppleness will increase and the posture will become comfortable. Changing the cross of the legs regularly means that they will develop evenly on both sides.

Focus

- When bending the knee, to avoid straining and to create space, use the fingers to draw the top of the calf muscle and the bottom of the back thigh muscle away from the back of the knee.
- For painful knees, place a strap at the back of the knee and pull on it as you take the leg into Padmasana.
- If the right knee doesn't reach the floor, support it on a foam block, then take the left leg into Padmasana.

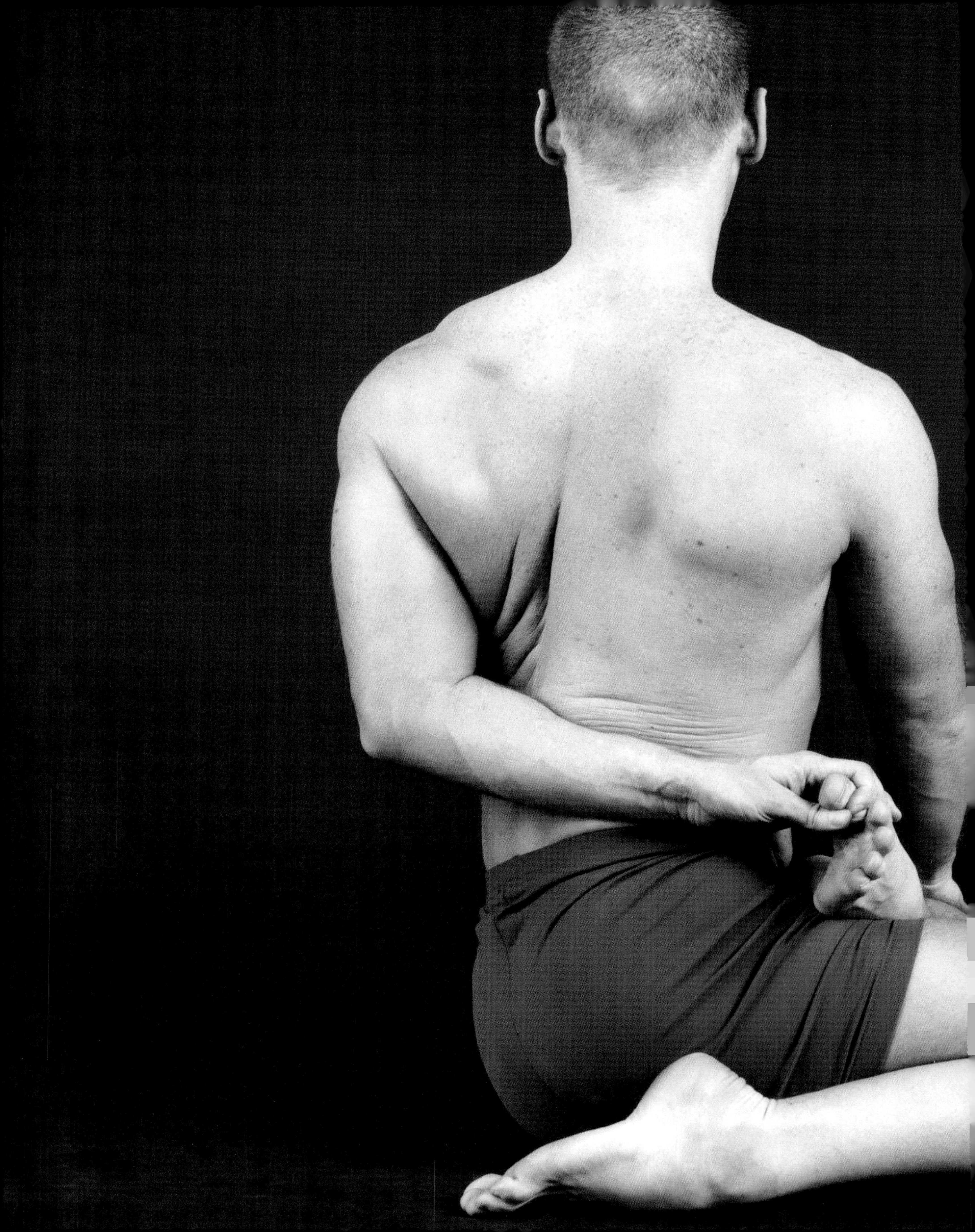

Twists

All lateral extension postures (twists) create flexibility in the spine and shoulders. They activate and nourish the pelvic and abdominal organs, and bring relief to back, hip and groin problems. As the spine becomes more supple, blood flow to the spinal nerves improves, and energy levels are raised. When practising twists, lift the spine first, and then turn the abdomen, chest and finally the head. Moving the shoulder blades into the back will improve the turn.

Standing Twist
STANDING MARICYASANA

This posture reduces stiffness in the neck and shoulders. It improves the alignment of the spine and strengthens the spinal muscles. It also relieves lower back pain and sciatica.

1 Put a stool near the wall. Stand in Tadasana with the wall on your right. Bend the right knee and place the foot on the stool, keeping the right thigh against the wall.

Inhale, stretch the left leg strongly up and keep the toes of this foot facing forwards. Extend the trunk towards the ceiling. Exhale, turn the front body to face the wall, and place the hands on the wall at shoulder level.

Inhale, extend trunk further, exhale, press the hands into the wall to enable the trunk to turn more to the right. Turn as far as you can, look over the right shoulder. Hold for 20–40 seconds, release, and repeat on the other side.

Focus
- Don't allow the front body to lean towards the wall.
- Move the shoulder blades into the body and downwards towards the waist to open the chest.

Easy Pose Twist
SUKHASANA (TWIST)

In this easy, cross-legged twist, use the breath to lift and turn. Relax the shoulders, moving them away from the ears and into the body.

1 Sit in step 1 of Sukhasana, with the fingertips on the floor.

2 Place the palm of the left hand on the outer right thigh. Inhale, press the right fingertips into the floor and extend the spine upwards. Exhale, press the left palm into the thigh and turn towards the right.

3 Look over the right shoulder. Hold for 30–40 seconds, release and repeat to the other side, changing the cross of the legs.

Hero Pose Twist
VIRASANA (TWIST)

This pose strengthens the abdominal muscles and relieves indigestion. Lower backache is eased the hips become more flexible and the hamstring muscles more supple.

1 Sit in Virasana with the soles of the feet facing the ceiling, and the palms on the feet.

Sit on a foam block or folded blanket if this helps.

2 Put the left fingertips on the floor/block beside the left hip, and put the right palm on the left thigh.

3 Inhale, press the left fingers into the floor and lift the trunk. Exhale, press the right palm into the left thigh and turn to the left. With each exhalation, turn the abdomen, waist, chest and shoulders further to the left and look over the left shoulder.

Hold for 30–60 seconds, release and repeat on the other side.

Focus
- Keep the shoulders relaxed, moving them down, away from the ears and into the body.
- Try to turn a little more with each exhalation.
- Use the breath to lift and turn.

Modification
- Sit on a wooden or foam block and use another block to place the fingertips on, behind the body.
- As with all directional poses, start with the right side and repeat on the left.

Simple Twist Using a Chair

BHARADVAJASANA (CHAIR)

This twist is an easier version of Bharadvajasana I. The chair is used to allow a safe and effective rotation of the trunk. It relieves a stiff back, neck and shoulders, and exercises the abdominal muscles.

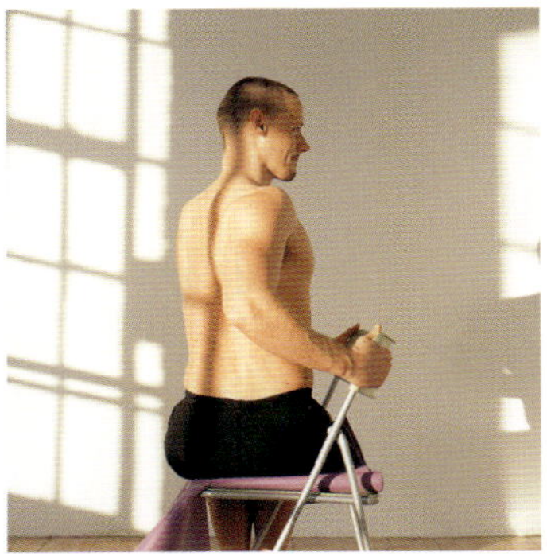

1 Sit on a chair with the right side of the body facing the chair-back. Keep the knees and feet together. Sit up straight and look straight ahead.

2 Inhale, extend the spine up and put the hands on the back of the chair.

3 Exhale, and turn the trunk to the right, using the hands to help you turn.

Inhale, lift the spine further, take the shoulder blades into the body and open the chest. Rotate the spine further so that the chest is parallel to the back of the chair. Keep the neck free from tension or strain.

4 Exhale, turn the trunk more and look over the right shoulder. Grip the back of the seat for leverage. Hold for 20–30 seconds, exhale, release the hands, face forwards and repeat on the other side.

Focus

- Press the feet firmly into the floor to lift the trunk.
- Press the left buttock down towards the seat of the chair – it wants to lift. Use the inhalation to extend the spine; use the exhalation to turn it.

Modification

- This twist can be made easier by raising the feet, or by placing a block between the knees.

Simple Twist

BHARADVAJASANA I

This twisting posture creates flexibility in the neck and shoulders and relieves lower back pain. It reduces pain in the knees and tones the abdominal organs, particularly the kidneys, liver, spleen and gall bladder.

1 Sit in Dandasana on a support.

2 Bend both legs to the left, placing the feet beside the left hip. Put the left foot on top of the arch of the right foot.

3 Keep the soles of both feet facing the ceiling.

Extend the trunk and spine up. Put the right fingertips beside the right hip and the palm of the left hand on the right knee.

Inhale, press the right fingers into the floor to lift the spine.

Exhale, press the left palm against the right knee to turn the trunk to the right.

4 Repeat, turning the abdomen, waist, chest and shoulders further with each exhalation.

Look over the right shoulder, hold for 30–40 seconds, exhale, release and repeat on the other side.

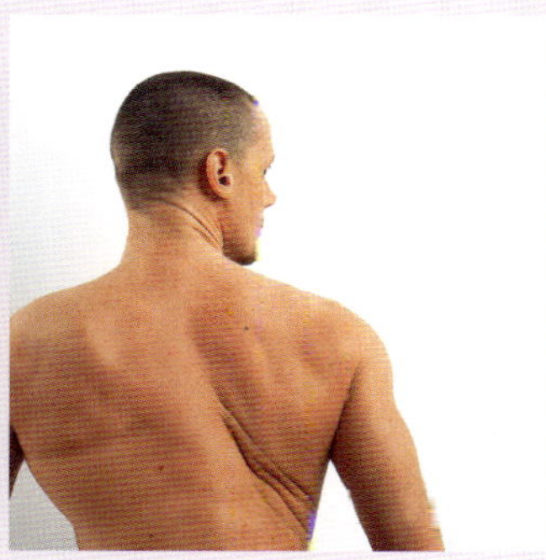

Focus

- Rest the left foot over the instep of the right foot.
- Press the left buttock down towards the floor to get the whole spine turning.
- Use the breath to lift and turn.
- Draw the shoulder blades down and into the body to lift the spine and open the chest.

Catching Arms Behind

MARICYASANA I (TWIST ONLY)

This spinal twist removes stiffness in the shoulders and spine and reduces lower backache. As there is an increased blood flow to the abdominal organs, digestion improves and the organs become toned.

1 Sit in Dandasana on a support. Keep the fingertips pressing into the floor beside the hips. Bend the right leg so that the knee faces the ceiling and the right heel is in line with the right buttock bone, toes pointing forwards.

Extend the left leg along the floor. Turn the trunk to the left and take the right elbow in front of the right knee (fingers pointing to the ceiling). Rotate the trunk more to the left.

Modification

- To ease your body into this posture, use a block under the floor hand and a lift to sit on.
- If you cannot reach your hands behind your back, use a strap. Fold the strap in two and grasp it firmly behind you, pulling the arms around.

2 Press the left fingertips into the floor to lengthen the spine. Wrap the right arm around the right leg and take it behind the body.

Turn the left shoulder slightly back and swing the left arm behind the back, catching hold of it with the right hand. If the hands don't reach, use a strap.

Turn the trunk as far as possible to the left, turn the head and look over the left shoulder. Move the back ribs and shoulder blades into the body to open the chest, and turn more. Extend the front of the body from the pubis to the chin. Hold for 20–30 seconds, then release and repeat on the other side.

Focus

- Keep the knee of the bent leg facing the ceiling throughout, and the heel close to the body.
- Press the sole of the right foot into the floor to lift the spine as much as possible.
- Move the shoulder blades into the body and down towards the floor to extend and rotate the spine more.
- The full posture, and Maricyasana II, combine a twist with a forward bend suitable for advanced yogis only.

Sitting Twist
MARICYASANA III

This stronger twist increases energy levels. As there is a vigorous rotation, the abdominal organs such as liver, spleen, pancreas, kidneys and intestines are toned and massaged, improving their performance and function.

1 Sit in Dandasana on a support. Lift the spine upwards.

2 Bend the right knee up towards the ceiling, and put the sole of the foot on the floor in line with the right buttock bone. Turn to the right. Put the fingertips of the right hand on the floor/block behind the right hip. Bend the left arm and place the elbow on the outside of the right knee.

3 Try to get the left armpit closer to the knee. Inhale, press the right fingers into the floor and lift the spine.

Exhale, press the left arm against the knee and the knee against the arm, and turn further to the right.

Repeat the lift and turn. Move the spine into the body, take the shoulder blades into the back and turn further. Look over the right shoulder. Rotate the left side of the ribcage, the left armpit and the left hip towards the right to increase the turn of the spine. Keep the chest lifted and open by moving the shoulders down and the shoulder blades forwards.

Hold for 30–60 seconds, release and repeat on the other side.

Focus

- Press the right foot firmly into the floor, especially the big toes and inner heel, and press the back of the left leg into the floor and stretch it forwards, toes facing up.
- Use the breath to lift and turn.
- Ensure that the bent knee stays facing the ceiling – when placing the bent arm over the knee, don't push it out of alignment.

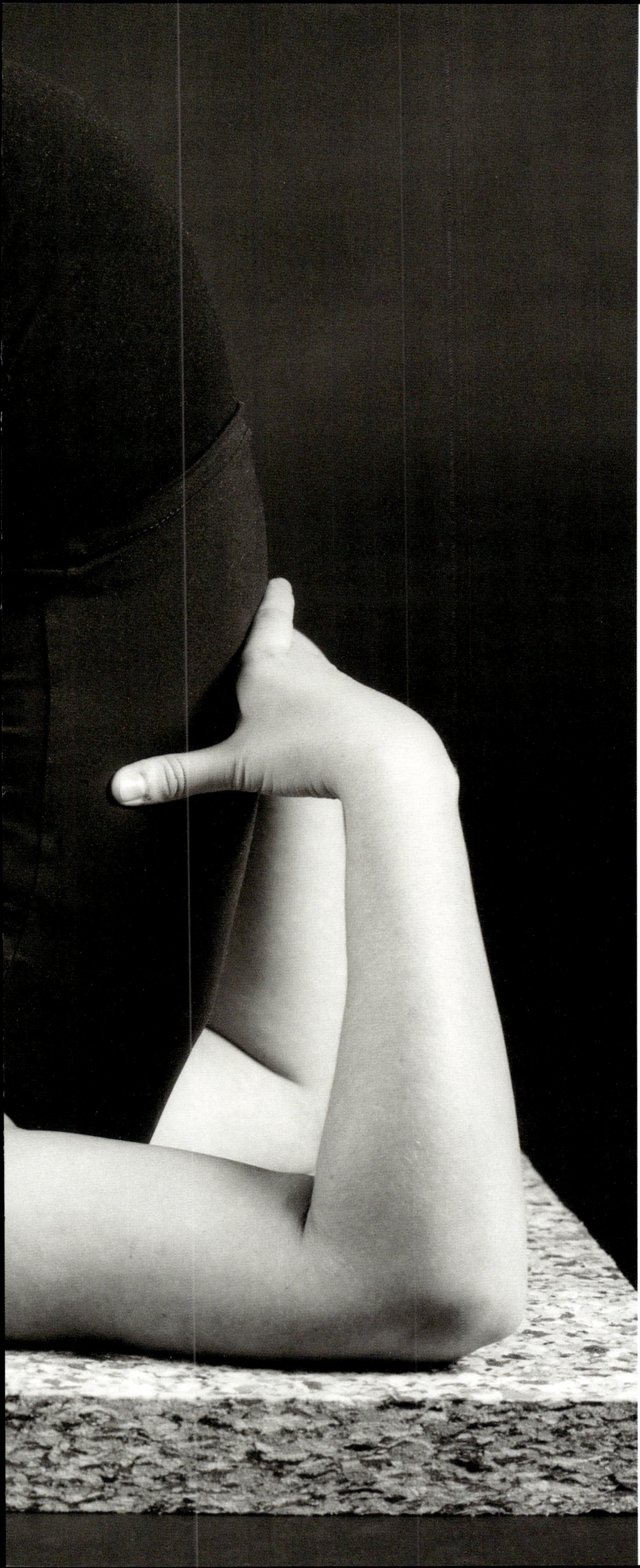

inverted Asanas

All inverted postures revitalize the entire system of the body. Because the internal organs are inverted, they become energized, and the brain is nourished as blood flow towards it is increased. Since there is no weight on the legs, inversions bring relief to tired, strained legs. Women should not practise any inversions during menstruation as this interferes with the natural flow of blood at this time.

Legs Up the Wall Pose

VIPARITA KARANI

This restorative pose calms the brain, opens the chest and rests the legs. It helps reduce respiratory problems, eases headaches and relieves indigestion and nausea. It is also beneficial for preventing varicose veins.

1 Put a wooden block against the wall with a bolster in front and a folded blanket in front of the bolster.

2 Sit on the bolster, sideways to the wall with the hip touching the wall.

3 Swivel the trunk around, using the hands to balance. Take one leg up the wall, keep the buttocks against the wall and straighten the second leg.

Focus

• Keep the inner edges of the feet together so that the soles of the feet are parallel to the ceiling.

• Keep the abdomen soft and press the shoulders into the floor.

4 Once both legs are up the wall, carefully take the trunk down and lower the shoulders and head on to the floor. Keep the backs of the legs and buttocks against the wall and open the chest.

5 Take the arms over the head, breathe evenly and relax. Hold for 5–6 minutes and then come down.

Supported Shoulder Stand

SALAMBA SARVANGASANA

This is known as the queen, or mother, of the postures. It supports the thyroid gland, frees the body of toxins and is beneficial for relieving respiratory problems such as asthma, congestion and sinusitis.

1 Place four small, or one large, foam block and a folded blanket on the mat for comfort. Lie with the shoulders and arms on the support and the head on the floor.

Stretch the arms towards the feet and move the shoulders away from the head.

2 Bend the knees towards the chest. Press the fingertips into the floor, and take the knees towards the head.

3 Lift the hips and trunk and immediately support the back with the palms of both hands. Straighten the legs and move the hands up the back towards the shoulder blades to increase the lift of the chest. Bring the chest towards the chin and stretch the whole body straight up. Look towards the chest. Hold for 2–5 minutes.

Focus

- Press the hands into the back to move the back ribs towards the front of the chest and to lift the trunk. Press the upper arms into the support.
- If the elbows slip apart, tie a belt around the upper arms (just above the elbows) to keep them shoulder-width.
- Stretch the legs up and keep the soles of the feet parallel to the ceiling – rest the toes on a wall for balance.

Supported Shoulder Stand

SALAMBA SARVANGASANA (AGAINST WALL)

This is an easier version of the shoulder stand. If pressure is experienced in the head while in Salamba Sarvangasana, come down immediately and try the pose against the wall or using a chair.

1 Sit as close as possible to the wall and place a foam block just under your left buttock.

2 Lean back, swivel the trunk around and take one leg, and then the second, up the wall. Keep the buttocks against the wall, the shoulders near the edge of the support and the head on the floor.

3 Press the feet into the wall and raise the hips and chest. Support the back with the hands and move the elbows towards one another.

4 Straighten the legs, press the heels firmly into the wall and lift the chest, trunk and hips. Hold for 2–5 minutes, bend the legs and come down.

Modification

- If you cannot manage Salamba Sarvangasana alone or against a wall, get someone to assist you by holding your legs upright. Begin by resting your feet on their thighs, then allow them to correct your alignment.
- Once you have done the posture with help, you may find it easier to achieve on your own.

Shoulder Balance in Chair

CHAIR SARVANGASANA

In the classic Salamba Sarvangasana posture, the hands support the back. In this modified version, a chair is used and this allows the pose to be held for longer with minimal strain on the neck and back.

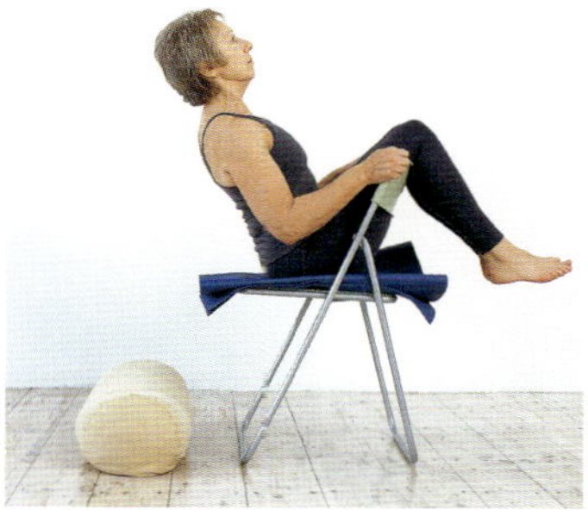

1 Place a bolster on the floor parallel to the front legs of the chair. Fold a mat and put it on the seat of the chair.

2 Sit on the chair and bend the legs over the back of the chair. Hold on to the sides of the chair. Lean the trunk slightly back.

3 Lower the back on to the seat of the chair. Slide the buttocks and back towards the front edge of the chair seat. Carefully rest the shoulders on the bolster and the back of the head on the floor. Hold the back chair legs.

Focus

- As with other inversions, Chair Sarvangasana should not be practised during menstruation.

4 Straighten one leg at a time. When both legs are straight slide the hands further down the back chair legs to increase the stretch of the arms. Move the shoulders away from the ears and the shoulder blades towards the head to open and lift the chest.

Breathe normally and look towards the chest. Hold the pose for up to 5 minutes, keeping the back of the neck soft.

Coming out of the posture

- Return first one leg, then the other, to step 3. Begin to release the grip of the hands on the chair legs and gently push the chair slightly away.
- Slide the back then buttocks on to the bolster, pushing the chair by the seat. Rest for a moment, roll over to the side, slide off the bolster and come up.

Half Plough Pose

ARDHA HALASANA

This supported version of Halasana reduces the effects of fatigue, anxiety and insomnia, and relieves stress-related headaches. If you have lower back pain, practising Ardha Halasana will not aggravate it.

1 Place a chair/stool over the head before going into Salamba Sarvangasana. From this pose, take the legs down on to the stool to support the thighs.

2 Straighten the legs and support the spine with the hands.

3 Take the arms over the head and relax. Hold for 2–5 minutes, bend the knees, slide the thighs off the stool and come down.

Plough Pose

HALASANA

This inversion relaxes the brain. It is beneficial to practise it when you have a cold, and it improves the functioning of the thyroid and parathyroid glands.

1 Go into Salamba Sarvangasana with the shoulders on a folded blanket or foam support. Take the legs down over the head and put the feet on the floor.

Keep supporting the back with the hands, lift the back and keep the chest open and lifted. Straighten the legs, extending them away from the hips.

Relax the eyes, hold for 2–5 minutes and come down.

Modification

- If the back hurts, put a support under the toes.
- The tips of the toes press into the floor or bricks. Lift thigh bones towards the ceiling and stretch the heels away from the head.

Shoulder Stand Bridge Pose

SETU BANDHA SARVANGASANA (SUPPORTED)

This pose opens the chest and gives a mild extension to the spine. It calms the brain, reduces depression and relieves headaches. Digestion is improved and the internal organs are strengthened.

1 Lie on the floor with the knees bent and the toes pointing towards the wall.

2 Keeping the head, neck and shoulders on the floor, press the feet down and lift the hips from the floor. Put a wooden block vertically under the sacrum near the tailbone.

3 Straighten one leg at a time and place the feet on the wall at whatever height is comfortable for the lower back.

Focus

- Maintain a strong stretch on the back of the legs from the buttock bones to the heels.
- There should be no tension in the neck.
- Lift the breastbone towards the chin.

4 Open the chest, and extend the arms towards the feet, which are pressing firmly into the wall. Roll the tops of the shoulders towards the floor and move the shoulder blades towards the front cf the body to open the chest.

Hold for 1–2 minutes, then bend the legs, remove the block and come down.

Modification

- If the wooden block is uncomfortable on the sacrum (lower back), use four stacked foam blocks.
- If the lower back hurts, support the feet on wooden blocks or a bolster.

supine and prone Asanas

There are two types of supine/prone postures: some are restful and are used for recuperation, while others strengthen the back, arms and legs. In all of them, the abdomen is stretched and the spine and hips gain flexibility.

Fish Pose
MATSYASANA (SIMPLE)

Here the muscles of the spine and abdomen are fully stretched. Flexibility in the hips, knees and ankles develops and the chest lifts and opens, so the depth of the breath improves.

1 Sit in Sukhasana (simple cross legs), crossing the right shin-bone over the left.

2 Lean back by resting on the elbows and then lie down. Soften the groin to allow the knees to release towards the floor.

3 Take the arms over the head, straighten the elbows and extend the arms strongly back.

Extend the trunk towards the head and the knees away from the head. Keep the lower back long (don't arch it) and move the shoulders away from the floor and towards the ceiling to lift and open the chest.

Hold for 1–2 minutes, come up, change the cross-over of the legs and repeat.

Modification

- If the groin is painful, support each knee with a foam block or bolster.

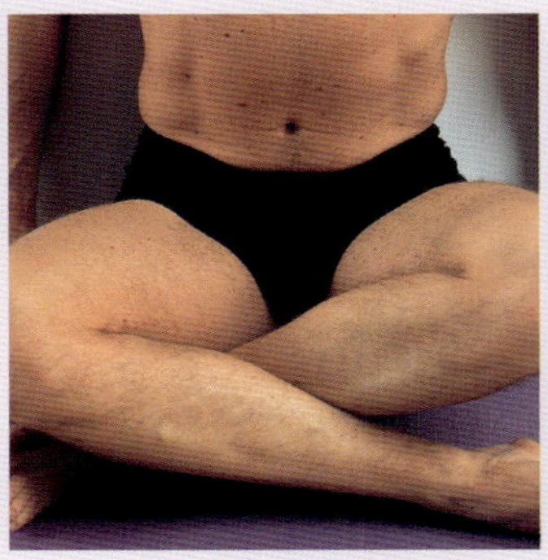

Focus

- Cross the legs evenly at the shins, not at the ankles, and change the cross.
- Don't overarch in the lower back – lengthen it by extending the sacrum towards the feet.

Cross Bolsters

This pose gently stretches the back and soothes the brain. As the back ribs are supported by the vertical bolster, the chest opens and breathing deepens, the abdomen extends and the whole body relaxes.

1 Place two bolsters on the floor, the first one horizontal and the second lengthways on top. Sit on the top bolster where it crosses over the bottom one, and bend the knees.

2 Lie back by resting on the elbows, placing the lower back on the highest part of the top bolster. Lower the shoulders down on to the floor.

3 Extend the legs forwards, take the arms over the head and relax them.

Hold for 2–5 minutes, then bend the knees, slide back towards the head, roll over to the side and get up.

Modification

- The shoulders must rest on the floor. If this is difficult, put a folded blanket underneath them.
- If the lower back aches, lift the feet and place them on two or three foam blocks. It may be easier to lie on top of the bolsters placed separately lengthways.
- To make the posture more relaxing, tie two straps around the legs, one at the ankles and one across the middle of the thighs.

Supine Cobbler Pose
SUPTA BADDHAKONASANA

This recuperative pose is particularly useful for women, especially during menstruation. The strap around the lower back lengthens the spine, and the bolster lifts the chest. This pose also helps sciatica.

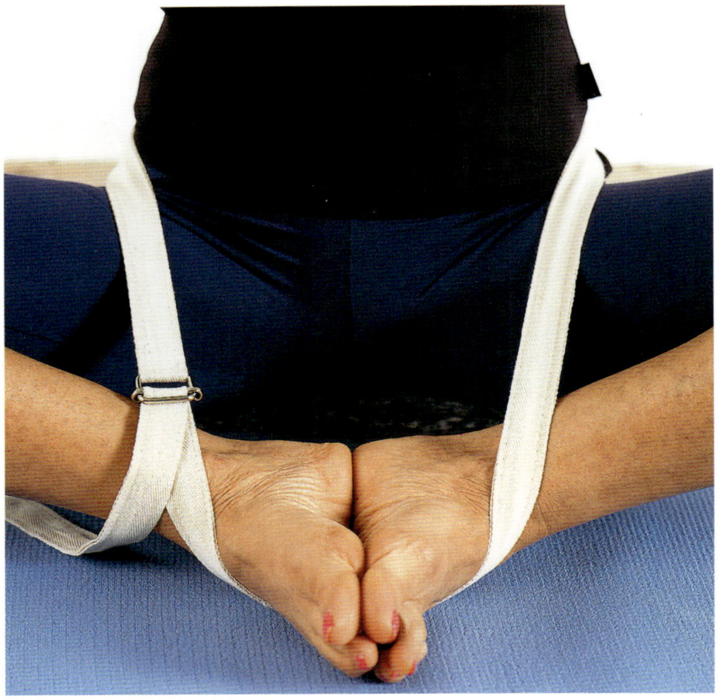

1 Place a bolster lengthways on the floor with a folded blanket at the top end. Sit in front of the bolster with the edge in contact with the lower back. Bend the knees out to the sides, take the soles of the feet together and draw the heels as close to the pubis as possible. Loop the strap across the lower back, over the hips and bind the soles of the feet together at the ankles.

Modification

- If the back is aching, put more support on the bolster and under the head.
- If the groin is uncomfortable, support each knee with a foam block or bolster.
- If the back aches in this posture despite the extra support, come out of it and lie over the bolster with the legs crossed as in Sukhasana.

2 Lie back over the bolster, keeping the edge touching the lower back, and support the head and neck with the folded blanket.

Feel the bolster gently moving the spine into the body and the resultant broadening, lifting and opening of the chest. Allow the shoulders to roll down towards the bolster. Keep the face, mouth and throat relaxed.

Take the arms out to the side, keeping the palms facing upwards. Relax them and close the eyes.

Hold for 2–5 minutes, focusing on the breathing, then open the eyes and come up.

Focus

- Make a circle with a strap and place it over the head. Bring it down to the hips, and hook it over the feet.
- As you lie back, the strap will keep the feet as close to the body as possible.

Reclining Hero Pose

SUPTA VIRASANA

This restful posture stretches the abdominal organs and the pelvic region. It also relieves aching legs and is good for digestion. If the back aches despite extra support, lie over the bolster with legs crossed.

1 Place a bolster lengthways on a mat with a folded blanket at the top end to support the head. Sit in Virasana on a foam block placed against the bolster.

Hold the bolster against the lower back and lie over the bolster, supporting the head and neck on the folded blanket. Take the arms out to the side, palms facing upwards. Hold for 3–5 minutes and come up.

Modification

- If the knees or lower back are painful, put another bolster under the first one.
- Keep the shoulders back, the chest open and raised.
- If necessary, place more blankets under the head.

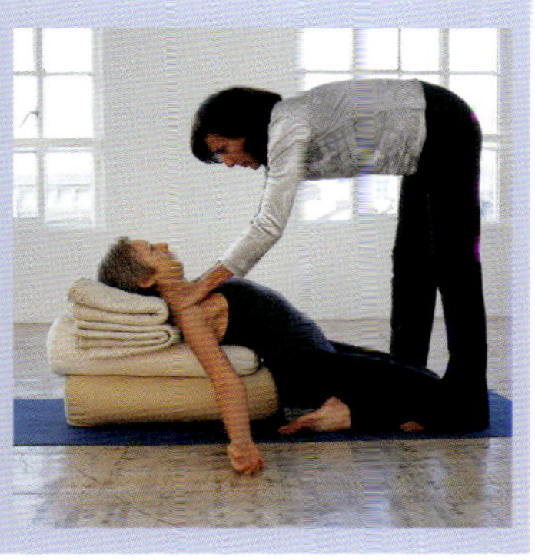

Legs Stretched to 90 Degrees

URDHVA PRASARITA PADASANA

This pose strengthens the lower back and gives relief to tired legs. The brain stays calm while focusing on the breath.

1 Sit sideways to the wall and move the right hip and buttock as close to the wall as possible. Lean back, swivel the trunk around and take both legs up the wall. The head should be in line with the tailbone.

Lie down and allow the wall to support the legs. Extend both arms over the head, keep the hips down, and stretch the legs up the wall. Hold for 40–60 seconds and come up.

Focus

- Extend the backs of the legs towards the ceiling and press them into the wall.
- Keep the lower back and hips moving towards the floor.
- Take the shoulder blades into the body to open the chest.
- This is considered a supine, relaxing pose, while Viparita Karani raises the hips and back off the floor, and is therefore considered an inverted posture.

Prone Leg Stretches
SUPTA PADANGUSTHASANA I & II

These postures are good for stretching the hamstrings. They strengthen the knees and hip joints, and help to relieve sciatica. The pelvic area is aligned, removing stiffness from the lower back and easing backache.

1 Lie down on a mat or blanket, with the soles of both feet touching the wall.

2 Bend the right knee towards the chest, and grab the big toe with the right thumb and forefinger.

3 Supta Panangusthasana I – Stretch the right leg straight up towards the ceiling while pressing the sole of the left foot more firmly into the wall. Keep the right leg at a 90-degree angle. (If the back is painful, take the leg to a 60-/70-degree angle.)

Lengthen the back of the right leg from the buttock bone to the heel. Press the back of the left leg into, and along, the floor. Pull on the foot to open the chest. Hold for 30–40 seconds, come down and repeat with the left leg.

4 Supta Padangusthasana II – following the instructions as before, extend the leg up to 90 degrees and then stretch the right leg and arm sideways to the right. Take the right leg towards the floor without disturbing the alignment of the head, trunk or left leg.

Press the sole of the left foot into the wall and the back of the leg into the floor. If the whole body rolls over towards the right, put a support under the right foot to control the descent of the leg (if using a strap, pull on it with the right hand) and extend the left arm out to the side.

Open the chest. Hold for 30–40 seconds and repeat on the other side.

Modification

- Students with tight hamstrings can use a strap around the foot, rather than catching the big toe.
- If difficulty is experienced with the leg to the side, rest the thigh on a bolster.

Dog Pose

ADHO MUKHA SVANASANA

Dog pose is a good all-over stretch. It extends the legs and strengthens the ankles. It also eases stiffness in the neck, shoulders and wrists. Staying longer in this pose removes fatigue and restores energy.

1 Get on to all fours (hands and knees). Place the palms on the floor, hands shoulder-width apart, with the middle fingers pointing forwards. Take the knees hip-width apart and tuck the toes under.

Press the hands firmly into the floor, particularly the thumbs and index fingers. Fully straighten the arms, extending them from the floor towards the shoulders. Move the shoulders away from the ears and the shoulder blades into the body to open the chest.

2 Raise the hips, straighten the legs and extend the heels towards the floor. Press the thighs back. Straighten both elbows, lift the shoulders towards the waist and stretch the trunk up.

Relax the head towards the floor. Keep the arms and legs firm. Push the heels towards the ground.

Hold for 20–30 seconds, bend the knees and come down.

Modification

- For an easier version of this posture, work with the hands or feet supported by a wall.
- Turn the hands out and place the palms on the floor with the index fingers and thumbs against the wall.
- Alternatively, start with the back to the wall, rest the heels up the wall and come into the pose.
- If there is strain in the head or neck, rest the forehead on a bolster for a more restful version of this posture.

Dog Pose (head up)

URDHVA MUKHA SVANASANA

This pose strengthens the spine, relieves backache and sciatica, and tones the internal organs. It also helps to expand the chest and increase flexibility in the neck and shoulders.

1 Lie face down on the floor and stretch both legs back, pressing the tops of the feet into the floor. (If the lower back hurts, tuck the toes under.) Place the palms on the floor beside the chest and spread the fingers.

2 Inhale, raise the head and chest, straighten the arms and lock the elbows.

3 Lift the hips, thighs and knees a few centimetres/inches off the floor, bringing the tailbone and sacrum forwards.

Keeping the elbows straight, roll the shoulders back, lift the chest further and curve the trunk back between the arms. Lengthen the back of the neck, take the head back slightly and look up. Stay for 30–40 seconds, breathing evenly.

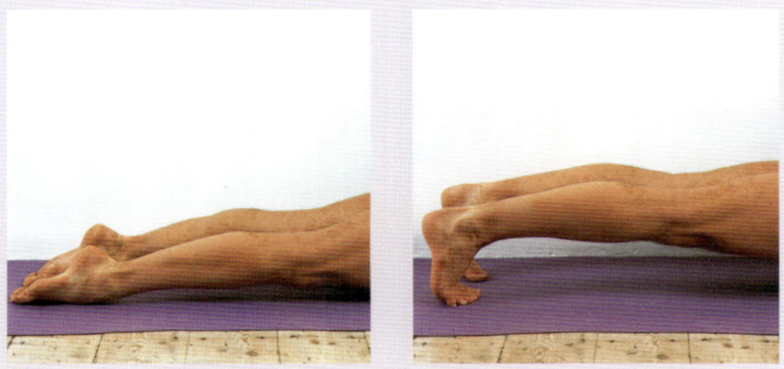

Focus

- Keep the toes pointing backwards, and lift the legs off the floor. If difficulty is experienced lifting the legs off the floor, tuck the toes under and then lift up.
- To lift the trunk and chest more, put each hand on a wooden block.

Locust Pose

SALABHASANA I

Salabhasana strengthens the back and improves flexibility in the spiral muscles. The abdominal muscles become stronger, improving digestion. Stiffness is reduced in the neck and shoulders

1 Lie face down on the floor with the arms beside the trunk, feet together, knees straight and the toes stretching back. Turn the palms up. Stretch the arms and raise them so the hands are parallel to the floor. Press the sacrum down and raise the head, chest and legs as high as they will go without causing any back pain.

2 Extend the trunk forwards, the legs and arms back and lift the chest.

Balance on the lower abdomen, look straight ahead and breathe normally. Hold the pose for 20–30 seconds and then release and lower the chest, head and legs.

Focus

- In everyday life we are continually bending forwards, but have little reason to bend backwards. Back bends help to extend the heart muscles, stretch the front side of the lungs and maintain flexibility in the respiratory muscles, thereby increasing lung capacity. They are also useful for nourishing and toning the abdominal organs and stimulating the adrenal glands.
- Back bends have not been featured here, as they are advanced postures that should be carried out only under the supervision of an experienced and qualified teacher. For a preliminary back bend try Ustrasana, over the page, in the moderated version at first.

Modification

- Don't raise the arms and legs too high, as this will cause pain in the lower back.
- Stretch the shoulders back, keeping the arms parallel.
- Keep the legs together and the knees straight.
- If it is difficult to do the pose with the feet together, place a foam block between the feet, press the inner edges of the feet into the block and lift the legs.
- In order to open the chest more, and increase the extension in the arms, put a wooden block on the palm of each hand. Imagine the blocks are heavy weights, and without actually lifting the hands any higher, push the palms into the blocks as if trying to lift them.

Camel Pose
USTRASANA

Although neither supine nor prone, this posture is preparation for more advanced back bends. It strengthens the spinal muscles and enables you to understand the curvature of the spine.

1 Kneel with the knees and feet hip-width apart. Press the shin-bones and tops of the feet firmly into the floor. Place the hands on the waist, and lengthen the trunk upwards.

2 Exhale, keep the chest lifting and curve the spine back, moving the spine deeply into the body. Extend the arms towards the heels and hold the heels with the hands.

3 Keep the neck long and take the head back. Look behind you. Keep lifting and opening the chest.

Hold for 15–20 seconds, inhale, raise the head, release the hands and lift the trunk.

Focus
- Move the back ribs and shoulder blades more deeply into the back to open the chest more.
- Straighten the arms and hold the heels more firmly to activate the shoulders.
- Finish this pose by leaning forwards to extend the spine in the opposite direction.
- Keep the thighs perpendicular to the floor.

Modification
- Students who cannot reach their heels can arch over bolsters propped on a chair, or place a rolled-up blanket under the tops of their feet so the heels are easier to reach.

Corpse Pose

SAVASANA

After performing the asanas, this relaxation pose helps to release tension in the muscles, settle the breathing and calm the mind. Energy flows into and through the body, recharging it and removing stress.

1 Sit in the centre of the mat with the knees bent and the feet on the floor. Put a folded blanket at the head end of the mat.

2 Lower the trunk down, rest on the elbows and check the body alignment, then carefully lower the trunk on to the floor. Place the centre of the back of the head on the support.

3 Straighten one leg at a time and, when straight, keep the legs and feet together.

Release the tension in the legs and allow the feet to drop out to the side.

4 Stretch the arms out to each side, slightly away from the sides of the trunk, and turn the palms so that the knuckles of the little fingers are on the floor as much as the knuckles of the index fingers. Shut the eyes by lowering the upper eyelids towards the lower eyelids.

Relax the eyes and facial features and allow the body to sink into the floor. Breathe evenly and focus on the breath in order to keep the brain calm and passive. Don't go to sleep.

Hold for 5–10 minutes, then slowly open the eyes, bend the knees, roll over to the side and slowly come up.

Focus

- Let your body go and surrender to the floor.
- Relax the fingers and palms of the hands.
- Keep the head straight, with the bridge of the nose facing the ceiling.
- Relax the thigh muscles and let the legs roll away from one another.
- Draw the organs of perception (eyes, ears and tongue) inwards so that the mind and body become one and inner silence is experienced.

Breathing

UJJAYI PRANAYAMA

In Pranayama the brain becomes quiet which allows the nervous system to function more effectively. It generates a store of energy in the body, while strengthening and increasing the capacity of the lungs.

1 Normal Inhalation/Extended Exhalation

Lie in Savasana on a bolster or blanket, with another folded blanket under the head. Cover the eyes with a bandage. Spend a few minutes becoming aware of your normal breathing. Exhale, relax the abdomen. Inhale normally.

Exhale slowly, quietly and smoothly, lengthening the breath without straining. Inhale normally again. Exhale slowly, deeply and smoothly.

If breathlessness or fatigue is experienced in between cycles, take a few normal breaths before proceeding. Continue in this manner for 5 minutes. Return to normal breathing to allow the lungs to recover.

Focus

- Beginners should master the postures and gain control over the body before attempting Pranayama.
- Keep the face, eyes, mouth and throat relaxed.
- Keep the chest and ribcage lifted throughout.
- Keep the shoulders moving away from the ears.
- Keep the abdomen soft in inhalation and exhalation.
- Soften the palms of the hands and relax the fingers.
- If the mind is racing, an eye bandage will aid calmness.

2 Extended Inhalation/Normal Exhalation

Exhale, completely emptying air from the lungs.

Take a slow, soft inhalation, filling the lungs from the bottom to the top.

Don't strain or jerk the chest, breathe smoothly and lengthen the breath calmly.

Exhale normally. Inhale once more, slowly drawing the breath into the lungs.

Exhale normally.

Repeat these two cycles for about 5 minutes, then return to normal breathing. Once you've returned to normal breathing, check that there is no tension in the shoulders, throat, mouth or hands.

Exercise caution when practising Pranayama – incorrect practice may strain the lungs and diaphragm.

These two cycles can be practised separately or together and should be done for a few months before proceeding to breathing with extended inhalation and extended exhalation.

3 Extended Inhalation/Extended Exhalation
Exhale, completely emptying the lungs of air. Inhale slowly and smoothly, lengthening the breath.

Maintain the lift of the chest, and exhale slowly and deeply without straining the throat.

Control the flow of breath so that the body doesn't shudder or strain. Take a few normal breaths.

Repeat for about 5 minutes. Return to normal breathing.

To end the above cycles, bend the knees, roll over to the side and remove the bolster. Lie flat, with the head still supported, in Savasana for 5 minutes, keeping the brain quiet and releasing the body to the floor. Slowly open the eyes, turn to one side, stay for a moment, then turn to the other side. Come up and sit in Adho Mukha Virasana before getting up.

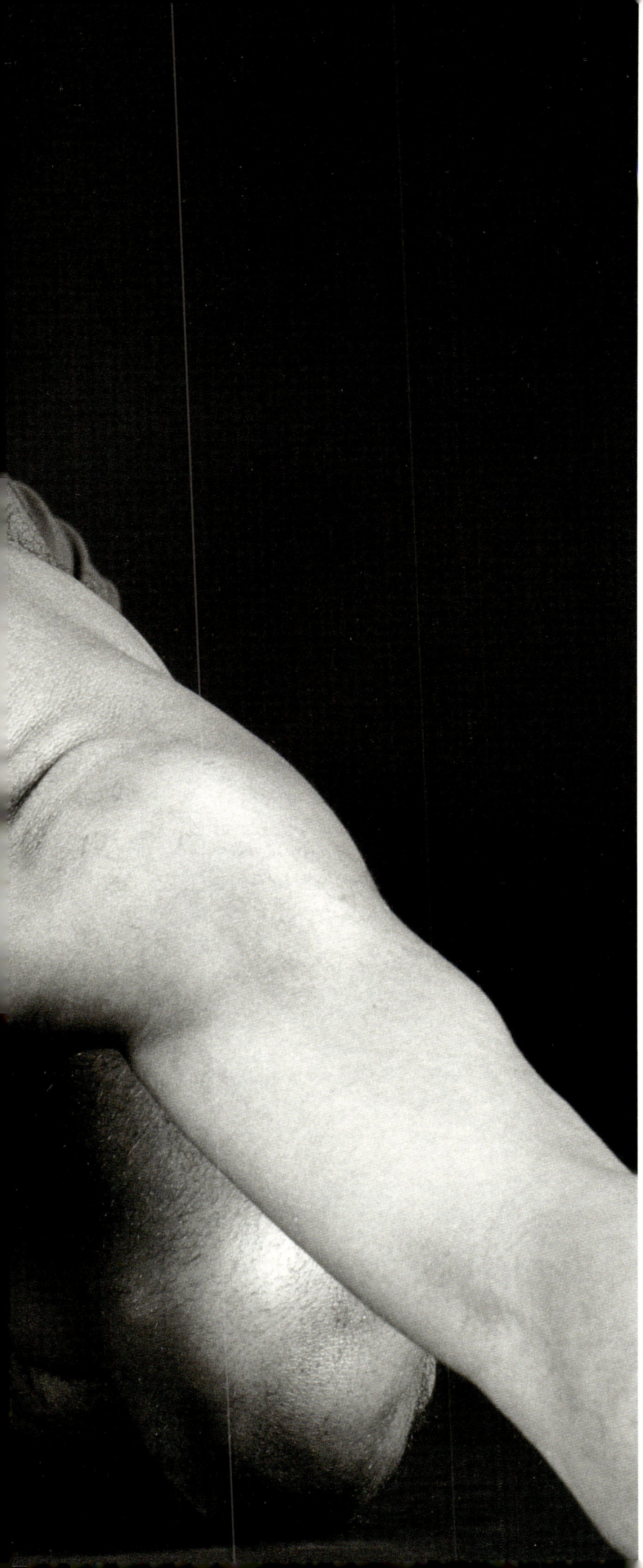

routine Practice

The sage Patanjali states in Yoga Sutra 11.47: "Perfection in an asana is achieved when the effort to perform it becomes effortless, and the infinite being within is reached."

Practising postures in a set order increases their effectiveness as well as the student's understanding of each posture. The subtleties and details of the poses and their effect on the mind and body become more obvious as one's practice becomes more established.

Routines and Sequences

The practice of postures has a beneficial impact on the entire body. The postures tone the muscles, tissues, ligaments, joints and nerves, as well as maintaining and improving the health and functioning of all the body systems. It is important to keep practising until you become familiar with, and comfortable in, the postures. When this happens, the full benefits are felt. This is why routines should be practised as often as possible.

Classification of postures

Broadly speaking, standing postures are dynamic and exhilarating. They refresh both body and mind by removing tension, aches and pains. The standing postures form the basis of all other postures, and, through them, practitioners become familiar with various parts of their bodies, their muscles and joints, and use their intelligence to bring action and awareness to these parts. Most routines begin with standing postures in order to waken the physical body – the arms, legs and spine – and stimulate the brain by connecting movements to specific areas of the body. They also build stamina and strength as well as determination.

The seated postures are introduced after standing postures to rest and remove strain from the legs. Seated forward bends are calming. They remove fatigue, soothe the nerves and calm the mind. In standing postures the brain is stimulated; in seated postures an agitated, fluctuating mind becomes passive.

Twisting postures extend and rotate the spine. These postures are good for relieving backache and stiffness in the neck and shoulders. The internal organs are stimulated as the trunk turns, and this improves digestion.

Inverted postures energize the entire system. They relieve strain in the legs, activate and nourish the inner organs, stimulate the brain and improve the respiratory, circulatory and nervous systems. Standing, seated and twisting postures prepare the body and mind for inversions. Women should not practise inversions while menstruating.

Supine, prone, or lying-down postures are also known as abdominal postures, and a routine should never begin with these. Standing postures tone the stomach muscles so they can be used correctly, and inverted postures protect the organs so they are not damaged when doing abdominal postures, so these should be done before attempting abdominal postures.

Savasana (relaxation) should be done for 5–10 minutes (depending on time) at the end of each routine.

Suggested practice plan

The following routines are suggested to enable students to practise systematically and progressively. It is more beneficial to practise for a shorter time each day than a longer session once or twice a week. Attend a regular yoga group with a qualified teacher, as they can make sure you are progressing at the correct pace.

Each routine can be practised daily, starting with Sequence 1 on the first day and progressing to Sequence 5 by the end of the week. Repeat the first 5 sequences over a 2–3 week period to consolidate the postures, then continue with the Sequences 6–10. Ultimately, discrimination should be used with regard to the length of time and which postures to

left Try to get to an organized class, led by a qualified teacher, at least once or twice a week, and supplement this by practising at home every day, and you will feel the difference very quickly.

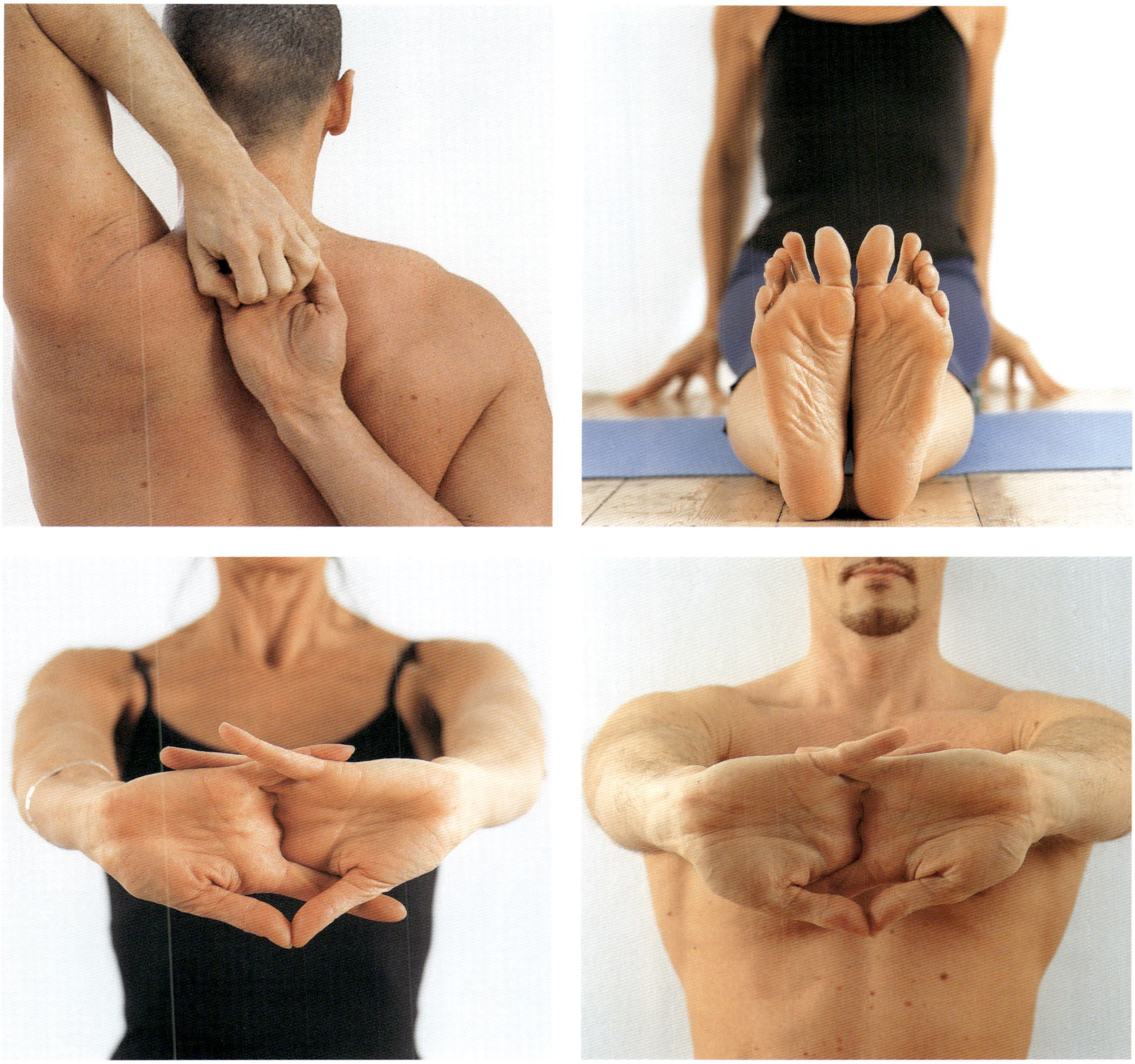

above Time and patience are required to understand the subtleties and technical requirements of the postures.

practise, the aim being to have a physical and spiritual rhythm to your practice. Confidence is gained by working at an even pace, learning about the postures and their effects on the body, and then proceeding with knowledge and understanding on to the next routine. Move on to the next set of routines only when you feel able to do so.

As you progress in your practice, flexibility and stamina improve and the postures can be held for longer periods of time. The effects of the postures are not instant, and timing is dependent on energy, intelligence and awareness. However, if time doesn't permit it, you can tailor your practice to suit the circumstances.

Sequence 1 – Simple Standing Postures

In this first sequence, the shapes of the postures should be studied and worked on. Then, as these become more familiar, detailed instructions should be incorporated to make the postures more correct and to feel the effects. Think about keeping the spine long in all postures. If fatigue or exhaustion is felt, do supported Uttanasa I to recover.

1 **Tadasana**

2 **Tadasana** with hands in Parvatasana

3 **Vrksasana**

4 **Utthita Trikonasana**

5 **Utthita Parsvakonasana**

6 **Virabhadrasana II**

7 **Uttanasana I** (s)

8 **Adho Mukha Virasana**

9 **Sukhasana**

10 **Savasana**

Focus

- Where the moderated posture is used it is marked (s) for supported or (w) if the wall is used.

Sequence 2 – Simple Seated Postures

In this group of seated postures, one supine pose (Adho Mukha Svanasana) and two inverted postures (Setu Bandha Sarvangasana and Viparita Karani) have been introduced, but inversions should not be done if you are menstruating. It is advisable to sit on a support in the seated postures, as this helps to lift and extend the spine. The lower back should not be arched forwards, but lengthened upwards towards the head. In Virasana, ensure that the support under the buttocks is high enough so that there is no pain in the knees. If any discomfort is felt in the lower back in Setu Bandha Sarvangasana, raise the feet higher so as to remove strain from the lumbar region.

1 **Sukhasana**

2 **Uttanasana I**

3 **Adho Mukha Svanasana**

4 **Sukhasana**

5 **Virasana with Parvatasana**

6 **Gomukhasana**

7 **Setu Bandha Sarvangasana**

8 **Viparita Karani**

9 **Savasana**

Focus

- Each routine can be practised daily, starting with Sequence 1 on the first day and progressing to Sequence 5 by the end of the week. Then repeat over a 2–3 week period before progressing to sequences 6–10.

Sequence 3 – Consolidation of Simple Standing Postures

Parsvottanasana has been introduced here, in which the back foot is turned in much more than in the other standing postures. Ensure that both hips are level and facing in the same direction. Use wooden blocks to support each hand in this posture, and lengthen and extend the spine upwards. Begin to increase the timings in these postures.

1 **Sukhasana**

2 **Tadasana**

3 **Tadasana** (Parvat.)

4 **Vrksasana**

5 **Utthita Trikonasana**

6 **Utthita Parsvakon.**

7 **Virabhadrasana II**

8 **Parsvottanasana** (s)

9 **Uttanasana I**

10 **Adho Mukha Vir.**

11 **Savasana**

Sequence 4 – Introduction of Salamba Sarvangasana and Ardha Halasana

Virabhadrasana I is brought into this routine as a slightly more challenging standing posture. It is very important to have the back leg well turned in and both hips turned to their maximum in this pose. The back leg in all standing postures is strong and stable – this leg is the "brain" of the posture. If Salamba Sarvangasana is uncomfortable, just lie with the legs up against the wall. Do not do Salamba Sarvangasana or Ardha Halasana if you are menstruating.

1 **Tadasana**

2 **Tadasana** (Parvat.)

3 **Vrksasana**

4 **Utthita Trikonasana**

5 **Utthita Parsvakon.**

6 **Virabhadrasana II**

7 **Uttanasana I**

8 **Virabhadrasana I**

9 **Parsvottanasana** (s)

10 **Uttanasana I** (s)

11 **Adho Mukha Vir.**

12 **Gomukhasana**

13 **Salamba Sarv.** (w)

14 **Ardha Halasana**

15 **Savasana**

Sequence 5 – Quiet, Calming Practice

This routine focuses on postures with the head supported and the chest lifted. If you are feeling tired or out of sorts, this quietening practice will help. Try to hold the postures for as long as possible in order to experience their calming effects. Keep the face relaxed throughout and the breathing normal, but be aware of the change of depth and rhythm of the breath as you relax. In Adho Mukha Svanasana, keep the spine ascending to the ceiling even though the head is down. Move the shoulders towards the front of the chest in order to broaden and create space in the chest cavity.

1 **Cross Bolsters**

2 **Matsyasana**

3 **Uttanasana I**

4 **Adho Mukha Svanasana**

5 **Setu Bandha Sarvangasana**

6 **Savasana**

Sequence 6 – Hamstring-stretching Poses

In these standing postures, pay attention to the feet by ensuring the soles of the feet make maximum contact with the floor. Stretch all five toes of each foot into and along the floor, and extend the legs strongly up from the ankles to the hips. In Utthita Hasta Padangusthasana (I & II), ensure the front of the trunk is lengthening up towards the ceiling, and the sides extending. In Prasarita Padottanasana, extend and lengthen the spine forwards before taking the head towards the floor. Pay attention to the feet in this posture. If they roll on to the little toe side, extreme discomfort will be felt on the side of the shin-bones, so ensure that all four corners of the feet are pressing equally into the floor.

1 **Virasana with Parvatasana**

2 **Utthita Hasta Padangusthasana I** (s)

3 **Utthita Hasta Padangusthasana II** (s)

4 **Tadasana**

5 **Vrksasana**

6 **Utthita Trikon.**

7 **Utthita Parsvakon.**

8 **Virabhadrasana II**

9 **Virabhadrasana I**

10 **Parsvottan.** (s)

11 **Prasarita Pad.** (s)

12 **Adho Mukha Vir.**

13 **Gomukhasana**

14 **Salamba Sarvang.**

15 **Ardha Halasana**

16 **Savasana**

Focus

- Repeat the Sequences 1–5 over a 2–3 week period to consolidate the postures, then continue with Sequences 6–10. Ultimately your discrimination should be used with regard to the length of time and which postures to practise.

Sequence 7 – Sitting Postures with Simple Twists

In the twisting postures, the spine must first be extended and lengthened, and then turned. Move the whole trunk around when you turn, keep the shoulders moving away from the ears, and turn your head without tensing the neck. In Virasana with Parvatasana, ensure that the shoulders move away from the ears so the neck can lengthen and extend.

1 **Standing Maricyasana**

2 **Bharadvajasana chair**

3 **Sukhasana**

4 **Virasana with Parvatasana**

5 **Gomukhasana**

6 **Garudasana** (s)

7 **Adho Mukha Svan.**

8 **Chair Sarvang.**

9 **Halasana**

10 **Savasana**

Focus

- Halasana is introduced without a stool for support. If the back aches or the neck becomes painful, use a support (Ardha Halasana) until the discomfort goes away.

Sequence 8 – Introduction of Utkatasana and Garudasana

When the arms are extended, ensure that they stretch from the tops of the shoulders to the tips of the fingers, and keep the palms of the hands broad. Virabhadrasana I can be attempted, but if this causes backache, put the hands on the hips. Garudasana may be done standing in Tadasana, but gradually work towards doing the full posture.

1 **Adho Mukha Vir**

2 **Adho Mukha Svan.**

3 **Tadasana**

4 **Utthita Trikon.**

5 **Utthita Parsvakon.**

6 **Virabhadrasana II**

7 **Uttanasana I**

8 **Virabhadrasana I**

9 **Uttanasana I**

10 **Parsvottanasana**

11 **Garudasana**

12 **Utkatasana**

13 **Adho Mukha Svan.**

14 **Virasana/Parvat.**

15 **Adho Mukha Vir.**

16 **Chair Sarvang.**

17 **Halasana** (s)

18 **Savasana**

Sequence 9 – Relaxation Practice

Ensure that the chest is lifted and open in these postures. The brain should remain passive, with the mind quietly focusing on the breath, throughout the poses. These postures can be held for 3–5 minutes to gain maximum benefit. If the muscles of the groin are painful in Supta Baddhakonasana, place foam blocks under each thigh to lessen the stretch. If the back and/or knees hurt in Supta Virasana, add as much support as is needed to relieve the discomfort. To eliminate visual distractions, close your eyes and keep them still, focusing on the breath.

1 **Cross Bolsters**

2 **Matsyasana**

3 **Supta Baddhkonasana**

4 **Supta Virasana**

5 **Adho Mukha Virasana**

6 **Adho Mukha Svanasana**

7 **Salamba Sarv.** (w)

8 **Ardha Halasana**

9 **Sukhasana**

Focus

- Practise Sequences 6–10 by repeating them over several weeks and learn to increase timings before proceeding to the next five.

Sequence 10 – Introduction to Seated Forward Bends

Sit on a support for these seated postures to help lift the spine. The forward bends are done with a concave back, an action achieved by lifting and opening the chest, moving the shoulders away from the ears and moving the shoulder blades towards the front of the body. If the back hurts, hold a strap caught around the foot, so the angle between the trunk and the leg lessens and the backache is relieved. Keep the arms straight when holding the strap. In Urdhva Prasarita Padasana, the entire backs of both legs (from buttock bones to heels) should be against the wall.

1 **Uttanasana I**

2 **Adho Mukha Svanasana**

3 **Dandasana**

4 **Janusirsasana**

5 **Trianga Mukha. Pascimottanasana**

6 **Pascimottanasana**

7 **Ardha Halasana**

8 **Setu Bandha Sarvangasana**

9 **Urdhva Prasarita Padasana**

10 **Savasana**

Sequence 11 – Standing Poses Held for Longer

This sequence consolidates the standing postures and should be done with more awareness and attention to detail. If discomfort is experienced, try to locate it, think about what has caused it and, by understanding the technique of the pose, try to remove it. Try to hold each posture for a little longer than you have done previously.

1 **Utthita Hasta Padangusthasana I** (s)

2 **Utthita Hasta Padangusthasana II** (s)

3 **Tadasana**

4 **Vrksasana**

5 **Utthita Trikonasana**

6 **Utthita Parsvakonasana**

7 **Virabhadrasana II**

8 **Virabhadrasana I**

9 **Uttanasana I**

10 **Ardha Chandr.** (s)

11 **Parsvottanasana**

12 **Prasarita Pad.** (s)

13 **Adho Mukha Vir.**

14 **Salamba Sarvang.**

15 **Halasana**

16 **Savasana**

Focus

- This sequence should take longer than the others so far, as the timing of each posture is increased.

Sequence 12 – Increased Timings in Seated Forward Bends with Concave Back

Doing the forward bends with a concave back improves the elasticity of the spine and helps to open the chest. The whole trunk must be lengthened. When looking up, be careful not to compress the back of the neck.

1 **Uttanasana I**

2 **Adho Mukha Svanasana**

3 **Dandasana**

4 **Paripurna Navasana** (s)

5 **Janusirsasana** (s)

6 **Trianga Mukha. Pascimottanasana**

7 **Pascimottanasana**

8 **Salamba Sarvang.**

9 **Halasana**

10 **Savasana**

Focus

- In Paripurna Navasana, lift the trunk upwards. If the lower back becomes painful, do the posture with the fingertips on the floor.

Sequence 13 – Basic Standing Postures and Introducing Seated Postures

Try to practise the standing postures with less strain and more composure. By now the technicalities of the poses should be physically ingrained, so try to just "be" in the posture and allow the psychological effects to emerge.

1 **Adho Mukha Svan.**

2 **Uttanasana I**

3 **Tadasana**

4 **Utthita Trikonasana**

5 **Utthita Parsvakon.**

6 **Virabhadrasana I**

7 **Virabhadrasana II**

8 **Ardha Chandr.** (s)

9 **Parsvottansana**

10 **Virasana**

11 **Sukhasana**

12 **Baddhakonasana**

13 **Upavistakonasana**

14 **Adho Mukha Vir.**

15 **Chair Sarvang.**

16 **Halasana** (s)

17 **Savasana**

Sequence 14 – Twists and Seated Forward Bends

After doing the first two twists, which allow the spine to extend and rotate, the forward bends become easier. In this sequence, full forward bend poses are done, where the trunk is extended and, if possible, the foot of this leg is caught with the hands. If you cannot reach the foot or the lower back is painful, catch a strap around the foot.

1 **Standing Maricyasana**

2 **Bharadvajasana (chair)**

3 **Adho Mukha Svanasana**

4 **Dandasana**

5 **Janusirasana**

6 **Trianga Mukha. Pascimottanasana**

7 **Maricyasana I**

8 **Pascimottanasana**

9 **Malasana**

10 **Salamba Sarvang.**

11 **Halasana**

12 **Savasana**

Sequence 15 – Relaxing and Recuperative Postures

This sequence should not be rushed and the postures can be safely held for up to 5 minutes. The chest should be lifted and open, the eyes soft and closed, the facial features relaxed and the brain calm and focused on the breathing. Do not fall asleep, just relax and breathe. The back should feel comfortable in all the poses, so use support if necessary.

1 **Cross Bolsters**

2 **Matsyasana**

3 **Supta Baddhakon.**

4 **Supta Virasana**

5 **Uttanasana I**

6 **Salamba Sarvangasana**

7 **Ardha Halasana** (s)

8 **Setu Bandha Sarv.**

9 **Vipariti Karani**

10 **Savasana**

Focus

- Consolidate these postures, going back to the ones you find more difficult and practising them again until they feel easier.

Sequence 16 – Standing Postures and Standing Forward Bends

This routine can take up to two hours to complete. If fatigue is experienced, do Uttanasana I in between to rest the brain and allow the body to recover. Increase timings in the postures, especially Salamba Sarvangasana and Halasana.

1 **Utthita Hasta Pad. I & II** (s)

2 **Tadasana**

3 **Utthita Trikonasana**

4 **Utthita Parsvakonasana**

5 **Virabhadrasana I**

6 **Uttanasana I**

7 **Virabhadrasana II**

8 **Ardha Chandrasana**

9 **Virabhadrasana III** (s)

10 **Parsvottanasana**

11 **Prasarita Padattonasana**

12 **Padangusthasana**

13 **Adho Mukha Svan.**

14 **Adho Mukha Vir.**

15 **Salamba Sarvang.**

16 **Halasana**

17 **Savasana**

Sequence 17 – Stronger Forward Bends and Floor Twists

Lift, open and broaden the chest in all these seated poses. Sit on a support to help with the lift of the spine. While practising the twists, make sure the spine is extended and lengthened before twisting. Both buttock bones should remain on the support in the twists. Increase the timing of the forward bends and keep the brain passive.

1 **Uttanasana I**

2 **Virasana**

3 **Gomukhasana**

4 **Baddhakonasana**

5 **Upavistakonasana**

6 **Paripurna Nav.** (s)

7 **Ardha Navasana**

8 **Janusirsasana**

9 **Trianga Mukha.**

10 **Maricyasana I**

11 **Pascimottanasana**

12 **Bharadvajasana I**

13 **Maricyasana III**

14 **Salamba Sarvang.**

15 **Halasana**

16 **Savasana**

Focus

- In Paripurna Navasana and Ardha Navasana, try to straighten the legs. If the back hurts, practise these postures with bent knees.

Sequence 18 – Progressively More Difficult Postures

At this stage of practice, your stamina, endurance and flexibility should have improved, so this sequence of postures should be challenging but manageable. Practise Virabhadrasana III with only the hands supported, and fully extend the back (lifted) leg away from the head while the arms stretch strongly towards the fingertips.

1 **Utt. Hasta Pad. I & II**

2 **Tadasana**

3 **Utthita Trikonasana**

4 **Utthita Parsvakon.**

5 **Virabhadrasana I**

6 **Virabhadrasana II**

7 **Ardha Chandrasana**

8 **Virabhadrasana III** (s)

9 **Parivrtta Trikonasana**

10 **Parsvottanasana**

11 **Prasarita Padottanasana**

12 **Uttanasana I**
13 **Savasana**

Sequence 19 – Relaxation

In this relaxation routine, forward bends are practised with the head supported. Once the head touches the support, the brain should become calm and passive, allowing you to focus on the breath. Do not strain or create tension while practising supported forward bends, just allow the body to take on the shape of the posture and let go.

1 **Cross Bolsters**

2 **Virasana**

3 **Janusirsasana**

4 **Trianga Mukha.**

5 **Pascimottanasana**

6 **Maricyasana III**

7 **Salamba Sarv.** (w)

8 **Ardha Halasana** (s)

9 **Savasana**

Focus

- If the sequences are becoming too challenging, go back to Sequence 1. There is no race to get through all the sequences as quickly as possible. It is more sensible to work slowly, methodically and intelligently than to rush ahead and lay yourself open to pain and injury.

Sequence 20 – Prone Poses and Basic Standing Poses

Urdhva Mukha Svanasana is one of the preparatory postures for backbend work. In this posture the centre of the tops of the feet should be on the floor, the inner legs should lift up towards the ceiling, and the elbows and knees should be locked. If difficulty is experienced with lifting the body off the floor, use blocks under the hands and tuck the toes under.

1 **Adho Mukha Svan.**

2 **Urdhva Mukha Sv.**

3 **Adho Mukha Svan.**

4 **Urdhva Mukha Sv.**

5 **Utthita Trikonasana**

6 **Utthita Parsvakon.**

7 **Virabhadrasana II**

8 **Virabhadrasana I**

9 **Parsvottanasana**

10 **Vrksasana**

11 **Garudasana**

12 **Utkatasana**

13 **Supta Virasana**

14 **Salamba Sarvang.**

15 **Halasana**

16 **Savasana**

Focus

- As a result of opening the chest and extending the spine upwards, the standing postures require less effort and are improved.

Sequence 21 – Seated Postures and Knee Work

Practising Padmasana incorrectly may result in severe knee problems, so never force the knee. Practise Sukhasana a few times prior to Padmasana in order to "lubricate" the hip and knee joints, and then practise Padmasana with one leg in Sukhasana – be patient, consolidate your practice and, with courage and determination, you will achieve your goal.

1 **Sukhasana**

2 **Virasana with Parv.**

3 **Padmasana**

4 **Dandasana**

5 **Uttanasana I**

6 **Virabhadrasana II**

7 **Pascimottanasana**

8 **Urdhva Pras. Pad.**

9 **Salamba Sarvang.**

10 **Halasana**

11 **Savasana**

Sequence 22 – Standing, Reverse Standing and Seated Postures

This group of mixed postures requires stamina, strength and flexibility and should be practised with care. Rest in Uttanasana I between the standing postures if necessary. You should set aside at least two hours to do this practice, doing the directional postures twice on each side, and at the end of the sequence practise Savasana for 10 minutes.

1 **Tadasana**

2 **Utthita Trikonasana**

3 **Utthita Parsvakon.**

4 **Virabhadrasana I**

5 **Virabhadrasana II**

6 **Parivrtta Trikon.**

7 **Parivrtta Pars.**

8 **Parsvottanasana**

9 **Janusirsasana**

10 **Trianga Mukha.**

11 **Maricyasana I**

12 **Pascimottanasana**

13 **Salamba Sarvang.**

14 **Halasana**

15 **Savasana**

Sequence 23 – Relaxation and Pranayama (Breathing)

Increase the timings in this group in order to open the chest more and deepen relaxation. Never strain the lungs or become agitated in Pranayama – both inhalation and exhalation must be smooth, calm and flowing. The quality of your Pranayama is more important than the quantity. If you feel uncomfortable and tense, return to normal breathing.

1 **Cross Bolsters**

2 **Matsyasana**

3 **Supta Baddha.** (s)

4 **Supta Virasana**

5 **Adho Mukha Vir.**

6 **Uttanasana I** (s)

7 **Adho Mukha Svanasana** (s)

8 **Chair Sarvangasana**

9 **Ardha Halasana**

10 **Setu Bandha Sarvangasana**

11 **Savasana**

12 **Pranayama**

Sequence 24 – Standing Postures to Consolidate your Practice

In this sequence, focus on fully stretching the backs of both legs. Spend time in Tadasana, analysing and correcting the posture from the feet to the head. Repeat each standing posture twice using the "information" acquired from Tadasana to deepen your understanding and execution of the poses. Extend timings in Salamba Sarvangasana and Halasana.

1 **Utt. Hasta Pad. I** (s)

2 **Utt. Hasta Pad. II** (s)

3 **Supta Pad. I**

4 **Supta Pad. II**

5 **Tadasana**

6 **Utthita Trikonasana**

7 **Utthita Parsvakon.**

8 **Virabhadrasana I**

9 **Virabhadrasana II**

10 **Ardha Chandr.**

11 **Parvottanasana**

12 **Prasarita Pad.**

13 **Adho Mukha Vir.**

14 **Salamba Sarvang.**

15 **Halasana** (s)

16 **Savasana**

Sequence 25 – Seated Postures

Practise Adho Mukha Svanasana and Urdhva Mukha Svanasana three times, opening the chest and lengthening the spine progressively. In Urdhva Mukha Svanasana, look up without compressing the back of the neck and keep the head in a comfortable position. In Dandasana, Paripurna Navasana, Ardha Navasana and Pascimottanasana, fully stretch and lengthen the backs of the legs and keep the thighs and knees pressing towards the floor. In Baddhakonasana – and Upavistakonasana, keep the front of the body extending from pubis to chin and move the shoulder blades towards the front of the trunk to lift and open the chest. Twist further and breathe more deeply in Bharadvajasana I.

1 **Uttanasana I**

2 **Adho Mukha Svan.**

3 **Urdhva Mukha Svan.**

4 **Virasana**

5 **Dandasana**

6 **Paripurna Nav.** (s)

7 **Ardha Navasana**

8 **Pascimottanasana**

9 **Baddhakonasana**

10 **Upavistakonasana**

11 **Bharadvajasana I**

11 **Salamba Sarvang.**

Sequence 26 – Standing and Prone Postures

After the standing poses in this routine, Adho Mukha Svanasana is followed by Urdhva Mukha Svanasana,which prepares the spine for Salabhasana. In the latter two poses, the pubis and sacrum move towards the floor to avoid a painful pinching sensation in the lower back. Salabhasana should be practised with the legs together, though if the back is painful, you should separate them slightly. Extend both legs strongly towards the heels, keeping the soles of the feet long and broad. Lengthen the arms from the shoulders and stretch back towards the fingertips, keeping the palms broad and facing the ceiling. Lift and open the chest as much as possible and look straight ahead, keeping the eyes soft. After Salabhasana, practise Urdhva Mukha and Adho Mukha Svanasana quietly to release the spine gently. Ensure that the back is comfortable in Ardha Halasana. If it is sore in Savasana, rest the legs on a stool.

1 **Tadasana**

2 **Utthita Trikonasana**

3 **Utthita Parsvakon.**

4 **Virabhadrasana I**

5 **Virabhadrasana II**

6 **Parsvottanasana**

7 **Adho Mukha Svanasana**

8 **Urdhva Mukha Svanasana**

9 **Salabhasana**

10 **Urdhva Mukha Svanasana**

11 **Adho Mukha Svanasana**

12 **Ardha Halasana**
13 **Savasana**

Sequence 27 – Relaxation

Try to let go while practising these poses. When in each posture, settle the body and focus on the breath. If the body becomes restless, the brain will follow. Once the head is resting on the support in the forward bends, soften the abdomen, relax the shoulders and back, keep the face, mouth and throat passive, and unite the breath with the mind and the mind with the breath. Extend the Pranayama practice without causing strain or tension.

1 **Uttanasana I**

2 **Adho Mukha Svanasana** (s)

3 **Janusirsasana** (s)

4 **Pascimottanasana** (s)

5 **Salamba Sarvangasana** (w)

6 **Ardha Halasana**

7 **Setu Bandha Sarvangasana**

8 **Savasana**

9 **Pranayama**

Surya Namaskara – Sun Salutation

In this short routine the postures are linked together in a flowing movement. It can be practised only when the individual postures have been learnt and understood, which may be after completing the previous 27 sequences. The cycle of postures can be repeated 4–12 times, depending on the time available and the energy of the practitioner.

Surya Namaskara involves quick postures and movement, with each pose held for a few breaths only. Regular practice improves mobility, alertness, agility and speed, while developing willpower and physical strength. The brain becomes active and refreshed.

1 **Tadasana**

2 Exhale, extend into **Uttanasana I**

3 Step back into **Adho Mukha Svanasana**

4 Inhale, roll forward into **Urdhva Mukha Svanasana**

5 Exhale, come back to **Adho Mukha Svanasana**

6 On the next exhale jump forwards into **Uttanasana I**

7 Exhale, release the arms and come back into **Tadasana**

Focus

- People with heart problems and women who are menstruating should not practise this routine.
- Breathe normally for 3–4 breaths before jumping or stepping into the next posture.
- Synchronize the inhalation and exhalation as you move from one position to another.
- Repeat the routine 4–12 times.
- After completion, rest in Uttanasana I to recover.

yoga Therapy

"Yoga's system of healing is based on the premise that the body should be allowed to function as naturally as possible. Practising the recommended asanas will first rejuvenate the body, and then tackle the causes of the ailment."

B.K.S. Iyengar

Therapeutic Yoga

Yoga can help to improve and heal parts of the body that are injured, traumatized or neglected. Movement of the body in asanas stimulates injured joints, muscles or organs by increasing the flow of blood to these parts. The practice of yoga also increases the pain threshold. This chapter on therapeutic yoga is based on the sequencing of selected postures to treat specific minor ailments. The postures are adapted by using props and are therefore accessible to all students, regardless of their complaints or the condition of their bodies.

Healing with yoga

When the body is tired and lethargic as a result of minor illness or injury, your regular yoga practice need not be discontinued. Even if you feel unable to follow your sequence of postures in the normal way, practising with props helps to improve the posture and maintain balance, and allows you to stretch fully while experiencing a state of relaxation during practice. This feeling of peace and tranquillity is the beginning of the healing process.

In some cases, the practice of yoga will not result in a complete cure, but in most cases it will alleviate some of the suffering and discomfort associated with the condition, and boost confidence and morale. Practising the asanas with dedication and patience calms the brain and soothes the nerves. This feeling of relaxation reduces the anxiety that is created by the pain, which in itself helps to reduce the actual pain and improve your pain threshold.

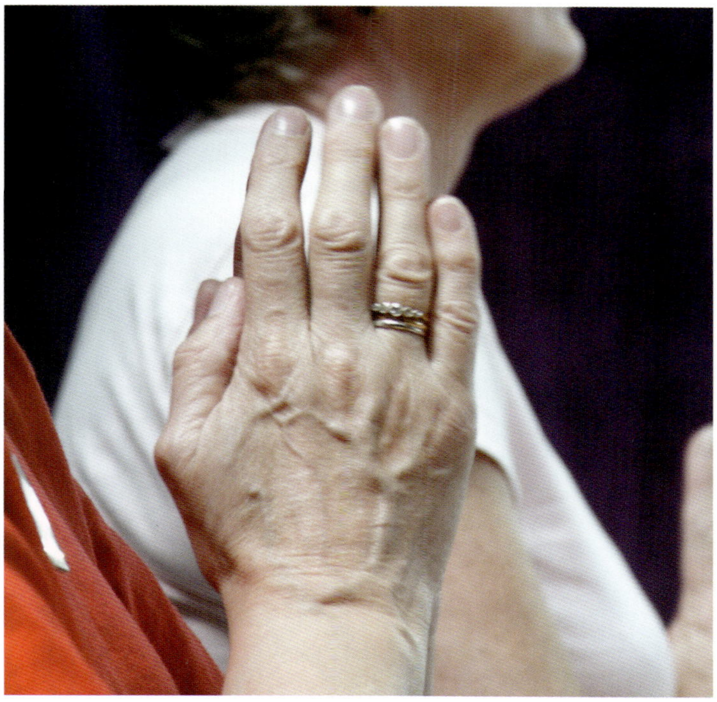

Working through a sequence of postures using the necessary supports can effect remarkable changes in both your physical and mental state, At the end of your practice you are likely to feel more flexible and fluid, with greater mobility, a lessening of pain and a renewed sense of serenity and peace.

This chapter offers programmes for a range of minor ailments and common problems. It does not include sequences aimed at alleviating any serious medical conditions, as these should be done only under the guidance and supervision of a suitably qualified Iyengar teacher. The student of yoga will readily understand the tremendous need to include yoga in their daily life, and the suggestions that follow show how it can be used effectively with conventional medicine, or alone, to improve or alleviate many common disorders.

The postures for everyday ailments are shown on the following pages. The props and supports used are explained in detail, but you may also find it useful to refer back to the original descriptions of the postures and the various modifications suggested there.

Commonsense should prevail when you are practising these adapted postures, and the poses should be held for only as long as is comfortable. When following a sequence for a specific condition, it is best to continue with this programme until some relief is obtained. If difficulty is experienced with a programme, it is advisable to consult an experienced teacher.

left Iyengar Yoga is a gentle and supportive system of exercise that can help to fend off illness and keep the body supple, whatever the age of the practitioner.

above Clockwise: correcting the alignment of the trunk in Parivrtta Trikonasana; sitting in Baddhakonasana, lifting the chest; supported Adho Mukha Svanasana, with the head resting on a bolster; supported Prasarita Padottanasana – a quiet, passive posture that allows the brain to stay calm. These postures are all potentially therapeutic when used in conjunction with an appropriate routine.

Mental Fatigue and Exhaustion

Stress and physical exertion contribute to fatigue and exhaustion, and if this is not checked it can develop into chronic fatigue syndrome. The pace of daily life has an impact on the body and the emotions.

1 Supta Baddhakonasana using a bolster and folded blanket to support the head and neck and a strap to keep the feet close to the body.

2 Supta Virasana with as much support as is needed placed under the spine, neck and head to allow the back and knees to release. Keep the chest open and up, and the shoulders relaxed and back.

3 Virasana with Parvatasana extending the palms towards the ceiling.
4 Adho Mukha Virasana with the head and trunk supported on a bolster and/or blanket.

5 Pascimottanasana with the forehead supported on a stool to avoid straining the back.
6 Standing Maricyasana using the wall and the stool for support.

7 Janusirsasana with the head, elbows and knee supported on bolsters, and using a strap.
8 Maricyasana I sitting on a support to aid the lift of the spine, and turning the chest.

Focus

• In yoga, strong emotions are linked to hormonal imbalances, which leave one vulnerable to infections and illness. This sequence works on stimulating and nourishing the internal organs and the nervous system to pacify and calm the nerves, body and mind.

9 **Bharadvajasana (chair)** using the chair to increase the turn. Keep the feet on the floor, parallel to one another, to stabilize the hips. Turn from the waist, moving a little more with each exhalation.

11 **Adho Mukha Svanasana** with the head supported on a bolster to calm the brain.

10 **Tadasana** standing against a wall. Use the wall to aid balance, keeping the feet parallel and together and the heels against the wall. Lift the chest, keeping the face and eyes soft.

12 **Ardha Halasana** with the legs supported on foam blocks on a stool, and the brain quiet.

13 **Viparita Karani** using a wooden block and a bolster to support the lower back and hips.
14 **Savasana** with the head and neck supported on a folded blanket, and bandaged eyes.

Headache/Migraine

A headache may be a result of tension in the neck muscles and scalp after a stressful event, or due to fatigue and lack of rest. In the case of migraine, an intense throbbing pain in the head may be accompanied by nausea and vomiting.

1 Adho Mukha Virasana with the head and trunk supported on a bolster and blanket.
2 Janusirsasana with the forehead and arms supported on a stool.

3 Pascimottanasana with the forehead and arms supported on a stool.
4 Prasarita Padottanasana with the head, trunk and arms supported on a stool and blankets.

6 Uttanasana I with the head and forearms supported on a stool softened with a blanket. This posture, with the head lowered, allows more blood to flow to the area, helping to relieve any discomfort.

5 Adho Mukha Svanasana with the head supported on a bolster, or a pile of blankets, in order to keep the brain calm.

7 Ardha Halasana with the legs supported on a stool, the height adjusted with foam blocks.
8 Supta Baddhakonasana with a strap around legs, bolster under spine, and head supported.

Focus

- These postures for relieving headaches and migraines increase blood flow to the brain and restore the stability of the nervous system. While doing the postures, be aware of lengthening the muscles of the neck and try to keep the brain as quiet as possible.

9 **Supta Virasana** with the spine, neck and head supported on two bolsters and two folded blankets.

11 **Viparita Karani** with the backs of the legs against the wall and the body lying over a bolster and wooden block. Use a blanket for comfort under the head, arms extended over the head, palms facing upwards.

10 **Setu Bandha Sarvangasana** using foam blocks to support the sacrum and a bolster to support the feet, arms extended over the head, palms facing upwards.

12 **Savasana** with the neck and head supported on a folded blanket. A bandage firmly tied around the head and/or eyes is very soothing and calming when experiencing headache.

Stress/Anxiety

These postures work on tense muscles and encourage blood to circulate. This stabilizes the heart rate and blood pressure. Shallow, fast breathing becomes deeper, slower and more rhythmical, which results in a higher intake of oxygen, and this helps to remove stress.

1 Uttanasana I with the head supported on a blanket and stool. When one part of the body is strained and tense, circulation to that body part is decreased – increasing it again will help to calm the mind and body.

3 Adho Mukha Svanasana with the head supported on a bolster to keep the mind quiet.

2 Prasarita Padottanasana with the head supported on a wooden block. If the hands don't reach the floor, use foam blocks under the palms to raise the level of support. It may be necessary to use more blocks under the head as well.

4 Adho Mukha Virasana with a bolster and blanket supporting the trunk and head.

5 Janusirsasana with the head and arms supported on a bolster and a strap around the foot. If necessary, you may also use a bolster to support the bent knee.

6 Pascimottanasana with the head and forearms supported on a bolster and using a strap around the foot. Keep the eyes closed and the mind still and quiet.

8 Supta Baddhakonasana with bolsters and blankets supporting the spine and head, and a strap around the legs and feet. The thighs are supported with rolled-up blankets.

7 Setu Bandha Sarvangasana with four foam blocks under the sacrum, feet resting on a bolster and head and shoulders supported on a folded blanket – arms over head, palms facing the ceiling.

9 Cross Bolsters with the feet resting on blocks. This gentle arch opens the chest.

10 Savasana with a folded blanket supporting the head and neck, and with the eyes covered.

Focus

• Postures here are done with a support under the head. This allows the brain to become quiet and calm. Breathe normally throughout and focus the mind on the breath. Keep the face, mouth and throat relaxed.

• In order to deal with stress and anxiety, both the mind and body must be treated. Tension associated with stress is stored mainly in the muscles, diaphragm and nervous system and if these areas are relaxed, stress is reduced.

Insomnia

The physiological symptoms of insomnia – raised or lowered blood pressure and exhaustion – can be dealt with by doing these postures with the face, mouth, throat and stomach soft and relaxed, in order to keep the mind and brain quiet.

1 Uttanasana I with the head and arms supported on a stool.
2 Prasarita Padottanasana with trunk, arms and head supported.

3 Adho Mukha Svanasana with the head supported on a bolster.
4 Adho Mukha Virasana with the forehead and trunk supported.

9 Ardha Halasana with a stool and foam blocks for support.

5 Pascimottanasana with the forehead and arms supported.
6 Janusirsasana with the forehead and arms supported, using a strap.

10 Setu Bandha Sarvangasana using foam blocks and bolster.
11 Cross bolsters supporting the feet on foam blocks.

7 Supta Baddhakonasana using a strap and bolster support.
8 Chair Sarvangasana shoulder stand using a chair and bolster.

12 Viparita Karani legs against wall, support under lower back.
13 Savasana head and neck supported, eyes bandaged.

Depression

While performing the postures, there needs to be a balance between the mind, body, emotions, and soul. Since the head is supported in these postures, the mind becomes calm and the heart is energized, bringing about courage and a healthier mental state.

1 Uttanasana I with the head and forearms supported on a stool. This position encourages an increased flow of blood to the head, which helps to calm the mind.

2 Prasarita Padottanasana with trunk, head and arms supported.
3 Adho Mukha Svanasana with the head supported on a bolster.

4 Chair Sarvangasana using a bolster for the shoulders.
5 Ustrasana with a chair and bolsters supporting the spine.

6 Supta Baddhakonasana with a strap and supports.
7 Supta Virasana with several bolsters for support.

8 Pascimottanasana with the head and arms supported on a bolster.
9 Janusirsasana with forehead and arms supported, using a strap.

10 Setu Bandha Sarvangasana with supports under sacrum/feet.
11 Cross Bolsters This gentle arch helps breathing.

12 Viparita Karani with legs up the wall and a bolster for support.
13 Savasana using support and with the eyes covered.

Colds

In some of the postures listed below, the head is down, which helps to drain the nasal passages and sinuses. In others, the chest is supported and lifted to facilitate easier breathing.

1 Uttanasana I with the head and forearms supported on a stool softened with a blanket. Broadening the chest in this posture will facilitate easier breathing.

2 Prasarita Padottanasana with the arms and trunk supported on a stool, bolster and blankets.
3 Adho Mukha Svanasana with the head supported on a bolster.

4 Supta Baddhakonasana using a strap and bolster support.
5 Supta Virasana with bolsters and blankets supporting the spine.

6 Setu Bandha Sarvangasana with foam blocks supporting the sacrum.
7 Ardha Halasana with thighs supported on a stool and shoulders on a foam block.

8 Chair Sarvangasana with the shoulders and neck supported on a bolster.
9 Ardha Halasana with the thighs supported on a stool and the shoulders on a foam block.

10 Viparita Karani with the legs against the wall and the lower back raised with block and bolster.

Focus

- In the sequences for colds and asthma, attention should be paid to opening and broadening the chest while in the postures. Breathing should be normal and the brain passive. Regular practice of these routines will build up the strength of the respiratory system.

11 Savasana with the head supported and eyes covered. Arms out with palms facing upwards. Allow the body to let go completely in this posture. Sink towards the floor. Focus on the breath.

Asthma

These postures facilitate dilation of the air passages in order to make exhalation easier during an attack. They also help to prevent constriction of these passages, thus reducing the number and intensity of further attacks.

1 Dandasana with the inner edges of the feet together and the backs of the legs pressing into the floor.

2 Baddhakonasana with the soles of the feet pressed together, sitting up, lifting and opening the chest.

3 Upavistakonasana sitting on a foam block for lift, and using the wall to support the back.

4 Supta Baddhakonasana with the head, neck and spine supported by bolsters and blankets.

5 Supta Virasana supporting the spine with several bolsters and blankets.

6 Setu Bandha Sarvangasana with four foam blocks supporting the sacrum and a bolster to support the feet.

7 Adho Mukha Svanasana supporting the head on a bolster.

8 Uttanasana I with the head and arms supported on a stool softened with a blanket.

13 Chair Sarvangasana using a chair to support the spine and a bolster for the neck and shoulders. Stretch the arms through the chair and pull on the legs to open the chest, keeping the shoulders back.

9 Tadasana with the hands in Parvatasana, using the wall to support the body.
10 Tadasana with the hands in Namaste, opening the chest.

14 Cross Bolsters with two bolsters crossing to help lift and broaden the chest.
15 Viparita Karani with the legs against the wall and support for the back.

11 Adho Mukha Virasana with the trunk and head supported.
12 Ustrasana using a support for the spine as it arches back.

16 Savasana using support for the head and with the eyes covered.

Indigestion

Digestion problems occur as a result of the sluggish movement of food through the stomach and the intestines. In these postures there is increased blood flow to the abdominal organs, which improves the functions of the digestive system.

1 Adho Mukha Svanasana with the head supported on a bolster. This posture can also be done with the heels resting on a wall for balance.

3 Uttanasana I with the head and forearms resting on a blanket and stool. If you do not have a Halasana stool, use a chair and blocks.

2 Prasarita Padottanasana with the legs apart and with the head supported on a wooden block or several foam blocks.

4 Virasana sitting on a support. Use a rolled-up blanket under the feet if they are painful.

5 Virasana (twist) sitting on a support, turning the trunk, resting the back hand on a block.

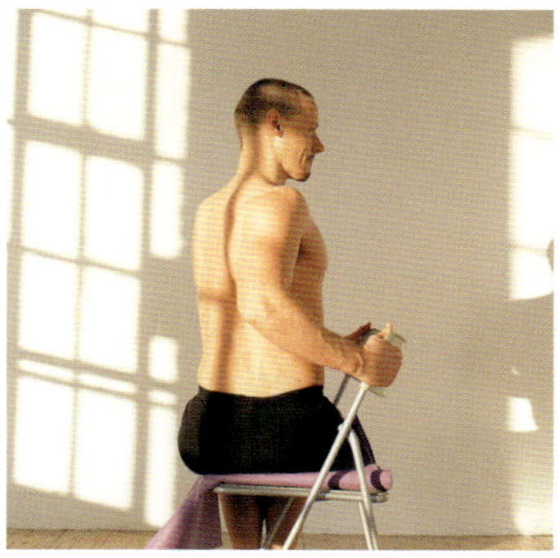

6 Standing Maricyasana using the wall and stool as support.

7 Bharadvajasana (chair) using the back of the chair to turn.

8 Adho Mukha Virasana with the head and trunk supported on a bolster and folded blanket.

10 Supta Baddhakonasana with bolsters and blankets supporting the spine, head and knees, and a strap around the legs and feet.

9 Janusirasana (concave) using a strap around the foot and keeping the back concave. Hold the strap in a "V" shape, one end in each hand.

11 Supta Virasana using the support of two bolsters and several folded blankets as necessary for comfort.
12 Setu Bandha Sarvangasana supported sacrum and raised feet.

13 Viparita Karani with the legs against the wall, bolster and block supporting the lower back.
14 Savasana with the head supported by blankets and the eyes covered.

Constipation

In these postures the abdominal organs are compressed and massaged and this improves their digestive, absorptive and excretory functions. In the inverted poses, there is a positive displacement of the abdominal organs, which helps to relieve stress and strain.

1 Uttanasana I with head and forearms supported on a stool.
2 Prasarita Padottanasana with the head supported on a wooden block.

3 Adho Mukha Svanasana with a bolster to support the head.
4 Utthita Trikonasana against the wall, using a block to support the hand.

5 Utthita Parsvakonasana against the wall, using a wooden block.
6 Ardha Chandrasana against a wall supporting the leg with a stool.

7 Adho Mukha Virasana supporting the head with a bolster and blanket.
8 Janusirsasana supporting the head and knee with bolsters and strap.

9 Pascimottanasana supporting the head on a stool.
10 Chair Sarvangasana using a bolster to support the shoulders.

11 Ardha Halasana using a stool and blocks to support the thighs and a block for the shoulders.
12 Setu Bandha Sarvangasana supporting the sacrum, and feet.

13 Viparita Karani with the legs against the wall and a block and bolster to support the lower back.
14 Savasana with a blanket supporting the head and neck. Palms are open and up.

Diarrhoea

This condition is often accompanied by abdominal pain or fever. In the postures below, the abdomen should remain soft and the brain passive and calm. A combination of restful and stretching postures will aid comfort.

1 Supta Baddhakonasana with a strap around the feet and legs, and support for the spine and legs.
2 Supta Virasana supporting the back and body on bolsters and blankets.

3 Setu Bandha Sarvangasana supporting the sacrum with foam blocks.
4 Supta Padangustasana II using a strap around the foot, and pressing the other foot to the wall.

5 Chair Sarvangasana using a bolster to support the shoulders and neck. Inversions will help to relieve any stress on the bowels and abdomen.

6 Viparita Karani with the backs of the legs against the wall and a bolster and wooden block supporting the lower back. Use a folded blanket to support the head and shoulders.

7 Savasana with the head and neck on a folded blanket, and the eyes loosely covered. Keep the whole body relaxed, allow the feet to drop and the arms to be loose, with the palms facing the ceiling.

Focus

- These sequences to aid digestion include standing postures that stimulate, as well as twists and forward bends that "squeeze" and massage the abdominal organs. While performing these postures, ensure that the abdomen is not restricted or cramped.

Backache

The following five sequences offer poses that will strengthen bones, stretch muscles and help to free and release the affected areas. Flexibility and mobility improve with sustained practice, and pain and discomfort diminish.

1 Bharadvajasana (chair) with hands on chair back to help rotate the spine safely. Try to turn a little more on each exhalation, turning from the waist. Use a block under the feet if they don't touch the floor easily.

2 Standing Maricyasana using a stool to support the foot of the bent leg and the wall to support the hands in order to turn the trunk.

3 Utthita Trikonasana against the wall for balance, using a wooden block to support the hand.

4 Utthita Parsvakonasana against the wall, using a wooden block to support the hand.

5 Ardha Chandrasana against a wall, using a stool for the foot.

6 Uttanasana I against a wall, with the arms supported on a stool.

7 Adho Mukha Svanasana with the head supported on a bolster.

10 Ardha Halasana using a stool and blocks to support the thighs.

8 Supta Padangustasana I with a strap around the foot and the other foot against the wall.
9 Supta Padangustasana II using a strap around the foot, the leg going out to the side.

11 Viparita Karani with the legs against the wall and a block and bolster to support the lower back.
12 Savasana with a blanket supporting the head and neck. Palms are open and up.

Focus

- Back problems are caused by a number of factors – stiffness in the lower back muscles, weak abdominal muscles, muscle strain, arthritis, slipped discs or inflammation of muscles and tendons.
- The spine is made up of 32 vertebrae, which work in unison. Weakness and strength is transmitted from one vertebra to another. If one of the vertebrae is overworked it weakens itself, and the other bones – and the muscles and ligaments – have to take the strain until they too begin to weaken.
- When doing postures for backache, the spine must always be lifted, particularly in the lower back. Never hold the breath – breathe normally in the postures, and keep the neck and facial muscles relaxed.

Sciatica

This condition is due to inflammation and compression of the sciatic nerve. The postures in this sequence help to strengthen the leg muscles, increase flexibility in the hips and improve circulation in the legs.

1 Supta Padangustasana I with a strap around the foot and the other foot against the wall.

2 Supta Padangustasana II using a strap, the leg going out to the side.

3 Utthita Trikonasana against a wall for balance, and using a wooden block to support the hand.

4 Utthita Parsvakonasana against a wall, using support for the hand.

5 Ardha Chandrasana against a wall, using a foam block on a stool to support the extended leg.

6 Bharadvajasana (chair) with the feet parallel on the floor and using the hands on the chair to increase the turn.

7 Standing Maricyasana against a wall, with the foot on a stool. Push the hands into the wall to turn.

8 Ustrasana using a chair and bolsters to support the arch of the spine. Lean back, allowing the head and neck to relax backwards.

10 Setu Bandha Sarvangasana using a wooden block, feet pressing into the wall.

9 Chair Sarvangasana using a bolster to support the neck and shoulders.

11 Savasana relaxing with a blanket supporting the head and neck, and the eyes loosely covered.

Tense Shoulders and Neck

These postures, which tone and stretch the trapezius muscles and release tension in the neck, must be done with attention to rolling and extending the muscles at the back of the neck down the back, and drawing the shoulders away from the ears.

1 Tadasana standing up straight and moving the shoulders towards the body. Keep the feet together, tuck in the bottom and sacrum, and keep the legs strong and active.

2 Tadasana with hands in Namaste Stand in Tadasana and place the palms of the hands completely together behind the back. Move the shoulders into the body, keeping the hands as high as possible.

3 Utthita Trikonasana against a wall with a wooden block for support.
4 Utthita Parsvakonasana against a wall with a wooden block.

5 Ardha Chandrasana against the wall, with the foot supported by foam blocks on a stool.
6 Adho Mukha Svanasana with the head supported on a bolster.

7 Standing Maricyasana using the stool, raise one foot up, and use the wall to turn the spine.

8 Bharadvajasana (chair) with the hands on the chair back to increase the turn in the spine.

9 Virasana (twist) sitting on a support, and using another foam block for the hand if necessary.

10 Maricyasana I sitting on a foam block as a support and using another block to support the back hand. Press into the block to turn the spine.

11 Chair Sarvangasana holding on to the back legs of the chair.
12 Ardha Halasana with the thighs supported on a stool.

13 Setu Bandha Sarvangasana using the wall to raise the legs.
14 Savasana with the head and neck supported on a blanket and the eyes covered.

Knee Problems

These postures bring flexibility to the knee joint. Distortions of the knee joint caused by tears in the cartilage or knee injuries will be relieved. When practising the postures, try to concentrate on creating space in the knee joint.

1 Supta Padangusthasana I & II with a strap around the raised foot.

2 Janusirsasana (concave) with a strap around the foot.

3 Pascimottanasana with one hand holding the other wrist.

4 Standing Maricyasana using a stool and the wall to help twist.

5 Virasana using as much support as necessary to relieve the knees.

6 Upavistakonasana leaning against the wall and using straps.

7 Baddhakonasana sitting on a support, with the feet together.

8 Utthita Trikonasana against a wall, and using a wooden block.

9 Ardha Chandrasana against a wall, the foot supported by a stool.

10 Adho Mukha Svanasana with the head supported on a bolster.

11 Ardha Halasana with the thighs supported on a stool.

12 Chair Sarvangasana supporting the shoulders.

13 Viparita Karani with the sacrum on a block and bolster.

14 Savasana relaxing with the head and neck supported.

Focus

- When practising the standing postures, ensure that no sudden jerky movements are made (such as jumping).
- Draw the thigh muscle strongly up towards the top of the leg to create space in the knee joint.

Stiff Hips

The hip joint is prone to stiffness as it bears a great deal of body weight. As you get older, the spinal and hamstring muscles become stiff and the range of movement in the spine and hip joint is reduced.

1 Bharadvajasana (chair) using a block between the knees.
2 Standing Maricyasana using a stool to raise the foot.

3 Utthita Trikonasana against the wall with the hand supported.
4 Utthita Parsvakonasana against the wall using a wooden block.

5 Virabhadrasana II using the wall for support.
6 Virabhadrasana I with hands on hips to protect the back.

7 Utthita Hasta Padangusthasana I & II using the stool for support.
8 Supta Padangusthasana I & II using a strap to hold the foot.

9 Upavistakonasana sitting on a foam block against the wall for support, with straps around the feet.

10 Supta Baddhakonasana with a bolster and blanket supporting the spine and a strap around the feet.
11 Chair Sarvangasana with the shoulders and neck supported.

12 Savasana relaxing with a blanket supporting the head and neck.

Focus

- Flexibility is increased as a result of stretching the hamstring muscles.
- The seated postures create elasticity in the hip joints and can thus prevent the onset of arthritis.

Menstruation

Inversions and standing poses should be avoided when menstruating as you should not exert yourself physically during this time. Forward bends are extremely beneficial as they help to control the flow of blood and keep the brain quiet and passive.

1 Supta Baddhakonasana using a bolster and folded blankets to support the head and trunk. Keep the strap around the hips to hold the feet in towards the groin and use rolled-up blankets to support the knees.

3 Baddhakonasana sitting on a support with the soles of the feet pressing together and the spine stretched up.

2 Supta Virasana using two bolsters and several blankets to support the head, neck and spine. The same effect can be acheived by using thick, rolled-up blankets, or cushions.

4 Upavistakonasana sitting on a support against the wall. Stretch the legs towards the heels.
5 Adho Mukha Virasana with a bolster and blanket supporting the head.

6 Janusirsasana with the head, arms and knee supported on a bolster.
7 Pascimottanasana sitting on a support, the forehead on a bolster.

8 **Adho Mukha Svanasana** using a bolster or a pile of cushions to rest the head. The sitting bones should be stretched towards the ceiling, with the heels extending towards the floor.

10 **Setu Bandha Sarvangasana** using four foam blocks to support the sacrum and raised feet.

Focus

- Menstruation is not an ailment but may cause discomfort in the form of backache, stomach cramps and bloating of the abdomen. Forward bends regulate menstrual flow, massage the reproductive organs, keep the brain passive and increase blood supply to the pelvic area.

9 **Uttanasana I** with the head and arms supported on a blanket and stool. If the back is uncomfortable, or the hamstrings painful, increase the height of the support.

11 **Savasana** with the head and neck supported on a folded blanket and the eyes covered to keep the brain quiet. You can use a specialist bandage, but a scarf or small bean-bag would be adequate.

Prolapsed Uterus

A prolapsed uterus occurs when muscles and ligaments of the pelvis weaken and the uterus changes position. The postures listed below strengthen the supporting ligaments and the forward bends create space in the pelvic area.

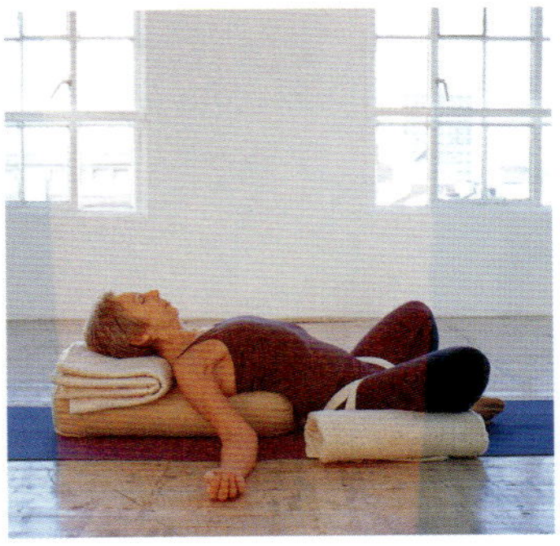

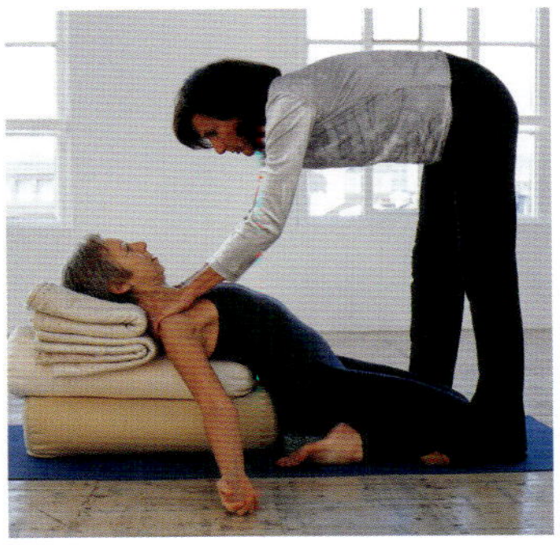

1 Supta Baddhakonasana with a bolster to support the body and rolled blankets under the knees.

2 Supta Virasana with bolsters and blankets to support the spine.

3 Supta Padangustasana II using a strap in one hand to reach the foot, keeping the opposite arm outstretched to keep the body flat on the floor.

4 Janusirsasana (concave) keeping the back arched.

5 Prasarita Padottanasana with the head supported on a block (use more support if necessary).

6 Tadasana stand up as straight as you can, drawing the crown of the head towards the ceiling. Keep the feet together, and the legs strong, knees lifted. Raise and open the chest, keeping the shoulders down.

7 Ardha Chandrasana using the wall for support in this posture, keeping the foot supported on a stool with foam blocks raising it to the correct level for your height. The hand is supported on a wooden block.

8 Chair Sarvangasana with the neck and shoulders on a bolster and the head on the floor. Reach the hands through to the back legs of the chair and use the pull to open the chest further.

9 Setu Bandha Sarvangasana using a wooden block to support the sacrum, with both feet pressing into the wall. Make sure that the block is under the tailbone, not in the lower back.

10 Viparita Karani pressing the legs against the wall and supporting the lumbar spine and sacrum with a block and a bolster. Arms stretched over the head, palms up.

Focus

- Symptoms of a prolapsed uterus include a dragging sensation in the pelvic area and backache. In this sequence, the abdominal muscles are strengthened and the body is inverted, which improves this discomfort.
- The forward bends, done with a concave back, create space in the pelvic area and lift the uterus.

11 Savasana relaxing with a folded blanket to support the head and neck.

Menopause

The menopause occurs with changing hormonal balance. The following postures create a soothing sensation in the nerves, keep the brain passive, improve the flow of blood to the pelvic area and help to lessen many of the symptoms.

1 Upavistakonasana sitting on a support against the wall. Keep extending inner legs to heels.
2 Baddhakonasana sitting on a support with the soles of the feet together.

3 Supta Baddhakonasana with a bolster and blankets supporting the head, spine and knees.
4 Supta Virasana supporting the body on bolsters and blankets.

5 Supta Padangusthasana I & II holding a strap in one hand to reach the foot, stretching the leg up first, then out to the side for the second of the postures, while keeping the other foot against the wall.

Focus

• The menopause usually takes place between the ages of 45 and 55 and is accompanied by changes in the hormonal balance of the body. Symptoms include mood swings, depression, insomnia and hot flushes. Forward bends and inversions can be particularly beneficial.

6 Prasarita Padottanasana with the head supported on a wooden block. If the hands do not reach the floor, put foam blocks under the hands so that the palms can press down.

7 Adho Mukha Svanasana against the wall. Turn the hands out so that the thumbs and index fingers are pressing into the wall. Support the head with a bolster if necessary.

8 Uttanasana I with the head and forearms supported on a blanket and stool. Keep the feet parallel and hip-width apart, legs strong with the knees lifted.

13 Setu Bandha Sarvangasana with a wooden block under the sacrum and the feet raised on the wall. Support the head and neck on a folded mat or blanket.

9 Janusirsasana sitting on a support and resting the head on a bolster.
10 Pascimottanasana with the head and arms supported on a bolster, and a strap around the feet.

11 Chair Sarvangasana with the shoulders and neck on a bolster.
12 Ardha Halasana with the thighs supported on a stool.

14 Viparita Karani with the legs raised and pressing into the wall. A wooden block and bolster support the lumbar spine. The arms are stretched along the floor, palms facing upwards.
15 Savasana relaxing with the head and neck supported on a folded blanket and the eyes covered.

Pilates

This section includes a broad range of simple but effective Pilates techniques for a strong, lithe and healthier body. All the exercises are designed to be practised safely at home by beginners.

Emily Kelly

Introducing Pilates

What is it about Pilates that makes it such a favourite in gyms and dance schools and such a respected and popular activity? With all the different exercise videos and books on the market, what makes this technique special?

Maybe the answer can be summed up in one word: commonsense. This section is designed to be an accessible manual that you can integrate into your life. It explains the key elements of Pilates and takes you by the hand through a comprehensive range of exercises. The programme aims to be very user-friendly: it is designed for beginners to Pilates but more advanced variations of many exercises are included so that you can have greater challenges as you progress.

The "first position" in each exercise is the most basic option. If you are new to Pilates then always start with this one, otherwise you will not have mastered the control and the focus needed to perform the exercise correctly. During a Pilates session your main concern should be the feeling that you get from doing the movement correctly, not how many repetitions you can do. The "second position" should only be attemped after you have a clear understanding of the first position. For some people this may take two or more months. For others, it may take as little as three weeks. Everyone is different. It is not a competition, just progress at your own rate. The "third position" is a more intense variation still.

above Pilates combines stretches and strengthening exercises, making it one of the safest and most effective forms of exercise.

above Pilates helps to re-define posture, creating a relaxed, confident stance. It is worth remembering that the correct posture can give an illusion of a 6 lb weight loss.

You may find that you progress faster with some exercises than with others. This is perfectly normal. For example, you may have a slight imbalance in your body that is being strongly challenged by the movement. Have faith in your knowledge of how your own body feels.

The holistic approach

This section aims to get you to look at exercise in a holistic way and to help you integrate it into your daily life with only minimal disturbance. It does not set out to turn you into an Olympic athlete. It might, however, give you that little push you need to start exercising by explaining just why it is important, not just for aesthetic purposes but to help you avoid pain and injury, to make you feel good about your body and to increase your self-esteem.

The intention is that you will find the programme clear, logical and simple to remember, so that it will be quite easy to make it a regular part of your daily routine – just like brushing your teeth – because exercise really should be a matter of course. It's just common sense. You need to take care of your body at least as well as you take care of your car. You probably expect your car to last you six or seven years, and oil changes, tune-ups and wheel alignments are common practice for every car owner. How long do you want your body to last you?

Everyone can benefit

So who can benefit from this programme? Basically, Pilates has something to offer everyone, whatever your age or current fitness level. Although you will get stronger all over, one of the main benefits of Pilates is an increase in core strength. This is a phrase that is used over and over again in connection with Pilates, and it refers to the important abdominal and back muscles at your centre that support your whole body whether moving or at rest. As these muscles are strengthened, your posture will improve and you will find it easier to go about your daily tasks.

If you are completely new to Pilates, you will find these exercises different from others you may have tried. First of all, Pilates is a series of movements that flow into one another without pauses. Most conventional exercise starts and stops: you might do 12 repetitions of a move, rest, and then start up again with the next sequence. Pilates concentrates on the body as a whole, stretching some muscles, strengthening

right Pilates creates a strong, lean, balanced body. This reduces the risk of injury and helps to elimate nagging aches and pains.

others and, by helping you to function more effectively, reducing the risk of injury, not only while you are exercising but in everything you do.

Many people who take up Pilates are pleased to discover that only a small number of repetitions are needed per exercise in comparison with other conventional methods. If you are performing the movements correctly, up to ten repetitions will be more than adequate. This means that you can give each repetition your full effort and concentration: you will be maximizing the potential of the exercise without growing tired or bored with continual repetitions.

The importance of focus

Another distinguishing feature of Pilates is that to practise it you must be totally focused and concentrated, and this concentration creates a mind-body connection. This doesn't mean that conventional exercise can be done without thought of course, but it does mean that Pilates needs all your attention and focus in order to get the best results. If you sometimes feel overwhelmed by everyday problems and stresses, giving all your attention to the movements of a Pilates sequence can help to still the insistent clamour of your daily life, acting like meditation to calm your mind and help you see things more clearly. This total concentration and attention to alignment and detail makes Pilates quite unique and very satisfying.

Be kind to yourself

When you start the programme, it is important that you do not place any expectations on yourself. Pilates is about the feeling you are getting from the exercise, not about how many repetitions you can do, how long you exercise for or how many advanced exercises you can work through. Some of the movements are very subtle and to an observer it may appear that you are doing very little. You should check throughout the exercises that

below Within weeks of beginning regular Pilates practice, you will see a clear improvement. Pilates creates long, lean muscles with no risk of developing a bulky, overdeveloped physique.

right Pilates should be combined with healthy eating and regular cardiovascular exercise for optimum results.

your spine is in neutral (unless otherwise stated), that the abdominals are contracted, that you are not holding your breath at any time, that the muscles not involved in the movement are relaxed (it is common to hold tension in the jaw and shoulders), and that the movements are controlled. All these factors are the key elements that make Pilates so effective, and they are fully explained on the following pages.

Pilates is a very personal experience. Listen to your body and stop if anything feels uncomfortable or causes pain – though this should not be confused with an exercise being challenging. It could be that a particular exercise is not right for you at this time; you can always come back to it on another occasion, or try the less intense version of the same exercise. If you simply cannot focus on an exercise during a session, choose another exercise from the same category; don't waste your time and create negative feeling for a movement.

The endorphin effect

You will sometimes hear regular exercisers talking about the high they get from activity: what they are describing is the production of endorphins, chemicals in the brain that are stimulated by exercise and have similar effects to that of opiates. If you need any more encouragement to get started, consider this: tests have shown that people who suffer from illness and depression are significantly helped by taking exercise.

As well as describing each exercise in detail, the section gives advice on putting together a sequence to help you achieve the benefits you are seeking, and on incorporating Pilates into an all-round fitness regime of exercise and healthy eating. Start investing in the present and future health of your body, today.

left Regular practice of Pilates will help you achieve a long, lean, strong physique.

The History of Pilates

Recently it has become almost impossible to open a magazine and not find mention of a Pilates-based exercise programme. Everyone is talking about this "new" form of exercise, especially having seen the way it has sculpted celebrities such as Courtney Love, Sophie Dahl, Madonna and Melanie Griffiths. We jogged in the 70s, did aerobics with Jane Fonda in the 80s, took up weight-training in the 90s; in the new millennium we are discovering the mind-body experience.

In reality, Pilates has been around for a century. For ballet dancers, it has been a well-kept secret as the perfect way to become strong and centred without building bulk. Only in the past few years has the fitness world embraced Pilates, and this accounts for its sudden and well-deserved popularity as a form of exercise.

Joseph Pilates was born in Germany in 1880. He was a sickly child and suffered from asthma, rickets and rheumatic fever, which left him with a burning desire to become physically stronger. By the age of 14 he was an avid body-builder with a well-sculpted physique. He practised all types of sports, such as skiing, diving and gymnastics. At 32 he moved to England, where he made his living as a boxer, circus performer and self-defence instructor for detectives.

left The Pilates method was originally developed to build strength and increase immunity. Today, the many modified forms of the techniques still teach your body to work at its most efficient.

left Performing artists, such as singers, dancers, actors and models, have long used Pilates' methods to improve posture, align their body, gain strength and avoid injury.

When World War I broke out Pilates was interned in the Isle of Man. Being such a keen fan of exercise, Pilates decided that his fellow internees should get fit under his training. His efforts paid off, as none of his trainees succumbed to the massive influenza epidemic that killed millions after the war. He also worked as a hospital orderly, encountering many war casualties. He started working with some of the disabled patients, using his own body weight to move their limbs and devising special equipment to aid their progress. This consisted of springs attached to their hospital beds which gave gentle resistance to aid muscle strengthening and stretching: these were the prototypes of the machines that are used today.

Pilates believed that imbalances in the body and habitual patterns of movement cause injuries. He observed the links between weak areas of the body and over-compensation (if you are weak in one area the rest of the body has to support the imbalance), and the exercises he devised were based around re-education and the re-alignment of the body.

In 1926 Pilates and his wife Clara moved to New York where they set up an exercise studio. By 1940 the dance community had become aware of his fitness programmes, including George Balanchine and other members of the New York City Ballet.

Pilates had a number of students who went on to set up their own studios and so the method spread, each teacher adding their own personal twists, as they continue to do today. It would be rare to find two instructors who teach Pilates in exactly the same way.

Since Pilates' death, followers of his methods have modified the original 34 exercises and made them more user-friendly. The Pilates method is practised in one of two ways: using equipment called a re-former, an updated version of the original springs, or as free body exercises using only a mat. The latter is the version that you will be taught in this section.

The Benefits of Pilates

Muscles can be divided into two groups: prime movers and postural. The prime movers are those muscles involved in movement, such as the hamstrings at the back of the thighs or the deltoids in the shoulders. Postural muscles, such as the deep abdominal muscle called the transverse abdominis, work to maintain stability. This core stability is essential when the body is moving, for example, when creating a firm platform for keeping the pelvis still while running, or controlling the position of the shoulder blade while throwing.

Muscle imbalances can occur through repetitive strain or faulty mechanics, and result in an uneven pull of the muscles around a joint. This imbalance may eventually cause injury to that joint. The pain that results will inhibit the postural or stabilizing muscles around the joint and, as a result, these muscles weaken, making the injured joint even more unstable and still more susceptible to further injury and pain. And so the cycle repeats. Even when the area is no longer painful, these muscles do not automatically strengthen again. This is why injuries tend to reoccur. To recover fully from injury, the muscles in that area need to be specifically strengthened and their co-ordination retrained again.

Trunk or core stability requires strength, endurance and co-ordination of the stabilizing abdominal, pelvic floor and lower back muscles. Stability is necessary to

below The anterior and posterior views of the human muscular system show the main muscles of the front and back of the body. Although this is a simple diagram only, it will help you to gain a clear understanding of the location of the muscles used throughout your Pilates practice. Be aware, though, that Pilates uses many other supporting muscle groups during different phases of a movement.

THE MUSCULAR SYSTEM

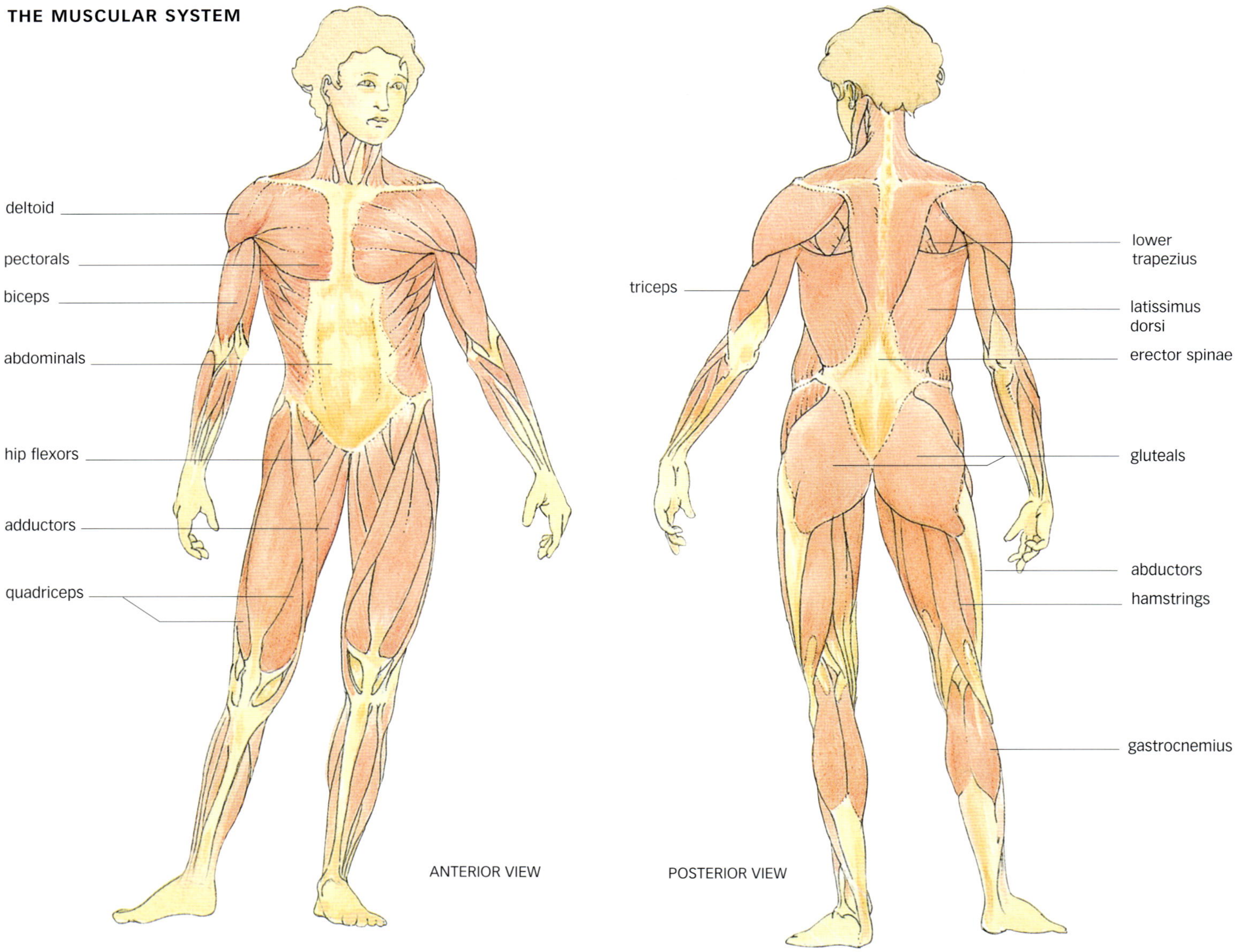

left Throughout the day try to give yourself a posture bodycheck. Try to pinpoint your bad habits as awareness is half the battle.

support and protect the lower back from injury, to help with general postural alignment and to allow the release of the hips for greater freedom of movement. Better core stability can therefore reduce the chance of injury. Improving it is often the way finally to get rid of niggling back problems that you may have suffered from for years. Core stability exercises are an important part of the Pilates method, which focuses on improving the strength and control of these stabilizing muscles.

The Pilates programme is very enjoyable and you should soon feel results which will motivate you to continue. If you adhere to it, you will be rewarded by improved posture, an enhanced feeling of balance, reduction in aches, pains and stiffness, greater flexibility and a longer, leaner, more toned body. As your posture improves, you will look as if you have lost weight, and one of the most frequently heard comments from people who are new to Pilates is that they feel "as if they have grown". This is because they have learned to lengthen up through the spine to its maximum potential, making them look slimmer and feel more confident.

Regular Pilates sessions will help your co-ordination and enhance your balance, which is of special importance through the aging process. You will gain strength in a balanced way, so that tight, tense areas are stretched and weak ones strengthened. The realignment of your body will also make it easier for you to use it correctly. You will feel more relaxed and less stressed and will possibly benefit from other "by-products" such as more refreshing sleep, more energy, extra alertness during waking hours and a general sense of well-being.

For the more experienced exerciser, Pilates can help to highlight imbalances throughout the body. The attention to detail and the concentration given to the movements can challenge even elite professional athletes, who often comment that they feel like beginners again after trying it. What appear to be the simplest of movements can be incredibly challenging when performed correctly, so do not worry if even the first position of an exercise seems hard to you: in terms of Pilates this is a good thing. As long as you work at your own pace, paying attention to how your body feels during the movement, Pilates is perfectly safe and very effective.

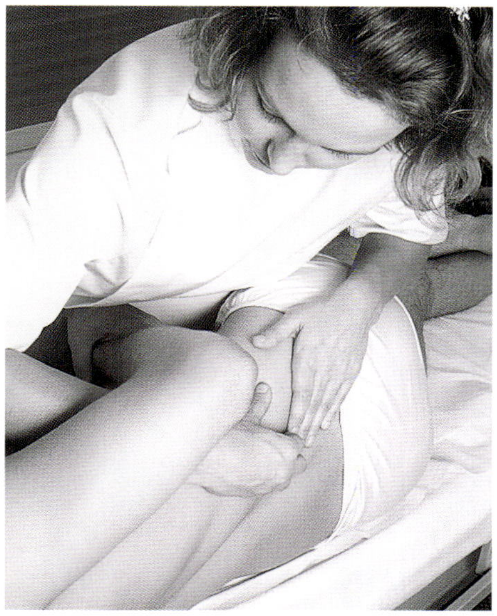

right Many osteopaths recommend Pilates to aid recovery and rehabilitation as well as a way of preventing possible imbalances or injuries. Remember though, if you feel pain or have an existing injury, always check with a medical professional before starting a new exercise programme.

PILATES AND OSTEOPATHY

My introduction to Pilates followed a serious back injury. I was eager to recover as quickly as possible, and for the injury not to recur. I am a competitive runner (a former International 400m runner), so I did not want the injury to affect my training. I found a class and was impressed by the specificity of the exercises and how much more stable my back felt after several weeks of regular sessions. Since maintaining a regular regime, my back has felt better and my sports performance has improved. I now incorporate clinically based Pilates exercises into the rehabilitation of my patients and recommend it to them as an excellent way to improve their own stability.

Alex Fugallo

DO, ND, Bsc (Hons) Osteopathic Medicine

Registered Osteopath

Key Elements of Pilates

Some concepts are referred to repeatedly in Pilates: these are the "key elements" that make it more than just a sequence of movements. Keep them in mind throughout your sessions, relating them to each exercise, and as you become more familiar with the technique they will start to make more sense to you. They will help you to get the most benefit from each movement, and also keep the exercises safe and comfortable. Some of these key elements will come more naturally to you than others, but do not feel discouraged. They will eventually become automatic and you will find yourself applying the same principles to other forms of activity, because they are based on attention to detail and alignment, safety and commonsense.

Breathing

Breathing is something you do unconsciously, but when you are relaxed and calm your breathing pattern is different from when you are tense, anxious or negative. At times of tension and stress, breathing is usually irregular and shallow, and does not completely fulfil your need for oxygen. If you learn to control your breathing while practising Pilates as well as during daily activity, it will help you to maintain your energy and stay relaxed.

Holding your breath causes tension in your muscles, which decreases when you exhale. For this reason, athletes learn to exhale when executing certain movements such as a tennis serve, a basketball dunk or a golf swing: they are programmed to exhale on the maximum effort. In sports that require a maximum effort during a longer period of time, such as power-lifting, elite athletes will hold their breath. This gives their muscles added stability but has several potentially negative effects on their blood pressure. Remember that these athletes are aiming at a particular goal: they want to win medals at all costs, sometimes even by endangering their health. You should never hold your breath when exercising. In Pilates, it is sometimes difficult to gauge which of the movements is the one that takes maximum effort. Most of the movements maintain tension in the torso at all times, but your breathing should always be regular and relaxed.

When starting out on this or any other exercise programme, strive to master the general movement first, then focus on the breathing patterns. It is often the case that correct breathing patterns start to come naturally as the body tries to help itself, but you can practise breathing control exercises when you are not moving to help you learn the correct technique. During the exercises try not to let the ribs flare up (push upwards and outwards away from your spine), which sometimes goes hand in hand with arching the spine. Aim to keep the ribs the same distance from your hips, just sliding them out to the sides and then back again as you breathe. This is described as breathing laterally.

Breathing exercise

Here is a simple breath control strategy that you can practise at any time. Regulating your breathing will enhance your body awareness and control and make you feel calm and centred.

1 Place your hands with your palms under your chest, on your ribs, and your fingers loosely interlocked. Inhale slowly and continuously through your nose, to a count of four. Do not strain, keep yourself relaxed.

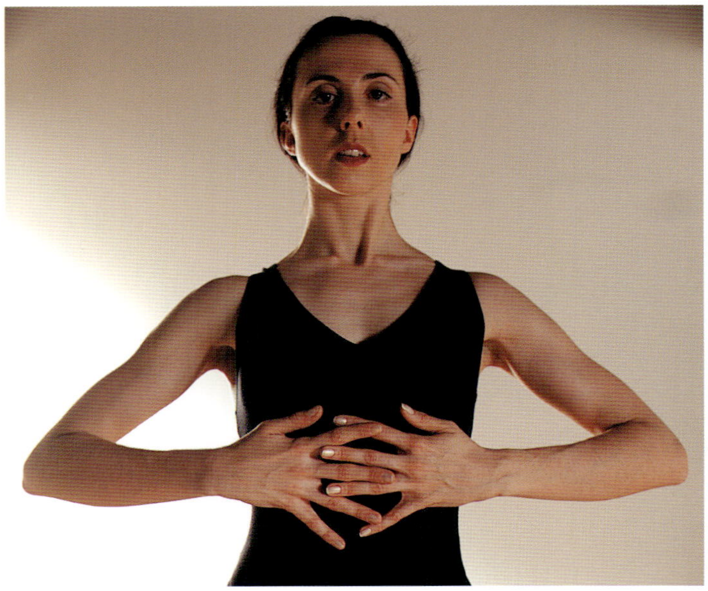

2 As you inhale concentrate on allowing your ribs to expand laterally: your fingers should gently part. Don't let your ribs jut forward. Exhale slowly, expelling all the breath from your lungs, then repeat.

left During your Pilates session you must give each movement your full concentration. Really focus and feel the muscles working.

right If you do not feel in complete control of a movement, then try a less intense version. Return to the more advanced variation at a later date.

Concentration

Your muscles respond better to a training stimulus if the brain is concentrated on the effort. Remember that it is the brain that sends out the signal to the muscle to contract. So, it is imperative that you concentrate on the work you expect the muscle to perform.

It is very easy to get distracted while exercising if you do not set the right mood, avoiding intrusive sounds or disturbances that will take your mind off what you are doing. It is also necessary to prepare yourself mentally to focus on your body and the work that it will be doing.

Control

All movements should be performed slowly and with absolute control. The faster you do anything, the less actual muscle mass you will use to do the exercise: instead, you will be using momentum. Most Pilates movements are not static; they should be continuous but at the same time controlled and precise.

Flow

Pilates movements cannot be likened to repetitions of a conventional exercise. They are continuous. Try to "link" one movement with the next, maintaining a steady flow of energy throughout the session. You will not be stopping and starting as in conventional exercise, but flowing like a steadily turning wheel.

above Maintain a steady flow of energy, keeping movements graceful and fluid.

Relaxation

Pilates is a gradual re-education of the body, and in order to benefit from it you must try not to create unnecessary tension. This would eventually create an imbalance in the body, which is the very thing you are trying to remedy. Watch especially for tension in the neck and jaw, but you may hold it anywhere – even in the feet. During a session, give yourself little mental checks from head to toe and you will start to see where you tend to hold tension. Awareness is half the battle.

Adherence

No exercise programme works unless you do it! Adopt this programme as part of your life and make it as much part of your daily routine as brushing your teeth: physical activity is as much a way of taking care of your body as personal hygiene.

below Try to begin and end each session with a few moments of complete relaxation.

above Pilates practice must be consistent in order for you to see and feel the benefits.

Core Strength

The principal aim of the exercises is to create core strength, which will be the powerhouse for the rest of your body. When you reach a level of understanding of core strength Pilates starts to feel like an altogether different form of exercise: you begin to get a feel for your body working as a whole in a very focused, concentrated way.

The abdominals and back form the centre of the body, from which all movements in Pilates are initiated. If you look at a ferris wheel in a funfair, there is movement around the wheel but the powerhouse is the centre because everything is controlled from there. This is how you should view your body. Your centre should be your first priority, because without sufficient strength in this area you are vulnerable to injury. So, what are these muscles and how do you locate them?

right The illustration displays the key abdominal muscles used in Pilates. These are the muscles used when we refer to "working from a strong centre" or developing "core strength".

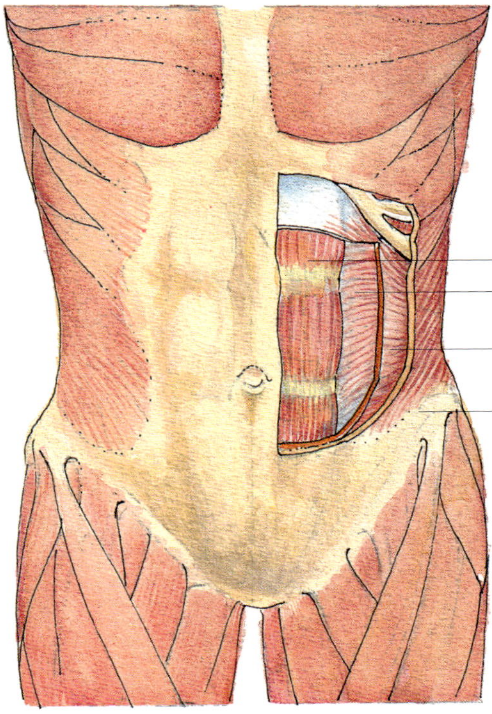

Muscles that stabilize the torso

Rectus abdominis: This is a wide and long muscle that runs all the way down from the sternum (breast bone) to the pubic bone. The rectus abdominis helps to maintain correct posture and allows forward flexion.

Obliques: These are located at the waist, and there are actually two sets: the internal and external obliques. They allow you to rotate at the waist as well as flexing laterally (to illustrate this, imagine that you are picking up a suitcase by your side).

Transverse abdominis: This muscle is located behind the rectus abdominis, like a "girdle" wrapped around your stomach. It is used when you draw your navel towards your spine, and is the muscle that contracts when you cough.

Building core strength

By stabilizing the torso you are creating a "co-contraction" between the abdominal muscles and the back muscles. This means that all these muscles are working together to create a stable entity. In most people they are weak, and in the back they can be tense and tight. In this situation the spine may be pulled out of alignment, causing improper posture and risk of injury. When the back muscles and the abdominals are strong and flexible it becomes easier to maintain correct posture. Pilates strengthens and stretches these core muscles, helping to correct imbalances and reducing the chances of suffering back pain.

left Pilates exercises are designed to build up your core strength.

Locating the transverse abdominis

Sit or stand upright, inhale and pull your stomach towards your back, imagining that you are wearing very tight jeans and trying to pull your tummy away from the waistband. This is what you will be doing during all the Pilates exercises.

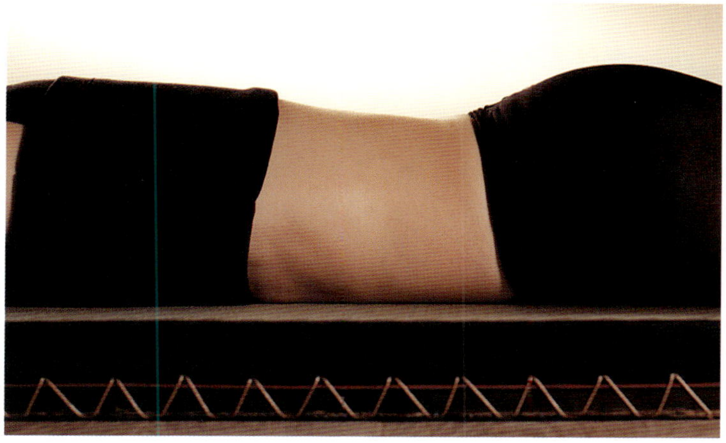

1 Lie on your tummy with your head relaxed and supported on your folded hands or on a small cushion under your forehead. Keep your head in alignment with your back and the back of your neck long, without shortening the front. Try to keep your hip bones on the floor and relax your shoulders.

2 Inhale, then as you exhale pull your navel towards your spine, trying to create an arch under your abdominals. You may not be able to lift very far up at first: this is not important as long as you understand the concept. Gently lift your shoulders back and draw your shoulder blades down your spine.

above If sliding your shoulder blades down your spine is a baffling request, practise this subtle movement by standing up with your arms by your sides. Keeping your back straight, push your fingertips towards the floor. Do not force your arms down or lock them into position. Try to keep the shoulder blades close to the back of the ribcage. This is very useful for limiting tension around the shoulders, which tends to make you pull your shoulders up to your ears.

above Every movement should be controlled via your abdominals. Keep bringing your attention and focus back to pulling your navel towards your spine.

Neutral Spine

A healthy spine has natural curves that should be preserved and respected but not exaggerated. The term "neutral spine" refers to the natural alignment of the spine. If you have any serious pain in your back, check with a physician before embarking on any exercise programme. The main curves are:

1 **The cervical spine**: the area behind the head, along the back of the neck, is concave; it should curve gently inwards.

2 **The thoracic vertebrae**: the largest area of the back curves very slightly outwards.

3 **The lumbar spine**: the lower back should curve slightly inwards; it should not be flat or over curved.

4 **The sacral spine**: the sacral curve is at the bottom of your spine and curves gently outwards.

It is important to allow the spine to rest in its natural position to prevent stresses and imbalances. During Pilates movements you should ensure (unless otherwise directed) that your back is not flat or pushed into the floor, although this can be tempting in order to achieve a flatter tummy. What you tend to do in this position is grip at the hip flexors (the muscles located at the top of the thighs) thus creating tension in a place that is commonly tight anyway. You must also try to avoid over curving your spine, as this pushes the abdominals forwards and tightens the muscles around the spine. "Neutral spine" lies in between these two extremes and echoes the natural and safe position that your spine prefers.

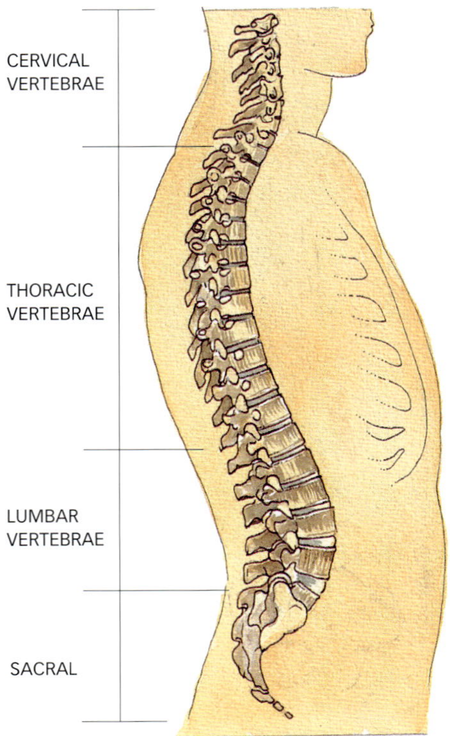

left The diagram shows the four natural spinal curves. These curves help to cushion some of the shock from our daily activities – even walking creates some mild stress. One of the key elements of Pilates is the close attention given to the alignment of the spine during all movements.

Finding neutral spine

The importance of neutral spine cannot be emphasized enough, as it allows your spine to elongate and relax. Before starting an exercise it can be helpful to roll gently between the two extreme positions and then try to fall comfortably between the two.

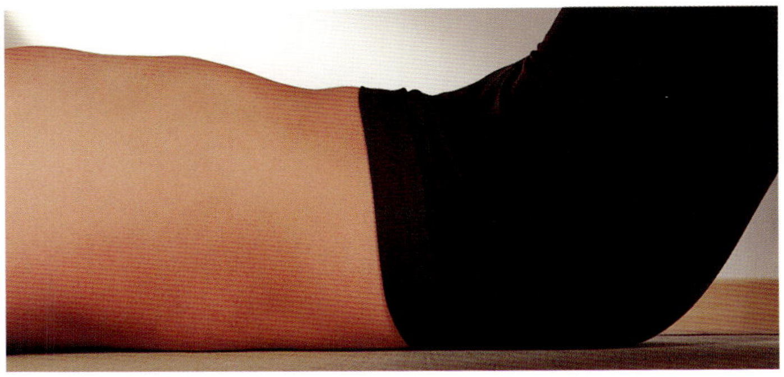

1 Tilt your pelvis, flattening your back into the floor.

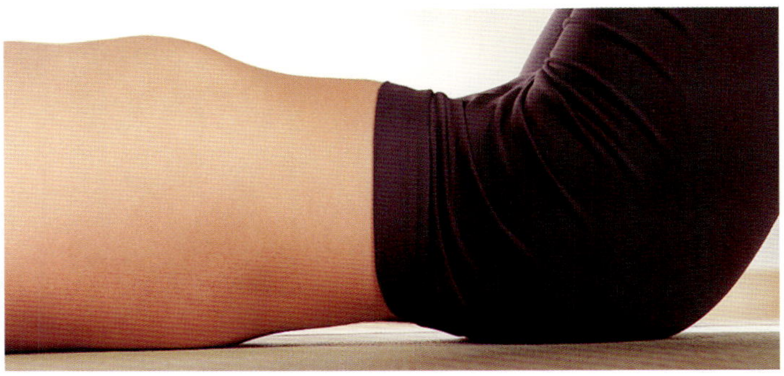

2 Tilt your pelvis in the opposite direction, creating an arch under your lower back. Make this movement slow and take care not to hold for too long or you may cause tension in your lower spine.

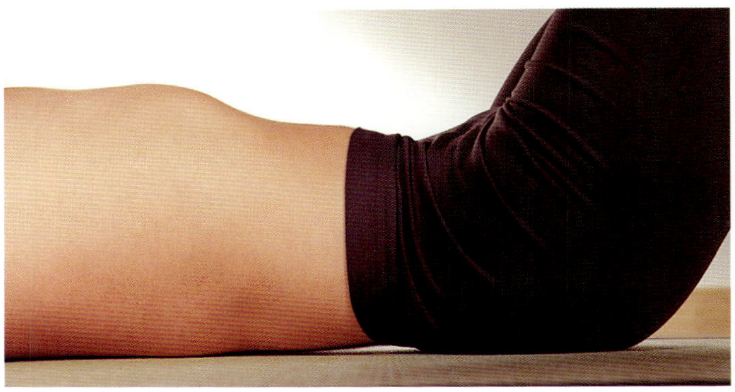

3 Find a position between these two extremes in which your back feels natural and comfortable: this is neutral spine. Unless otherwise stated, you should always work from this position during your Pilates routine.

Pelvic Floor Muscles

The pelvic floor muscles act as a dynamic platform at the base of the pelvis, functioning both as a support mechanism and as an aid to bowel and bladder function. Well-trained pelvic floor muscles may also improve orgasmic potential in women and erectile function in men.

Pelvic floor muscle activity is a "lift and squeeze" movement: it is the action used to stop midstream urine flow and to stop the passage of wind. It is essential to perform this movement accurately in order to improve the muscles. A woman can tell if she is using the correct muscles by examining herself with a mirror. During a pelvic floor muscle contraction she should see an anal squeeze and an upward movement of her perineum. Inside the vagina, she or her partner should be able to feel a vaginal pressure. A man should see an anal squeeze with the penis lifting at the same time.

Once you have found the correct movement, the next part of the strengthening process is to hold the contraction and to repeat it. At first, you may be able to perform only short holds, but the aim is eventually to hold each contraction for ten seconds. The number of times that you repeat the contraction also depends on your ability; the aim is eventually to repeat the hold ten times.

As well as these sustained holds, you should also practise short, sharp, fast contractions, again in sets of ten. To strengthen the muscles you will need to exercise them up to six times a day. To maintain the resulting change you should remember to exercise them to their full ability at least once a day.

As the brain controls the action of muscles in groups rather than individually, it is important when exercising to consider those muscles that work well together. It is now believed that the pelvic floor muscles work best in conjunction with the transverse abdominis, which is contracted constantly during Pilates exercises. Once you are familiar with Pilates movements you can add pelvic floor muscle lifting and squeezing as you contract your abdominals.

Jeanette Haslam
MPhil, MSCP, SRP

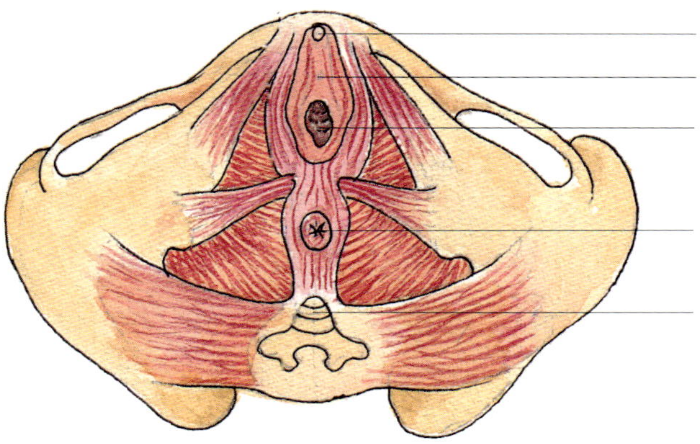

right The pelvic floor muscles are often ignored but are important to exercise. For maximum benefit, especially for women who have had children, the exercises should be performed daily.

above When you become more familiar with Pilates, try adding pelvic floor contractions as you exercise.

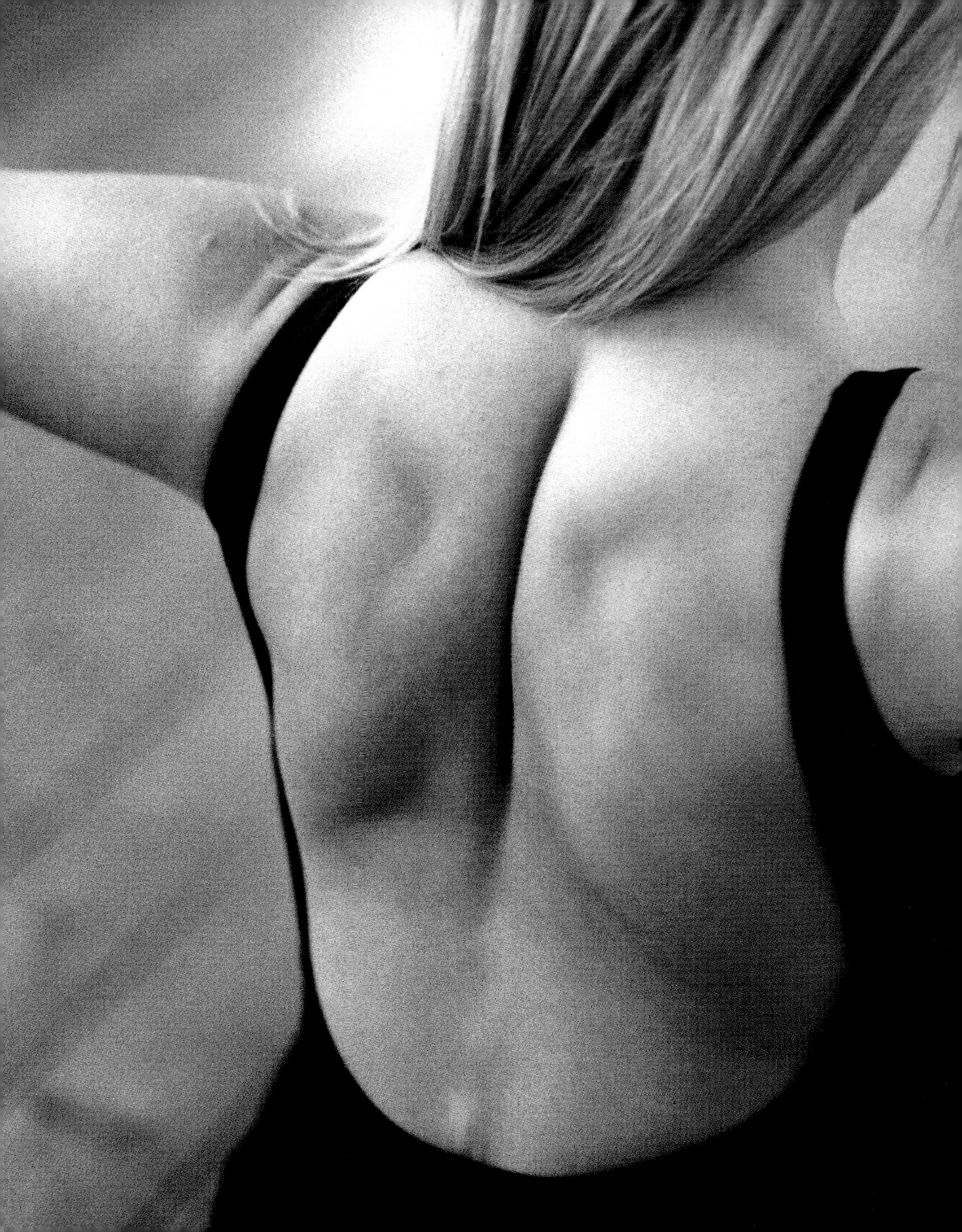

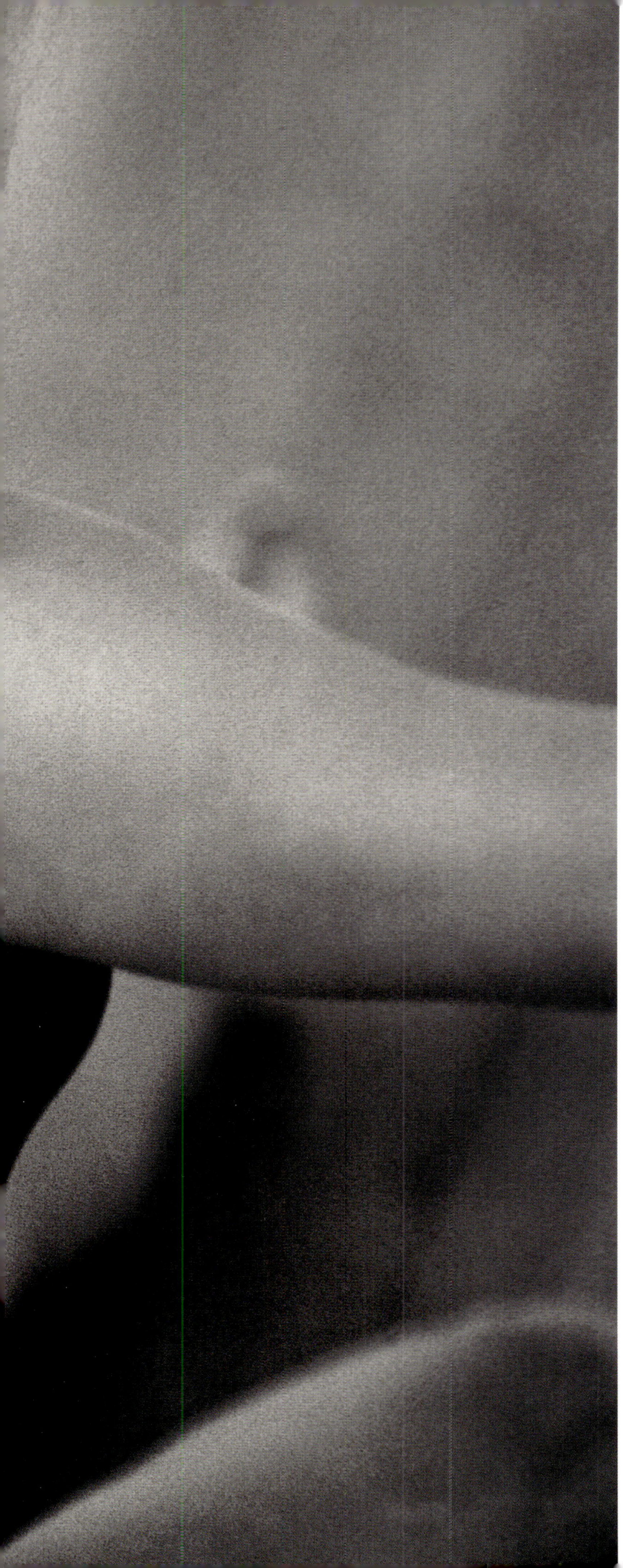

Warming up and Mobility exercises

This chapter is dedicated to preparing the body for the demands we are going to make on it. One of the benefits of warm-up exercises is that fluids are released into the joints, making the muscles more pliable, reducing the risk of injury as well as making muscular responses faster and more precise. By regularly practising mobilizing exercises, you decrease your risk of sustaining injuries when exercising and make even everyday activities easier to perform.

Exercises for Warming Up

The first part of any exercise routine should be a warm-up to raise the core temperature of your muscles. If you pull a cold elastic band too hard it snaps, but once it is warm it becomes more pliable and will stretch further. The same applies to your muscles. The warm-up prepares you psychologically for activity, getting you in the mood. It also increases the efficiency of the neuromuscular pathways, thus speeding up the signals sent from the brain to your muscles.

Keep your movements flowing and gentle during the warm-up: do not force your body or overstretch. Adopt the correct breathing patterns each time and keep the spine in neutral. Repeat each of the warm-up exercises five times.

Perform all exercises with flow and complete concentration. Work from a strong centre and avoid holding on to any unnecessary tension. Breathe wide and full.

Arm crosses

These are great for warming up the shoulders and upper back. The movement should be continuous and flowing: think of the graceful way in which a ballet dancer's arms move. As you do the exercise, watch for tension in the neck; your spine should stay in neutral and your abdominals hollowed. Imagine you are trying to reach both sides of the room and lengthen out through your arms and up through your spine.

1 Stand with your feet about hip-width apart and cross one hand in front of the other. Relax your shoulders and lengthen up through your spine, keeping your head in alignment.

2 Inhale to prepare and, as you exhale, take your arms out to the sides, palms up. Keep your shoulders relaxed and slide your shoulder blades down your spine as you lift your arms. Lower your arms to begin again. This should be performed at a moderately fast pace but should always be controlled and flowing.

Shoulder circles

A good way to relieve tension in the shoulders and upper back, this exercise also mobilizes the shoulders. It is a movement that many people tend to stumble on naturally when they are feeling stiff. Make the movement slow and controlled, breathing in wide and full through the ribs. Keep the spine in neutral.

1 Stand with your feet hip-width apart, lengthen up through your spine and do not let the abdominals sag. Inhale to prepare. As you exhale, roll your shoulders forwards up to your ears and then around.

2 Concentrate on trying to form a complete circle. Think about the shape you are making: is it a circle or an egg-shape? Create as big a circle as you can in one direction then the other.

Arm sweeps

This big, sweeping movement will wake you up and help with a "fuzzy head". It also mobilizes the spine, lower body and shoulders. Try to move in a fluid, rhythmic way at a constant speed.

1 Stand with your feet close together, knees and shoulders relaxed, keep the abdominals hollowed. Extend your arms overhead and lengthen up through the spine while keeping your feet flat on the floor and your head in alignment.

2 Inhale to prepare, then drop your chin to your chest and roll down through your spine, letting your arms flow behind you.

3 Bend your knees as your arms sweep back and again as you bring them forward and up over your head to begin again, lengthening up through your spine as you return to standing.

Walking through the feet

You may be surprised at how stiff your feet and ankles get, and this exercise is designed to wake up the feet, ankles and calves. It's a good idea to warn them gently of the activity to come, so that they provide a strong, secure base.

left From standing, lift the heel on one foot then the other in a natural walking movement, bending the knees. Keep the spine in neutral and the abdominals hollowed. Keep this movement rhythmic and continuous, always lengthening up through the spine.

Standing balance

This is a more advanced way to warm up the feet and lower legs, which may also challenge your balance. Try to keep your weight central and concentrate on each part of your foot as you rise and come back down on to your heels. This movement is performed at a moderately slow pace.

left Stand with your feet hip-width apart and make sure that your toes are not clenched but relaxed. Keep your spine in neutral, abdominals hollowed, and place your hands on your hips to help you balance. Keeping your head in alignment, come all the way up on to your toes. Hold the balance for a few seconds, then lower your heels slowly to begin again.

Relaxation position

This is not a movement, just a comfortable position. Try always to start and end your Pilates sessions with a couple of minutes in the relaxation position. It will help you focus and get in contact with your body, as well as making you feel relaxed and refreshed. Concentrate on each area of your body, from your head down, and try to observe any tension, particularly in your jaw and face, shoulders and hips. Some people even clench their feet. Just notice where your areas of tension are and gently focus on relaxing. Try to visualize your spine lengthening and sinking into the floor. Imagine you are lying on warm sand and let it support your spine. This position can also be used at any time during the day, whenever you get a chance to relax.

above Lie on your back with your knees bent and your feet flat on the floor. Your spine should be in neutral. Relax your shoulders and let your shoulder blades gently glide down your spine, but do not force them into position. Your head should be in alignment with your spine and your arms relaxed by your sides. Breathe wide and full laterally, in through your nose and out through your mouth.

Exercises for Mobility

During the aging process, our range of movements can decrease making everyday activities harder, increasing our risk of injuries. The following exercises guide you safely and effectively through a series of exercises that challenge mobility, so helping to keep the joints healthy and flexible. Some of the exercises also challenge your co-ordination, balance and strength.

Rolling down the spine

Now you are ready to start your Pilates session with some mobilizing exercises. This is a really effective movement for mobilizing the spine, and can be very refreshing if you have a stiff back. However, if you have problems with your spine take advice before doing it. If you find it difficult you can do it with bent knees or against the wall, and you can also keep your hands on your thighs. Keep the movement flowing and remember not to collapse into it: the abdominals should not sag. During a Pilates programme, you can use this as a transitional movement to transfer from a standing to a floor exercise, so that the feeling of flow is not lost.

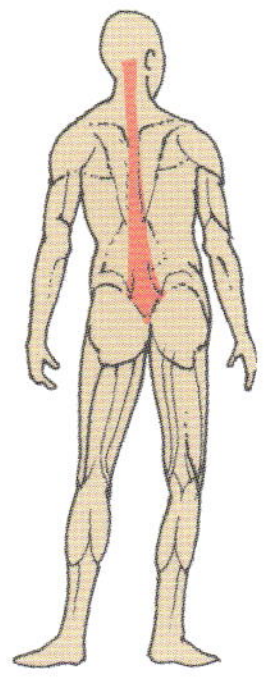

Purpose: To mobilize the spine and improve balance
Target muscles: Designed to loosen/mobilize the spine
Repetitions: Repeat 6 times

Checkpoints

- Create space between each vertebra
- Bend your knees and keep your hands on your thighs if required
- Create a C-shaped spine

1 Stand with your feet hip-width apart, balancing your weight evenly through your feet. Breathe in to begin and, as you exhale, lower your chin to your chest, and start to roll down towards the floor.

2 As you bend over from the hips, create a C-shape with the spine letting the arms hang towards the floor. Feel your head relax and your shoulders drop. Don't sway backwards or forwards as you roll down. Make the movement flowing and controlled.

3 Start to curl back up, tilting the pelvis and trying to mobilize each part of the spine, uncurling it bone by bone and creating as much length as possible between the vertebrae. Try not to lean backwards or forwards but keep your weight in alignment, with your feet flat on the floor. As you come up to standing feel the crown of your head float up to the ceiling.

One leg circles

Circling the legs mobilises the hip joints and also challenges core strength, as you aim to keep the hips still during movement of the lower body, your thighs get a workout too. Keep the abdominals hollowed throughout. Make sure your spine stays in neutral and your shoulder blades glide down your back. The ribs may move away from the hips in this position so keep gently reminding yourself to control them. Make the circles flow and keep the movement continuous: think of a ballet dancer's grace and poise.

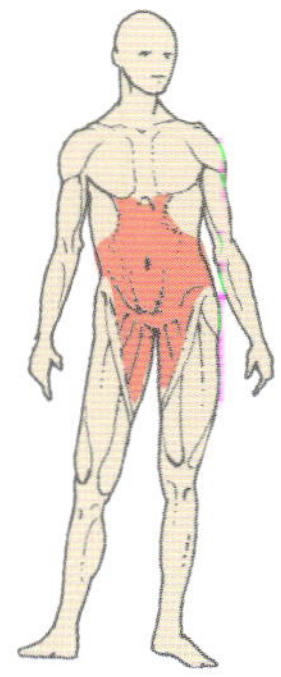

Purpose: To mobilize the hips and build core stability

Target muscles: Adductors, hip flexors and abdominals

Repetitions: Circle 5 times in each direction, then change legs and repeat

FIRST POSITION

1 Lie on your back with your knees bent and your arms by your sides. Keep your spine neutral, your head aligned and the supporting foot firmly on the floor, raise one bent leg. Ensure your hips are square and still. Then start to circle your knee. Make small circles initially then larger ones, using your abdominals for control. The breathing for this movement requires concentration: break each circle into semicircles, inhaling as your leg crosses your inner thigh and exhaling on the outer edge of the circle.

Checkpoints

- Keep the hips square: don't let them lift from the mat
- Keep the spine in neutral
- Make the circle as large as you can safely control

SECOND POSITION

2 Straighten the moving leg, keeping the other foot firmly on the floor. Lengthen up through your toes and try to make your leg as long as possible. If your hips start to move, you are not controlling the movement and would be better off continuing to work with a bent leg. Try to increase the size of the circle as you get stronger.

Checkpoints

- Keep the abdominals hollowed throughout the movement
- Extend the circle as you grow stronger

THIRD POSITION

3 Straighten the supporting leg and lengthen, as if you were trying to reach the end of the room. Continue to lengthen up through the circling leg. Make the circles only as large as you can control. This position is really tough, so do not try to progress to it until you feel you have complete control in the second position. Remember to work from a strong centre.

Checkpoints

- Guard against over-curving of the spine
- Lengthen through both legs

The shoulder bridge

A very popular exercise in almost every class, this is a good mobilizer with which to start your session and a wonderful way to ease a stiff back. After this exercise your spine should feel loose and supple and it will also work your abdominals and lower body. The aim is for each bone in your spine to lift off the mat in succession. You may find that, to begin with, your back lifts in two or three sections: try to create length between each vertebra. As you lower yourself, place each vertebra in turn on the mat, imagining a pearl necklace sinking on to a velvet cloth.

The hips should be perfectly level, and you should try to create as much distance between your hips and your shoulders as possible. Do not forget to tilt the pelvis as you begin the movement. To mobilize the spine fully be sure to return to neutral as you lower your back to the floor, just before you tilt the pelvis and start the next lift.

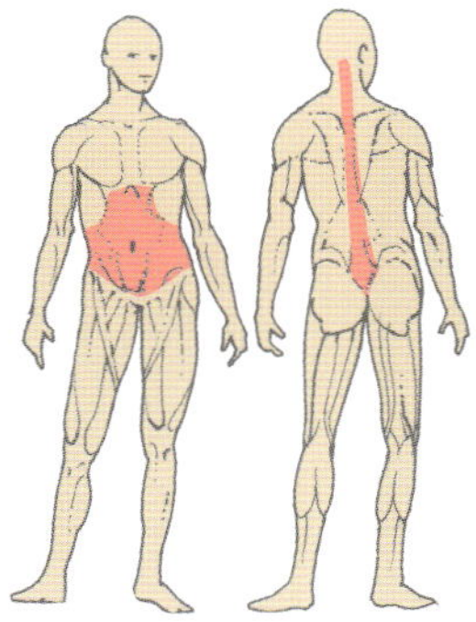

Purpose: To mobilize the spine and challenge the abdominals
Target muscles: Erector spinae, abdominals
Repetitions: Repeat 6 times

Checkpoints

- Keep the hips level
- Maintain the distance between the hips and the ribs
- Make the movement flow

1 Lie on your back with your arms by your sides, slide your shoulder blades down your spine and lengthen your arms away. Bend your knees and place your feet hip-width apart flat on the mat. Your head is in alignment and your spine in neutral.

2 Tilt your pelvis and lengthen the tailbone away. The whole length of your spine should be in contact with the mat.

3 Slowly peel your spine up off the mat bone by bone, raising your hips towards the ceiling and keeping the abdominals flat and drawn down. In this position it is common to flare the ribs, so concentrate on keeping a constant distance between the hips and ribs. Make the movement smooth and flowing, inhaling as you lift and exhaling as you come down. Once you get used to the movement you can increase the stretch by taking your arms over your head.

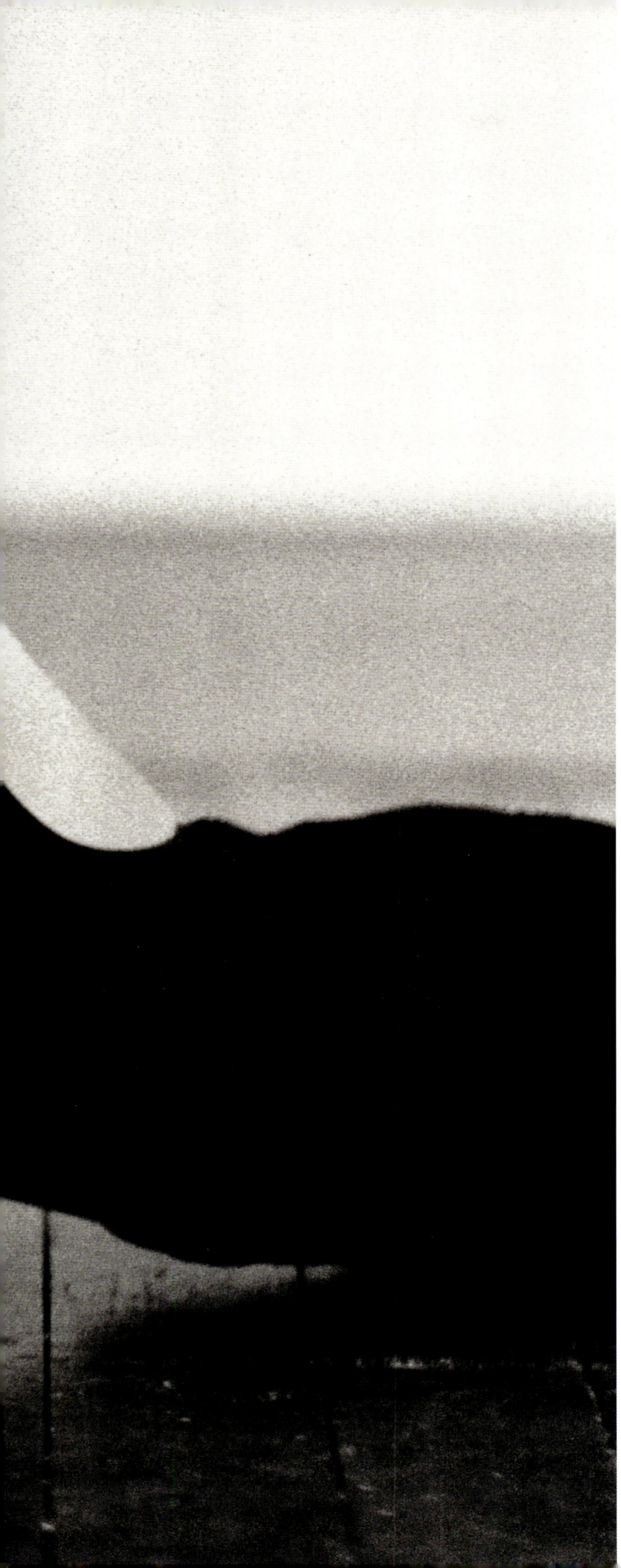

Abdominal and Back exercises

The following exercises concentrate mainly on the abdominals and back – the staples of Pilates – although of course the body works as a unit throughout every movement. Feel the abdominals getting stronger, flatter and firmer as you progress and watch your wardrobe change. Your back will respond by allowing you to live your life in comfort, free from the burden of aches and stiffness. Pay attention to the alignment of your body throughout the day, for optimum results.

Rolling Back

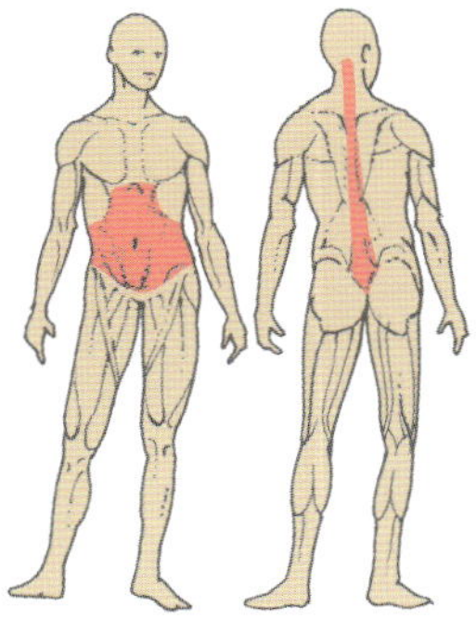

Once you have mastered this movement, it is bound to bring back memories of childhood. We all rolled back and forth when younger and it did wonders for our backs. But do remember that it may not be as effortless now that your back has stiffened up – and make sure you work on a mat that gives plenty of support. Once you have practised rolling down the spine with your hands on the floor, try progressing on to rolling back: you may not roll back up on your first attempt, but keep practising. When pulling in the abdominals, imagine you are squeezing a sponge held between your navel and your spine. Squeeze the sponge as hard as you can. Take care not to roll back on to your neck.

Purpose: To mobilize and massage the back and strengthen the abdominals

Target muscles: Erector spinae, abdominals

Repetitions: Repeat 6 times

FIRST POSITION

1 Sit with your spine in neutral and your knees bent with both feet flat on the floor. Place your hands near your hips with your fingers facing your feet. Inhaling wide and full through the ribs, draw your navel towards your spine. Lower your chin towards your chest then, using your hands for support, start to roll down to the floor. Try to place each vertebra on the floor, one by one. To do this, tilt your pelvis and curve your spine into a C-shape.

2 Once you have rolled down as far as you find comfortable, exhale and, using your core strength, return to the starting position. Pull up through the crown of your head to create a long spine, then repeat. Use your arms only as support and avoid transferring all your weight onto your triceps.

Checkpoints

- Keep your feet flat on the floor
- Lengthen up through the spine at the end of the movement
- Tilt the pelvis

SECOND POSITION

1 Sit upright with your spine in neutral. Lengthen up through the spine and imagine your head floating up to the ceiling. Place your feet flat on the floor and your hands just below your knees. Don't overgrip: keep your elbows bent and your chest open. Take care not to tense or grip around your neck.

2 Inhale as you tilt the pelvis and curve the spine into a C-shape to roll back, tucking in your chin and keeping your thighs close to your chest. As you exhale, use your abdominals to pull you back up to the starting position. Try not to use momentum, but make the movement flow at a consistent speed. Between each roll lengthen up through the spine.

Checkpoints

- Keep the chin tucked into the chest
- Do not grip the neck
- Use your abdominals to get you back to the starting position again

The Roll-up

In spite of the name of this exercise, you begin by rolling down. It is an excellent way to strengthen the abdominals but is very challenging, so ensure you are comfortable and confident with the first position before moving on. Although you are curving your spine do not collapse into the movement. Roll down only a little way at first to get the feel of the movement, then roll lower as you become stronger. At all times, do a mental check that you are not tensing other parts of your body, such as your neck or face. As you come back to an upright position imagine that you are sitting against a cold steel door.

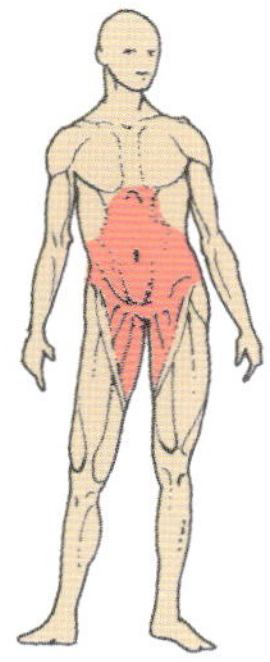

Purpose: To strengthen the abdominals

Target muscles: Abdominals, hip flexors

Repetitions: Repeat 10 times

Checkpoints

- Do not overgrip the legs, use them only as support
- Lengthen up through the spine in the starting position
- Feel the abdominals pull you up

FIRST POSITION

1 Sit upright with your feet flat on the floor and your knees bent. Hold the back of your thighs, with your elbows bent and your arms open; don't overgrip. Your spine should be in neutral. Lengthen up through the spine but do not grip the neck. Slide the shoulder blades down the spine.

2 Inhale and tilt your pelvis to create a C-shaped spine. Keeping your feet flat on the floor, roll down bone by bone, creating space between the vertebrae. Your hands are there to support you if you lose control but try to rely on abdominal strength to stabilize the movement. As you curl down, imagine your spine is a bicycle chain that you are placing down link by link. When you have lowered down as far as you can, exhale and contract the abdominals to roll back up to the starting position. Sit upright, keeping the spine in neutral.

SECOND POSITION

1 This time, hold your arms directly in front of you, level with your shoulders. Your elbows should be bent, arms rounded. Let your shoulder blades glide down your spine and feel the crown of your head "float" up towards the ceiling. Inhale and tilt your pelvis to begin the downward roll as before.

2 When you first progress to this position try a few small roll-downs to get the feel of the movement before going down further. Feel the support of the abdominals throughout the downward and upward roll. Keep your feet flat on the floor all the time.

Checkpoints

- Use the abdominals, not momentum, to pull you up
- Lower bone by bone
- Do not collapse into the movement
- Keep the feet on the floor

The Hundred

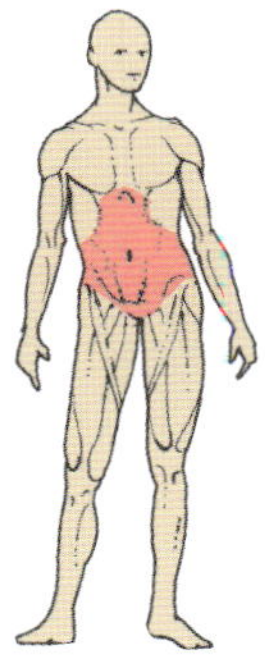

This static contraction builds core strength and is one of the most commonly taught Pilates exercises. Challenge yourself to reach a hundred.

The Hundred really tests your co-ordination. Try not to stagger your breathing as you count your taps: the breath should be flowing and even. Pay special attention to any tensing in the neck and face in this position. To help you do this exercise well, visualize a heavy weight balancing on your abdominals and pulling your navel down towards your spine.

Purpose: To strengthen core muscles, co-ordinate breathing patterns and build endurance.

Target muscles: Transverse abdominis, rectus abdominis, stabilizing mid-back muscles

Repetitions: 20 x 5 beats

FIRST POSITION

1 Lie on your back with your knees bent, your feet flat and your head in alignment. The spine should be in neutral and the abdominals hollowed, drawing the navel to the spine. Your arms are by your sides, lifted off the mat. Slide your shoulder blades down your spine. Inhale as you count to five then exhale for five. Gently tap your fingertips on the floor and co-ordinate your breathing with your taps. Breathe steadily and laterally into your ribs.

Checkpoints

- Keep your arms lengthened
- Draw the shoulder blades down the spine
- Keep the abdominals hollowed

SECOND POSITION

2 When you feel confident about the first position, lift your feet off the floor. Your knees should be directly above your hips and your feet level with your knees. Do not allow your knees to fall away as this will cause your spine to curve. If this is too much of a challenge you can raise just one leg, but do not twist your hips. Repeat the breathing pattern as before. Keep the abdominals flat throughout and maintain the distance between your hips and ribs.

Checkpoints

- Glide your shoulder blades down your spine
- Keep your knees above your hips
- Toes are pointed
- Feet stay level with knees

THIRD POSITION

3 Curl your upper body off the floor, dropping your chin towards your chest so that you are facing your thighs. Do not grip your neck and keep drawing your shoulder blades down your spine. Maintain the breathing pattern for a hundred beats as before. If you want a greater challenge, try straightening the legs. Lower your eyes in this position to check that your abdominals are flat and your ribs are not flaring up.

Checkpoints

- Release tension from the neck
- Do not clench your jaw
- Keep the abdominals flat

The Swimming

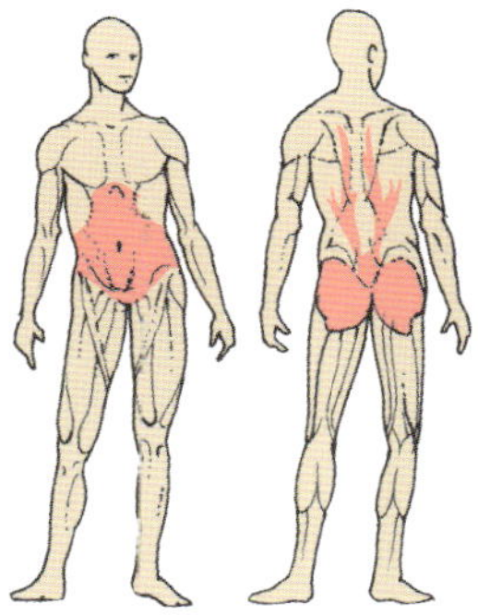

This exercise is a favourite with physiotherapists as it is a very effective way of developing strength in the core muscles. It is a very challenging exercise but is an easy one to cheat on, so read the instructions carefully to make sure that you are performing the exercise correctly. Ensure that you keep your abdominals lifted. Instead of just raising your arms and legs, visualize them lengthening away from your trunk. Do not try to lift them too high from the floor. Make your movements elegant and flowing and avoid throwing your arms and legs or collapsing back onto the floor on the way down. Take care not to lift your hips off the floor or to overbalance onto one side or the other.

Purpose: A strength exercise, challenging co-ordination and core strength

Target muscles: Abdominals, gluteals, erector spinae

Repetitions: Repeat 10 times

FIRST POSITION

1 Lie on your front, placing a small pillow under your forehead to keep your head in alignment with your spine, which is in the neutral position. Keep your neck long. Stretch your arms over your head and lengthen them away. Point your toes and lengthen your legs away. Breathe laterally, wide and full. Draw in your abdominals, imagining that there is a drawing pin on the mat that you are lifting away from.

Checkpoints

- Do not tip your head back
- Keep the abdominals lifted
- Breathe laterally

SECOND POSITION

2 Introduce a challenge to your core strength by lifting one leg. Exhale as you lift and inhale as you lower the leg. Keep both hips in contact with the floor, and do not try to lift the leg too high. Keep lengthening as you lift, maintaining the distance between the ribs and hips. Do not lose the lift in your abdominals. Take care not to twist the raised leg but keep your knee and foot in line with your hips. Repeat with the other leg.

Checkpoints:

- Lengthen as you lift the leg
- Do not twist the hips

THIRD POSITION

3 As you exhale, lift your opposite arm and leg together. When you lift your arm raise your head and upper body with the movement, but keep facing the floor so that your head stays in line with your spine. Lengthen through your arms and legs and keep your hips in contact with the floor. Remember the drawing pin under your navel: if you lose the lift in your abdominals, continue to work in the second position for a while longer.

Checkpoints

- Keep your head in line with your spine
- Do not twist the torso
- Lengthen from a strong centre

One Leg Stretch

Do not be fooled into thinking that this is a relaxing leg stretch – it is actually a very challenging movement which builds core strength and is also good for improving co-ordination. Keep your hips still throughout as if they were being held in a vice. Take care not to curve your spine and keep your shoulder blades pulled down your spine and close to the back of your ribs throughout. If you find the hand position difficult, you can lightly hold either side of your knee instead. Make sure that you are just making light contact and do not over grip as this causes tension in the neck and jaw. Your upper body should be stabilized by your abdominal muscles.

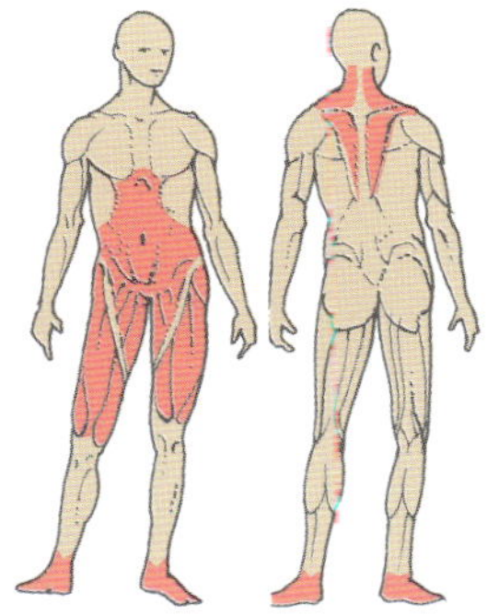

Purpose: To strengthen abdominals and improve co-ordination

Target muscles: Abdominals, stabilizing back muscles

Repetitions: Repeat 10 times on each leg

Checkpoints

- Hollow your tummy throughout
- Keep the hips still

FIRST POSITION

1 Lie on your back with your knees bent and your feet flat on the floor. Your spine should be in neutral and your head in alignment: do not shorten your neck by tipping your head back or dropping your chin to your chest. Draw the navel to the spine.

2 Lift one foot off the floor, keeping the knee bent, and pull the leg gently towards you, supporting it at the knee. Try not to overgrip, causing tension in the neck, and keep your foot in line with your knee. Take care not to let the ribs flare up. Repeat with the other leg, inhaling as you lift and exhaling as you lower.

SECOND POSITION

above When the first position is understood, curl the upper body off the floor and continue the same movement. Let the chin fall towards the chest, and try to limit tension in the neck. Keep the hips very still, controlling any movement from the hips via your abdominals. Breathe laterally. Keep the stomach hollowed throughout the movement, trying to make it as flat as possible.

Checkpoints

- Do not tip the head forward or back
- Watch for tension in the neck

THIRD POSITION

above This position really challenges your co-ordination. As you raise the right leg, place the right hand on the ankle and the left hand on the inside of the knee. Change hands as you change legs. As one leg comes in to the body the other leg lifts and lengthens away on an exhalation. Keep your toes pointed and stretch down through the straight leg. The movement is controlled by the abdominals: keep them hollowed, and maintain the distance between the ribs and hips. Do not twist the hips: imagine they are being held in a vice. Keep the pace slow and consistent.

Checkpoints

- Pull the shoulder blades down your spine close to the back of your ribs
- Lengthen the legs away
- The lower your straight leg, the harder your abdominals have to work

Leg Pull Prone

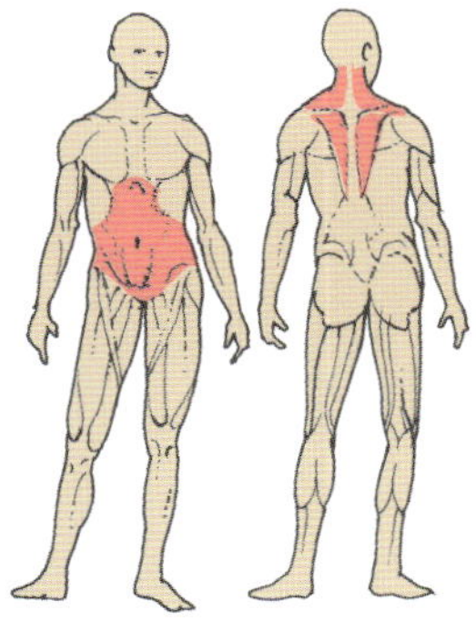

This is actually a yoga position as well as a modified Pilates position. You will gain a lot of torso strength and stability from this exercise, and if you do it properly it will feel as if every muscle in your body is being challenged. Remember to breathe freely throughout the exercise and do not hold your breath when holding the position. It is common to shrink down into your shoulders in this position so try to maintain the length in your neck throughout. Keep checking for tension around the neck, face and shoulders. Focus on your abdominals which should be stabilizing your whole body. You could try to visualize a drawing pin inserted through your navel and attaching to your back.

Purpose: To strengthen the abdominals and spine and challenge the upper body
Target muscles: Abdominals, stabilizing back muscles
Repetitions: Repeat up to 10 times

FIRST POSITION

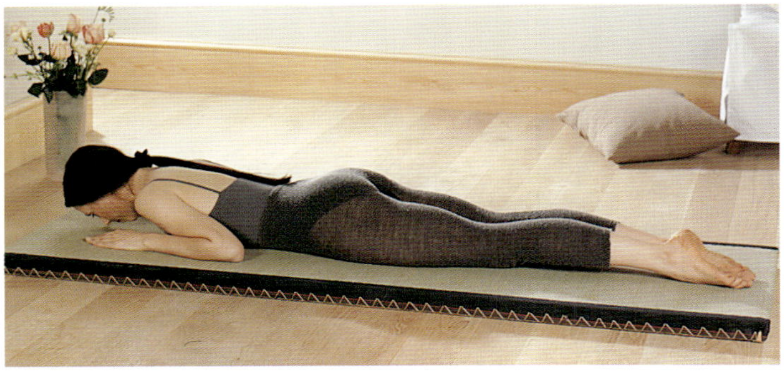

1 Lie on your front with your head in line with your spine. Bend your arms and keep your upper arms close to your body. Lift the abdominals off the floor, imagining that you are creating an arch under your stomach. Breathe wide and full. Focus on this abdominal lift and aim to hold it for one minute before relaxing again.

Checkpoints

- Slide your shoulders down your spine
- Keep the upper arms close to your body

SECOND POSITION

2 Your elbows should be directly under your shoulders. Do not push your buttocks towards the ceiling or arch your spine. Keep your head in line with the spine and lengthen it away: don't sink into your shoulders or squeeze the shoulder blades together. Make sure that your hips stay square. The abdominals are lifted throughout. If this is too difficult, lower your hips and curl just your upper body off the floor. Try to hold this for one minute.

Checkpoints

- Maintain a straight line from your head to your knees
- Do not let the abdominals sag

THIRD POSITION

3 Lift up on to your toes, straightening your legs. This is a real challenge, so be sure to have worked on the first and second positions for quite some time before progressing. Take care not to transfer all the weight into your shoulders or upper body, and keep your hips square. Pull your navel to your spine, maintaining the distance between ribs and hips, and breathe laterally. Aim to hold for up to one minute.

Checkpoints

- Keep a straight line from your head to your heels
- Do not transfer all your weight into your upper body
- Draw your shoulder blades down your spine

The Side-kick

This is another good exercise for core strength, concentrating on the lower body. Have patience and work gradually through the progressions to achieve the best results.

When performing the Side-kick take care not to use momentum to lift and lower your leg. It may help to visualize moving your leg through mud as this will slow you down.

Your foot or knee should stay in line with your hip throughout the movement. Be aware of the alignment of your hips and keep them stacked on top of one another as it is common for the hips to roll forwards and the posture to collapse. This movement is stabilized by the abdominals and the obliques (the muscles at the side of the waist). Try to keep a constant connection with their involvement.

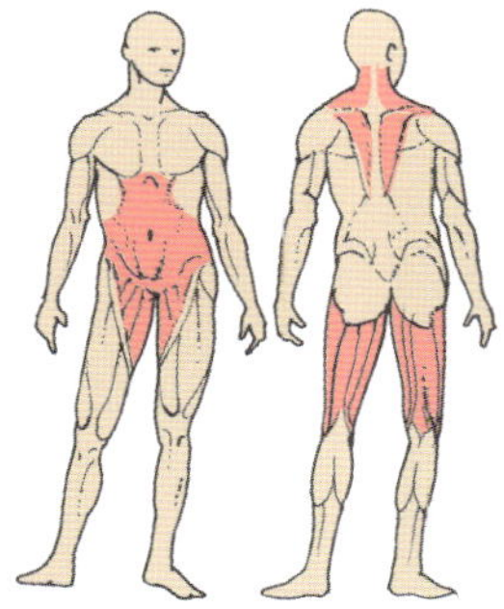

Purpose: To challenge core strength and work the lower body

Target muscles: Hamstrings, hip flexors, abdominals, stabilizing shoulder muscles, abductors

Repetitions: Repeat 10 times each side

Checkpoints

- Do not transfer all your weight into the arm in front
- Keep your abdominals flat

FIRST POSITION

1 Lie on your side, resting your head on your outstretched lower arm. Keep your head in line with your spine, which is in neutral, and your hips stacked vertically: they must not roll in or out. Your knees are bent, one on top of the other. Place your free hand in front for balance but do not lean into the supporting arm or transfer your weight forward.

2 Lift the top knee directly above the other knee. Inhale and, with your toes pointed, move the knee back as you exhale until it travels behind your body. The challenge is to keep your hips stacked and your abdominals hollowed. Your shoulder blades should be pulled down your spine and your ribs should not be pushed up. You should feel this in your side. To increase the challenge, straighten the top leg, keeping the toe pointed.

SECOND POSITION

above Straighten both legs. This is very challenging so be sure to advance only after working with the previous position first. Bring the bottom leg forward slightly from your hip, it should not be in line with your spine. Keep the hips vertical and lengthen out through both legs. The control comes from your centre. Exhale as the leg travels backwards.

Checkpoints

- Do not let the hips collapse
- Lengthen out through the legs

The Side-squeeze

This exercise will shape the waist and abdominals, so it is especially good for the area that hangs over your waistband when you wear fitted clothes. As you lift, check for tension in your neck or other parts of your body, and watch that your ribs stay down. Do not let the abdominals sag but hold them taut throughout.

If you wish to add an extra challenge, raise the top knee, keeping it in line with your hips – no higher. Make this a slow, controlled movement. Take care not to overgrip with your hands. Perform the movement with flow, avoiding any jerky movements when lifting and lowering.

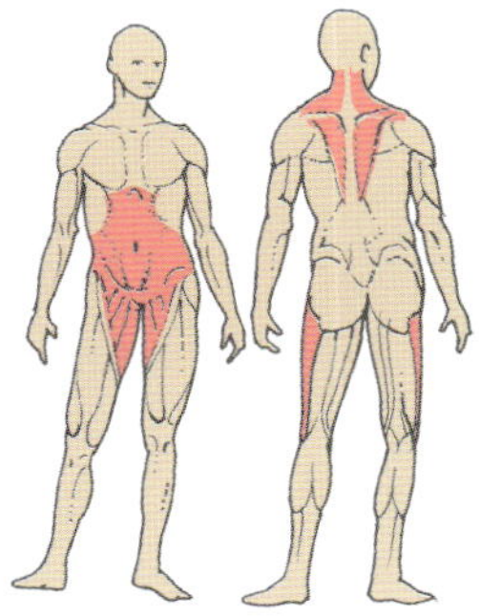

Purpose: To strengthen the waist and mid-section, stabilizing and improving balance.
Target muscles: Obliques, shoulder stabilizers, abdominals and abductors
Repetitions: Repeat 10 times on each side

Checkpoints

- Do not allow the abdominals to sag
- Keep your hips stacked
- Maintain the distance between your ribs and hips
- Really feel the muscles in your side working

1 Lie on your side with your knees bent and in line with your hips. Your hips are stacked and your abdominals hollowed. Place your hands on your head, directly opposite each other. Do not tip your head back or drop your chin to your chest. Breathe in.

2 Exhale as you lift your upper body off the floor and inhale as you lower. Make the lift slow and controlled. Don't jerk your neck or grip too hard with your hands. Maintain the length through your spine and take care not to let your hips collapse, but keep them stacked. Make sure your knees stay level with your hips. Draw your shoulder blades down your spine.

The Side Bend

This movement may look simple but it creates a marked improvement around the waistline if you practise it regularly, as well as developing core stability and balance. Feel the movement being controlled by your torso.

Take care in this position not to let the hips roll either inwards or outwards. Imagine that you have a red dot on your hips that should always face the ceiling as you lift. Maintain the length in your neck and avoid sinking into your shoulders. You may not be able to lift very far off the floor initially but do not worry as the real benefit comes from maintaining the correct alignment and performing the exercise accurately. You might find that this exercise is less challenging on one side than the other: it is common for one side to be a little stronger.

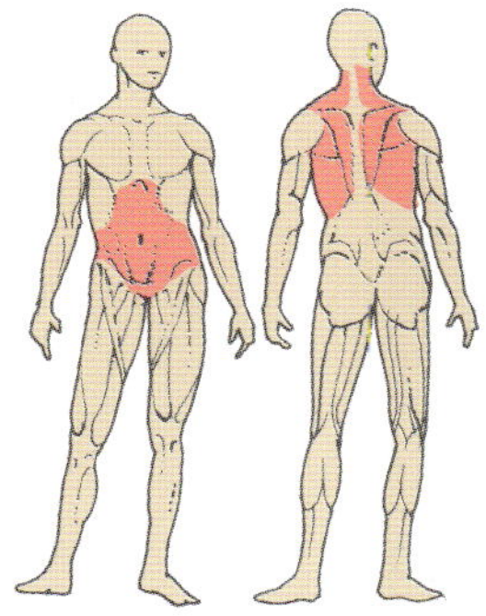

Purpose: To strengthen the abdominals and sides and improve balance

Target muscles: Obliques, abdominals, stabilizing shoulder muscles and latissimus dorsi

Repetitions: Repeat up to 10 times on each side

FIRST POSITION

1 Lie on your side with your legs bent, knees level with hips and feet in line with knees. Imagine there is a rod running vertically through your hips. Rest on your elbow, which should be directly under your shoulder, and bring the other arm in front for support. Resist the temptation to push all your weight on to the supporting hand or the resting elbow.

2 Inhale, breathing laterally, and as you exhale lift your hips off the floor. Use the muscles in the side closest to the floor to initiate the movement and control it via a strong centre. Hollow the abdominals, drawing navel to spine, slide your shoulder blades down your spine and ensure that your ribs are not pushing up.

Checkpoints

- Initiate the movement via a strong centre
- Do not transfer all your weight on to your arms
- Keep the neck soft

SECOND POSITION

above Progress only after reaching a level of ease in the first position. If you feel ready, straighten your legs and lengthen them away. Cross one foot over the other, with the toes pointed, to support you as you lift your hips. Keep your head in line with your spine and lengthen up through the top of your head.

Checkpoints

- Make sure the hips do not collapse
- Keep the abdominals hollowed
- Lift straight up, not veering to either side
- Keep the movement flowing

Upper and Lower Body exercises

Although Pilates is a holistic form of exercise, these movements concentrate particularly on upper and lower body strength. A number of repetitions is recommended for each exercise, but work at your own pace: if you can perform a movement accurately only twice, do so, increasing the repetitions as you grow stronger. Work your way through the progressions gradually – don't try to do too much too soon.

Push Ups

This is a classic exercise for shaping the upper body: the shoulders and biceps. If it is performed properly your abdominals will get a workout too. Once you progress beyond the first position, if your previous exercise was a standing one you can preserve the flow of movement and loosen up the spine by using a transitional move to get to the floor: follow the instructions for the mobilizing exercise called "Rolling Down the Spine" and, once your hands are hovering at floor level, bend at the knees, place your hands on the floor and move into the starting position for push-ups.

In every position, pull the abdominals in, never allowing them to sag, and keep your spine in neutral. Check for tension in your neck. Build up gradually to the full push-up.

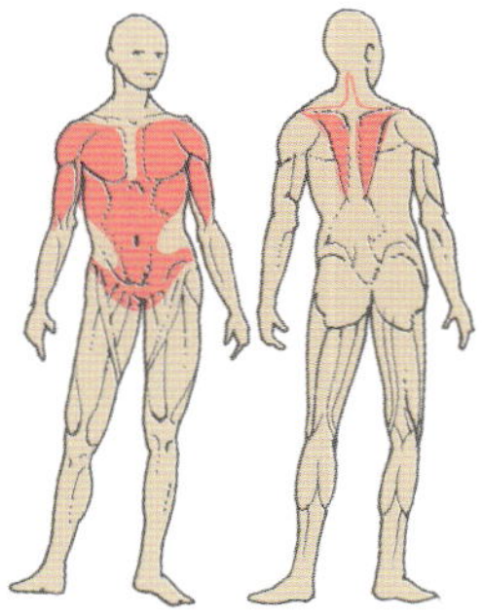

Purpose: To strengthen the upper body

Target muscles: Deltoids, pectorals, biceps, stabilizing back muscles and abdominals

Repetitions: Repeat up to 10 times

Checkpoints

- Keep your head in line
- Do not allow the abdominals to sag

FIRST POSITION

◀ **1** Stand facing a wall and place your hands on it. Your hands should be level with and just wider than your chest and flat against the wall, with the fingers pointing upwards. Your feet stay flat on the floor. Keep your spine in neutral and lengthen up your body, feeling your head "float" towards the ceiling.

◀ **2** Bend at the elbows to bring your chest towards the wall. Keep your head in line with your body, slide your shoulder blades down your spine, and check that you are not pushing up your ribs. Push away from the wall to come back to your starting position. Keep the movement slow and controlled.

SECOND POSITION

1 Position yourself on all fours, knees directly under your hips and hands directly under your shoulders, with the fingertips facing forwards. Keep your spine in neutral and don't let your head sink into your neck.

2 Keeping your head in line with your spine, exhale as you lower your chest to the floor between your hands by bending your elbows. Do not allow the abdominals to sag. As you push up, straighten the arms without locking the elbows.

Checkpoints

- Do not lock the elbows
- Lower only as far as you can control
- Keep your chest at hand level and your head forward of your hands

THIRD POSITION

▲1 Drop your hips so that there is a straight line from your head to your knees. Your fingertips should be facing forwards and hands directly under the shoulders. Keep the abdominals strong and your hips square.

▶ 2 Exhale as you lower and inhale as you lift. Keep your head in line with your spine and forward of your hands. Don't let your ribs flare up. Keep your weight evenly distributed between your knees and your hands.

Checkpoints

- Keep a straight line from your head to your knees
- Do not let your buttocks stick up
- Do not arch or curve your back

FOURTH POSITION

▲1 Form a straight line from your head to your feet, supporting yourself on your toes and hands. The fingertips should face forwards and your head should be in alignment with your spine.

◀ 2 Lower your chest to the floor between your hands, then push up, keeping your elbows soft. Keep the movement controlled and continuous. Lower only as far as you can control.

Checkpoints

- Keep your shoulder blades down the spine
- Make it a controlled, flowing movement
- Breathe laterally

Tricep Push Ups

A common complaint is the lack of muscle tone at the back of the upper arm: this is excellent for challenging this area. It works by adapting the classic push-up to work on the triceps. The movements may look the same but there are subtle – but very important – differences. The elbows stay close to the body this time. To help you keep your elbows into your sides, visualize doing the movement in a narrow space between two walls. Try to maintain a constant, and slow, speed throughout the exercise, although this can be very difficult to maintain on the last few repetitions.

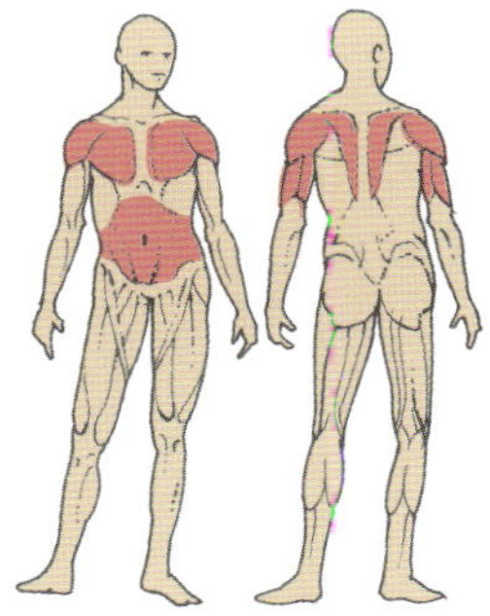

Purpose: To strengthen the upper body and the abdominals

Target muscles: Triceps, pectorals, deltoids and abdominals

Repetitions: Repeat up to 10 times

Checkpoints

- Do not let your elbows "wing" out to the sides
- Watch for your shoulders moving up towards your ears
- Lengthen up through the top of your head

FIRST POSITION

▶ **1** Stand facing a wall. Place your hands flat against the wall, fingers pointing upwards. Your hands should be level with and just wider than your chest. Your feet stay flat on the floor. Keep your spine in neutral and slide your shoulder blades down.

▶ **2** Bend at the elbows to bring your chest towards the wall as you exhale. Unlike the classic push up your elbows should remain close to the body and pointing down at all times. Keep your head in line with your body and check that you are not pushing up your ribs. Push away from the wall to come back to your starting position.

SECOND POSITION

1 Position yourself on all fours, with your hands directly under your shoulders, fingertips facing forwards. Keep your spine in neutral and maintain a straight line from your head to your hips. Don't let the abdomen sag.

2 Exhale as you lower your chest to the floor. This time, bend at the elbow and ensure that your elbows point towards your feet, with your upper arms staying close to your sides. As you push up, straighten the arms without locking the elbows.

Checkpoints

- Keep your chest level with your hands
- Keep your head forward of your hands
- Keep your feet flat on the floor

THIRD POSITION

1 Drop your hips so that there is a straight line from your knees to your head. Glide your shoulder blades down your spine. Your fingertips should face forwards.

Checkpoints

- Do not let your buttocks stick up
- Feel the movement in the back of your upper arms
- Do not rely on momentum

2 Exhale as you lower and inhale as you lift. Keep your head in line with your spine. Ensure that your head stays the same distance from your hands and that the elbows are pointing in the direction of your feet. Try to perform the exercise with flowing, continuous movements.

FOURTH POSITION

Checkpoints

- You should really feel this in the triceps
- Keep your body in alignment
- Hollow the abdominals
- Maintain a straight line from your head to your feet

above Make sure you have been practising the modified positions for some time before progressing to this position. This time your whole body should be in one straight line. Don't let your head sink into your shoulders. Lower the chest to the floor, keeping your elbows pointing towards your feet and using the same breathing pattern as for the previous positions.

Tricep Dips

This exercise is indispensable for firming up the muscles at the back of the arms. The tricep runs from the shoulder to the elbow and can be hard to work, but if neglected, this is the part of your arm that wobbles when you wave. Before you begin, find a chair that offers support at the correct height and check that it will not slip away from you. Work through the full range of the movement by straightening the arms, but take care not to "lock out" the elbows. Lengthen up through the top of your head.

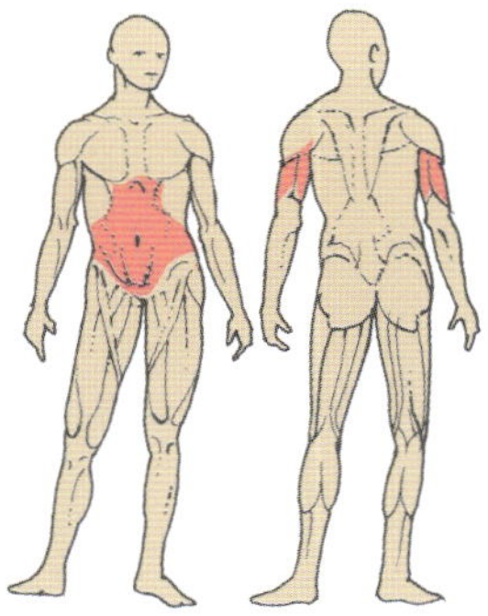

Purpose: To tone the triceps

Target muscles: Triceps, abdominals

Repetitions: Start gently but work up to 20 times

Checkpoints

- Keep your back close to the chair
- Do not lock your elbows
- Keep your head in line

FIRST POSITION

1 Place yourself in front of the chair with bent knees and feet flat on the floor. Support yourself on your hands with your fingers pointing forwards. Lengthen up through your spine, which is in neutral. This is your starting position. Make sure that your abdominals are hollowed throughout the exercise.

2 Bend your elbows and lower your body as you inhale. Glide your shoulder blades gently down your spine and watch that your ribs do not push up. As you return to the starting position on an exhalation, take care not to "lock out" your arms, just straighten them. Keep your back close to the chair and make sure your elbows travel backwards rather than out to the sides. Execute the movement with control.

SECOND POSITION

left Start in the same basic position as above, but this time put your legs straight out in front of you with your toes pointed. Keep your back close to the chair, your elbows pointing straight behind you and fingers pointing down. In this advanced position it is very tempting to let the elbows travel out to the sides, particularly if you are tired, or not paying full attention. Ensure that your head does not sink into your shoulders and remember to breathe fully. Your breathing should be wide and full allowing your ribs to expand fully, but your abdominals should be hollowed out throughout. Aim to keep the movement flowing and continuous, and don't let the pace speed up or down. In this way you will work the muscle harder and get the most benefit from the exercise.

Checkpoints

- Do not use momentum
- Keep the abdominals hollowed
- Maintain an even flow

Exercises for Thighs

The following exercises pay attention to the inner thighs and hips. Although you will be predominantly toning the lower body, you should still focus on hollowing out the abdominals. Ankle weights can be added to both of these exercises. Alignment is very important for these exercises so follow the directions carefully, letting the movements flow rather than "throwing" the leg.

The outer thigh blaster

If practised regularly, this exercise will really firm up the outsides of the hips and thighs and strengthen the lower body. Do not let the abdominals sag, and slide your shoulder blades gently down your spine. Maintain a constant distance between your ribs and your hips and keep the hips square, moving only your leg. Watch for tension elsewhere in the body as you do the exercise.

◀ **1** Stand facing the wall with your hands at chest level and flat against the wall. Bend one leg at the knee so that your foot is level with your knee and both knees are in line. Your spine should be in neutral and your foot flexed. Check that there is a straight line from your head to your feet, resisting the temptation to lean into the wall or bend at the hip.

◀ **2** From this starting position, take your knee out to the side. It is important to keep your foot flexed and your knees aligned. Exhale as your leg travels away from your body, inhale as you bring it back. You should not swing the leg. Don't "sink" into the supporting leg, but keep lengthening up through the spine.

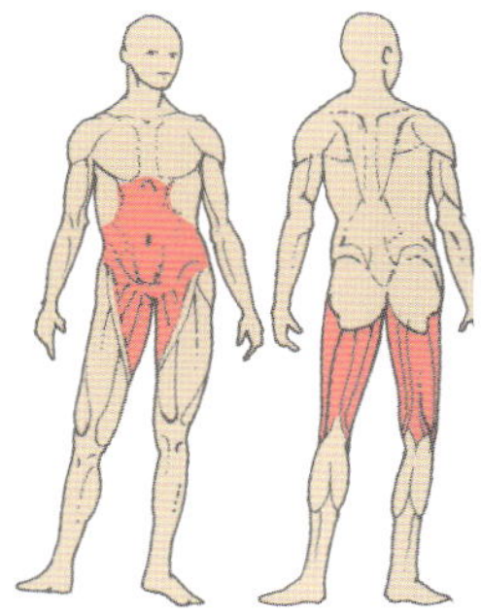

Purpose: To tone the hips and lower body

Target muscles: Abductors, abdominals, adductors and hamstrings

Repetitions: Repeat 10 times with each leg

Checkpoints

- Keep your lifted foot in line with your knee
- Keep the rest of your body still; only move the working leg

The inner thigh lift

This is a popular exercise that is often done badly. However, when it is performed correctly it works wonders with that much complained about area, the inner thigh. To progress the exercise you could use ankle weights, but you should really get a feel for the inner thigh initiating the movement before moving on.

1 Lie on your side, supporting your head on your outstretched arm. Your hips should be stacked and your other hand can rest in front of you on the floor for support. Bend the top leg and rest your knee on the floor. Straighten the lower leg and lengthen it away on the floor with the foot flexed. Do not curve your back or allow your ribs to jut forwards. Glide your shoulder blades down your spine.

2 Inhale and, as you exhale, lift the bottom leg as high as you can, keeping the abdominals hollowed all the time, then lower it. Make the movement flow, trying to avoid any jerky movements or, worst of all, swinging your leg. You should feel the muscle of the inner thigh doing the work. Take care not to twist the knee. Keep your foot in line with your leg: there is a tendency to lead with the toes in this position.

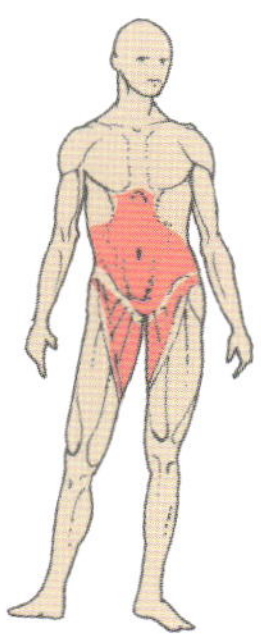

Purpose: To tone the inner thigh

Target muscles: Adductors and abdominals

Repetitions: Repeat 10 times on each leg

Checkpoints

- Do not roll hips
- Do not curve the spine

The Open V

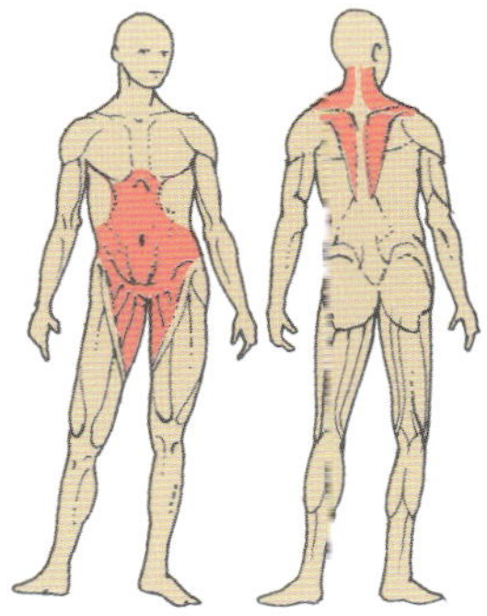

This is not one of the most graceful-looking movements, but it works wonders for the thighs, especially the inner thighs, and also benefits the abdominals. It is very important to pay special attention to keeping your knees (and feet in the second and third positions) directly above your hips at all times. If your feet fall towards the floor, your lower back may curve upwards which could cause stress. Check that you are not holding any tension in the shoulders or neck. To create an extra challenge try placing a cushion between your knees. Of course, you won't be able to open your legs so far.

Purpose: To firm up the inner thighs

Target muscles: Adductors, hip flexors, abdominals and stabilizing back muscles

Repetitions: Repeat 10 times

Checkpoints

- Check that your feet do not drop down
- Keep your feet flexed
- Do not curve your spine

FIRST POSITION

1 Lie on your back, with your knees bent and directly above your hips, and your feet level with your knees. Your feet should be flexed. Your arms are on the floor, lengthening away, your shoulder blades slide down your spine, and your head is in alignment with your spine. Start with your knees apart.

2 Keeping your feet in line with your knees, bring your knees together and squeeze to feel your inner thighs working. Hold for a few seconds, then return to the starting position. Keep your abdominals hollowed throughout and your spine in neutral.

SECOND POSITION

1 The basic movement is the same as before, but is done with straight legs. Lengthen up through your heels and keep your feet flexed. Start with your legs apart.

2 Bring your legs together and squeeze to work your inner thighs. Keep the hips still via the abdominals, which are hollowed throughout. Keep your arms strong, and really feel your inner thighs working.

Checkpoints

- Do not allow your legs to drop away from your body
- Do not let the legs open too far
- Squeeze the knees together

THIRD POSITION

above Curl your upper body off the floor, watching for tension in the neck and shoulders. Don't let your head sink into your shoulders, but glide your shoulder blades down your spine. Watch that your ribs do not flare up. Keep hollowing the abdominals: you can glance down and check that they are held flat. Squeeze the legs together as before.

Checkpoints

- Watch for tension in the neck
- Lengthen the arms away
- Lengthen up through the heels
- Slide your shoulder blades down your spine

Cleaning the Floor

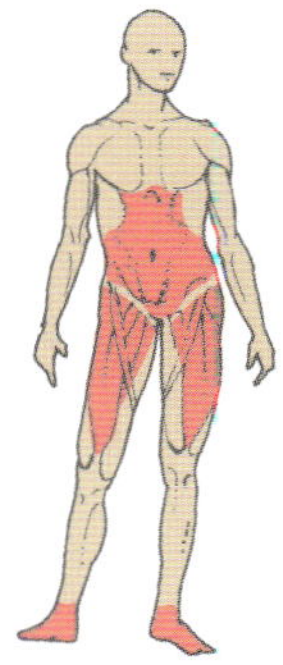

This movement will improve your balance and strengthen your lower body and all the small muscles in your feet and ankles – it is great for weak ankles. Initially, you may find the balance quite challenging. If so, it may help to look at a fixed point on the wall. It is common to find that your balance is better on one side than the other as most people favour one side. One of the objectives of this exercise is to balance any subtle differences in strength. Concentrate on maintaining the alignment between your foot and knees. If it helps, imagine that your supporting leg is held between two narrow walls.

Purpose: To strengthen lower body, feet and ankles

Target muscles: Quadriceps, supporting muscles around feet and ankles, abdominals

Repetitions: Repeat up to 10 times on each leg

Checkpoints

- Watch for your knees rolling inwards or outwards
- Keep your supporting foot flat on the floor
- Lengthen up through the spine
- Make the movement smooth and continuous

FIRST POSITION

◀ **1** Stand up tall and imagine the crown of your head floating up to the ceiling. Feel your spine lengthening. It should stay in neutral throughout. Keep your abdominals as flat as possible. Place your hands on your hips and keep your head in line with your spine. Keeping your knees in line with one another, let one foot hover above the floor as you balance evenly on the other.

◀ **2** Bend the supporting leg and lower your body as far as you can control. Do not collapse into the movement. The supporting foot may feel a little wobbly at first. Check that the knee of the supporting leg stays in alignment with the foot. Inhale as you come back up to standing. Keep your upper body strong and watch that your ribs do not travel away from your hips.

SECOND POSITION

left Bend your knee and lower as far as you can into the position as before. This time, you are going to hold this position and then very carefully lower your chest towards the floor. Bend only a little initially. To get back to the starting position, straighten your torso first then come back up to standing. Keep your head in line.

Checkpoints

- Do not try to lower too far
- Do not collapse into the movement
- Keep lifting the abdominals

One Leg Kick

This core exercise really challenges your co-ordination as you cannot see the movement – you just feel it. It is fantastic for toning up the lower body while challenging core strength. A good way to visualize the movement is to imagine that you are squeezing a pillow between your hamstrings and your calf. Try to resist just placing the leg: really feel the hamstrings working. This is a deceptively hard movement so do not worry if it takes practice. You may find it easier to get a feel for the movement first, then add the correct breathing pattern and work on lengthening down through the other leg.

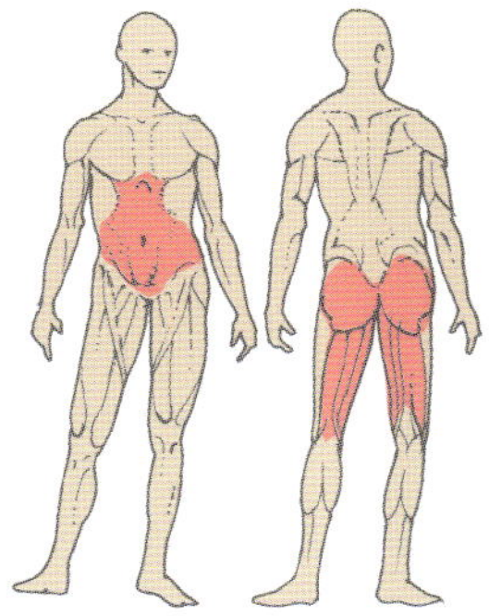

Purpose: To tone lower body and develop core stability and strength
Target muscles: Hamstrings, erector spinae (when upper body is lifted), abdominals, gluteals
Repetitions: Repeat 10 times with each leg

Checkpoints

- Keep the movement swift and continuous
- Limit any movement by keeping the abdominals hollowed throughout
- Slide the shoulder blades down your spine

FIRST POSITION

1 Lie on your front, supporting your forehead on your folded hands to keep your head in alignment. Draw your navel to your spine, trying to form an arch under your abdominals.

2 Relax the neck. Avoid clenching the jaw. Relax your shoulders and slide the shoulder blades down your spine. Bend one leg at the knee. This is your starting position.

3 Inhale and, as you exhale, point your toes and make a stabbing movement with your foot towards your buttocks. Keep your knees together and lengthen through the legs.

4 Ease out of this position then repeat, this time with your foot flexed. Then extend your leg back to its original position. Meanwhile, the supporting leg on the floor should be lengthening away at all times.

SECOND POSITION

left Perform the same movements, but this time curl your upper body off the floor and rest on your elbows. Slide the shoulder blades down. Keep your neck long throughout and watch that your ribs do not travel away from your hips. Lengthen through the spine. If you feel a pinch in your spine in this position, stay with the first position for a while.

Checkpoints

- Keep your neck in line throughout the exercise
- Breathe wide and full
- Do not push all your weight into your arms

Stretches

Throughout your Pilates sessions you will be stretching and lengthening, but here is a whole chapter to take you by the hand through one of the most popular parts of most classes – the stretches. Notice how your range of movement will re-adjust, giving you more freedom and mobility in your daily tasks. Stretching is also linked to a reduced risk of injury – something everyone can appreciate. Many people notice a distinct "lift" in their mood after stretching, feeling refreshed and invigorated, with a general sense of well-being.

Spine Stretch

If your back feels tight or if you just want a healthy and mobile spine then this is the stretch for you. You will feel longer, stretched and more flexible. This is a flowing movement, not a static stretch. To keep your spine lengthening up and to stop you collapsing into the stretch, imagine that you have a beach ball in front of you, and lift up and over the ball. As you come upright again, imagine that your back is rolling up a pole, vertebra by vertebra, and take care to keep this alignment from your head to your hips: do not lean forwards or away from the imaginary pole.

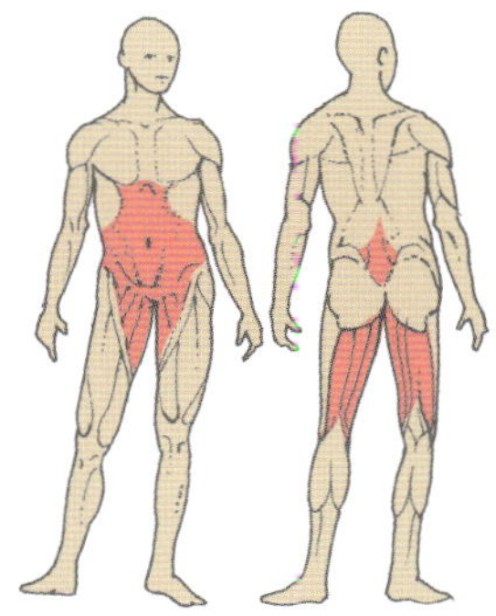

Purpose: To stretch the spine
Target muscles: Erector spinae, hamstrings, adductors and abdominals
Repetitions: Repeat 10 times

Checkpoints

- Do not collapse into the stretch
- Keep the movement flowing and continuous
- Let your head float up to the ceiling

FIRST POSITION

1 Sit upright with your knees bent and your feet flat on the floor. Create as much length through your spine as possible. Keep the shoulders relaxed.

2 Let your chin gently drop to your chest, then roll down bone by bone through your spine. As you do so, gently reach forwards with your hands. Keep your abdominals hollowed throughout. Roll back up to the starting position and lengthen up through your spine. Do not collapse into the stretch, but lift up through the abdominals and spine. Exhale as you lower into the stretch.

SECOND POSITION

left The movement is the same as before, but this time straighten the legs and flex your feet, lengthening the heels away. Bend the knees slightly if you find this uncomfortable. The legs should be parted as far as is comfortable. As you roll up create as much length as possible between the vertebrae. Keep your buttocks on the floor.

Checkpoints

- Do not have the legs too far apart
- Visualize reaching up and over a beach ball
- Roll up vertebra by vertebra

Spine Twist

A deceptively challenging movement, this twist will stretch the waist and lower back while strengthening the abdominals. To gain the maximum benefit, it is important to keep your bottom on the floor throughout this movement. Let your head float up to the ceiling and pull your navel towards your spine. Try to keep the movement smooth and continuous. On your first attempts at this exercise you may be surprised how hard it is to sit correctly aligned. We all develop certain postural habits and this exercise challenges them so it will feel intense at first. It gets easier with practice.

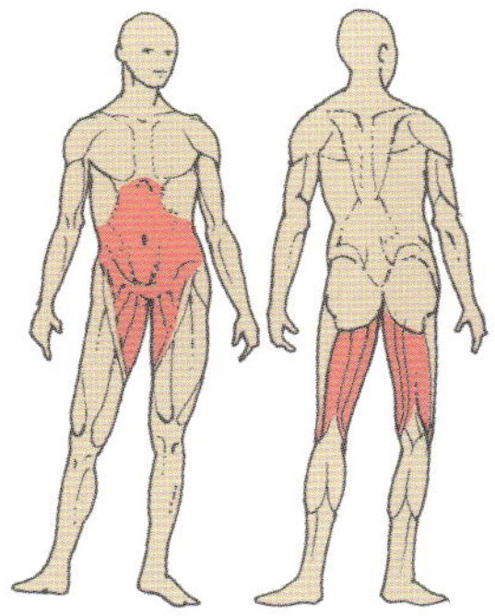

Purpose: To stretch the sides, strengthen the abdominals and promote thoracic mobility

Target muscles: Obliques, abdominals, adductors and hamstrings

Repetitions: Repeat 10 times on each side

FIRST POSITION

1 Sit upright, lengthening up through the spine, with your knees bent and feet flat on the floor, legs slightly apart. Cross your arms loosely across your chest. Maintain a straight line from your head to your bottom.

2 Breathing laterally, inhale and, as you exhale, turn the upper body to one side, keeping your buttocks firmly on the floor. Repeat on the other side. Remember that this is a flowing movement, not a static position.

Checkpoints

- Keep the movement flowing
- Hollow the abdominals
- Lengthen up through the spine

SECOND POSITION

left The basic movement is the same but is performed with straight arms, lengthening out through the arms from the shoulders. Take care not to drop them. Now you are stretching in two directions: lengthening out through your arms and up through your spine. Slide your shoulder blades gently down your back and keep your feet flat on the floor.

Checkpoints

- Do not collapse into the movement
- Keep the whole of your buttocks on the floor
- Do not curve the spine

THIRD POSITION

left The movement is the same but this time straighten the legs and point your toes. You are now stretching in three directions: up through your spine, out through your arms and through your legs. Be sure to keep your buttocks on the floor. You may be tempted to lean into one side as you turn.

Checkpoints

- Lengthen all the way to the toes
- Feel the abdominals working

Lower Back Stretch

This is a good warm-up stretch. Taking deep breaths can help you to relax into the stretch and you may find your muscles becoming more pliable, allowing you to ease yourself further into the movement. The stretch is great for easing mild tension in the lower back, which is a common complaint. Some people find it beneficial to rock slightly from side to side while in this stretch as this can gently mobilize the lower back. To do this, keep your upper body on the floor and make the movement very subtle. Although a number of repetitions are recommended, these are only a guideline until you are confident about your instincts. Hold the stretch for longer or repeat if you need to.

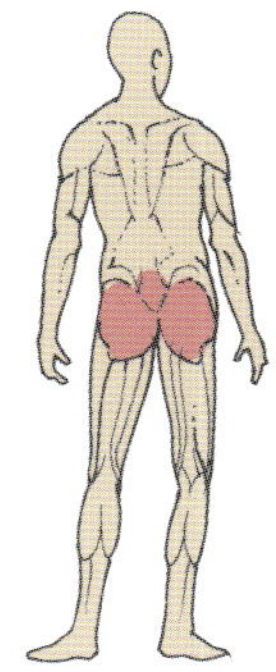

Purpose: To stretch the lower back

Target muscles: Erector spinae and gluteals

Repetitions: Stretch twice; hold for 30 seconds each

FIRST POSITION

left Lie on your back and bring both knees up towards your chest. Support your legs with your hands, just below your knees. Relax your shoulders and feel the stretch in your lower back. Remember to keep your abdominals hollowed. Inhale to prepare and exhale as you lift your legs.

Checkpoints

- Check for tension in the neck and shoulders
- Relax into the stretch
- Do not overgrip with your hands

SECOND POSITION

left Curl your head and shoulders off the floor, imagining curling up like a ball. Keep your neck soft: do not force your head forwards to your knees. Take care not to overgrip – keep your elbows open.

Checkpoints

- Curl up and down slowly
- Make sure your mat is thick enough to protect your back

Spine Press

This movement mobilizes and stretches the lower spine. It is a good one to try whenever your lower back feels stiff, especially if you have been sitting for a long period, at your desk for example (and it can be done very discreetly). The curve of the spine should be very subtle. Take care not to over curve your spine as you may "pinch" the muscles in the lower back. If it feels uncomfortable to curve your spine, or you have problems with your lower back, you may want to perform the second part of the movement only. When you tilt your pelvis, initiate the movement by imagining you are pressing your navel towards your spine. Avoid collapsing into the movement by lengthening your spine.

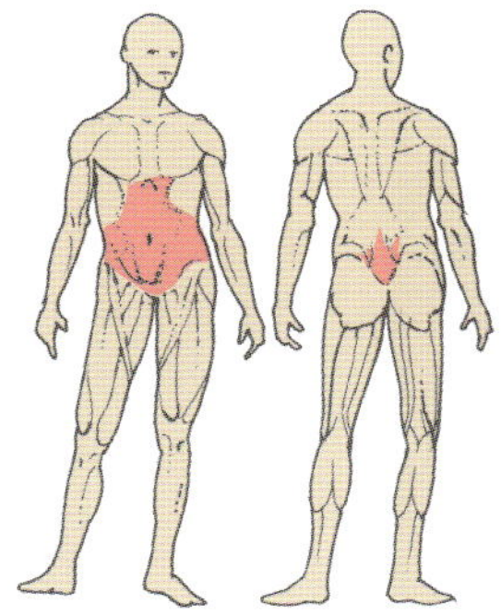

Purpose: To mobilize and stretch the lower back

Target muscles: Erector spinae and abdominals

Repetitions: Stretch twice; hold for 30 seconds each

Checkpoints

- Do not overcurve your spine
- Keep the abdominals hollowed
- Keep your head in alignment

1 Stand a short distance away from the wall, with your back against it, your knees bent and your arms by your sides. Lengthen up and glide your shoulder blades down your spine.

2 Inhale and, as you exhale, push your spine flat against the wall by tilting your pelvis and contracting your abdominals. Keep your head in alignment. Try not to collapse into the movement: keep your abdominals hollowed.

Simple Stretches

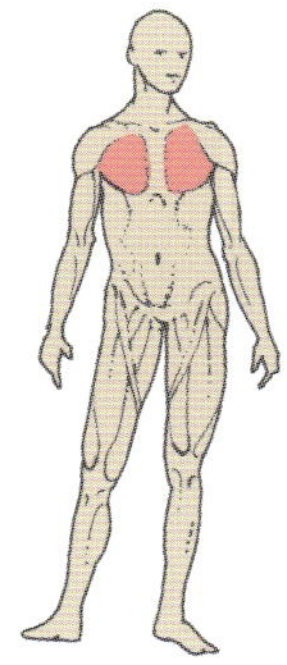

The following stretches are great for lengthening fatigued, tense muscles. The two upper body stretches are great for opening up the chest; this is ideal if you have been sitting at a desk for a long period of time. On the first Chest Stretch, the wrist is also being slightly stretched. If this is uncomfortable, turn your hand round so that your fingertips point to the ceiling. In the Deep Chest and Back Stretch, slightly bend your knees if your legs are stretched beyond the comfort zone. When performing the gluteals stretch, be sure to keep your bottom on the floor or you will not stretch enough.

Chest stretch

This feel-good stretch is great for relieving tightness in the chest and uses the wall for support. It can be done almost anywhere to relieve tightness in the chest.

Purpose: To stretch the chest
Target muscles: Pectorals
Repetitions: Stretch twice; hold for 30 seconds each

Checkpoints

- Keep your spine in neutral
- Feel the stretch in your chest
- Relax your shoulders

1 Stand sideways to a wall. Extend one arm and place your hand flat on it. Keep your hand in line with your chest and your feet in line with your hips. Draw in your abdominals; your spine stays in neutral.

2 Now turn your hips away from the wall, so that you feel a stretch in your chest. Relax your shoulders and enjoy the stretch. Change sides and repeat the movement.

Gluteals stretch

This stretch is reasonably easy to do and promotes a greater range of movement in the lower body. It is also a valuable stretch to do before many different sports that involve a lot of lower body work.

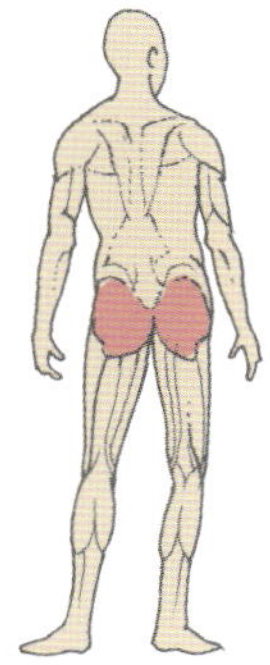

1 Sit on the floor and position one leg in front of the other (the legs are not crossed). Relax your arms in front of you. Lengthen up through the spine, creating space between the vertebrae. Don't worry if your knees don't fall to the floor, just relax and let the knees fall into a natural position.

2 Drop your chin towards your chest and curl down the spine while pushing the arms forwards and keeping your buttocks on the floor. Curl up again, switch the positions of the legs and repeat on the other side. Do not collapse into the movement; keep the abdominals pulled in throughout.

Purpose: To stretch the lower body
Target muscles: Gluteals
Repetitions: Stretch twice; hold for 30 seconds each

Checkpoints

- Keep your buttocks on the floor
- Replace the spine bone by bone
- Create length between the vertebrae

Deep chest and back stretch

This stretch is ideal for easing tightness in the chest and back. Try to relax your shoulders and neck into the stretch. Remember, if this stretch is too intense, you can bend your knees.

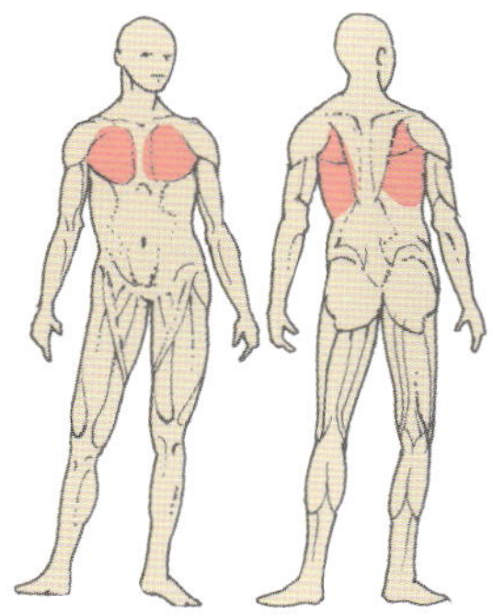

1 Stand facing the wall with your feet together and place your hands flat on the wall level with your shoulders, just wider than shoulder-width apart. Lengthen up through the spine.

2 Inhale, then as you exhale lower your chest by bending from the hips, to feel a stretch in your chest and back. Keep your head in line with your spine. Keep the spine lengthened and the abdominals hollowed.

Purpose: To stretch the chest and shoulders
Target muscles: Pectorals and latissimus dorsi
Repetitions: Stretch twice; hold for 30 seconds each

Checkpoints

- Keep your head in line with your spine
- Keep your hips over your knees
- Bend the knees if necessary

Abdominal stretch

This is a very popular stretch that is similar to the "cobra" in yoga. It is very good for stretching the abdominals after all the hard work they have done. Take care not to throw your head back in this stretch. Keep facing the floor and lengthen up through the top of your head to avoid sinking into the shoulders. If you feel any pinching in your lower back ease gently out of the stretch.

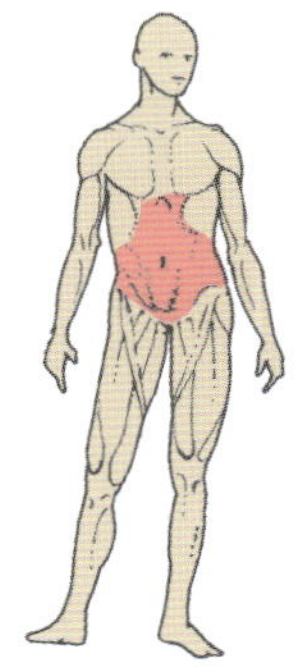

1 Drop your hips so that there is a straight line from your knees to your head. Glide the shoulder blades down your spine. Your fingertips should face forwards.

Purpose: To stretch the abdominals
Target muscles: Abdominals
Repetitions: Stretch twice; hold for 30 seconds each

2 Inhale and, as you exhale, lift your upper body off the floor, resting the weight on your arms. Keep the abdominals hollowed and lifted, and take care not to overcurve the spine. Keep your hips on the floor. Do not sink into your neck, but lengthen up through your spine. Watch for tension in the neck. If you feel a pinch in your lower back ease out of the stretch.

Checkpoints
- Do not overcurve your spine
- Keep your head in line with your spine
- Keep your hips on the floor

Hip flexor stretch

The hip flexors tend to be one of the tightest muscle groups, and when these muscles get overly tight they can cause discomfort and eventually imbalances. People involved in most sports benefit from this stretch, especially runners.

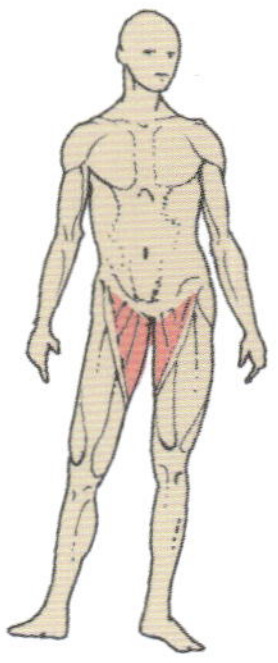

1 Kneel down on the floor and take one step forwards, using your hands for support. If you need extra cushioning, place a pillow under the supporting knee.

2 Lunge carefully into the front leg, exhaling as you lunge forwards. Make sure your raised knee is directly over your foot. Lengthen up through the spine and keep the abdominals hollowed. You should feel this stretch at the top of the rear leg. Change legs and repeat.

Purpose: To stretch the hip flexors
Target muscles: Hip flexors
Repetitions: Stretch twice; hold for 30 seconds each

Checkpoints
- Take care not to collapse into the stretch
- Lunge into the stretch
- Keep your head in alignment

Waist lifts

This is a good movement to stretch and mobilize the spine. If it feels too intense or uncomfortable to have your arms overhead, then stretch with them by your side.

1 Lie on your back with your arms overhead or, if this is difficult, by your sides. Lengthen through your feet, spine and arms: visualize two cars pulling you in different directions. Draw the navel in to the spine.

2 Carefully lift your waist. This is a very subtle movement; take care not to create a big curve in your spine. Keep the abdominals strong and the head in alignment. Watch for any gripping in your lower back. If you feel any pinching in your back, ease out of the stretch.

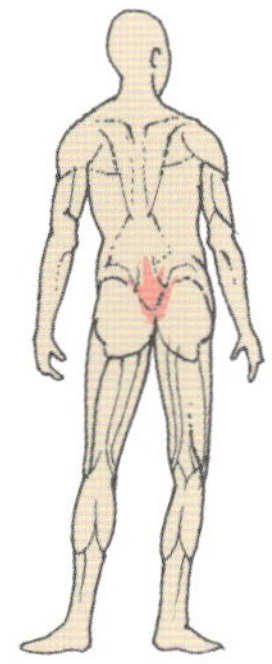

Purpose: To stretch and mobilize the spine
Target muscles: Erector spinae
Repetitions: Stretch twice; hold for 30 seconds each

Checkpoints

- Ease out of the stretch if any pinching occurs
- Keep the abdominals strong
- Lengthen out the spine

Side stretch

This feels good at any time. No wonder cats and dogs are always stretching – it relieves the body of unwanted tension and liberates the spine and joints.

left Sit on the floor with one leg in front of the other (the legs are not crossed). Inhale as you prepare. Exhale as you raise one arm and lengthen up through the spine, then stretch into one side from a strong centre, taking care not to collapse into the stretch. Feel the stretch in your back. Pull the navel to the spine and keep your buttocks on the floor. If this leg positioning is uncomfortable, bend your legs and keep your feet flat on the floor.

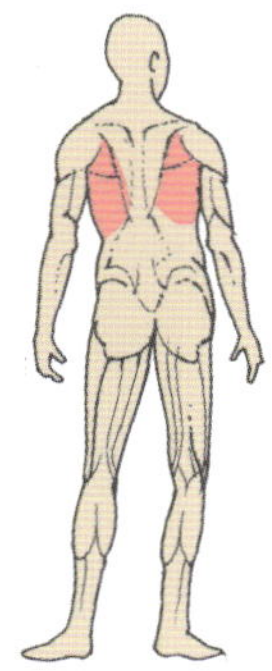

Purpose: To stretch the back
Target muscles: The latissimus dorsi
Repetitions: Stretch twice on each side; hold for 30 seconds each

Checkpoints

- Keep your buttocks on the floor
- Lengthen up through the spine
- Don't let the abdominals sag

making Pilates a part of your Life

To be effective, any exercise needs to be organized into a programme that is easy to remember and that you will want to do regularly. This chapter offers you guidance on devising a successful Pilates programme that will help you achieve your goals, and shows you how Pilates can become integrated into your daily life. Keep your programme balanced. Combine it with cardiovascular work and good nutrition to give you a total fitness plan.

Designing a Programme

With Pilates, it can be difficult to identify the muscles that are being challenged as most movements involve a combination of several muscle groups all working together. A Pilates exercise may be overtly working the arms or the legs but at the same time it may be demanding a constant stabilization process from the torso. So you will find that even though a movement is targeting a certain muscle group, you will often feel it in other parts of your body as well.

In general, Pilates movements can be divided into three main categories:

1 **Strengthening exercises** that concentrate on making certain muscle groups stronger and more toned.

2 **Flexibility exercises** that improve the range of motion around a joint.

3 **Mobility exercises** that train the body to move more easily.

left Flexibility exercises will increase your range of movements and help to prevent sports injuries.

Classifying the movements

The exercises described in this section are grouped according to both the action that is being reinforced and the dominant muscles that are being used. For ease of reference, the following lists repeat this classification to help you choose a selection of movements from each group to make up a well-rounded programme. If you find an exercise listed under more than one heading it is because it involves a combination of various actions.

Exercise groups

Exercises that strengthen the upper body

- Push ups (deltoids, pectorals, biceps, abdominals and stabilizing back muscles)*
- Triceps push-ups (triceps, deltoids, abdominals and pectoral muscles)
- Leg pull prone (abdominals, stabilizing back muscles)*
- Triceps dips (triceps, abdominals)

Exercises that strengthen the lower body

- Cleaning the floor (quadriceps, supporting muscles of the feet and ankles, abdominals)
- The shoulder bridge (buttocks and abdominals)*
- The open V (adductors, abdominals, hip flexors and stabilizing back muscles)
- The outer thigh blaster (abductors, abdominals, adductors and hamstrings)
- One leg kick (hamstrings, abdominals, lower gluteals and erector spinae)*
- The inner thigh lift (adductors, abdominals)

Exercises that strengthen the abdominals and back

- One leg stretch (abdominals and stabilizing back muscles)*
- The side kick (hamstrings, hip flexors, abdominals, abductors and stabilizing back muscles)*
- Leg pull, prone (abdominals and stabilizing back muscles)*
- The roll-up (abdominals, and hip flexors)*
- The side bend (obliques, abdominals, stabilizing back muscles; stretches the latissimus dorsi)*
- One leg circles (adductors, abdominals, and hip flexors)*
- The side squeeze (internal and external obliques, abdominals, shoulder stabilizers and abductors)
- The hundred (abdominals and stabilizing mid-back muscles)*
- Swimming (abdominals, gluteals and erector spinae)*

Exercises that promote flexibility

- Gluteals stretch (gluteals)
- Chest stretch (pectorals)
- Side stretch (latissimus dorsi)
- Hip flexor stretch (hip flexors)
- Spine twist (obliques, adductors and hamstrings; promotes thoracic mobility)*
- Abdominal stretch (abdominals)
- Spine stretch (erector spinae, hamstrings, adductors)*
- Deep chest and shoulder stretch (pectorals and latissimus dorsi)
- Lower back stretch (erector spinae and gluteals)
- Spine press (erector spinae)

Exercises that promote mobility

- The shoulder bridge (spine)*
- Rolling back (spine)*
- Spine twist (spine)* and Spine press (spine)
- Spine stretch (spine)*
- One leg circles (hips)*
- Rolling down the spine (spine)*

Core exercises have been marked with an asterisk (*).

above Consistency is one of the key elements in creating and maintaining a strong, healthy physique. Regular Pilates sessions, combined with cardiovascular exercise and healthy eating habits, will ensure positive results.

Core exercises

There is an adaptation process involved in this as in any other exercise programme. This means that your body will need a few sessions to get used to the movements. You will therefore get the best results if you choose a few "core" exercises – movements that are considered pure Pilates exercises – and concentrate on these for a period of time, say four to six weeks, giving your muscles a chance to adapt to the work that is being asked of them. Start with these, and once you feel that you have mastered them (not necessarily advancing to a higher level, just feeling comfortable and confident about the movement), add on a few more.

As you add exercises, try to keep a balance between the main muscles being used: choose one from each group in turn until you have tried them all.

Planning your exercise programme

How much time do you need to dedicate to your Pilates programme? How can you design a programme that will be well-rounded and complete, as well as motivating and enjoyable? When should you change the programme? What if you don't always have time to do it all? To answer these questions you need to take several factors into account.

left You can loosen and liberate your body with the regular practice of Pilates.

1 The time factor

In a perfect world, you would dedicate at least one hour to your Pilates programme and 30–40 minutes to a cardiovascular work-out, and you would do both activities three times a week. However, on those days when there is no time for a complete training session, a short, 25-minute workout is better than none at all.

2 Desired results

Are you trying to win a sporting event or do you just want to get a little fitter? Dramatic results require dedication, time and effort. But an hour of Pilates three times or even twice a week, as well as a weekly minimum of three cardiovascular workouts of 30–60 minutes duration, will raise your fitness level, giving you very acceptable results in a relatively short time.

3 Daily life

Do you have an active job? Do you live at the top of several flights of stairs? Do you drive everywhere or walk? The things that you do when you are not working out also count: your body does not care whether you are in a gym lifting weights or carrying a heavy box to the attic. Obviously, the more sedentary your daily life, the more conscientiously you will have to carry out your fitness plan.

Sample Programmes

The majority of the exercises need to be repeated approximately ten times each (or, in the case of unilateral exercises, ten times per side). Apart from some exceptions – the Hundred is performed for one hundred taps on the mat and the Plank is held for 60–90 seconds – when putting together a programme you can safely estimate that each movement will take about five minutes. A certain group of muscles may need more attention because of, for example, muscular imbalances or repetition of a certain activity. You also need to take into account the initial warm-up, final stretch and a short relaxation period at the end. As an example to get you started, two basic plans are suggested here.

Vary your programme from time to time so that you do not get bored. If you dislike an exercise or it does not feel right on a particular day, do a different movement that targets the same muscle groups. Always listen to your body. Most of the exercises have variations, so work your way progressively through the different levels of intensity.

The short programme

What if you don't have time for a session lasting a whole hour? You can plan a mini programme lasting 25 minutes to do on those days when you just cannot find more time. However, do try to base most of your sessions around the hour-long plan and use the short plan only when you really have to. Twenty-five minutes is not ideal, but it's better than skipping the session entirely. Obviously, you will have to shorten the length of time spent on each exercise, as well as doing fewer of them: aim to achieve five to seven repetitions of each movement.

1

◀ **Warm-up**
8-10 minutes
(p64)

2

◀ **Push-ups**
3 minutes
(p84)

3

◀ **Swimming**
3 minutes
(p75)

4

◀ **Rolling back**
3 minutes
(p72)

5

◀ **Spine stretch**
3 minutes
(p96)

6

◀ **The Hundred**
3 minutes
(p74)

7

◀ **Relaxation**
2 minutes
(p66)

The one-hour programme

In this sample format, the exercises chosen include some of the "core" movements; this would be a good programme to start with while you are learning and adapting to these exercises. As with most Pilates programmes, the emphasis is on the strengthening of the torso.

After a few weeks, you can change some of these movements for others; try always to do some movements from each of the different categories so that you are working on all parts of the body and developing strength, flexibility and mobility.

1

◀ **Warm-up**
8-10 minutes
(p64)

2

◀ **The shoulder bridge**
5 minutes
(p69)

3

◀ **Swimming**
5 minutes
(p75)

4

◀ **Side squeeze; right side**
5 minutes
(p80)

5

◀ **Side squeeze: left side**
5 minutes
(p80)

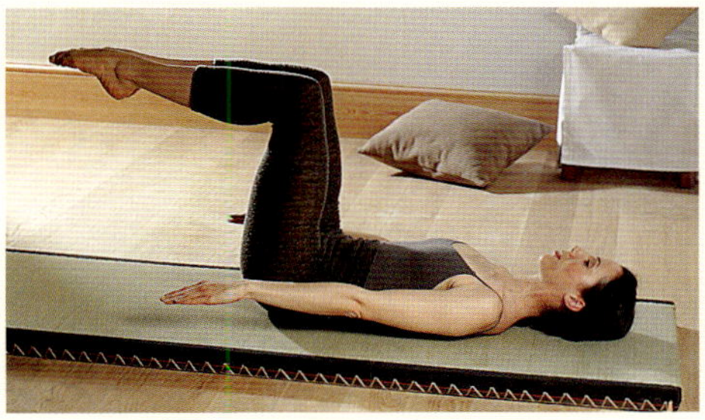

6

◀ **The hundred**
5 minutes
(p74)

7

◀ **Spine stretch**
5 minutes
(p96)

8

◀ **Push-ups**
5 minutes
(p84)

9

◀ **Rolling back**
5 minutes
(p72)

10

◀ **The roll-up**
5 minutes
(p73)

11

◀ **Relaxation**
5 minutes
(p66)

Assessing Common Postural Faults

The human body is a fantastic machine. It is designed to walk, run, jump, push and pull. It is autonomous and multifunctional and can adapt to many different situations - for instance, by strengthening or lengthening its muscles or adding a layer of fat to protect it from the cold. Unless you were born with a particular physical challenge, your body began life as a symmetrical and co-ordinated unit.

Unfortunately, in adult life many bodies are no longer aligned or symmetrical. The two sides function differently, with some muscles overworked and tight while others are weak and overstretched. So what does a perfectly balanced body look like? First, both sides of the body have equal strength and flexibility. The shoulders, hips and ankle joints are level and symmetrical and the shoulder blades are back and down.

Posture check

Stand in front of a full-length mirror and look at your reflection. Just relax and take up your usual stance without thinking about your posture. Assess your stance honestly – or ask a trusted friend for their assessment. Here are some common misalignments of the body. Do you recognize any of these?:

- The head may be tilted to one side, jut forward or tilt backwards.
- The legs may sway backwards.
- There may be a curved "C" shape in the spine.
- The back may be over arched.
- The shoulders are not level or parallel: one may be rotated forward or elevated or both shoulders may be rounded.
- The palms of the hands are turned backwards
- The hip joints are uneven, tilted backwards or forwards or to one side
- The knees and ankles may be rolling inwards or outwards and are asymmetrical
- The feet turn in or out
- The weight is not evenly distributed between the feet
- The arches in the feet are collapsed

There are many reasons why your body has become misaligned. When any part of the body becomes dysfunctional the whole unit is affected. Even though some muscles are not doing their job effectively, you still have to get on with your day-to-day life so other muscles compensate for weaknesses. Using your body in a faulty manner reinforces these imbalances. Eventually you may start to ache in those areas that need to compensate. Aches and pains are the body's

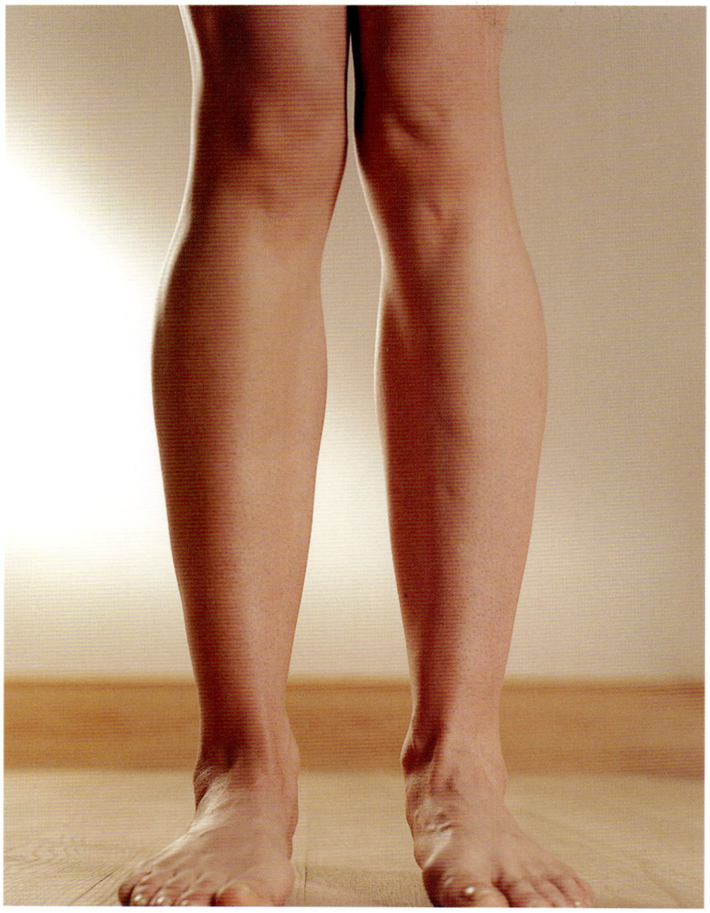

above The knees or ankles may roll inwards or outwards, or may be asymmetrical.

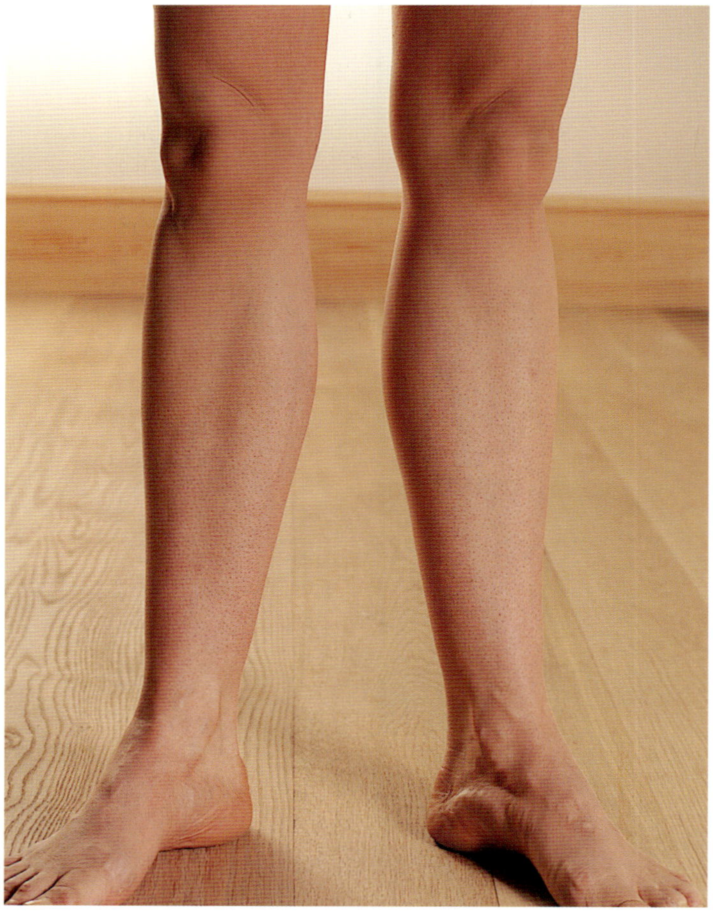

above The feet may be turned inwards or outwards.

left The hip joints may be uneven, with the weight unevenly distributed between the feet.

right The head may be tilted to one side, creating muscular imbalances in the neck and back.

way of alerting you to a problem. You may even get injured or at best suffer chronic pain, commonly in the neck, back, knees, hips or shoulders. It is advisable to get an accurate assessment of the imbalance from a trained professional whilst it is still in its early stages as it is best to try to remedy the problem before your body overcompensates.

Think about the way you feel when you sit for long periods of time. Is your neck sore on one side? Does your lower back ache? This is not the way you are supposed to feel. If your body is doing its job correctly, you should not be experiencing pain or discomfort at any one place in your back or neck from sitting or standing for long periods.

So why are our bodies not doing what they were originally intended for? Most people live in a stress-filled environment. Life has become faster, more is expected, and in order to cope many devices have been designed for increased convenience and reduced effort. Devices like remote controls, lifts and cars have meant that we are less physically active than previous generations. This lack of activity has led to a rise in obesity levels and conditions such as heart disease. We can no longer rely on general activity to keep us healthy, so we have to look at increasing our exercise levels. Stress and tension in the body can be very damaging, causing imbalances that make muscles overtight and this can lead to movement becoming restricted.

You can tell a lot about your body from your shoes. Look at a pair of your own shoes with leather (not rubber) soles. Are they more worn on the inside or the outside? Does the sole of one shoe look older than the other? Are the toes pushing against one side of only one of the shoes? Most people have slightly misaligned feet but, if this is a distinct pattern or causes discomfort, it may be worth checking with a qualified specialist. You may have an actual postural deviation that inhibits the maintenance of correct posture. If so, this should be dealt with by a medical practitioner.

right The head may jut forward out of alignment with the spine.

Improving Your Posture with Pilates

The body must be re-educated to cope with the stresses of daily life. In cases where the postural fault is severe, or there is pain, you should see a specialist before attempting this or any other exercise programme. Pilates is not meant to be an alternative to the prescription of a medical professional, but it can be a useful tool to accompany the recommendations of a specialist.

Commonly when people train in a gym they tend to choose exercises randomly, concentrating on the areas of the body they like the least, or doing exercises that they find easy to do: this can reinforce existing misalignments. Unless the body is trained as a whole, as in Pilates, its weaknesses will only be reinforced. The regular practice of Pilates strengthens and stretches all the core postural muscles, making correct posture far less of a muscular effort and more of an unconscious act.

To understand the whole picture it is essential to realize the importance of the torso. Every step you take, every weight you lift and every movement you make must be stabilized by the muscles of the abdominals and the back to protect the spinal cord against injuries. It does not matter how strong your arms are, unless your torso can protect you by stabilizing internally, your strength will be limited. Think of your body as a chain of muscles: you are only as strong as your weakest link.

If your posture is not good, your muscles will have been working in an incorrect manner for a long time. You cannot force them into place in a few sessions; there will be a period of adaptation. Always seek medical advice if you feel pain either during or after exercise. However, it is good to learn to differentiate between sore muscles and pain. Muscle soreness is par for the course

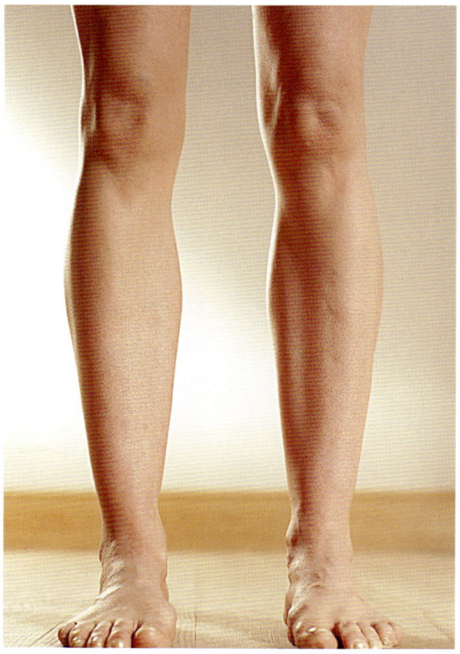

right When you are standing in the correct manner, the knee and ankle joints are symmetrical and the knees face forwards.

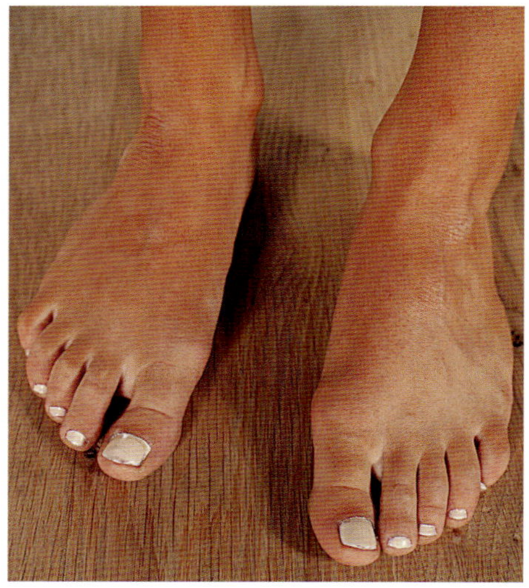

above The weight of the body should be equally spread between all four "corners" of the feet. Weakened muscles or rapid weight gain may have led the arches in the feet to collapse.

right Pilates works by strengthening the key postural muscles, making it physically more comfortable to maintain the correct alignment.

right Stand in front of the mirror and carefully check your posture. Pay special attention to your hips, arms, shoulders, spine and weight distribution

when you begin to exercise; you will feel it most about 48 hours later. Stretching out the muscles at the end of a session helps, as can a hot bath. You may also want to try some of the wide variety of gels and creams designed to ease muscular tension. Ask your pharmacist for a recommendation.

So take up your stance in front of the mirror again. Only this time adopt what you consider to be "good posture". You should note the following points. Can you see them in your reflection?:

- Shoulders are level
- Hip bones are equal and symmetrical
- The thumb side of the hand faces forward
- The knee joints are symmetrical and face forwards
- The ankle joints are symmetrical
- The weight of the body is equally distributed between all four "corners" of the feet
- You are lengthening through your spine

below Become aware of how people respond more positively to you as your posture changes.

Pilates in Everyday Life

There would be little point in spending time exercising if you did not take a fresh look at your posture throughout the day, as you could still be reinforcing imbalances in the body that you are now dedicating time to amending. Pilates will help to strengthen and lengthen the muscles needed to maintain good posture but you also need to learn how to carry your body in the most efficient, safest way possible all the time.

Posture

Your posture, the way you hold yourself, says a lot about you. When you watch someone with very good posture enter a room, observe how your eye is drawn to them and the assumptions you can find yourself making about their lives. They seem to be in control, confident and capable.

Psychologically you are also affected by your own posture: notice how much more positive and alert you feel when you sit or stand upright. Try this when making a business telephone call, it will immediately give you more confidence. Everyone is naturally more drawn to someone who seems comfortable with themselves, and research shows that we consider people with good posture to be more attractive. But most of the time you are probably unaware of the way you carry your own body; most people think about their posture only when they start getting back aches and sore necks.

right Ask an honest friend to assess your posture as often we are unaware of our postural habits.

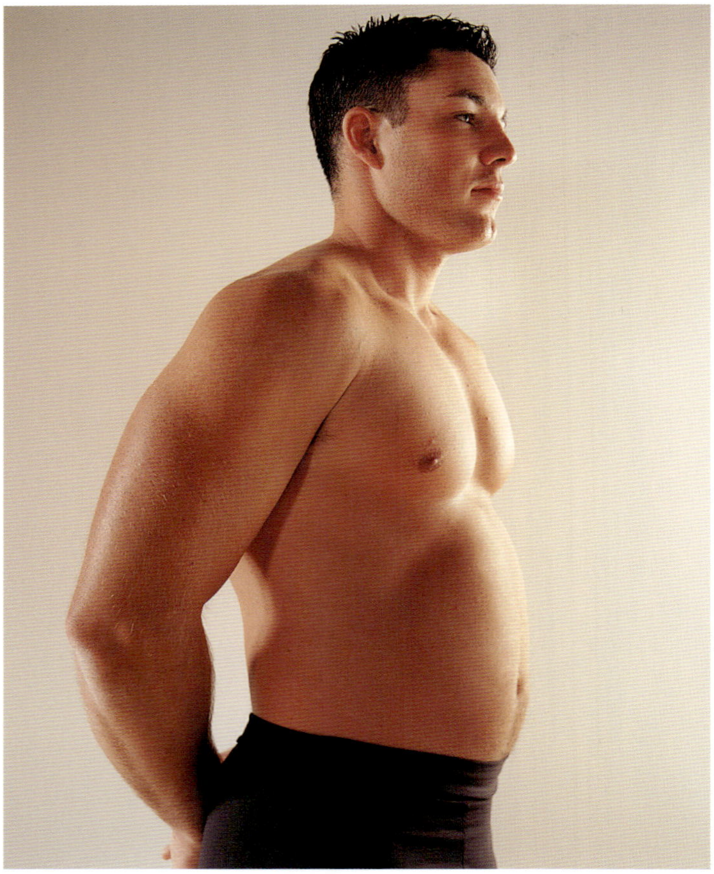

above Posture has a dramatic effect on our appearance. In this picture, the tone of the abdominal muscles has been completely abandoned. This lack of tone makes the model look slightly overweight.

above By correcting his posture and restoring tone in the abdominals, the model looks 5-6 lbs lighter. His whole appearance has changed, presenting a slimmer and more toned physique.

left Avoid flexing forward over your desk. Lengthen up through your spine with your shoulders back and down, and keep your head in alignment. Do not let the abdominals sag. Your feet should be flat on the floor, with your knees directly over them.

Posture is not just a question of how you walk or sit. To get maximum benefit from your exercise sessions, you need to get your whole body to work at maximum efficiency all the time so that it can cope with the daily demands placed on it. This means reducing imbalances throughout the body. There is little point in doing Pilates or any other form of exercise to improve your physique if you reinforce imbalances by using your body incorrectly the rest of the time.

Sitting

If, like a large percentage of the population, you work in an office, you are likely to sit for long periods of time, usually in chairs that are not ergonomically correct. Practically every chair in the western world has a back rest to accommodate our slouching. In Japan, where it is common practice to sit on the floor with no support, the incidence of back pain is far lower than the estimated 80% in the West.

If you are working at a computer, writing or eating, you are likely to sit in a forward flexed position, with shoulders forward, head dropping, neck muscles tensed and spine arched. Over a period of time, this posture can become the one that you adopt every time you sit, reinforcing the muscular imbalances. It is really quite difficult to sit up straight. Your torso must be strong enough to maintain a static contraction in the back and abdominal muscles to hold your body in place. Correct alignment is the same whether you are sitting, standing or lying down: it should not change because you change positions. Whether you are standing or sitting, the shoulders should be back and down, the chest open, the abdominals contracted, the chin parallel to the floor, the feet flat on the floor.

Pilates will give you the strength to maintain correct alignment for prolonged periods of sitting. When sitting, the knees should be bent at right angles and the spine straight and lengthened but still in neutral. The legs should not be crossed. This posture can be especially difficult to maintain if you are concentrating on an activity in front of you, such as using a computer. VDU monitors that tilt and stools designed to make you sit correctly are worthwhile investments. A good way to remember your posture throughout the day is to simply write the word "posture" on your screen saver: notice the instant effect seeing the word has on you. You can also try to enrol the help of work colleagues: ask them to remind you throughout the day of your posture and to correct you if you slip into negative habits.

Whatever you are doing, stand and stretch at least once every hour. Raise your arms above your head and very gently arch and curve your back. You will feel an immediate relief in the lower back.

Standing

Very few people stand with their weight distributed evenly between both feet. Usually they favour one leg and then the other if they are standing for long periods of time. People with an exaggerated curve in the lower back quite often lock their knees and allow their stomachs to protrude. These habits usually result in back and knee pain. Here again, it is important to strengthen the torso in order to be able to maintain correct alignment. Refer back to the posture check and try to become aware of the way you stand throughout the day. Make a list of your natural tendencies and aim to work on one thing at a time, until you gradually adjust your habits. If it helps, tell someone close to you that you are working on your posture and get them to remind you every time they see you slump or stand on one leg.

left Try to avoid curving the spine and bending at the hips when lifting a heavy object.

left Stand close to the object, then bend at the knees and take the weight through your legs. Keep your spine in neutral with your head in alignment and keep the abdominals strong.

above When standing up, try not to favour one leg but keep your weight evenly distributed through your feet. Lengthen up through your spine with your head in alignment and your spine in neutral. Keep your shoulders relaxed.

Climbing stairs

Everyone tends to lean forward from the hips when going upstairs or walking up an incline. A certain forward flexion is normal but this should not be exaggerated as it can result in lower back pain.

When you are walking up steps or climbing a hill it is important to maintain an abdominal contraction to help stabilize the torso. Although you need to see where you are stepping, try to keep your chin parallel with the floor. Glance down at the steps with your eyes; do not lower your head.

Lifting a heavy object

It is imperative to maintain stability in the torso when you are lifting anything, whether it is heavy or not. In some situations - such as catching a child who is about to fall - there is no time to prepare or brace the body for the force needed to lift an object suddenly. For this reason it is important to train the abdominal and back muscles so that they are used to contracting and the movement becomes an involuntary action.

When you do have time to prepare for the lifting of a heavy weight, bend your knees and lower the body with the torso almost erect. Place your body close to the object and use your legs, not your back, to give you the force to lift. Maintain the contraction in your abdominals the whole time, and try to lift the object from the lowest point possible. This will protect your back muscles from strain.

Exercises To Do During the Day

Apart from your regular Pilates sessions, there are some exercises you can do quickly and easily wherever you are. Reassess your posture throughout the day and practise the key posture points: you could even pin up a list of these and check through it from time to time. Maintaining the correct posture in your Pilates sessions helps to re-balance the body and achieve optimum results.

Drawing in the abdominals

Whenever you get the chance, practise contracting your abdominals by drawing navel to spine. This action not only tones the abdominals but will get you used to the centring movement often used in Pilates exercises.

right Keep your back straight and in neutral. Inhale and, imagining that you are wearing a tight pair of trousers, as you exhale pull your navel away from the waistband, making your waist smaller. Lengthen up through the spine.

Wrist circles

If you have been working on a computer it is helpful to give your wrists a stretch to make them feel looser. Remember to take a short break from your typing or writing every 20-30 minutes.

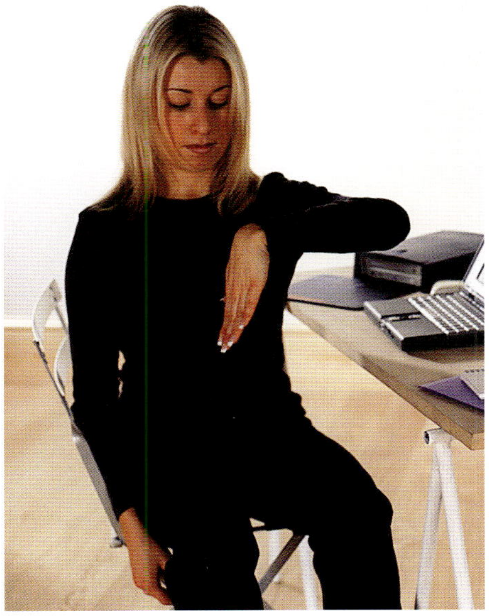

left Start by circling your hand. Support it with the other hand at your wrist if this feels comfortable. Circle in both directions, making a slow, full circle. Remember to keep the spine lengthened and the abdominals strong at all times.

Hand stretches

If you are working at a computer, writing or doing any other kind of repetitive movement with your hands during the day it can be beneficial to stop regularly and stretch out your hands.

left Keeping your hand straight and somewhat taut, draw your fingertips down towards the inside of your arm. Use the other hand to press them gently down. Now turn your hand in the other direction, drawing your fingernails towards your forearm.

Drawing the shoulder blades down the spine

This technique should be familiar from all your Pilates exercises. Standing or sitting, bring your arms to your sides with the thumbs facing forwards. Slide your shoulder blades down your spine, keeping them close to the back of the ribcage so that they are not sticking out. If you are not sure if they are sticking out or not, you can deliberately do the opposite and make your shoulder blades stick out.

right By gliding your shoulder blades down your spine, you will reduce the effect of any tension you are feeling in your neck and shoulders. Although hunching your shoulders up to your ears is a common reaction, it will exacerbate any discomfort you are already feeling in that area. Try to maintain the distance between your ear and shoulder at all times, unless otherwise stated. Throughout the day you can monitor the tension in your shoulders and try to become aware of situations that make them hunch up. For example, it is common for tension to increase when working at a computer for long periods of time, or when using the telephone, but by becoming aware of your habits and posture you can make a conscious and effective effort at reducing tension.

Neck stretch

When we sit for extended periods of time, especially while typing or writing, it is common to experience tension in the neck and shoulders. If you do store tension in your shoulders, it can be helpful to shrug your shoulders up to your ears, hold ... then let go. The following neck exercises will help to gently stretch and mobilize the muscles around the neck to help ease tension.

1 Keeping your spine in neutral and the abdominals strong, gently tip your head, letting your chin fall down towards your chest to feel a stretch in the back of your neck.

2 Turn your head slowly from side to side, taking care not to overstretch. Keep your abdominals strong and your spine in neutral.

Designing a Cardiovascular Programme

This section is intended to guide you through exercise in a healthy, balanced way. It deals mainly with Pilates-based exercises that will strengthen and stretch your body and give you better posture. However, in order to have a balanced programme and reach optimum fitness you also need to include exercise for the heart and lungs, known as cardiovascular exercise. There are three main components to a good fitness programme: strength work, flexibility training and cardiovascular exercise.

Cardiovascular exercise, also known as aerobic exercise, is necessary to stimulate the heart muscle. Regular cardio work will help reduce the incidence of certain diseases and will regulate blood pressure. It is also a great fat burner but this should not be your only objective.

You need to look at four important aspects of cardiovascular training when you are designing a programme: type of exercise, intensity, duration and frequency.

Type of exercise

To complement your Pilates training you can choose any kind of aerobic exercise that you enjoy doing and know that you will stick with. This could be walking, jogging, cycling, swimming, hiking, aerobic dance, step - the list is endless. The main point is that you should choose something that you will do consistently. It is no good saying that you are going to make rock-climbing your main form of exercise if you live in a city and do not have the time to travel.

If you prefer company, try to get friends to exercise with you, or join a club or gym that you like and that is convenient for you to travel to. You could book in just to use the sauna or get a beauty treatment if you want to check that a gym is right for you. Try classes on offer and ask for guidance from the staff. Team sports may appeal to you, or you could combine cardiovascular exercise with a practical skill such as martial arts. Home exercise equipment is widely available and need not be expensive: a skipping rope, for instance, costs very little.

above Cardiovascular exercise can be practised cheaply and effectively in the home environment. Try power walking, exercise videos or jogging. You can even dig out your skipping rope.

Make a list of all the activities you feel you would enjoy and try them all. Cross training - doing a variety of exercise types - is advised, as the risk of injury from overuse is less and your motivation will be kept high. You will also notice that your list will get longer as you get stronger. You will feel more capable and confident about doing different forms of activity and you will enjoy them more.

Intensity

How hard you should work depends on your present fitness level. The fitter you are, the more intense your workout can be, but it is important to keep the intensity of the activity suitable for your fitness level and this is sometimes difficult if you are not used to working out. It might be hard for you to distinguish between muscle fatigue and systemic tiredness. If, for example, you are cycling and your legs ache from pedalling, you may think that the exercise is very intense when really it is the weakness of your legs that is making you tired, not your heart and lungs working hard. This becomes easier to recognize over time.

During exercise, music can really help to motivate you. Try not to choose music that brings back memories as this may distract you. Select something upbeat and positive that is not too slow.

Heart rate monitors are not essential but can be helpful in setting goals and record keeping. They are widely available and relatively inexpensive. They can also help to record recovery rates (the rate at which your heartbeat returns to normal after exercise) which document changes in fitness levels.

below Aim to do cardiovascular exercise three to five times a week. There is no minimum amount of time for exercise, so if you can only manage 10 minutes it is better than none and will help to keep you motivated.

ASSESSING EXERCISE INTENSITY

Here is a simple way of gauging the intensity of a workout. Think of a scale between 1 and 10, where 1 is no effort at all (resting) and 10 is the maximum effort that you can exert (an all-out sprint or a powerful jump). Everything else is somewhere in the middle. Remember that you are the one who subjectively puts a number to each intensity. Your number 4 might be your grandmother's number 8. Here is an example:

Mary is 38 years old, walks regularly and doesn't smoke. Her scale is:

Scale	Activity
1	Lying in bed (very, very easy)
3	Walking: 3kph/2mph (easy)
4	Walking: 5kph/3mph (getting less easy)
5	Slow jog: 7kph/4½mph (taxing)
6	Faster jog: 9.5kph/6mph (hard)
7	Running: 10.5kph/6½mph (harder)
8	Running fast: 12.5kph/7½mph (very hard)
10	All-out sprint: 15kph/9mph (very, very hard)

Simon is 55 years old, sedentary and a heavy smoker. His scale is:

Scale	Activity
1	Lying in bed (very, very easy)
3	Walking: 2kph/1¼mph (easy)
4	Walking: 3kph/2mph (getting less easy)
5	Walking: 4kph/2½mph (taxing)
6	Walking: 5kph/3mph (hard)
7	Slow jog: 7kph/4½mph (harder)
9	Faster jog: 8kph/5mph (very hard)
10	Slow run: 9 kph/5½mph (very, very hard)

What Mary perceives as being easy, Simon feels is somewhat hard, as the two are in different physical shapes.

When working aerobically, you should try to work between a four and an eight (somewhat hard to hard) on this scale. This means that the work should be a challenge, but not impossible. You should not feel as if you have been run over by a truck after your workout. If you do, you are probably working too hard. The fitter you get, the faster and harder you can work while still working between a four and an eight.

As you get fitter, you can play with this scale and sometimes may go past your last effort. This will help you to raise your threshold and prepare you for harder work with less effort. If you are out of condition, start gradually and work your way up. Do not make a heroic effort to win any races on your first day.

above Exercising in the fresh air makes you more alert and for those whose work is mostly indoors, being outside can help ease stress.

right Joining a gym or health club may keep you motivated, but don't worry if this does not appeal to you as there are plenty of home videos available with high-standard aerobic exercise programmes for you to try.

below Cross training (which simply means taking part in a variety of activities) is one of the most effective ways of keeping fit. It reduces the risk of injuries, keeps you motivated and gives you the opportunity to develop a variety of muscle groups.

Duration

The longer, harder and more often you exercise, the more benefits you will reap, up to a point. You will burn more fat, your lungs will become stronger, your heart will get more conditioned. However, you must start at a level at which you feel comfortable: it can be very demotivating to start off doing too much and getting injured, which could mean taking breaks in your fitness programme to recover.

The point where the disadvantages of exercise start overcoming the advantages will be different for every person. Some people have the genetics to withstand hard training, and they can make great athletes. Other people's bodies break down more easily and they should listen carefully to what their body is telling them.

Try to exercise for between 15 and 60 minutes. If you are in good shape, you can go up to the 60-minute mark. If you are just starting out, keep your workouts shorter (and less intense, of course). Remember that there is no minimum. If you can really only spare five minutes one day then this is still better than nothing.

Nothing is set in stone. Do not feel that you must exercise for unrealistically long amounts of time. Set duration goals that you will be comfortable with. It is better to

do 20 minutes every other day than two bouts of 45 minutes and then never again. Obviously, the duration will be directly related to the intensity of the exercise. If you work at high intensity, you will not be able to work for very long and vice versa. Beginners should aim for longer duration with less intensity until they are strong enough to work a little harder.

Frequency

How often should you do aerobic exercise? Again, you must remember that added frequency will result in greater benefits. Three to four times a week is desirable, always allowing one day of rest in between. This rest day can be active, however: you do not need to stop moving, just change what you are doing. For example, if you walk briskly on Monday you can do Pilates on Tuesday. You are resting from your cardiovascular work but it is an active rest. Consistency is a key factor in maintaining your fitness level.

To get better results, try to do aerobic exercise at least three times a week and make the rest of your life as active as possible. This could mean taking the stairs whenever you can, walking up escalators or parking the car further away from your destination, or getting off the bus a stop or two earlier. Your daytime activity does make a difference and can be classesd as exercise if it is challenging for you. Walking to or from work can be a wonderful way to relax and unwind.

If you are going to be running or power-walking, start with a warm-up then go at a gentle pace for 3-5 minutes before increasing the pace slightly, giving your body time to adjust. Here is an example of a running programme for a beginner:

above Cardiovascular exercise need not be boring. Dancing the night away burns up many calories.

Week 1: Jog for 1 minute walk for 2 minutes

Week 2: Jog for 2 minutes walk for 2 minutes

Week 3: Jog for 3 minutes walk for 2 minutes

Week 4: Jog for 4 minutes walk for 2 minutes

Week 5: Jog for 5 minutes walk for 1 minute

Week 6: Jog for 6 minutes walk for 1 minute

The total amount of time you spend on this pattern will depend on how fit you are. Twenty minutes would be great but if you can only cope with 10 minutes or less, this is fine - work at your own level. Once you start you will be surprised at how quickly you can progress to jogging for 60 minutes. Carry on adding a minute week by week, decreasing your walking time, until you have reached a satisfying standard. It is important to keep setting yourself goals. Make sure you drink plenty of water before and after your run and never skimp on your warm-up or stretches as this may increase your chance of injury.

left Exercising with a friend can help to keep you motivated. Make regular times to exercise and choose someone with similar objectives.

Preparing the Body for Cardiovascular Exercise

Warming up the body before exercise is vital to prepare it for the work that it will be asked to do. In the case of cardiovascular work you must warm up the respiratory system (heart and lungs) as well as your muscles, to help reduce the risk of injury and to focus psychologically. In a warm-up it is a good idea to simulate the exercises that will be performed during the main part of the workout, but at a much less intense level, to prepare the body gradually. As in the case of Pilates, the warm-up helps to set the mood. For cardiovascular work this needs to be faster paced: it can help to listen to upbeat music, probably slightly louder than for Pilates. When you have completed the warm-up and the stretches, start your session slowly: walk for a few minutes then build up your speed and jog. Ease your body into activity. If you begin too ambitiously you may increase your risk of injury.

The warm-up

This general warm-up could be used for jogging, power-walking (fast-paced walking), skipping or dancing. Always warm up to prepare the body for activity, both mentally and physically.

One leg circles

This mobilizing Pilates movement helps to loosen the hip joint. Work at whichever level you are accustomed to in your Pilates sessions. Repeat five times in each direction then change legs. Remember to lengthen up through your leg and keep your spine in neutral.

right Lying on your back, circle one leg, keeping your hips very still. Start with small circles then increase the size, controlling the movement with your abdominals.

Knee hinges

This will mobilize your knees and warm up your ankles. Keep your spine in neutral and your abdominals strong throughout the movement. Relax your shoulders and neck. Repeat five times on each leg.

1 Lie on your back in the relaxation position. Lift one leg so that your thigh is at right-angles to the floor. Point your toe as you raise your foot.

2 When the leg straightens flex your foot. Push your heel up towards the ceiling, then lower the foot. Think of your knee as a hinge, keeping the thigh still and limiting any movement in the hips. Exhale as you lift, inhale as you lower.

Ankle circles

This will give you a wonderful loose feeling in your ankles and really wake them up. Repeat five times in each direction then change legs.

right Lie in the same position as for Knee Hinges, but this time rest one leg on the other. Slowly circle your ankle in one direction, then the other. Keep your toes pointed and make a full circle. Concentrate on the shape you are forming and perform this movement as slowly as you can bear. Keep the spine in neutral.

Stretches

As a guide, you should hold each of these stretches for 30 seconds, but if you want to increase your flexibility or if you are particularly stiff in any area you can hold the stretch for longer. Make sure you stretch both legs equally.

Gluteals stretch

You should not only tone the buttocks but also stretch it for best effect. Stretching lengthens the muscles and may help prevent injury. Stretch before and after cardiovascular exercise for optimum effect. It is also worth timing your stretching session occasionally as it is easy to rush through it when you are tired.

▲1 Lying in the relaxation position, place one leg across the other, holding the supporting thigh with your hands.

▲2 Exhale as you lift the supporting leg. Keep the abdominals strong throughout. Relax your neck and shoulders and do not overgrip.

Quadriceps stretch

The fronts of the thighs tend to get quite tight as you use them for most lower body activities. If they get overtight they can cause problems with the knees. The main mistake people make with this exercise is to bend at the hip, thus losing the stretch. If you find it difficult to hold your foot, loop a towel around it, and use this as an extension.

left Stand facing a wall or other support. Bend one leg and raise your heel towards your bottom, keeping your knees in line. Keep your abdominals hollowed. Exhale as you lift the leg. Watch for tension around the neck and shoulders, and keep your head in alignment.

Calf stretch

The calf muscles can get tight, especially if you do much walking or climb a lot of stairs.

above Standing up with your hands on your hips, take a big step forwards. Keep your spine in neutral and lengthen up. Push the back heel into the floor to feel a stretch in the back calf. Keep the abdominals hollowed and the head in alignment. If you cannot feel the stretch take a bigger step forwards.

Adductor stretch

This is a good stretch for the inner thighs. Stretching all the muscles in the legs helps to prevent knee and spine problems.

above From standing, take a big step out to the side. Bend one leg so that the knee is over the heel and keep the other leg very straight. Don't collapse into the stretch: or let the abdominals sag. Exhale as you stretch and feel the inner thigh lengthen.

Assisted hip flexor stretch

This stretch uses a chair for support, but make sure it does not slip. It is particularly good for runners, but many other people have tight hip flexors. You may feel the need to hold this stretch for longer than 30 seconds.

above Stand up and rest one foot on a chair (or something lower). Bend the leg and lean into the stretch on an exhalation, keeping your back heel on the floor. Keep your head in alignment, and your spine in neutral.

Assisted hamstring stretch

This is another stretch that benefits from an additional support. The hamstrings tend to be tight in most people, and can cause back pain if left inflexible. If they do feel tight hold the stretch for slightly longer.

above Standing on the floor, lift one leg and rest your foot on a support. Flex your foot and keep your leg straight, bending the supporting leg if this is more comfortable. Keep your head in alignment and your abdominals hollowed. Exhale as you ease into the stretch. Support just above the knee and try not to push down on your leg.

Nutrition: The Basics

Nutrition plays a huge part in how your body performs and how you feel about it. The more you know about food, the easier it becomes to follow a sound and sane diet.

above Not all types of fat are created equally. Some fats are essential so aim to eat monounsaturated fats, found in avocados, olive oil and fish.

Calories

People talk about how many calories there are in an apple or a piece of chocolate and they want to know how many calories they burn in exercise. But what is a calorie? One calorie is the amount of energy needed to raise the temperature of 1g water by 1°C. The same unit is used to measure the energy that food will give and the amount of energy used in activity.

Nutrients

Everything you eat or drink can be included under this common heading. Your diet should consist of a balance of proteins, carbohydrates and fats, together with small quantities of the other nutrients your body needs, such as vitamins and minerals.

Proteins are most commonly found in animal products such as meat, fish and milk, but are also found in vegetables, pulses and nuts. They help the body to repair and build tissue. According to most research, if you consume up to 15% of your total amount of calories per day as protein, you will have a balanced amount in your diet. Another way to calculate this is to allow 0.75g protein per day per kilogram of your body weight. Each gram of protein is equivalent to four calories, so if you know how many grams of protein you are eating, multiply by four to find out the number of calories. Remember that 100g/4oz of meat is not equal to 100g/4oz of protein. Meat, like most foods, consists of a number of different nutrients, as well as water, which make up the total weight. Most packaged goods will have the nutrients listed in grams as well as the total number of calories.

right Wholegrain carbohydrates are preferable to refined starches as they are richer in vitamins and minerals. They help to increase energy and provide a little protein for muscle repair. This becomes even more important when you start an exercise programme.

The main difference between vegetable protein and animal protein is that the latter is what is called complete: that is, it contains all the essential animo acids, which are those elements the body needs to take in because it does not form them internally. Vegetable proteins (except for soya beans) are not complete unless they are intercombined (grains with beans for example), which means that vegetarians need to be careful to include the correct combinations in their diet. Try to choose low fat proteins such as chicken, fish and tofu. Limit red meat and other higher fat protein sources.

Carbohydrates are the nutrients that give you immediate energy. They are found in bread, pasta, rice and cereals as well as fruits and vegetables. You should aim to eat about 60% of your total calories in carbohydrates, but you need to differentiate between simple and complex carbohydrates. The first

right Try to include lots of fruit in your diet. Carrying fruit around with you will mean you always have access to a healthy snack and are less likely to rely on high-fat, fast foods. Being organised, not obsessive, is a key factor in healthy eating.

(such as sugar and honey) metabolize quickly in the body and their energy is quickly "used up". The slower-metabolizing complex carbohydrates (such as pasta and rice) give you energy for longer periods of time, and at a much more even pace, maintaining a more constant blood sugar level than simple carbohydrates do.

Obviously, you should try to include more complex carbohydrates in your diet and fewer simple ones. The more refined (and usually sweet) a carbohydrate is, the simpler its composition. If possible, choose wholegrain cereals, brown rice and wholemeal pasta, which retain more of their original nutrients and also have the advantage of contributing fibre. Limit your intake of white flour, cakes and biscuits, as they tend to be high in sugar and fat. Also be aware that biscuits and cakes advertised as fat-free are not always healthier options as they can be loaded with artificial ingredients and sugar.

Fat is extremely concentrated in its energy power. One gram of fat equals nine calories; more than twice the amount of protein or carbohydrates. You need to take in fat for several reasons: it is an excellent, highly concentrated source of energy (a small amount of fat goes a long way, which was great for our ancestors but maybe not such a prized quality today); vitamins A, D and E are stored in fat; it also makes food taste better and gives you a satisfied feeling. It is because fat tastes good that people end up eating too much of it and pumping many surplus calories into the body. Processed food manufacturers know this and add a lot of extra fat and sugar to their products to make them more appealing.

So how much fat should you consume? Most authorities agree that less than 30% of your total calories should come from fat. This may sound a lot, but almost all foods (including fruits and vegetables) contain some fat, so the calories keep piling up.

The average western diet contains around 40% fat. This, together with a lack of physical exercise, is the main reason for our spreading waistlines and the ever-increasing incidence of obesity-related illnesses. All foods will make you fat if you eat too much of them. However, fat will do the job fastest. The sum is simple: calories in (food) should equal calories out (activity). If one side of the equation does not balance the other, weight gain or weight loss occurs. All calories that are not used will be stored. However, the storage process is easier for fat calories than for protein or carbohydrate calories. Fat likes to end up on your body, waiting to be used on that unlikely day when there is no food to be had.

left Include as many vegetables as you can with each meal. There are so many different types now available that it is easy to experiment for variety.

Fat is not intrinsically bad, but all fat is not created equal. Saturated fats contribute to the production of low-density lipoproteins, which cling on to the walls of your arteries, narrowing the passages and making them stiff and unpliable. The blood flows less freely and any particles that happen to be floating through can get trapped, possibly causing a heart attack or stroke. The message is to stay away from saturated fats. These are recognizable as they are almost always solid at room temperature, such as butter, lard and other animal fat. Some vegetarian products are also high in fat. Trans fats, found in margarine and some cooking oils, should be limited, as high consumption can lead to obesity and other debilitating illnesses.

Polyunsaturated fats are thought to help prevent skin complaints, heart disease and cancer. Essential fatty acids are present in fish oils, evening primrose oil, walnut oil and other polyunsaturates. Monounsaturated fats, found in olive oil, avocados, fish and nuts, are considered superior to other fats as they are linked to a decreased risk of heart disease, cancer and obesity. Most of your fat consumption should be from this last group.

Eating For Life

Everyone has advice to give on eating, especially if it concerns losing weight, but very few can advise you on maintaining weight loss. Even if you find it easy to lose weight, it is very difficult to keep it off if you don't formulate a sound plan. Anyone can stick to a diet of grapefruit for a few days, or even a few weeks, but no one could or would want to maintain that kind of regime for the rest of their lives.

It can be psychologically traumatic for your weight to yo-yo. Not only must you cope with a sense of failure when you return to your average body weight, but those around you will perceive you as fighting a losing battle. It doesn't help you, but many take a great interest in other people's weight gains or losses.

When you lose weight rapidly through manipulating your diet - especially if your weight drops uncomfortably below your genetic size - and then inevitably return to your average body weight, the proportion of fat in your body may actually be higher than before. This is because some of the weight loss would normally have included lean muscle mass. Therefore you are making further problematic weight gain more likely, as lean muscle mass consumes more calories even when the body is at rest.

left Try to involve your family and friends in your healthy eating habits. With their encouragement and support you are less likely to make poor choices. They may even have recipes or tips to share with you.

above Create time to sit and eat in a relaxed manner. Eating in a hurry can lead to eating poor foods.

So what should you do if you want to lose some weight? First of all, you need to assess whether you really need to lose it. Not everyone is built like a supermodel: most bodies are designed with some extra padding, like a little warehouse ready for pregnancy or even for keeping warm in winter. No matter how hard you diet or exercise, you cannot fool your body's genetic programming. Those little fat storage areas are put there for a purpose; you may not be fond of them but they are part of your body.

This does not mean that you cannot improve your body. A sound diet and an exercise programme will make it strong. Your genes are a given but the way you treat your body will make a big difference.

Maintaining your weight

The amount of calories you need to eat depends on how active you are. You want to keep fuelling your body; keep it happy and give it what it works best on. If you reduce your calorie intake too far, your body will interpret this as starvation and will react by slowing down its metabolism to save energy.

The main thing to keep in mind is that this is not a slimming diet - it is a way of eating for the rest of your life. It must be pleasurable and you must be able to lead a normal life. The plan is actually very simple: just avoid those foods that you know are high in fat and "empty calories" for most of the time and allow yourself a little more leeway for the occasional indulgence.

above There are so many excellent healthy-eating books on the market that it is easy to choose delicious but nutritious recipes.

UNDERSTANDING NUTRITIONAL INFORMATION

Try not to become obsessed with checking labels. Find products that taste good and satisfy your nutritional requirements, favour these then just check the labels of new foods. It can be psychologically damaging to over-analyse your diet – food should be enjoyed. Try to choose fresh, natural products, organically produced if possible. Beware of low fat processed foods as they can be full of additives, sugar and salt.

Fat

Food manufacturers may want you to believe that their products contain less fat than they really do. Take milk said to contain 2% fat. This actually means that fat makes up 2% of the total weight of the milk. But imagine a block of butter in a glass of water: if you measure fat as a fraction of weight, the butter (fat) is only a small percentage of the total. To measure the proportion of calories that come from fat, you need to know the total calories per serving and the weight of fat per serving. Take Brand X breakfast cereal:

Total calories per serving: 378

Grams of fat per serving: 14

There are 9 calories in a gram of fat, so 14 x 9 = 126. This is one-third of 378, so this product is 30% fat.

Calories

Calories are commonly listed in terms of serving size, which can be manipulated. The label on a chocolate bar may say it has 200 calories per portion, but there could be four portions in the bar. Some foods, such as avocados, are high in calories but also high in nutrients. Be sensible and base your choices on the percentage of fat, fibre and nutrients, rather than calories alone.

Sugar

Watch out for sugars that are not obvious, such as glucose, lactose or maltose. Of course, excessive sugar consumption not only causes dental problems but adds unwanted empty calories. A lot of fruit juices and carbonated drinks are full of sugar so try to stick to plain water for most of your daily liquid requirements.

Fibre

For a food to be classified as "high fibre" it should have a minimum of 5g of fibre per serving. Wholemeal foods, fruits, vegetables and pulses are all good sources. Fibre is important because it plays an important part in stabilizing weight and protecting against diseases such as bowel cancer.

Reduce oils in your diet but do not avoid them completely. Extra virgin olive oil, for instance, is very beneficial, but fats, cheeses, and cream should be monitored. Alcohol (seven calories per gram) is another source of empty calories. This does not mean that you can never have another glass of wine: it just means that you should enjoy a glass of wine once a week instead of once a day.

Never say never again. That will only lead to frustration and anxiety. Chocolate is great, but it is very high in calories and should be enjoyed sparingly. Do not make it part of your daily diet but do not cut it out completely. If you do, you will end up dreaming about chocolate.

You should eat, and enjoy what you are eating. Food is one of the great pleasures of life. You should feel satisfied and not hungry or deprived. Think about filling up on foods that you can eat in larger quantities without tipping the caloric equation. However, if you get the chocolate urge, go for it: anything else that you eat at that moment will not satisfy you. Just ask yourself if you really want to eat the whole bar or if a couple of squares would take away the craving. Remember the 20% rule: if you only eat higher fat foods for 20% of the time you will feel less guilty. You will be surprised if you really start listening to your body. Most people in the west eat because of mental rather than physical hunger.

Make sure that you are adequately hydrated during the day: sometimes when you feel hungry you are actually thirsty. Aim to drink 2 litres/3½ pints of water a day (this can include herbal teas) as, among other things, this will give you the added bonus of healthy glowing skin. If you are going to indulge in a treat, try to eat something that has nutritional value such as nuts, rather than empty calories such as sweets.

left Occasionally it is fine to eat foods that are high in fat. The key is balance. If you constantly deny yourself you will find your cravings increase.

Frequently Asked Questions and Answers

Will Pilates help me lose weight?

Losing weight - or rather fat - is a question of disrupting the energy balance, between calories in and calories out. A regular exercise programme will raise the body's metabolism, and although the amount of calories burnt per session may be quite small, over a period of time the average number of calories burnt will be greater. Pilates combined with a cardiovascular programme and a sensible diet will give you the results you desire.

I would like to get rid of the fat on my thighs and hips but every time I lose weight it goes from my face and breasts instead. What can I do to lose it from the right places?

Unfortunately, there is no such thing as spot-reducing. You cannot decide where you would like to remove fat, that is a decision that genetics takes for you. Many people think that by doing hundreds of abdominal exercises they will lose the fat around their middles but this is not the case. Just think about people who chew gum: if spot-reducing worked, they would have hollow cheeks! Instead of working incessantly on your lower body, you should also build up the upper body to draw attention away from the bottom half. Think what happens when you use shoulder pads - you look instantly slimmer.

I would like to start exercising again but last time I went to the gym I just got bulky and looked wider. I really dislike the current trend to be very muscular, can Pilates help?

Yes it can. Pilates builds long, lean muscles by keeping repetitions and resistance low. As it pays special attention to alignment, every move is designed to elongate as it strengthens, which is ideal for anyone who builds bulk easily. Think dancer's body rather than power-lifter's.

When will I start to see results? I have tried other programmes but I just cannot seem to stick with them long enough to see any real benefits.

If you are diligent about exercising and combine Pilates about three times a week with a cardiovascular programme and a sound diet, you should start seeing visible results within four weeks. Muscles you thought you did not have will peep through and your arms and legs will start to look more toned and streamlined. Your back will be stronger and your tummy may look flatter. However, the change won't only be visible. You will notice positive changes within yourself. You will start looking forward to your workouts and feel stronger in everything you do. You will sleep better and will most probably be in a better mood. Your aerobic sessions will become easier and you will be able to exercise for longer periods at a time. Give it a month: it's worth it.

above Regular Pilates practice will improve your strength and flexibility.

I have quite a sway back (lordosis) and frequently experience back pain just above the kidneys. Will Pilates aggravate that situation?

Anyone with an injury or back problem should seek medical advice before starting this or any exercise programme. Pilates is an excellent technique for correcting certain postural deviations and strengthening weaknesses. However, it should not be used as a remedial method unless supervised by a trained and certified professional. Pilates will aggravate a situation such as the lordosis described above if the movements are improperly executed.

I am worried about incontinence (urine leakage) when I work out. Are there any exercises to prevent this?

The muscles of the pelvic floor can weaken, especially after giving birth. Like any other muscle, these can be strengthened to prevent the problem of incontinence. During urination, stop the flow a few times. The muscles you are using are the pelvic floor muscles and this action is exactly what you should do to strengthen them. You can do this anywhere: on a bus, at the supermarket, standing in a queue at the bank. Read the section on pelvic floor muscles for more information.

I play golf every weekend and find that I often suffer from a stiff back and neck after a game. Which exercises would be helpful in relieving or preventing this?

Pilates is an excellent training method for golfers as the customary action in this sport is quite often a hazardous one for the back. You should follow the whole programme, as all the movements will be beneficial. You may be pleasantly surprised as you discover that your game is improving with your improved strength and flexibility.

I have never exercised at all but would like to start with this programme. Could this be dangerous? I am a 54-year-old woman, slightly overweight and a non-smoker.

You should seek medical advice before starting this or any other exercise programme if you have any injuries or risk factors. These would include coronary heart disease, diabetes, high blood pressure, high cholesterol, obesity, a heavy smoking habit or a very sedentary lifestyle. Women over 50 and sedentary men over 40 should also check with their doctors.

I am extremely thin and would like to gain a little weight. What can I do? Won't Pilates just make me look even slimmer?

You probably do not get much sympathy from others as this is the opposite of most people's problem. Most bodies are genetically programmed to store fat, but yours is designed to stay very lean. Try to take in extra calories whenever you can, but do not rely on empty calories from junk food. Drink fruit juices instead of soft drinks and carry nuts and dried fruits or other high-calorie but nutritious snacks with you at all times. You should still exercise to build muscle, to give you a more toned, stronger look. Keep your cardiovascular exercise to a moderate intensity.

I cannot seem to motivate myself to exercise or change my diet. I'd like to lose some weight and get a more toned body but I lack the stimulus.

It is important to set goals that are realistic, measurable, and with a definite time frame. This will help you to look forward and stop you from seeing fitness as unattainable. You can set both long- and short-term goals. For example, "Within four weeks I want to be able to do the Hundred without having to stop halfway," is both attainable and realistic. Another motivational tool is to make a written agreement with someone who you know will support your exercise regime. Write out a contract stating that you commit yourself to exercising X times per week for X weeks. Have the other person sign as well as yourself.

left Although we are not suggesting that you walk around balancing a book on your head, we are saying that regular Pilates practice will improve both your alignment and your posture.

above Pilates, combined with healthy eating and cardiovascular exercise, lengthens and stretches muscles creating a long, lean, strong physique.

Beware of people who may unconsciously want to sabotage your progress. Strange as it may seem, there are people who may not want you to succeed: friends who feel guilty about not taking care of themselves, mothers who are worried that you will do too much, jealous partners who worry that you will become too attractive to other people – odd, but true.

I am a single parent with no time for hobbies. I know I have to exercise but I often feel I have no free time.

When you have many demands on your time, it helps to examine all the reasons why you might choose to do something. Exercise can actually change your perspective, making you feel calmer and more in control. As they grow stronger, most people notice positive changes in their self-esteem and self-image. Headaches, backaches and depression can mysteriously disappear. With all these positive changes, exercise can become a treasured and necessary part of the day. Six weeks seems to be the point at which perspectives change. If you can reach a point where you feel you "want to" rather than "have to" exercise, it will take away the "chore" factor.

Don't forget that energy creates energy, and this will help you in your day-to-day activities. Pin up a big list of all the things that exercise will do for you, and keep it positive. For example, rather than saying "I want to be a size 10" say "I want to be confident and comfortable in my body". Do not underestimate the power of words and positive thought. Use affirmations to make you feel powerful. Sometimes it also helps to remind yourself that little is better than none at all, so start slowly and see what develops.

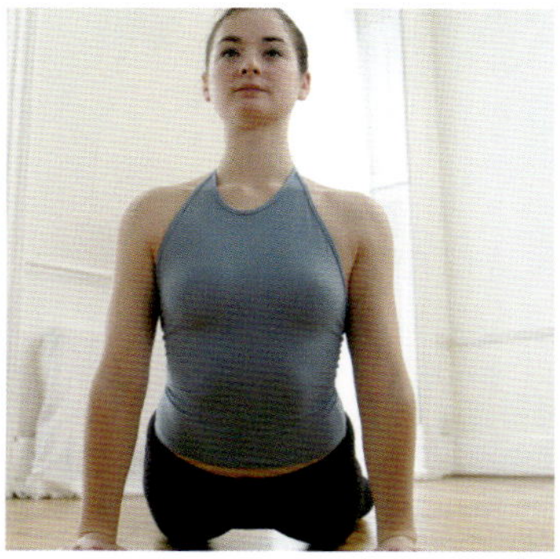

Yoga-Pilates

A dynamic fusion of two major disciplines, yoga-Pilates opens up a unique path to health and fitness. The postures feature easy and advanced variations, to suit everyone's level of flexibility.

Jonathan Monks

Introduction

Yoga and Pilates are both usually regarded as separate disciplines, and are practised as such. Normally, time is spent defining their individual theories and their origins to give them a distinct identity. This provides us with security in that we know what we practise; it's something definable and safe. The fact is, however, that each discipline you learn is as individual as the teacher you learn it from. It may be yoga of one of the many different varieties or Pilates from a highly qualified instructor, but it is still about feelings that are particular to each individual, and the responses that they will have to a given set of physical feelings.

This section is all about you, your body and how you relate to it. There is no in-depth history, proof of origins, or philosophy. In this section I offer you a method by which to find sensations in your body along with opportunities to feel and respond to them. It will allow you to create your own personal style – a personal form of exercise that you can take up, adapt and practise, wherever you are, whatever you are doing.

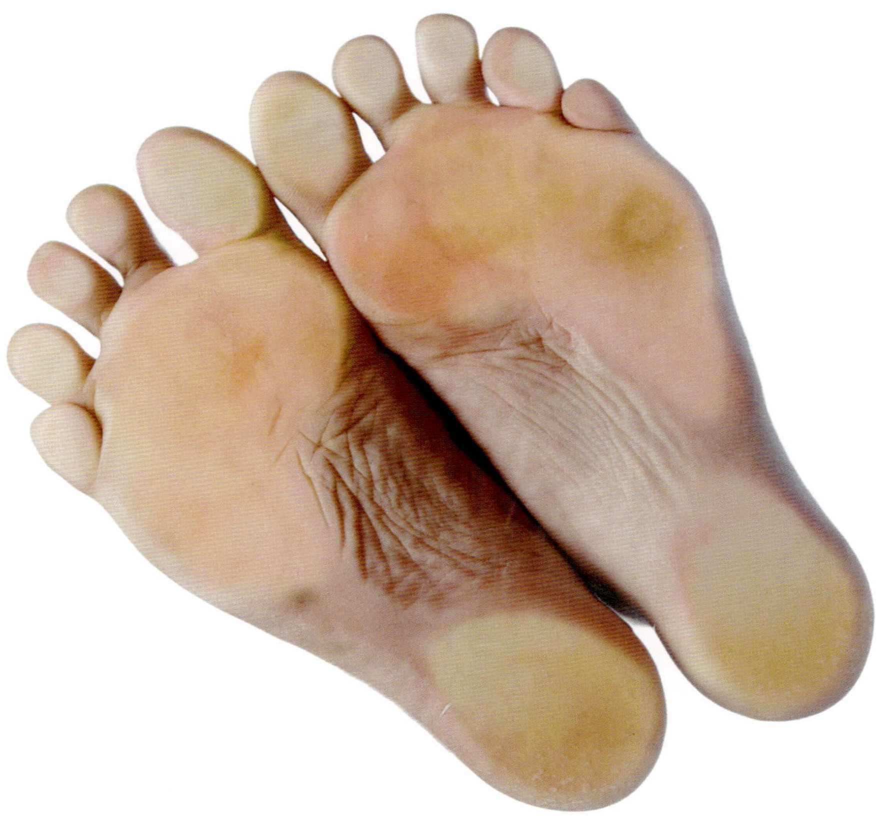

Why this section works

The information in this section can work only if you feel your body and begin to use it properly. This means that you have to practise regularly, taking an interest in what you are doing when you are doing it, not just going through the motions with the aim that all will be fine in the end. Pay attention to how you feel when you practise; are you a morning or evening person? Do you need twenty minutes practice every day or a thorough hour every other day? Only you can truly say what feels best for you.

I offer the contents of this section to young and old alike, but always with the aim of getting you to understand your body from the inside. When this happens I have seen long-term neck pain disappear in five minutes. I have seen better posture emerge through simple feeling and understanding in half an hour, and clients have dropped a clothes size in between three and six months. However, this is somewhat irrelevant for two reasons. The first is that these people have decided to practise because they enjoy it. They have changed their diet and drinking habits because they have felt they wanted to. They have grown into their bodies and now enjoy life through their bodies. The second reason why other people's stories are irrelevant is because they are not you. Be your own story: be your own body. Everything you've been looking for – the body beautiful – literally lies at your fingertips.

How to use this section

Read this section and, when you are ready, try it out and have a go. Try to exercise every day, even if it is only for a short period of time – little and often is best to start with. However, if you don't understand anything, take the time to reread that chapter, and break down the sentences until you

left It's hard to know where to begin on the journey of discovering your body, so I suggest you start off with what you truly know and feel. Take some time to discover how you use the ground beneath you, for in that knowledge you can unearth how and why you move.

can identify the body parts and movements I describe. You will find no visualizations or imaginative descriptions to aid you, since all this does is push your concentration farther inside your mind, the opposite direction of where all the action is actually going on: inside your body. Go through the first chapter, Core Strength, and become familiar with those sensations before you move on to the main postures.

Solid Grounding, is dedicated to reflecting on the imperfections of your body, and various ways of dealing with them. If you use this information in combination with the rest of the chapter on Core Strength, you may find the rare combination of stability and balance that solves your particular problems.

The chapter on sequences provides some ideal warm-up routines for you to begin with, but once again, be honest about the sensations your body is registering. If you find something hard work, try the easier option, and perhaps try it again the following day until it becomes easier. If you find it too easy, then spend more time in each posture, or try the harder option, extending your sequences for as long as you can manage to build stamina. Take a deep breath and begin your journey towards a stronger, leaner body.

A note on breathing

The subject of breathing fills many books. Such an important issue demands great attention. So how should you breathe? You have done a great job until now, because you are still here, but can you answer the questions, "How do I breathe?" and, "Where do I breathe from and to?" Pay attention to what you find.

Breathing is a marvellous way of removing toxins from the body. My own experience has taught me that sitting still and breathing deeply after an enjoyable (and indulgent) night out has helped me to feel a lot less cloudy headed. So pay attention to how you feel when you breathe a certain way. Use your breath to enhance your life.

Anatomically, remember that your ribs (which hold your lungs) are primarily behind you. See if you can breathe into your back and be aware of your response.

What you need

Yourself and an even floor are the essentials. A yoga mat is helpful, but by no means indispensable. Just make sure that the mat, rug or towel you have chosen stops your legs from slipping, to prevent unexpected split postures.

As for clothes, wear anything you find comfortable. I recommend a warm room and your underwear, since this is comfortable and allows you to watch your body move.

Listen to your body. It will tell you when you prefer to practise, but a good tip is that an empty stomach is less distracting than a full one.

Apart from these guidelines, you are your own boss. If spending lots of money helps to inspire you to practise then spend away, but remember – all you need is you and the floor.

A serious note on safety

This section is an outline of instructions. It is not a one-to-one personal training session. It cannot watch you or tell you when you are going too far, not working hard enough or using the wrong set of muscles. Only you can do this. Only you can check to see if the weight of your body is in your hips, not your lower back; if your knee is in line with your big toe and hip; if the pain you are feeling is that of muscle burn or a sharp pain that comes from a ligament strain or tear. Take responsibility for yourself; it is much more empowering in the long run. Take your time: feel. There are plenty of reminders along the way.

below These close-ups of parts of the body need to be joined together in order to see the bigger picture, then we are able to see how one thing can relate to another.

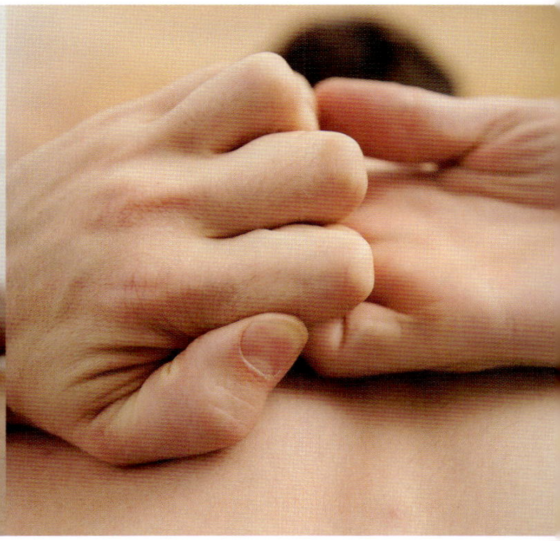

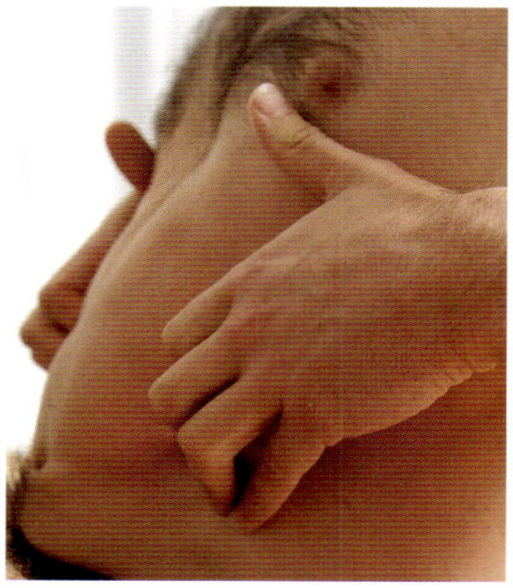

Core Strength

Strength in the centre of the body enables all the other parts to operate more easily. Learn how it feels to pull in the muscles of the abdomen. Combine this with flexibility in the hips and strength in the back, and you are on your way back to the centre of your body.

Flexibility or Strength

below Flexibility and strength go inextricably together. As bent, twisted and constricted as some of these postures may appear, the purpose is to help your body find its natural line and balance. Strong joints are the most supple, and strong muscles are the most elastic.

Try not to think of flexibility and strength as two quite separate concepts, or as an "either/or" option. The body is extremely clever so pay attention to what it is telling you.

Watch a young child standing, sitting and moving about freely and you will quickly recognize how far most adults have travelled from paying attention to their own bodies' guidance. Often, we are not even aware that we are setting an insidious pattern until it has become completely ingrained and we are suffering the effects of poor posture, tension and stress.

Flexibility comes from strength and the reason for this is simple. A joint sits between opposing muscles like a see-saw with the tight muscle holding the see-saw down. To create flexibility in a joint you must use the strength of the opposing muscle to stretch its partner.

The first reason why you have these problems is because the body has adapted itself to move, sit and hold itself in the way you have chosen (not how it may have told you to). So now it is the perfect manifestation of who and how you are. This is most obviously illustrated by the way we compensate for a physical injury, but it is actually also happening in ordinary, everyday life. The second reason is that the body tends to open up only when it truly feels safe to do so.

Releasing the body

There are three common methods of making the body feel safe and of releasing the tightness that hides a weakness. First, you can just collapse and relax, letting everything go, only to find precisely the same tensions and tightness return once you stop relaxing and re-adopt your habitual patterns and methods of movement. Second, you can have the tensions massaged, or manipulated, into letting go, but, once again, your habitual methods and patterns of movement will encourage the original tension back into your body. You could, however, create balance between your muscles, and since balance is most definitely safe, the body – your body – is more likely to open up and let go, altering your habitual patterns and methods of moving for the better. Only when a weakness is strengthened to balance a tense strength will the tension in the body be resolved.

As you practise, be aware of the imbalances in your body; learn to recognize them in everyday life so your work on the mat carries on all day, every day, changing your body from slouch to sleek. Until you balance the "see-saw" in everyday movement the imbalance will remain.

Try to be patient. Be honest about your weakness, then take time to strengthen it until your body makes it clear to you that the weakness is ready to let go.

Gravity – use the floor

What is the one thing that helps you stay on this planet? It is the same thing that shrinks us during the day and without which we would float away. Gravity beats us down and also provides us with all that we need to find a magical lift. Remember Isaac Newton: for every action there is an equal and opposite reaction. To find this lift up, against gravity's pull, all you need is a body and a floor.

No matter what part of your body is touching the floor or chair, you can find the lift up simply by pushing down a little. After all, we are designed with a foot that has natural balance owing to its arch and a spine that has curves to give us more spring. Gymnasts, yogis, dancers and athletes alike all perform feats that seem to defy gravity because they have found this lift.

More importantly than the ability to perform great feats, this lift shows us that you do not have to suffer under the seeming oppression of the weight of gravity. After all, if you measure yourself in the morning and again that evening there will be evidence that you have shrunk a little in between. This difference between the freedom and length of our spine before and after our day is a major reason why we get tired. The stress of gravity seems against us.

Push down to lift up

But how can levitation be achieved when gravity is so essential to all our lives? Well push down a little. Try and find where gravity is affecting your body, where the weak points are.

Try slouching when you sit and then pushing your bottom down on the seat. Stay there pushing and slouching until you feel the need to let go and you will find that there is a natural lift that accompanies the letting go. You will now feel upright and in line with gravity, not fighting against it. Try the same technique but standing this time and if the feeling remains elusive stay with the pushing and slowly let go with as much awareness as you can muster.

Feel this lift and as it becomes familiar let your actions and movements become filled and dictated by it; never slouching or stooping, always feeling a light long spine being filled with a lift. If you take away the stress and energy used in struggling every day against gravity, you can see how much easier living would be.

So we can forget about the long fight with gravity, and instead give in and work with this beneficial force, to use it to our advantage. Regardless of whether you use this natural lift to leap like a gazelle, stand on one hand or levitate, it will mean that as you age – the one thing you cannot avoid – you will not stoop, bow or give in to the pull of gravity. You will grow old gracefully.

below You don't have to know about Newtonian mechanics to understand how to use gravity to give you a lift up. See how the hand and the foot both have natural arches, which act like springs pushing up against gravity. Try simply pushing them down and waiting to feel a natural lift in reply.

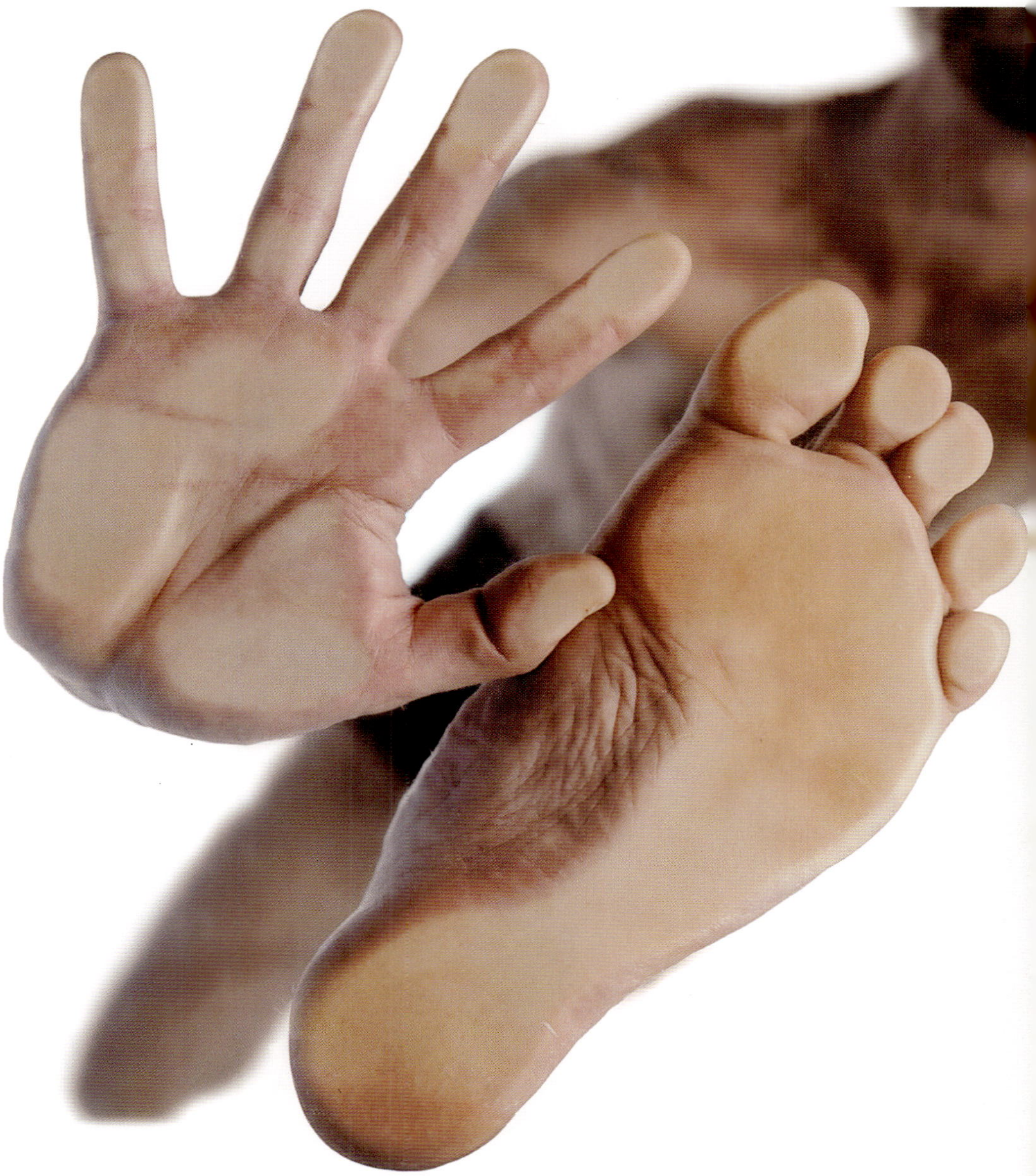

Pulling the Stomach In

The image of the body beautiful is constantly with us, whether in the media, with new looks of the rich and famous or in adverts for new and miraculous supplements or exercise fads. What is this image? Well it tends to have toned hips and legs with a pert bottom, a strong stomach and an open chest. Only the genetically gifted or determined fitness freaks seem to embody this ideal, and yet this is in fact how everyone is designed. We all have bigger muscles in our legs than our arms because nature intended us to use our legs as our means of transport. Around our middles are muscles in a similar shape to a girdle that hold our internal organs in the right place. Along our spines are muscles similar to struts that can hold the spine long. In the middle of our body we have a big hinge, the hips, surrounded and protected by big muscles (thighs, buttocks, hamstrings), which help us move around it.

So if we move using our hips as a hinge and our legs as support they will be fitter and toned. If we then hold ourselves upright using our "girdle" and maintain a long spine with our "struts" we will then not tend to let our stomachs bulge and our shoulders collapse.

Through rediscovering how our body is meant to move by feeling it from inside, the perfect body is achievable, and your own ideal body will emerge. You have to put time and intelligence into regular practice of course, but this can include walking, bending, playing games, entertaining and household chores, for they all involve you moving, and it is in this moving you can exercise, and enjoy discovering your body. Discovery does not have to be limited to set practice times for it is in the moments off the mat, sitting at your desk or doing the washing-up, that you understand the satisfaction of living correctly through your body.

Perhaps most interestingly, when you do start to move as you are meant to, your preconceptions of what you should look like fall away. An infinitely more satisfying feeling replaces them, that of a feeling of being at home within your own skin.

left To come out of the ape pose, really suck your stomach up and into your ribs. The position of the hips in relation to the spine is the reason we can walk tall. The more we can make our spine feel that it extends out of our hips, the more we will feel upright and evolved.

Ape or Man

Poor habits, sitting at a desk, leaning and slouching, can all result in standing incorrectly, putting strain on parts of the body. With poor posture, the weight of the world really does rest on your shoulders and will eventually push you into the ground.

1 Our bodies are remarkably similar to those of apes – we share similarly proportioned limbs and joints – and yet our posture is markedly different. Part of this is due to the way we use our spine, in particular our lower spine. Through playing at copying the stance of an ape we can understand how we became upright and perhaps more importantly what muscles are responsible for this step up in evolution.

To copy the ape stance, let your legs be slightly wider than hip-width as this will give your hips some space to move through, and let your arms hang down, opening your back. Give yourself permission to play and be silly; after all you will look ridiculous sticking your bottom out and letting your arms hang down, so you might as well have fun while you do it. To get back to an upright stance first try squeezing your buttocks and letting your hips come forwards. The feeling is almost as if the muscles of your bottom are pushing you forward (try not to slouch as you slowly stand upright). Repeat this as many times as you need to, until you begin to realize how important your bottom is.

2 The variations on upright vary with perception and reality, especially when our habitual patterns constantly reaffirm themselves in our posture. Take this slouch as an example. The weight of the world is beginning to fall off the rounded shoulders, making life uncomfortable for both the shoulders and the world that sits on them.

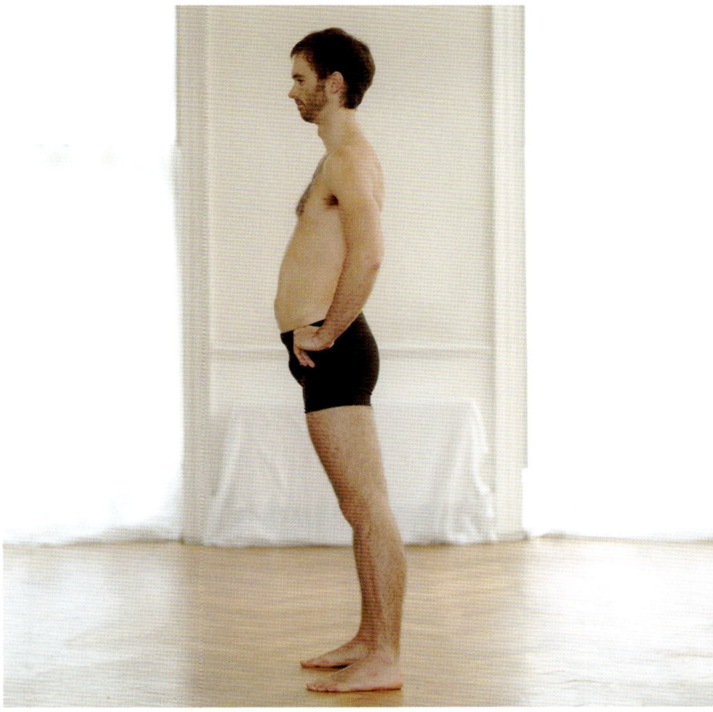

3 Look, too, at the slump here, in which the weight of the world sits happily on the shoulders but all the pressure falls to the middle, which begins to bulge as a result. Practise coming in and out of ape until you begin to feel the hinging of your hips forwards and backwards, since this is the reason we can walk tall, without bulges.

Abdomen Tuck

Most of the stomach exercises we are used to performing seem to make the abdomen bulge out, but the core muscles of the body are made active by pulling in. Therefore, begin by lying flat on the floor on your front.

1 Rest your forehead on your hands and feel the weight of your body on the floor. Feel the front ribs and pelvis pressing into it. You are going to try to pull your stomach up off the floor, keeping your ribs and pelvis down.

2 Begin by simply pulling the tummy up and lowering it down. How high can you pull your stomach up from the floor? Can you feel the lower spine lengthen? Have you created a gap underneath your body? When you feel confident with this, move on.

3 Keep the lower ribs firmly grounded on the floor and your hip bones and pubic bone flat on the floor. Now pull your tummy in as high as you can. Feel the lower spine lengthen and push your legs straight – so straight that you feel your toes spread.

► 4 Push your left hip and upper thigh up by squeezing the buttock and lifting your left foot off the floor. Is your tummy still in? Repeat, inhaling alternate legs up, exhaling them down. Can you begin to feel that the tummy can remain in, while the lower spine is kept long, even when you move your legs? Try to gain control of those pulling-in muscles as your limbs are moving.

Lengthen the raised leg from the thigh, as opposed to lifting by squeezing the buttocks. This exercise has the advantages of pulling your tummy in and of relieving tension from the front of your hips – a major cause of lower back pain. It can also lift the buttocks and add shape in quite a short time. With this, and all the exercises in this book, be sure to feel the exercise, not just in your head but throughout your body, so that the sensations make sense.

Stomach Curl

The pubic lift starts in the stomach. It is very easy just to squeeze your bottom to tuck in your tailbone, which provides the same action. Pay attention to the feeling of the correct action – allowing pressure to be equally distributed throughout the body will relieve problems.

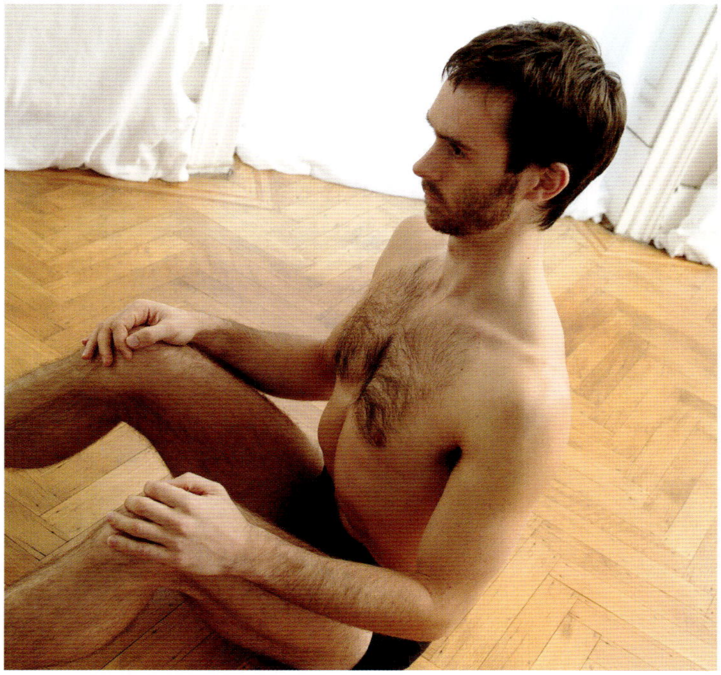

1 Sit with the soles of your feet on the floor and your knees in the air. Sit up as high as you can, pushing your sitting bones down into the floor. Cup your hands on your knees, so as not to use your arm strength to interfere with the exercise.

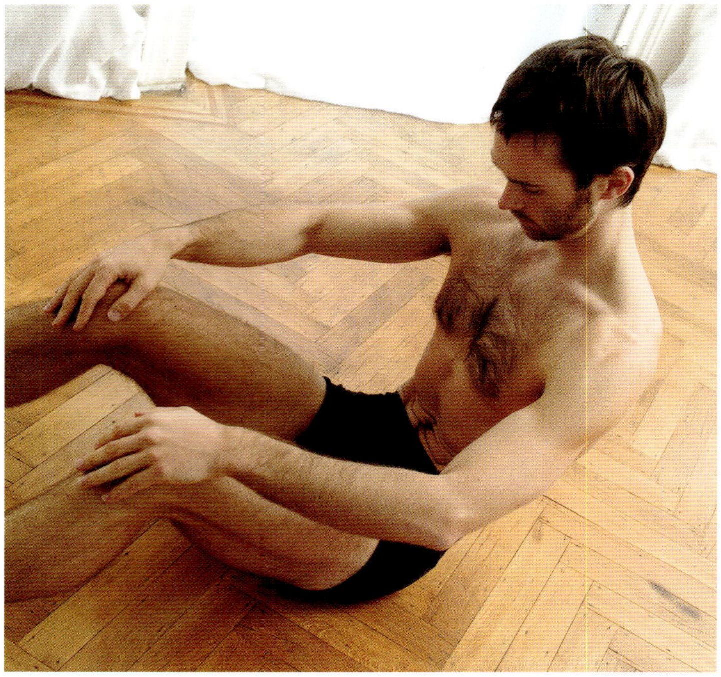

2 As you roll back, point your toes into the floor and feel your thighs work and lengthen and your knees push down towards the floor. As you come up, pull your heels towards your buttocks. The hamstrings and deep abdomen will engage to pull you up.

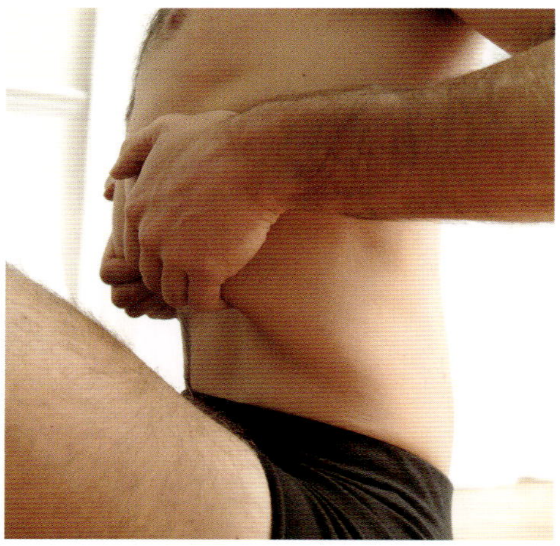

3 Look down at your stomach and pubic bone so you can see how you are moving. Using both hands, grab hold of your lower ribs and lift them up. Now suck in your stomach and all the muscles that connect from the pubic bone all the way up the front of the body.

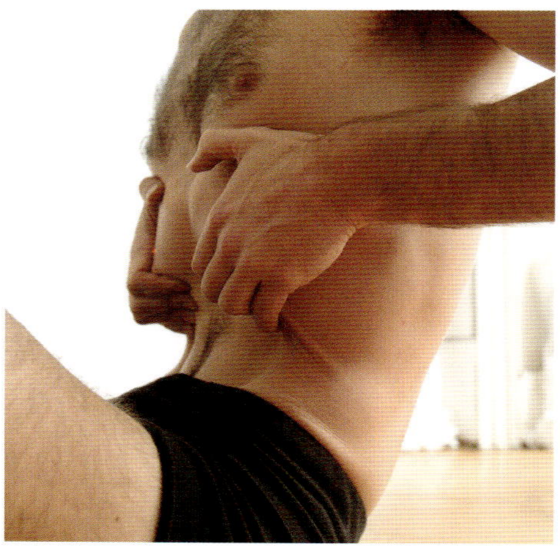

4 As you roll backwards, keep lifting your ribs. You will find that your stomach will pull in as before, but now also up into your rib cage, making it possible to feel a lift in the body as you roll down. Try to detect the origin of the movement in the groin. The fact that the tummy pulls in so hard gives a feeling that the pubic bone is lifted, which in turn tucks the spine between the buttocks and rolls you down.

incorrect If you simply lean back, rather than roll back, the tummy will bulge. If the arms lengthen before the pubic bone has rolled up, you will know that you have simply leaned back from your chest. This will most probably be accompanied by your abdomen pushing out. The pressure here is in your lower back, not spread evenly in the body, and will cause you problems and pain eventually.

Elbow Lift

In this exercise extend through your legs to your feet, feeling the work in the thighs. Push your chest high off the floor so you can feel the space between your shoulder blades. This will strengthen your stomach muscles, and train them to hold your insides in.

1 Lie on your front and tuck your toes under your heels. Place your hands together, thumbs on your sternum, tucking your elbows in towards your ribs and then push yourself up to balance on your elbows and toes.

2 Lift your pubic bone into your stomach, as in the stomach curl. Practise pulling your abdomen in and up without sticking your bottom out, as that will disengage the stomach muscles, which is the part of you that this exercise is designed for.

alternative If you find this too tricky, rest your knees on the floor, but make sure you really pull your pubic bone up into your stomach and lengthen the lower spine, or the hip flexors will get a good workout and nothing more.

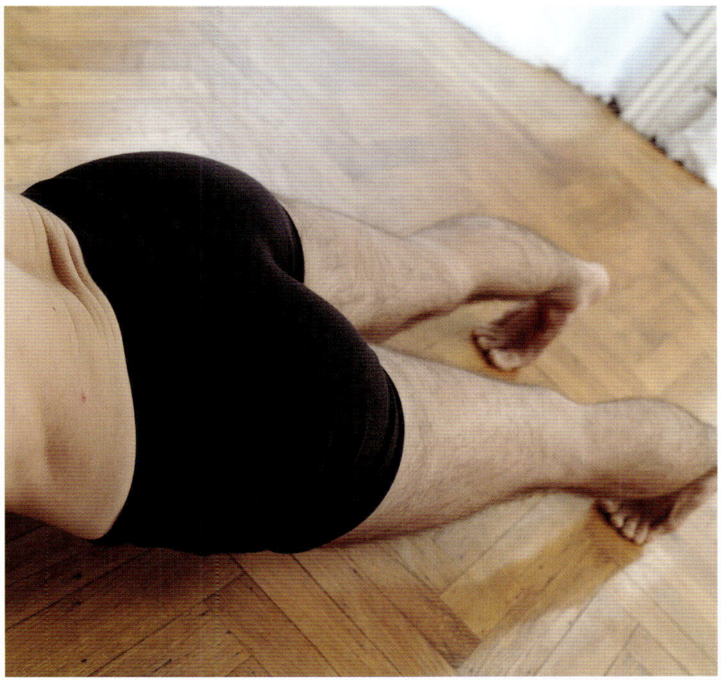

incorrect This shows the classic collapse that usually happens when people try this exercise for the first time. The extremities, especially the toes, take the weight of the body and the lower spine collapses and will soon begin to feel the strain.

Hip Flexors

In medical circles, hip flexors are known as iliopsoas. They are very powerful muscles and especially easy to overuse. You will have noticed in the Abdomen Tuck how difficult it was to lift the leg while pushing the hip down. This is caused by tight hip flexors. When they become permanently tight, the hip bones are constantly being pulled down, emphasizing a lumbar curve in the spine. This leads to a tight lower back and disengages and weakens the abdominal muscles. For this reason, you may feel most tummy exercises in the legs, particularly in the tops of the thighs. However, the more you work on pulling your tummy in and lifting your pubic bone, the more you will feel the abdomen engage, not just during exercises for the stomach but in all your postures. This is the beginning of finding a lift inside you. Don't give in to gravity: be part of it.

Loosening the hips

The hips are probably the most important set of hinges in the human body. Protected and worked by the largest group of muscles in the body, they set us apart from all other animals by giving us the ability to move around and function completely upright. The great versatility of the hip joint means that we can lunge forwards (Forward Bend), backwards (Back Bend) and perform any number of combinations of movements involving our legs.

In order to provide independence of leg from torso, there must be a certain level of openness and flexibility within the hips. Constriction limits both the range of movement and the flow of energy. First, let's find out how to improve the flexibility of the hips.

A note for women

Wearing high heels tilts the pelvis forwards, bringing a strong contraction of the hip flexors and a pronounced arch to the lower spine. This not only weakens the lower abdomen and tightens the lower spine, but can also severely limit the range of motion within the hips.

left To feel like your body is truly fluid and free, learn to extend your limbs and make space between them and your body. Open the space at the back of your neck, between shoulders and ears, lift your tummy to help you extend your legs, and then all postures will begin to make more sense.

Diamond Curl

This exercise stretches the lower back and loosens the hips. However, if you are doing it properly and rolling from the public bone, you will feel the main stretch in the muscles of your legs, especially the hamstrings, which stretch down the back of the thigh.

1 Sit on the floor, as you did for the Stomach Curl, but with your legs in a diamond shape. Place your hands firmly on your knees, pushing them down towards the floor. Feel the hip girdle move firmly forwards and backwards as you roll from the pubic bone.

2 As you roll back, don't be afraid of using your hands. Grab hold of your knees firmly if you need to. Remember to roll your pelvis and feel the movement of your hips between your legs. No matter how flexible you are, there is always room for improvement.

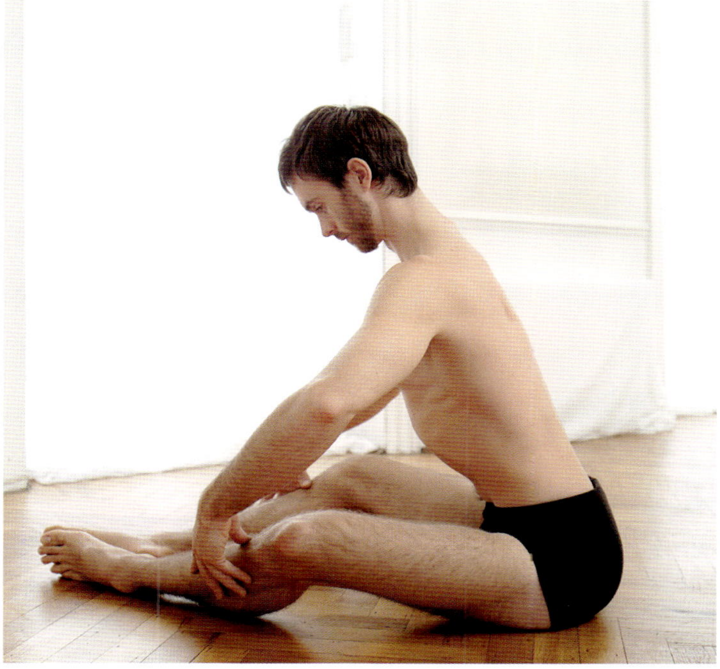

3 Really lean forwards, using your hips as a hinge and you will feel a tug in your hamstrings, the backs of your legs and the inner thighs, as you roll the hips up and over your legs.

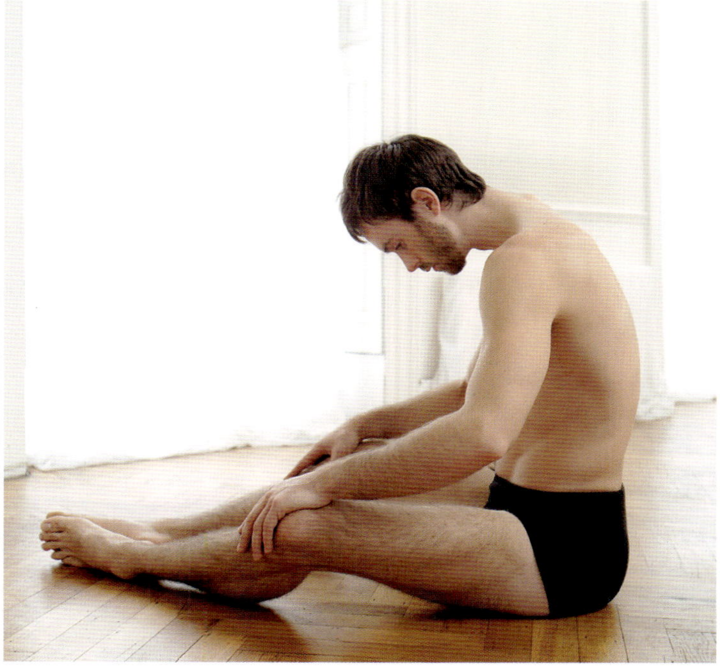

incorrect Leading with your head rather than moving your hips forwards will not exercise your lower back or stretch your leg muscles. Shift your awareness away from your head, which is so accustomed to leading most of the time.

Assembly Position

Remember sitting cross-legged at school? This exercise is very good for increasing flexibility in the hip joints and the elasticity of the spine. It also helps to stretch and strengthen the buttocks. Try to repeat this sequence at least twice a day and you will notice the difference very quickly.

1 Sit cross-legged. Keep tall, pushing your sitting bones down into the floor to find a lift up inside your abdomen. Place your hands on your knees and lower the shoulders, keeping the neck, shoulders and jaw relaxed.

2 The important step now is to hinge forwards and over your legs from your hips, not by simply collapsing your spine. Lean forwards and pull your stomach in tight. You should feel as though you are pushing your sitting bones backwards into the floor.

3 Lie on your back and bring your knees up into your chest in the Baby position. Begin by rolling your knees, one hand on each, down into your chest. As you do this, keep your bottom, sacrum and tailbone on the floor. If you can do this, you will find that the stretch enters your lower spine and buttocks, just where it should be. Keep the work close to the joint, in the flesh, not the bone.

When you find that the lower spine has released a little, grab hold of your heels by taking your arms inside your legs, then slowly pull your knees down to the floor. You should again play the game of keeping your lower back and top buttocks on the floor.

advanced If that was easy for you, try this. Place the ankles on the opposite knees, crossing the shins, and lean forwards from the hips as before. If possible, place one shin directly upon the other. If this is very comfortable, then draw the knees together until the knees sit inside the shins. The more you lean the greater the stretch you will feel in the top of the thighs.

When you have finished lengthening over both legs and opening both hips, roll onto your back and assume the Baby position to complete the stretch.

Pubic Lift

The hip flexors dominate your range of movement in this exercise, by using the strength in your abdomen, and bringing you a greater tilt into or openness of the front of the hips. Don't confuse this lift with tucking in your sacrum, pay attention to lengthening your lower spine.

1 Begin in a kneeling position, knees placed directly under your hips. The feeling you are after here is one of lifting your pubic bone with your stomach muscles. Do not be afraid to grab, poke or hold on to bits of you to help feel and discover how your body works.

It is easy just to squeeze your buttocks and tuck your tail under. However, there is another way that will show you the relationship between your tummy and your lower spine. Pull your stomach in.

2 Pull your abdominal muscles in and up as hard as you can, so that your pubic bone is pulled up between your legs. Repeat this in blocks of up to 21 repetitions. You may inhale as you pull your stomach in and up, as this can activate the stomach deeper, so lifting the pubic bone higher. However, if you find it easier to use the out breath to lift and the in breath to lower, then do so.

incorrect Poking your chest out and leaning back slightly will leave your hips in the same position without moving your pelvis. Instead, try to pull your tummy in, especially above your pubic bone. If you cannot find this feeling then go back to pulling in and up. Keep practising and it will appear.

The Back – It's Behind You

Your back is beautiful. It is the most amazing construction: 32 pillars stacked perfectly together, which not only hold your head high but also protect the spinal cord, allowing you to move your front so easily.

If we use our backs properly, we find we hinge in the right places. We hang our arms from our shoulders so that no tension is felt in the neck; we move with our backs so that our limbs are drawn into us, in a way that is centred, graceful and effortless. The back – our unseen part – can be our ultimate strength.

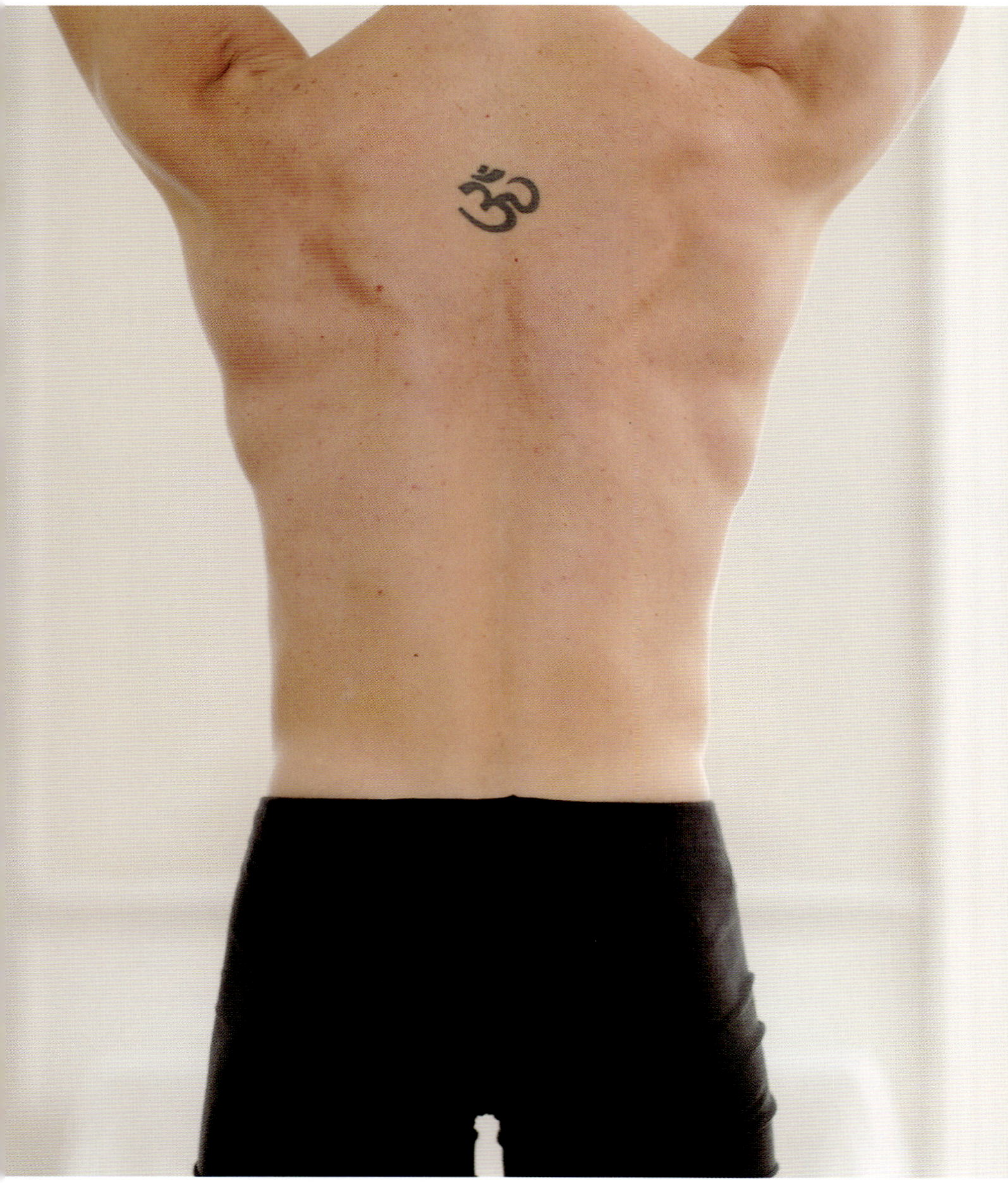

The problem is that our eyes point forwards and our backs are behind us. Consequently, we do not care for the one thing that we rely on – our backs. Since our backs are out of sight, they become out of mind to the extent that we cannot feel them; and if we cannot feel them, how can we be aware of changing or using them? The two main tools that you require to "find" your back are patience and practice.

Getting back to basics

Let's take a look at some games. First, can you lift your arms without using your neck muscles or the muscles that lie at the top of your chest or back? Most of us use the muscles at the top of the body, outside our core, to lift, pull, push or stabilize, whereas the body – which is very clever – has some muscles directly between the shoulder blades that can pull the shoulder blades down the back, so lifting the arms. What is the importance of this? Well, if you get neck ache, or even a headache, it is usually as a result of tension in the upper back and neck. Doesn't it make sense then that if there is no tension there, there will also be no pain? This simple exercise is one of the most fundamental steps in re-educating your body about where it stores its stress. The less stress that is stored around the head, the less stress is felt.

Raise your arms just above your head, so that your upper arms and body form a "Y" shape. Hold them there. Gradually your shoulders will open as the back gains strength, so less and less tension is felt in the top of the body. This will yield many benefits to your practice. Remember, the main reason behind all these exercises is to raise your awareness of your body, so try them out with the assurance that there is a purpose to them.

left Stand up straight and place your hands just above your head, with the arms active and outstretched. Keep your elbows bent and out to the sides. As you breathe regularly, feel your shoulders opening and the tension draining away from your upper body.

Ape Back

Lots of yoga postures were inspired by animals. This one mimics the ape. Copy the animal by leaning forwards and hanging your arms from your shoulder sockets as if your knuckles are about to drag on the floor. This will open your back and also relieve tension around the shoulders.

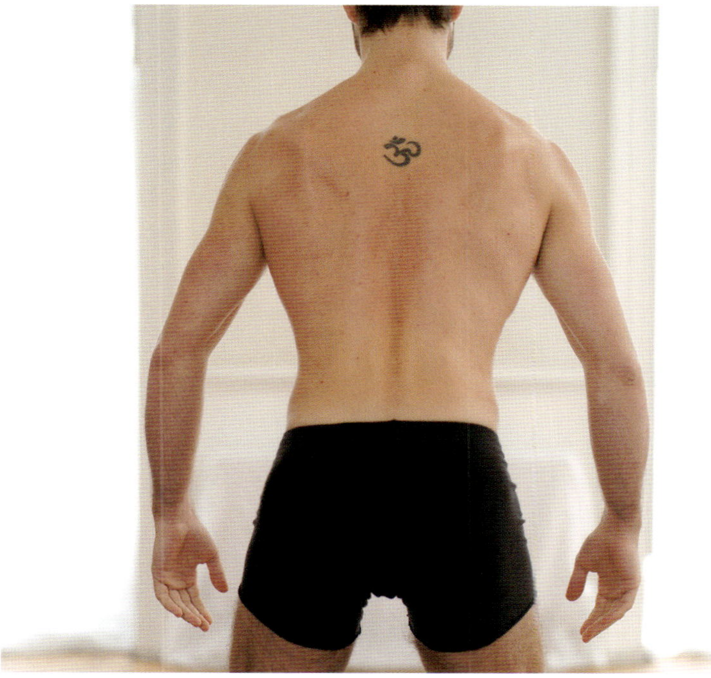

1 Let your body hang loose and you will feel all the weight in your legs from your hips to your bent knees. Your body should feel strong and open. But do not drop your chest, as this will pull all the weight of your head and upper body into your lower back muscles.

2 This profile captures the "dangle" aspect of the "ape man" pose. The chest is not drooping, so all the weight of the upper body is evenly distributed between all the back muscles that run along the spine and the legs and hips.

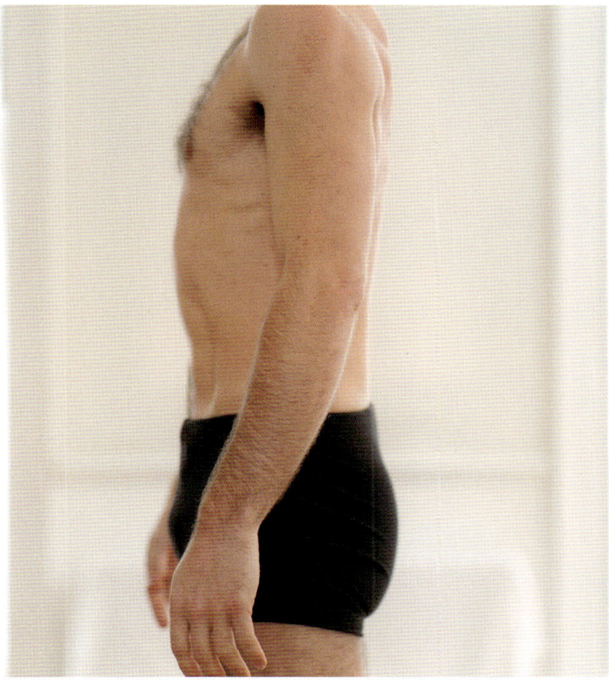

3 To get to the "man" part of this ape game is simple. Pull your tummy in and up hard so that this action will pull you into an upright posture. The challenge is to maintain that open feeling in between your shoulder blades and all the way down to your hands.

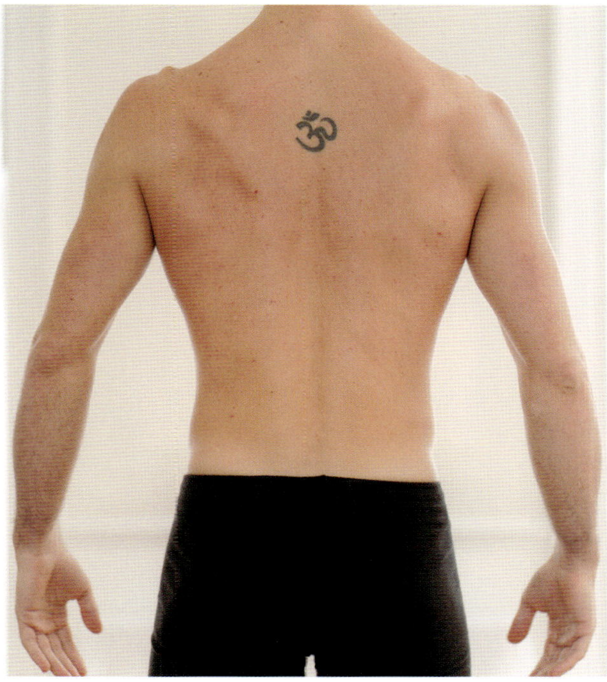

4 There is no squeezing or scrunching of shoulders to accompany the in and up tummy from "ape" to "man". In fact, the back hinges up in one long line from the hips without a bend, lean or slouch.

Drop the Chest and Feel the Lift

To lift the chest, you find the abdomen caves in and the back arches. However, there is another way. Let's return to training the abdomen. This exercise also helps to strengthen the muscles around the spine and relieves tension and aches in the back.

1 Lie on your front with your pubic bone and bottom ribs on the floor, lengthening the lower spine and engaging muscles of the stomach. Let your shoulder blades broaden and lift your elbows off the ground continuing to roll the shoulder blades down your back. Learn to recognize the feeling of an open chest and open back.

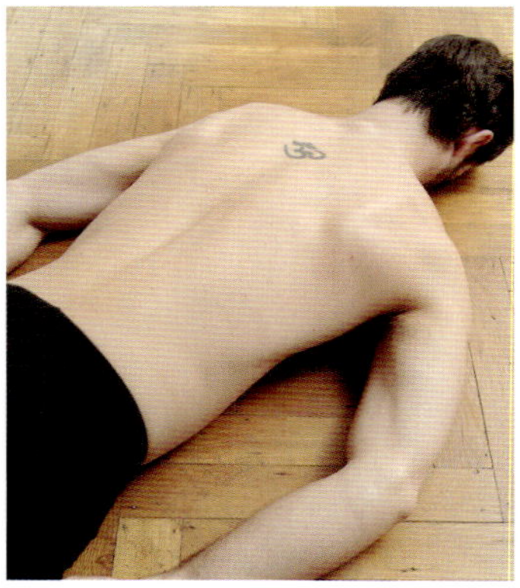

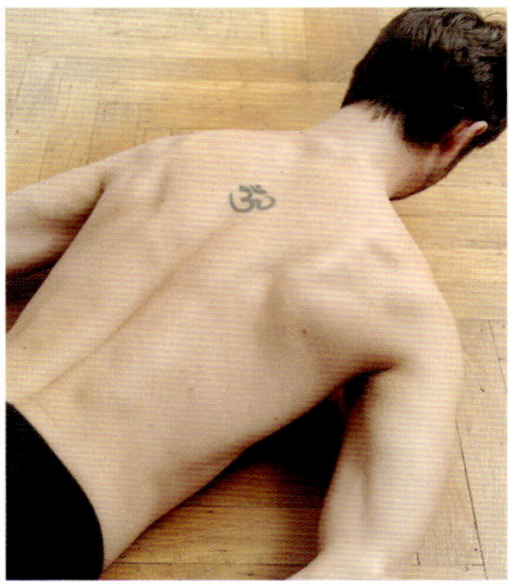

2 Now lengthen the back of your neck and continue to draw the shoulder blades down (you won't move much). The harder you contract the more the upper chest will lift. Keep your ribs and pubic bone down while lifting the stomach up. Simply inhale and try to lift the chest from the back and exhale, letting yourself down slowly.

3 Try to hold yourself up by the muscles that line the spine in between your shoulder blades and raise your legs alternately. Keep your tummy off the floor and raise the arms to the level of the body, but no more, palms uppermost.

Arm Lift

You can do this exercise standing up or sitting down, but, whichever you choose, it is worth checking yourself visually by watching the movement in a mirror. This will help you identify what you are feeling and allow you to take control of the way you move.

1 Begin with one arm and place the tip of the forefinger on your other hand on the end of your collar bone. Now simply lift your arm up until you find you are lifting your finger. Try to feel the shoulder blade drop down as you lift your arm.

When you have got the idea single armed, try with both arms, but watch and stop when either the top of the chest or the neck begins to become involved.

2 Relax your neck and shoulder muscles as you lift your arm. Looking in the mirror, notice the space that appears between your head and shoulder as you lift your arm. As you lower it, relax your neck and shoulder again and feel the tension disappear. Practise, raising the other arm in exactly the same way.

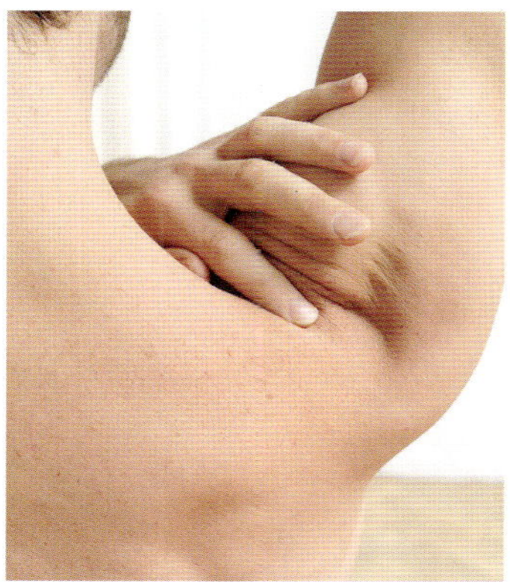

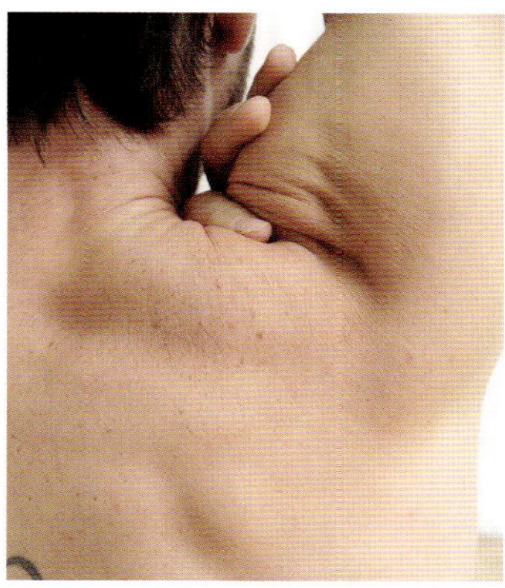

incorrect If your finger becomes squashed between the neck and shoulder, then you are not doing it correctly. In this picture the shoulder blades have lifted, and space is not being created in the armpit. Don't cheat, as this will stop you from feeling – the only way you will gain control and change the way you move.

Basic Back Bend

Now you have opened up the front of your hips, your lower spine should have lengthened down between the buttocks. All you need to do now is lengthen the rest of the spine on top of the hips and you will find yourself in a Back Bend without having bent your back.

1 Begin as you did in the Pubic Lift, kneeling down with your knees placed directly under your hips. Rest your hands on your hips.

2 Suck in your stomach muscles to lift the pubic bone up and through your thighs while you lift and extend your spine. This should keep your tummy tight and trim, and when you recognize that feeling, you can be sure that the spine is protected and long.

alternative If you find the Back Bend difficult, use your hands. Push your thumbs into your sacrum to help hinge the hips up and use your arms to help brace the back out long from the hips. If you feel pain or work in your lower spine, go back to practising Pubic Lifts.

▶ **3** Place both hands on your upper chest and push your hands up with your body. Keep the back of your neck long. Do not stop the lift in your tummy and pubic bone. The chest should feel as though it is moving forwards and upwards, rather than downwards and backwards. If you feel pressure or discomfort in your lower spine or it feels as if your lower back is doing all the work, go back to opening up the front of your hips and thighs, as this is still limiting the extension of your lower back.

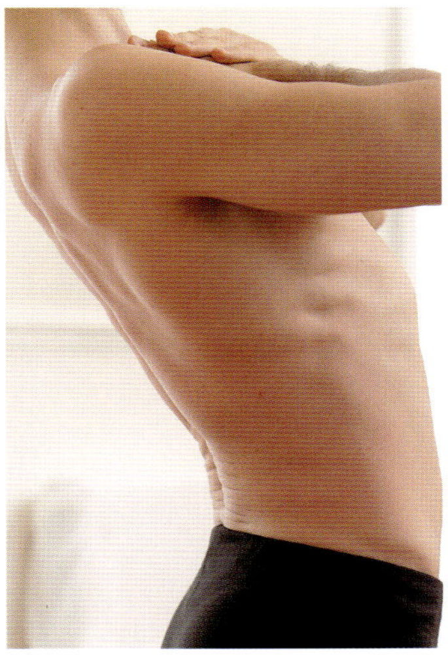

incorrect If you do not lift your pubic bone and simply lean backwards you will find that the back will bend a lot but you will only move backwards a little.

Back to Front

How can you tell what's going on behind you? Can you feel when your back is long? Without the aid of some friendly angled mirrors it is almost impossible to see your back. However, you do have the advantage of having a perfectly good mirror that is always in view, called your stomach. When you stand or sit, watch how your front behaves; as these three examples show, it will help you see what is going on behind you.

1 Arching spine

First there is the time when your stomach sticks out, especially the portion below your navel. Try it out, let your stomach relax forwards and you will feel your lower back begin to arch (see the illustration below).

This is for the simple reason that your stomach is pulling it forwards, and if the spine remains in this pulled position for too long you will feel an ache in your lower spine. The obvious solution to this is to pull your tummy back in, which will in turn allow the spine to move back and your weight to be carried evenly between the front and the back.

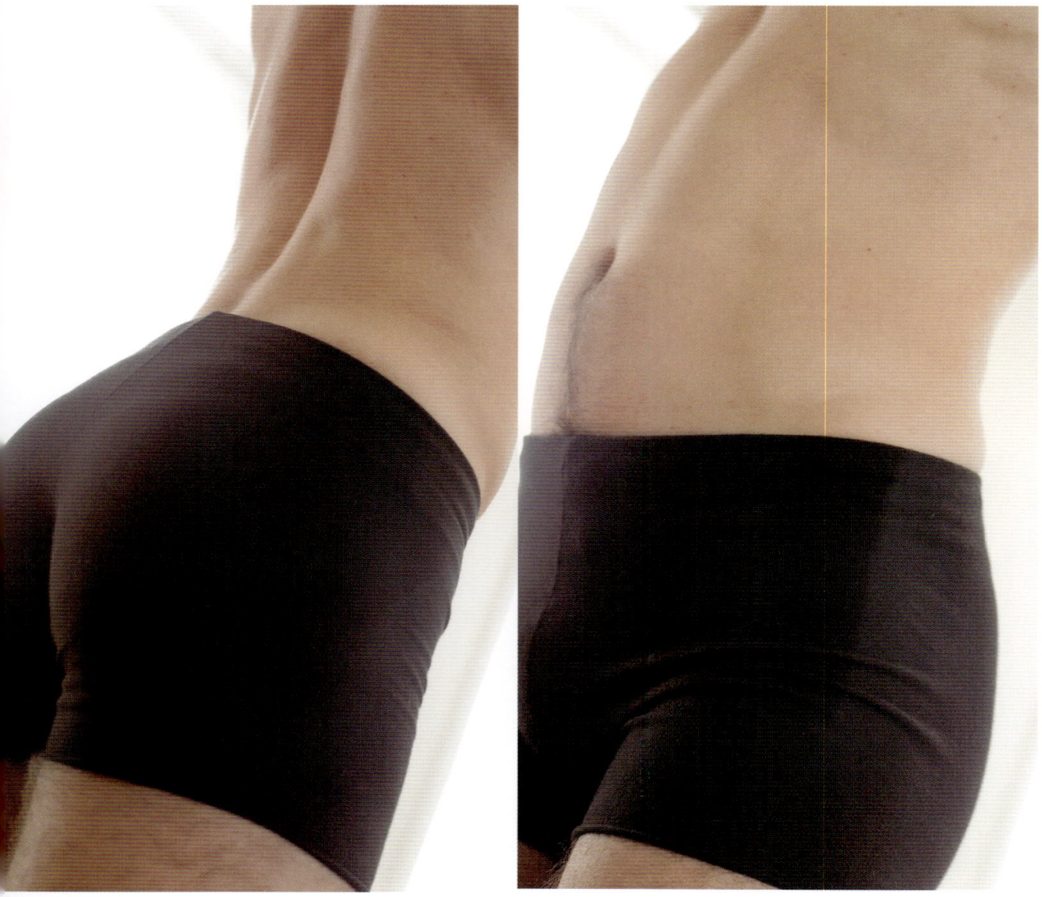

2 High chest

Next, try pushing your ribs forwards. A squeezing together of the shoulder blades normally accompanies this projection of your rib cage, so try that as well if you wish. If you now pull your shoulder blades down you will feel a collapsing sensation in your spine. This is due the middle area now being compressed. Picture 2 showing the back view shows this pronounced dip, which is rather worrying when you consider that your kidneys are being compressed. To bring yourself back into line, place your hands on your ribs and pull your ribs away from your hands. Combine this action with allowing your chest to soften while keeping your upper back long to iron out that middle back dip.

3 Hip balance

You can often see on people with a pronounced hip imbalance that one side of the waist is longer than the other. When this is the case you can guarantee that one side of the spine is longer than the other, and probably twisting, which can lead to back and hip problems. To get your hip bones even, push the sitting bone on the raised side down whilst keeping that side of the waist long. Sitting on the floor, or on your heels, is probably one of the best positions to do this since the floor will bring awareness to your sitting bones.

Keep an eye on these three principals as you practise and you will be able to know how to see when your hips are balanced and your spine is long.

1 back and front If your tummy pushes out and your hips rock forwards, then you know that there is a lumbar curve in your back. This is how so many lower back problems begin. Lengthen the abdomen to lengthen the spine and relieve the pressure caused by this constriction.

Balancing the Spine

These three examples show common ways that the back is misaligned. You might only be alerted to this imbalance of the back by the state of your front. Once you become aware of the pitfalls, a protruding chest, or distended stomach will alert you to more serious problems.

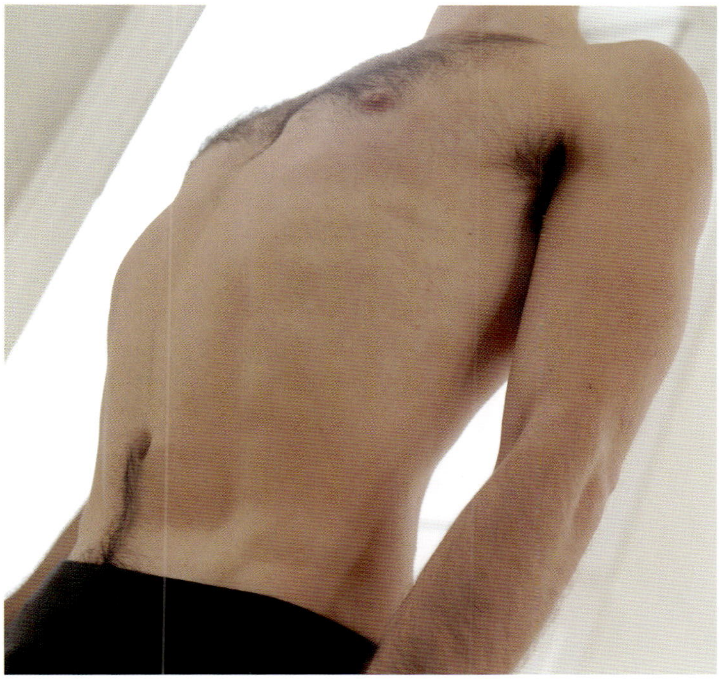

2 front If your chest puffs out and up, then you know you would see a heightened thoracic curve. You need to allow the chest to soften and the tummy to lift.

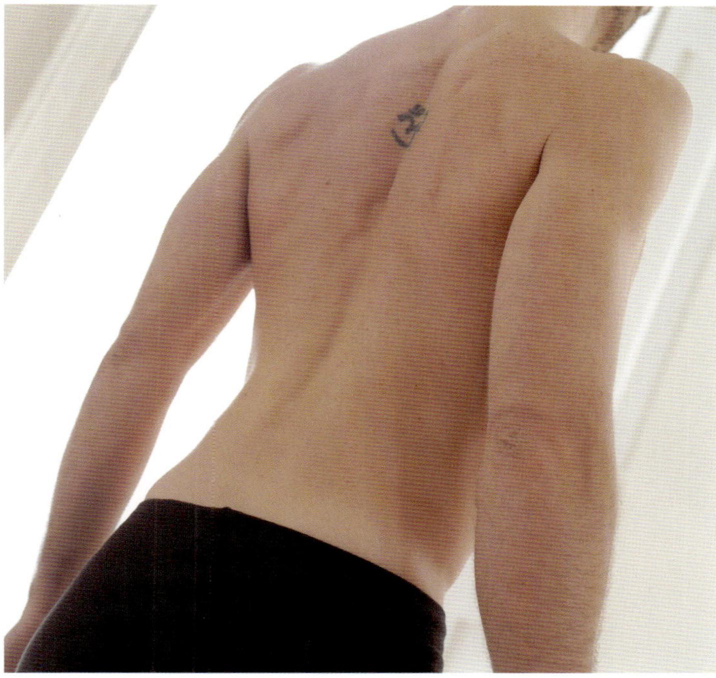

2 back Imagine that your kidneys are being squeezed by this curve in the lower back, and you will understand that it is worth correcting it. This is what happens when the chest is out.

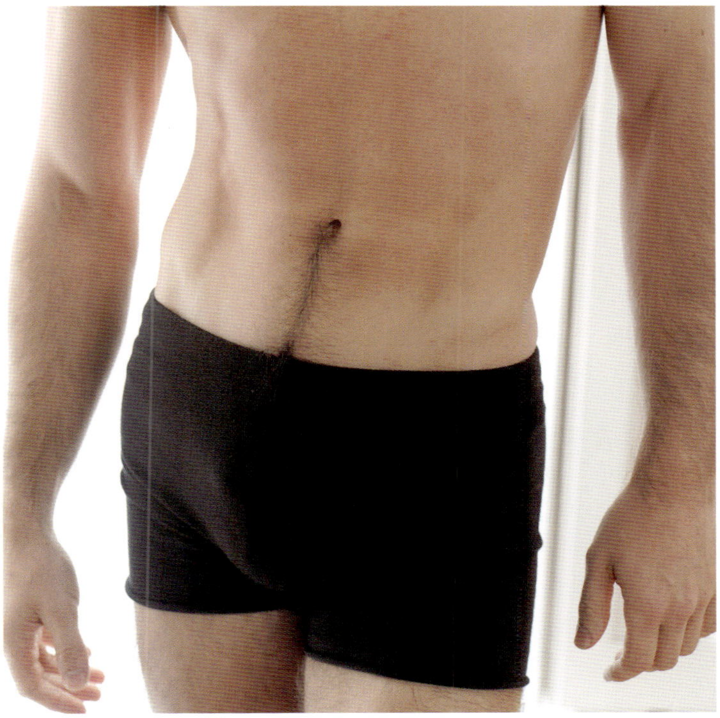

3 front If one side of your body protrudes and twists, it is merely mirroring the arc of your spine. You have to find out which of your sitting bones needs to lift, ground it, and then lift it into the rest of the body.

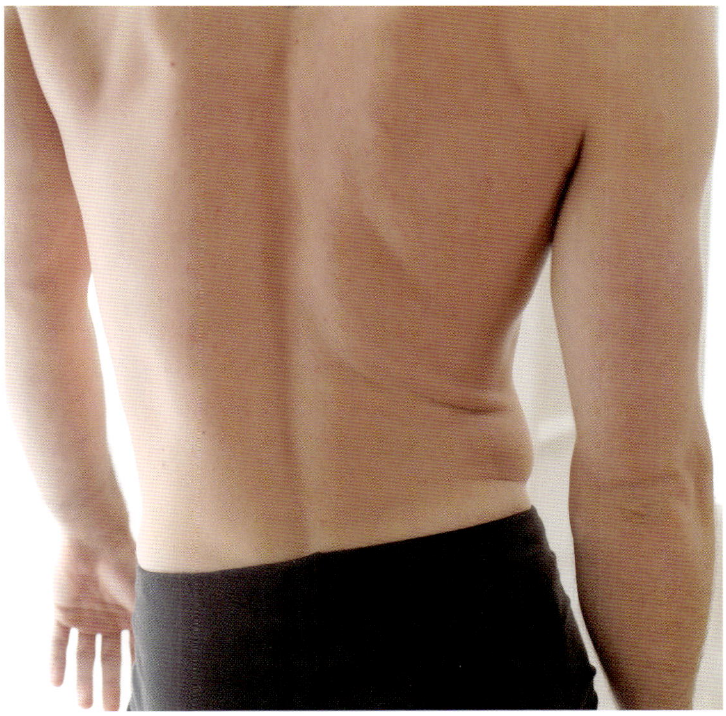

3 back If one side of your waist is longer than the other, as in this picture, then your spine is collapsing or bending to the opposing side. You need to push down the sitting bone to lengthen the waist to pull the spine back into line.

Solid Grounding

Even the most generally perfect bodies have at least one area that needs special attention. If you are reading this bemoaning how much of your body does not work, think about two things. First, your body is already fairly perfect because it has got you this far. Second, the work never stops for anyone; perfection is never achieved.

Be aware of the power of imbalances in the body. Continually repeating an action with an unbalanced shoulder or hip girdle will guarantee a habitual pattern that will twist and corrupt your body. You will not realize this until your body seems to give out for the smallest and most ridiculous of reasons: "I must have twisted strangely", or, "It happened just as I was getting out of bed."

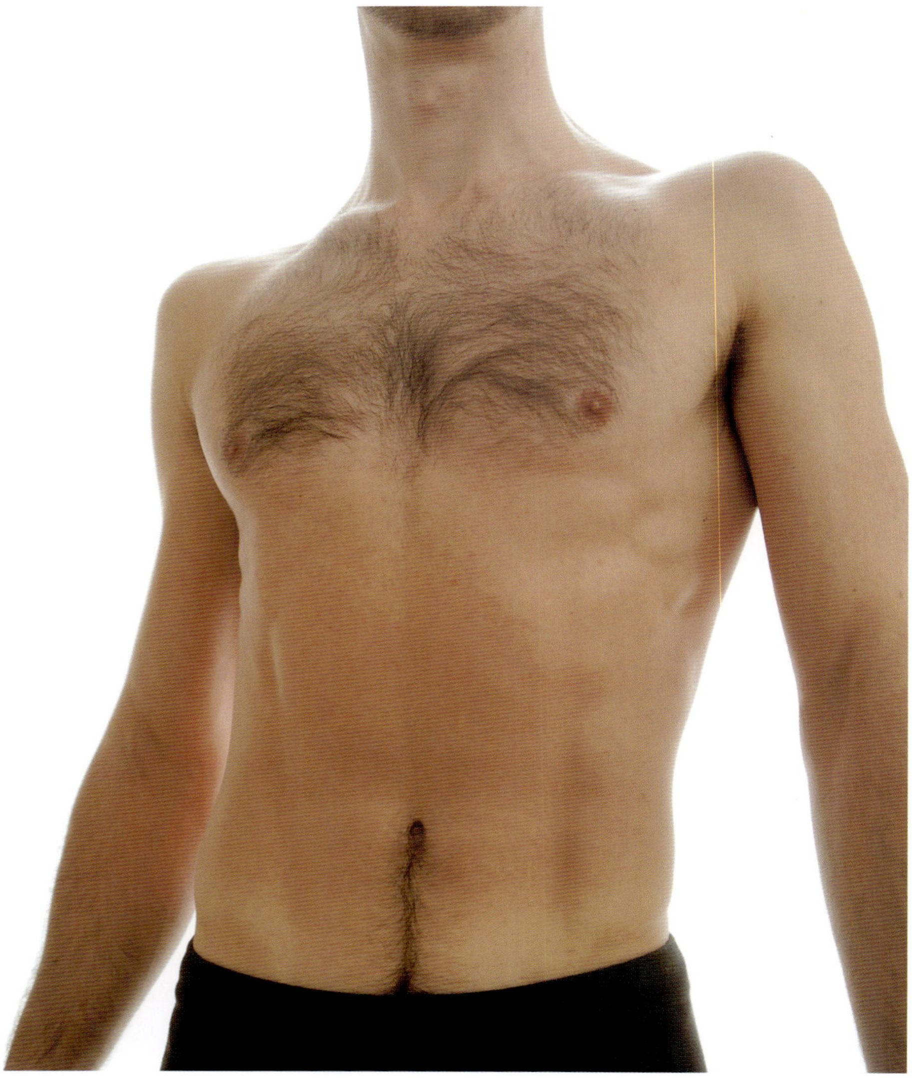

However, the good news is that there are many bodies that have gone from being round-shouldered, humped, arched and twisted to long, open, lithe and strong. You will need to be constantly vigilant and aware, but with this will come the joy of truly knowing your own body, of truly knowing yourself.

It is recommended that you find an excellent physiotherapist, as he or she will aid your awareness of where you are habitually tight or soft. He or she will recommend exercises, probably quite similar to the ones in this book, which you must practise regularly. Simply having a diagnosis and a list of exercises is not enough; if you do not put these exercises into practice, you will not change.

Keep changing

Change the way you use your muscles, for they are the main reason why you are pulled out of shape. Your body is not set in stone. The only limit to change is you.

Do not be scared of treating your body to a session at the physiotherapist or masseur/se to loosen your muscles. If you invest in your body, it should run well for a lot longer: you do that for your car, after all. By taking your body to a specialist in bodies – whether a doctor, a physiotherapist, or a masseur/se – you can find out how to take an interest in your speciality. But whatever their advice, make sure that it makes sense in your body.

Take pride in being special. You have the best reason to become exceptional: to make your weakness your strength. If you can be brave enough to find, accept, know and love your weaknesses, you will find an inspiration that could unlock far more than the balancing of your hips.

left Standing on one leg, wearing high-heeled shoes, slouching or sitting badly when you are working: all these things will contribute to poor posture. In the long run this may cause scoliosis, or curvature of the spine. It is never too late to take control of your habits, and your body.

Flat Feet – Flat Feeling

If your arches have collapsed then you will not be leaping around with a spring in your step. It is crucial to get your foundations correct, then you will have a stable support structure for the rest of your body.

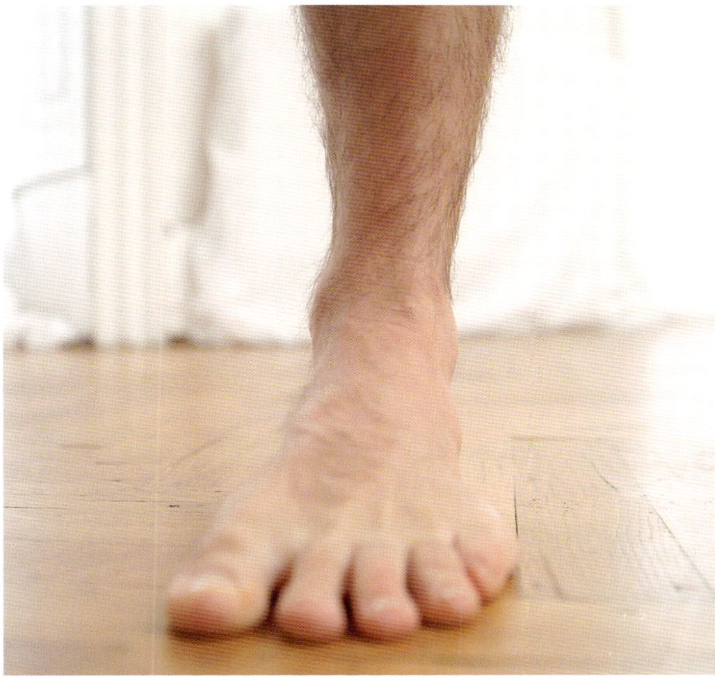

correct The ankle is in the middle of the foot with the toes spreading the weight of the body evenly across the entire ball and heel of the foot. When the foot looks like this, there is a natural spring to it, as opposed to flat and floor bound. To find this balance and placement of the ankle on the foot, have a look at the Jimmy Choo posture.

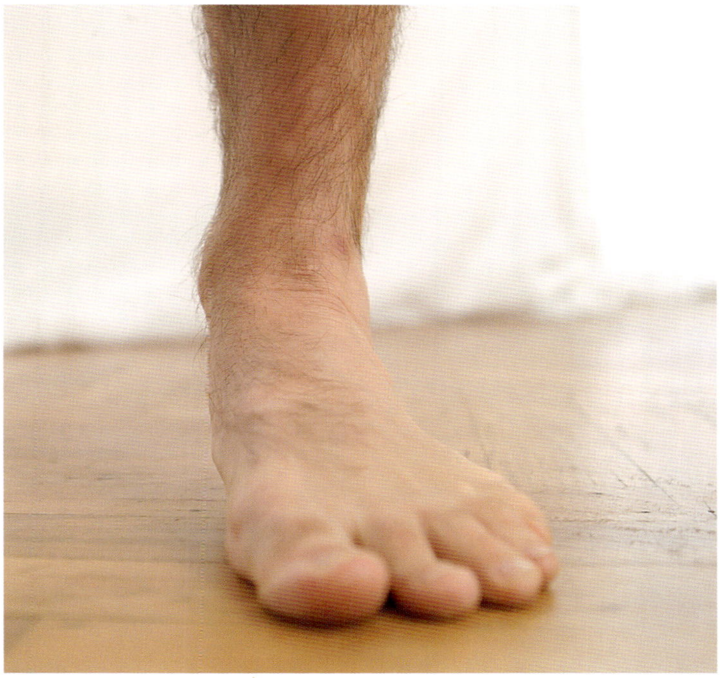

incorrect Look how the ankle bone is falling away from the centre of the foot. This collapse not only brings about a collapsed arch – flat feet – but also gradually pulls the big toe towards the outside of the foot. This will eventually affect the inside of the knee – knock knees – and then affect the hip as it travels up the leg.

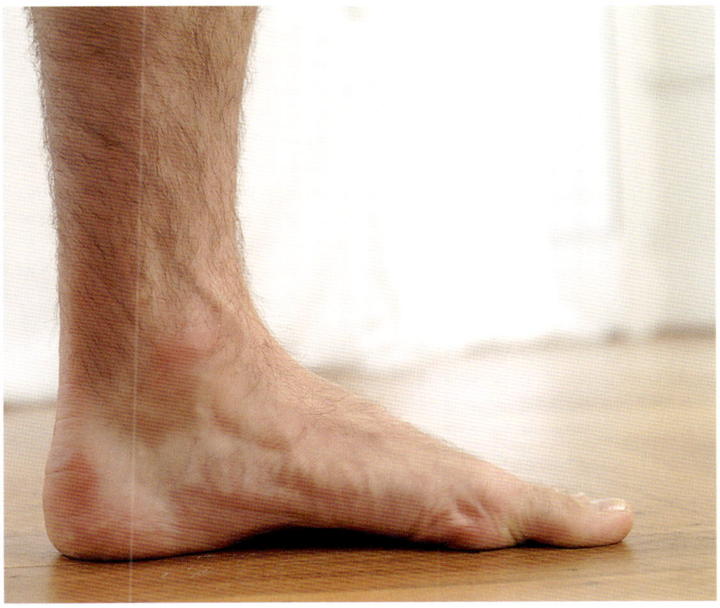

correct Compare the picture on the right with this and you will see the muscles in this foot holding up the arch and the ankle in the middle of the foot. The arch is there in most of us, but if it is not, in most cases it just requires us to condition the muscles of the foot for the arch to appear.

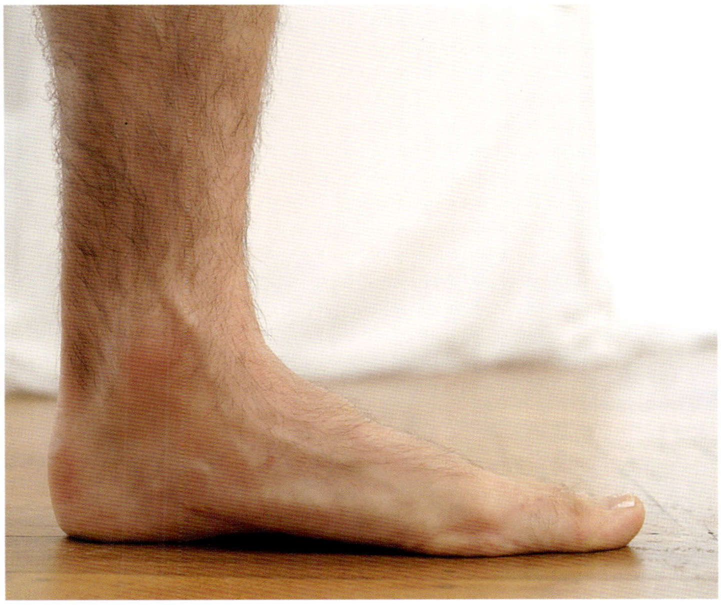

incorrect Look how little gap there is between the floor and the foot. In such little space, it is hard to feel a lift or bounce. The lift has to start where your body is in contact with the floor, and if the foot has collapsed, there will not be much lift. Try doing the Jimmy Choo exercises whenever you can to correct this condition.

Ankles, Knees and Hips

Let's begin with the ankles. Get a mirror and get honest. Have a good look. Which ankle corresponds to which picture?

You will probably find that one ankle lies differently from the other. When you stand, your feet probably do not point forwards at the same angle. This imbalance is repeated each time you step, walk or run, winding its way up through your knee to your hip and into your spine.

To correct the imbalance, let's use the mirror, your feet and some of your concentration.

Knees

Whether you are bow-legged or knock-kneed, by paying attention to the relationship between your ankles and your hips you can literally lengthen your legs. When you maintain the lift in your arches, your ankles will not want to collapse. Down Dog is a perfect posture in which to work on knees and ankles. After all, you can look at them from the best position. Practise rolling your ankles and playing with the feet, until you feel the relationship between your hips and your heels.

Hips: learn to be here

When someone claims that one of their legs is longer than the other, it is almost always actually the case that they are holding one of their hips higher than the other. Do you cross one leg in preference to the other? Do you stand with your weight on one hip? These habits mirror and reinforce an existing imbalance. This is not to say that you must sit or stand properly on both sitting bones or feet for the rest of your days, only that you need to become aware of your body.

Go back to feeling. Are your hip bones even? Go back to the hip opening sequence at the beginning of the book.

The Jimmy Choo

This exercise is named after the designer of beautiful, but unfeasibly high-heeled shoes. it is designed to help you overcome fallen arches. Simply lift and lower your heels, keeping everything in line – it's harder than it sounds – and your feet should wake up. You can use something to help you balance, but if possible keep your hands on your hips and see if you can feel a lift in your tummy as you raise and lower yourself. This will bring your awareness to the connection between your feet and you.

left Down Dog is the best posture to examine the relationship between your feet, ankles and knees because you are looking straight at them. Play inside this posture. Try collapsing your ankles followed by bringing them into the middle of the foot. As you do, feel your knees move in and out of line and maybe even become aware of the use of the muscles in your groin. It is up to you to make time within this and all postures to learn how best your body works.

The Jimmy Choo

It really doesn't matter if you can't get your heels as high as is shown in the picture on the left. Push the balls of the big toes down and feel the lift of the heels up. As long as you feel this, you are heading in the right direction. With this feeling you will begin to make your foundations firm.

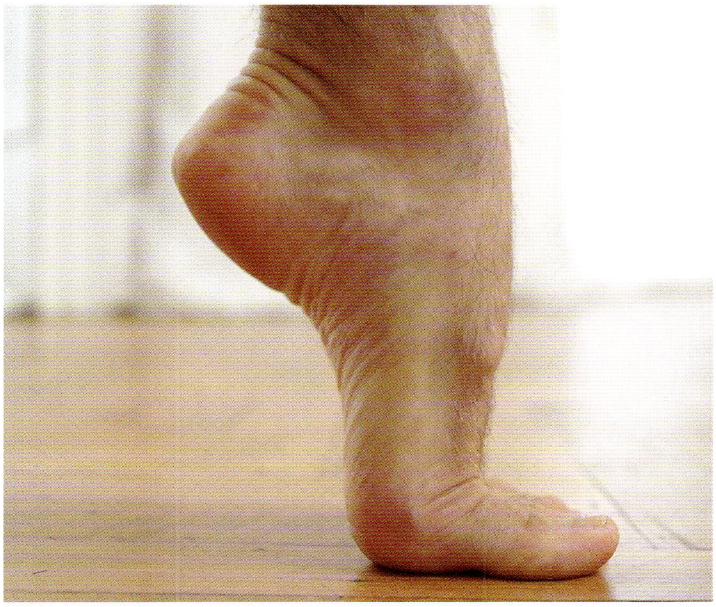

1 Stand with your feet facing forwards directly underneath your hips, everything perfectly parallel. Lift your heels up tall, on tiptoes (demi-point). Try to lift them directly above the balls of your big toes. Make sure that the ankles do not fall to the left or right and you will find that the feet are stimulated, the arch stretched and strengthened and strong lines formed from the foot through the ankle to the knee and hip.

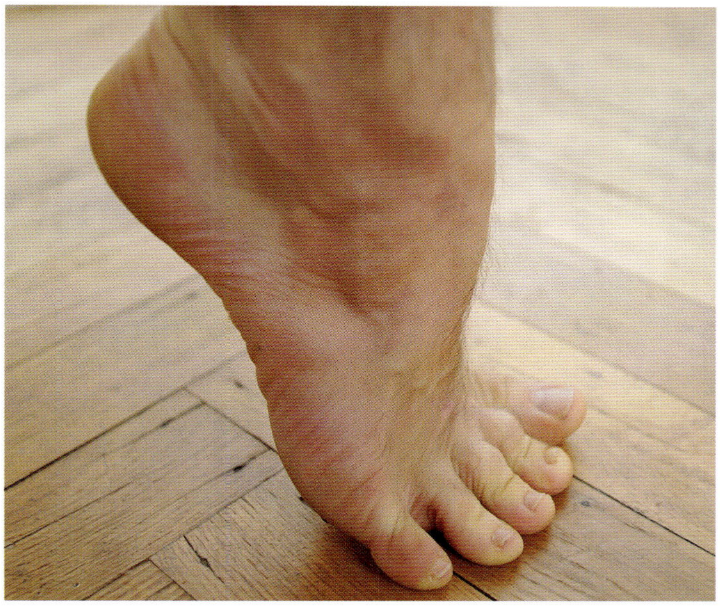

2 Open your toes and spread them wide to give you a firm base, pressing them down to help you balance. When you have risen up and down on your toes enough to feel familiar with the action, concentrate on going straight up, trying not to lean forwards each time you lift up. Use the wall to help if you need to, but when you lift up directly, you will feel the direct stimulation of the arches of the feet.

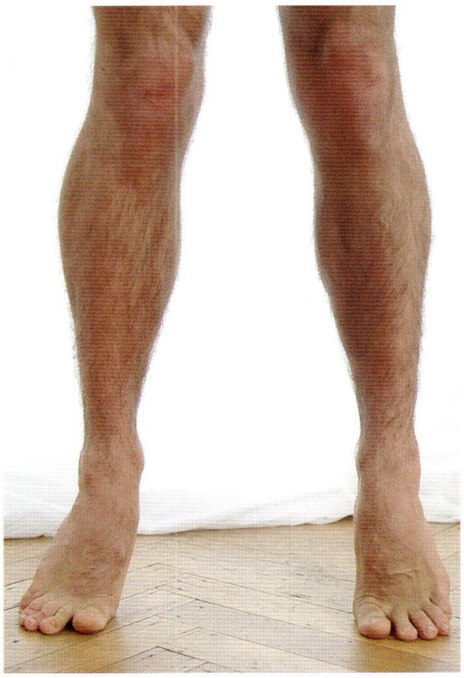

3 If your ankles collapse inwards stretch your little toes to keep your ankles in the middle of your body.

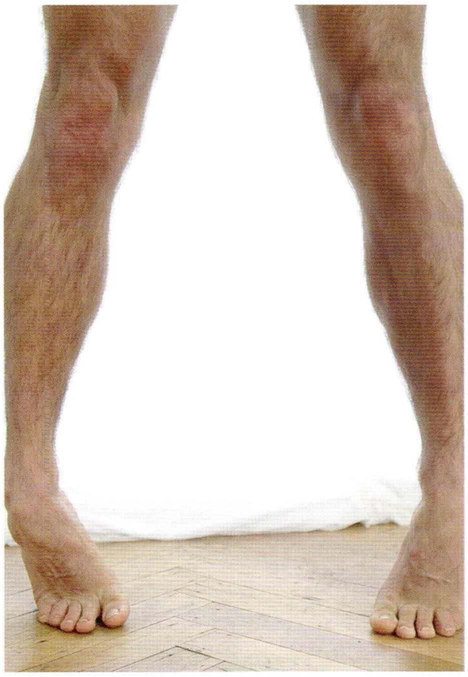

4 When your ankles fall out press the ball of your big toe into the floor and stretch your big toe forwards.

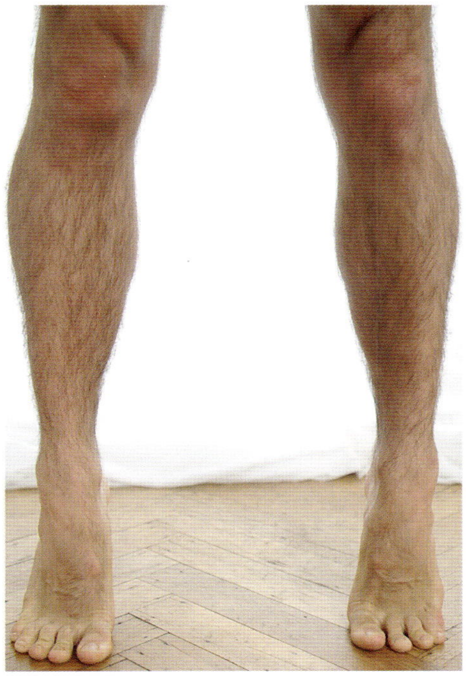

5 When both ankles are over the ball of your foot push your ankle forwards to help stimulate your arches.

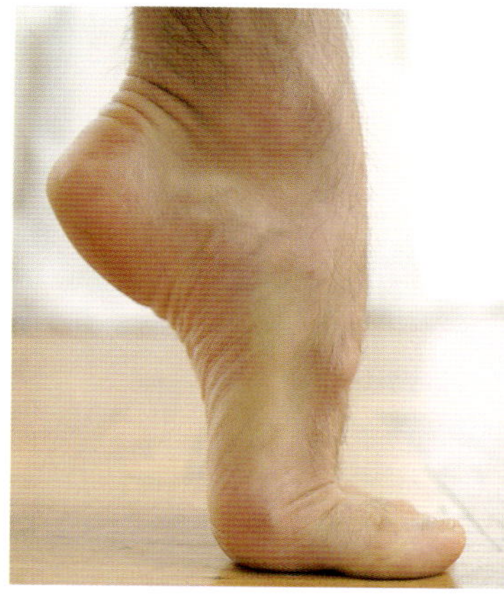

Standing
postures

Now you have found where the core strength of your body is centred, it is time to begin your practice with the standing postures. Some of these may be a challenge to your body, so begin gently and gradually build up, holding the poses for slightly longer periods of time.

Standing Start

By now you should have successfully figured out how to feel and use your core strength. You can hold yourself, warm up your body, move and, most important, feel when your body is working happily. Now it is time to challenge your body with standing postures.

To begin with, the demands made on the body by these postures will feel unnatural. But remember the idea of flow around the body. By using your core strength to hold you up, you begin to use the body as a pump to increase the flow of energy. So you should approach this chapter in two ways, looking at both individual shapes and postures and how you flow between them.

There are instructions on where you will feel each posture most, but it is important that you really look at the pictures and trust that your brain will make sense of them and interpret them into your body – it might help to use a mirror. Remember, there is no wrong feeling, only you, at that moment. If you look and read carefully you will have more than enough information to decide whether what you are doing is as beneficial as it can be. Bear in mind that you will fully feel a posture only after practice over time.

Flowing movement

The standing postures are designed to flow together. You can take a quick look through the book to see the bigger picture, but just as you are made up of little pieces, so is the sequence. Try to enjoy putting the sequence together, much as you might have enjoyed putting yourself together with your core in the first section.

Do not be scared to stop, play, or notice when something in you begins to feel. If you feel really comfortable, enjoy the feeling of your body working, flowing, not giving in to gravity. When a posture is hard, try the alternative version. When it is easy, stay longer, go deeper, extend further. If you feel discomfort, you should check that your core is working properly and that you are being true to your alignment and flexibility. Do not persist with a posture that is causing you pain, but carefully check the instructions and pictures again. Remember that almost all injuries happen when you are not listening, feeling and being honest.

left Build on your ability to feel and use your core strength as you move on to standing postures. After reading the instructions and looking at the photographs, listen to your own body as you practise the postures.

right Be aware of the flow of energy as you move from one standing posture to another and make use of your core strength to increase that flow. Not only will this be beneficial, it will also make your practice more enjoyable.

Lunge

Learn to love this posture. Inside it are myriad possibilities, all held static by the lift in the pubic bone and extensions through the thighs. The back heel in demi-point will stimulate the arch of the foot, which in turn allows you to open the hip. Lift the heel and drive the thigh back.

1 Stand with the feet together, extend forwards and touch the floor beside the feet with your fingertips. Look up, lifting the chest, and stretch one leg out behind you. Push one knee forwards and the other backwards (only one way makes sense) and feel the length between the back of your head and heel.

2 Place your hands on your knee as shown here. Put all your emphasis on lifting your pubic bone, lifting the back heel and opening the hip. The arms are down, but are your shoulder blades down too? This is the easy option, so if your legs are tired or if you want to give your tummy a helping hand, stop at this point.

▸ **3** Prop the shoulder blades to lift your arms and regain the feeling of freedom in the neck and shoulders. You should feel as though the torso is exactly the same as when standing, so the legs are required to hold you elegant and tall. The more power there is in your legs, the more lift and openness you will feel in the hips and body.

◂ **incorrect** The front thigh is lower, so all the weight of the body is being carried at the bottom of the lower back, instead of in the hip and thighs. The bulging tummy mirrors the overarched spine, something guaranteed to create an ache if held for too long. Notice also the back foot. Keep the hip and ankle happy by opening both.

Pert-buttocked Warrior

This posture carries straight on from the Lunge. Lower the arms to shoulder height from the full Lunge, and turn to face the side, rather than the front. This posture will help to open the hips, strengthen the legs and knees and reinforce the core strength that you have built up.

▶ **the full posture** From a Lunge, roll the back heel to the floor and allow the hip to follow. If you keep the front knee and hip in the same place you turn flat and into Pert Buttocked Warrior. The pertness comes from a lift in the pubic bone and a rolling backwards of the thigh muscles. This back view shows you the length of the spine which comes from the lift in the pubic bone, the evenness of the hips and the breadth of the back. Notice that the shoulder blades are down and that the neck is free.

◀**close-up** Here is a close-up of the buttocks, because you need to really feel how lifting the pubic bone and rolling the thighs backwards affects the hips. Put your hands on your bottom and feel this work. You will also notice that the strength of this posture cannot fail to open even the most stubborn of closed hips. The right angle in the knee can be sacrificed for the sake of good buttocks, since stubborn hips are far more important to feel and open than trying for perfection without knowing where it is.

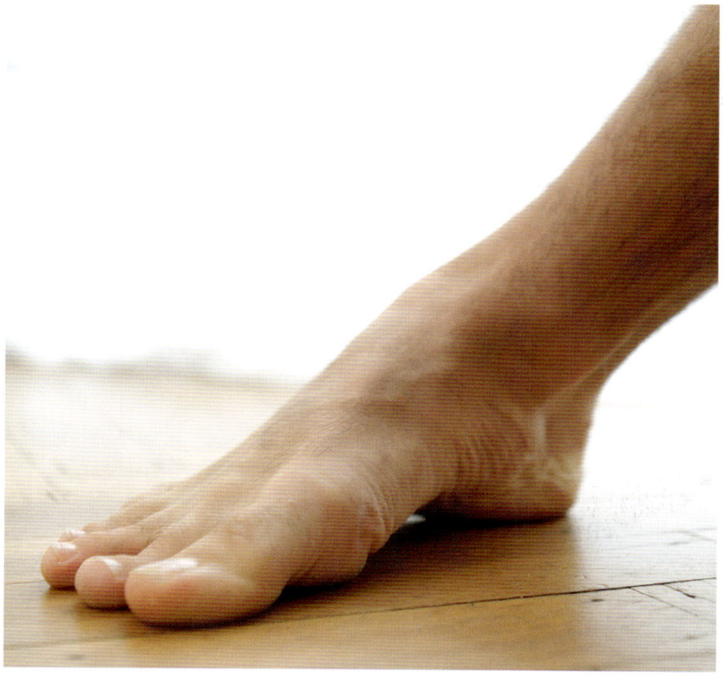

close-up The back foot is again very important. After it has been stimulated in the Lunge, you should keep a lift in the ankle while pushing the heel and ball of the big toe down. This will allow you to feel the body supported by both legs, rather than just by the front thigh. The more you can activate the muscles of the back leg, the easier it will be to feel the connection between the foot and groin. Try it and ground yourself. Through activating the arch of the back foot you will be able to feel the support of the back leg.

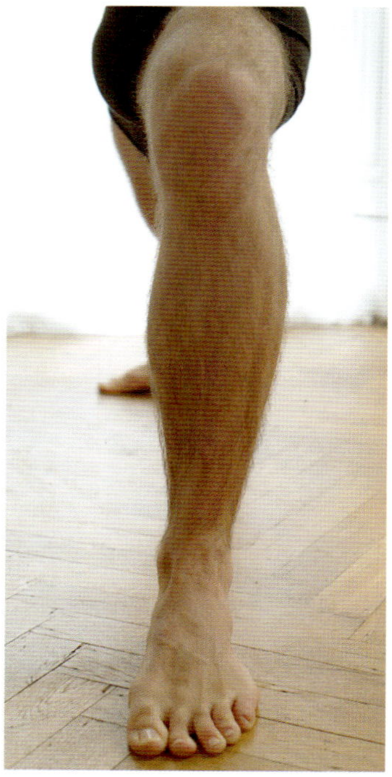

correct Look at the long line from the big toe to the knee to the hip. Notice also how the hips are facing flat to one side. Try to make yourself flat in this posture to benefit your hip flexibility and core strength and for the sake of your knee joint.

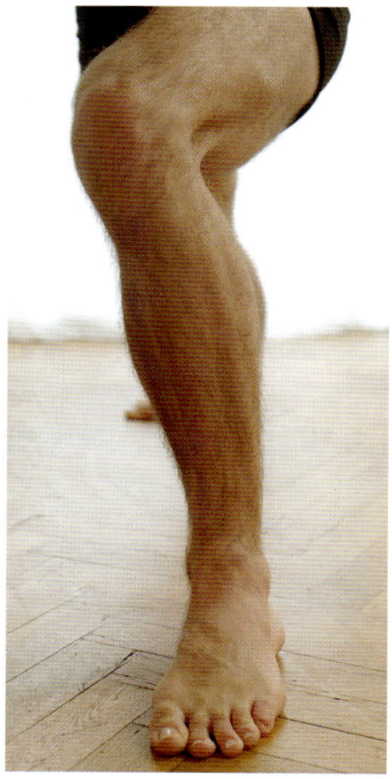

incorrect Look at the lines. See the stress on the inside of the front knee and how hard the outside of the shin has to work. The arch of the foot has also diminished. The back hip has rolled forwards so the hip cannot be opening as much.

Side Lunge

In this posture, the front leg has not changed position since the Lunge; the body has just moved around it. When the muscles work together, you will feel how they hold you long and upright and how the opposing forces of your legs provide balanced stability.

1 From the Warrior, lean the body towards the bent knee. Although the elbow is resting on the knee, the length is maintained along both sides of the waist. The hand on the bottom allows the sitting bone to be pulled backwards, and the knee to be pushed forwards.

2 In a simple Side Lunge the arm is lifted until the bicep reaches the nose. Notice the long line from head to heel, and the breadth to the back. Shoulder blades should be kept down and the back of the leg long. Beginners should stop at this stage of the posture.

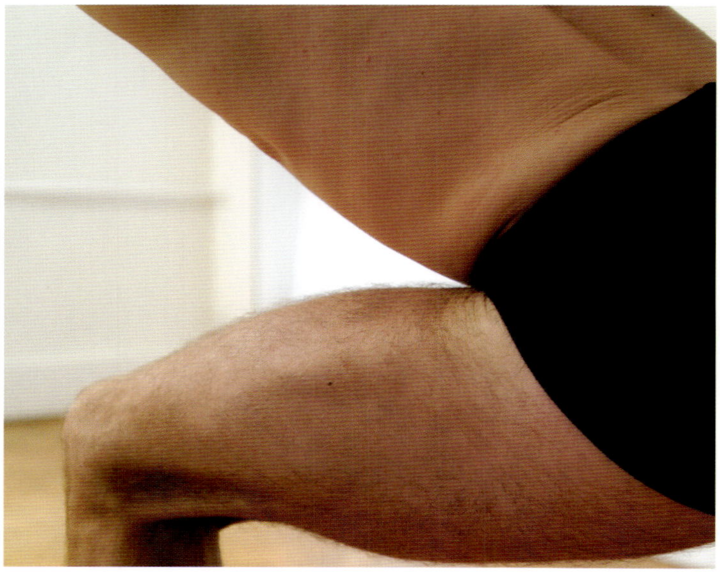

close-up Notice how the length in the side of the waist is mirrored by that in the spine. The legs, both pushing forwards and pulling backwards, allow the hip to hinge and become stable at the same time, two opposing forces balancing one another to leave stillness. Remember your stomach: keep it off your thigh.

incorrect A nice try with the arms, but a lot of collapse everywhere else. See how the angle between the thigh and waist is not sharp, meaning that the spine has to bend to take the body over. The weight of the body is therefore being held by little muscles, those of the curved spine.

▶ **3** Raise the left arm above the head, keeping the shoulders relaxed and down. The angle from above demonstrates why this posture feels so good. Look at the line from the back of the head. It feels as though the line grows from the floor and allows the back to broaden and separate. Notice the gap between the arms and ears, meaning that tension is held away from the head.

Thigh Lunge

From the Side Lunge, turn the body to face the front foot. Body weight should be distributed equally between the front and back leg. It is called the Knee Trembler, because the weight of the body is directly over the front thigh and when this thigh gets tired the knee begins to tremble.

1 Keeping the back heel flat on the floor forces you to feel your inner thigh and back leg. Even though your hands and arms are helping to support your torso, keep your tummy up and in. Try not to collapse and stick your bottom out. Beginners can stop here.

2 Take your arms back like a bird, but spread your wings – your shoulder blades – to cpen your back. Remember that you are never trying to constrict the body, so squeezing your shoulder blades together to "fly" your arms back simply draws tension to your neck.

close-up This back view explains the essence of the posture. The length in the back must mean that the front of the body is long as well. Lean forward from the root of the back heel, but always keep your body free and let it hinge from the front knee and hips.

incorrect The collapse in the upper back means there is even more weight in the lower spine. If your back is feeling the weight, lift your chest and pull your tummy in until your thighs begin to burn gently. Notice how the shoulders are around the ears. Drop your shoulders and extend your neck. Remember the length from your head to your heel.

▶ **3** Raise the arms over the head. Notice that the neck is long, the shoulder blades are low, so again there is no tension in the neck. Notice how the tummy is drawn in and up, helping to maintain the length of the lower spine. Notice, too, the long, straight line through the body. Enjoy separating the knees – one forwards, the other back – and using your back to stabilize yourself. Here's a quick challenge. Can you use your tummy so that you feel buoyant?

Dog Split

This posture – a cross between Down Dog and the splits – is really quite tricky. My advice is just to go ahead and do the posture. Make sure that you stretch from your back heel to your top toes. In fact, once you're there, it is actually quite fun.

1 After the Thigh Lunge, place your hands on the floor and straighten your leg. Do not blindly push your knee straight, but push your heel down and lift your bottom up. Create some space and some lift off the floor. A quick challenge. Can you lift your leg up between your hands?

2 This is how the Dog Split is most often performed. The leg is lifted back until it makes a long line from wrist to toes. To lift the leg, squeeze your bottom and lengthen your hip. Try looking at your ankle over the bottom foot. Is there a line all the way from your big toe, ankle, knee and hip bone? Beginners, stop at this point.

incorrect This version of the posture is a common mistake. Inflexibility in the chest means that it is hard to keep the shoulders open and arms correctly positioned. A desire to lift the back leg high results in a lifted hip and an inability to detect whether the back leg is straight. The head is up, so welcoming neck tension, and the back heel is down, adding to the collapse.

▶ **3** Feel the floor under your hands and push all the way from your wrists to your toes. Keep your shoulders braced, even and away from your ears. Your hips should be even and your ribs slightly contracted.

◀ **advanced** You should not attempt this advanced version unless you can already do the splits. If you can, bounce the back foot forwards, root your heel and extend as much as you can through the front hip. Push your bottom up with your thigh (not with your arms, as this tends to lead to constriction), and your abdomen can help. You can use your head and a relaxed neck as a weight to pull the leg up.

Press Up

This posture's very mechanical nature makes it a constant challenge. Sometimes known as the Staff pose, the body is held long by the torso muscles and, primarily in this posture, the back. If your shoulder blades pop up away from your ribs, try and perfect the easy version.

1 From the Dog Split, bring yourself to this position, pushing your chest high off the floor and lifting your pubic bone up into your abdomen. This will hold you up and away from the floor. To lower yourself, just bend your elbows, nothing else.

2 As you lower your body by bending the elbows, notice that the shoulder blades have not lifted and the chest is still lifted off the floor. Feel this posture in your tummy and back, not your shoulders and chest. If you are just beginning, keep your knees on the floor.

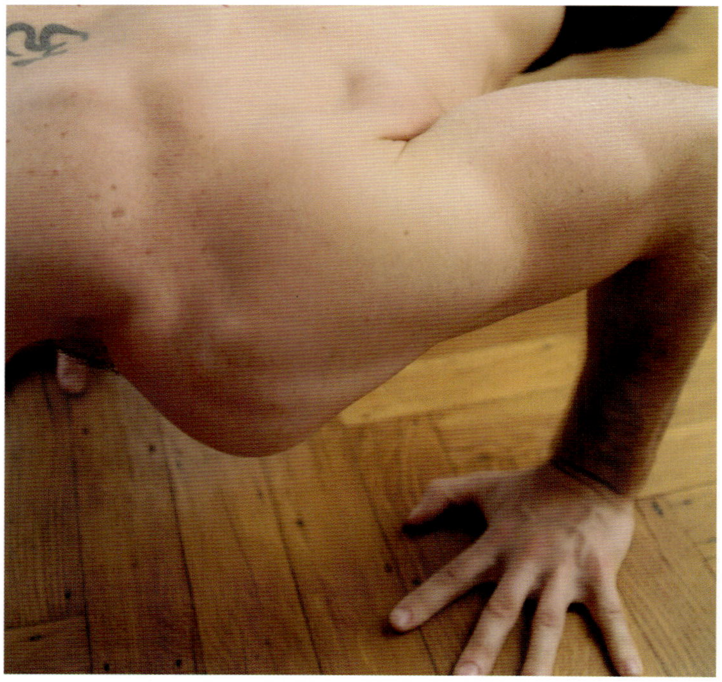

close-up Your back is your strength in this posture. Tuck your shoulder blades down and away from each other to activate your back. Look at the shoulder and the muscle that leads to the neck; there is very little tension in there.

incorrect This is a case of being head bound – when you move your head you think that all of you has moved. People think that the most important part of this posture is to get down and so sacrifice all integrity to get there: collapsed shoulders, chest taking the weight, flaring elbows which detach the arms from any back strength, and a soggy middle.

▶ **3** The arms go no deeper than in this illustration, keeping the shoulders in line with the elbows. Any lower and the chest will constrict and the integrity of your shoulder stability will be compromised. This posture should have no constriction anywhere in the body; in fact, you should actively open your chest, shoulders and back.

Up Dog

The more you understand the Press Up, the easier and more enjoyable Up Dog will become. Since the work was in the back in the Press Up, you now know just where to lift from to take you into this posture with your chest and shoulders open.

1 The width between the shoulders can be achieved only when the work is inside the back, allowing the chest to open. Notice how the tummy is pulled in and up. The elbows are open, rather than the arm, shoulder and back muscles taking the weight of the body.

2 The thighs are raised off the floor. The shoulders are wide, but follow the "V" shape down the abdomen and you can see that the muscles are pulled in and the pubic bone is lifted up, keeping the thighs off the ground.

incorrect Can you spot the mistakes? The neck is not long, so something is wrong. The chest and shoulders are narrowed forwards, when this posture is meant to open them. The thighs are resting flat on the floor, offering no protection to the lower spine.

incorrect The head thrown back without any support means that the cervical (neck) vertebrae are compressed. It is obvious that the chest is not open, and the position of the arms means that there is little hope of involving the back to help lift. Get your wrists beneath your shoulders and push the floor away from you.

▶ **3** See the breadth of the back. The shoulder blades are contained within the back and as wide as they can be to let the head float on top. The redness in the back shows the level of exertion. Use your shoulder blades to lift you and keep your tummy in and legs strong to protect your lower spine.

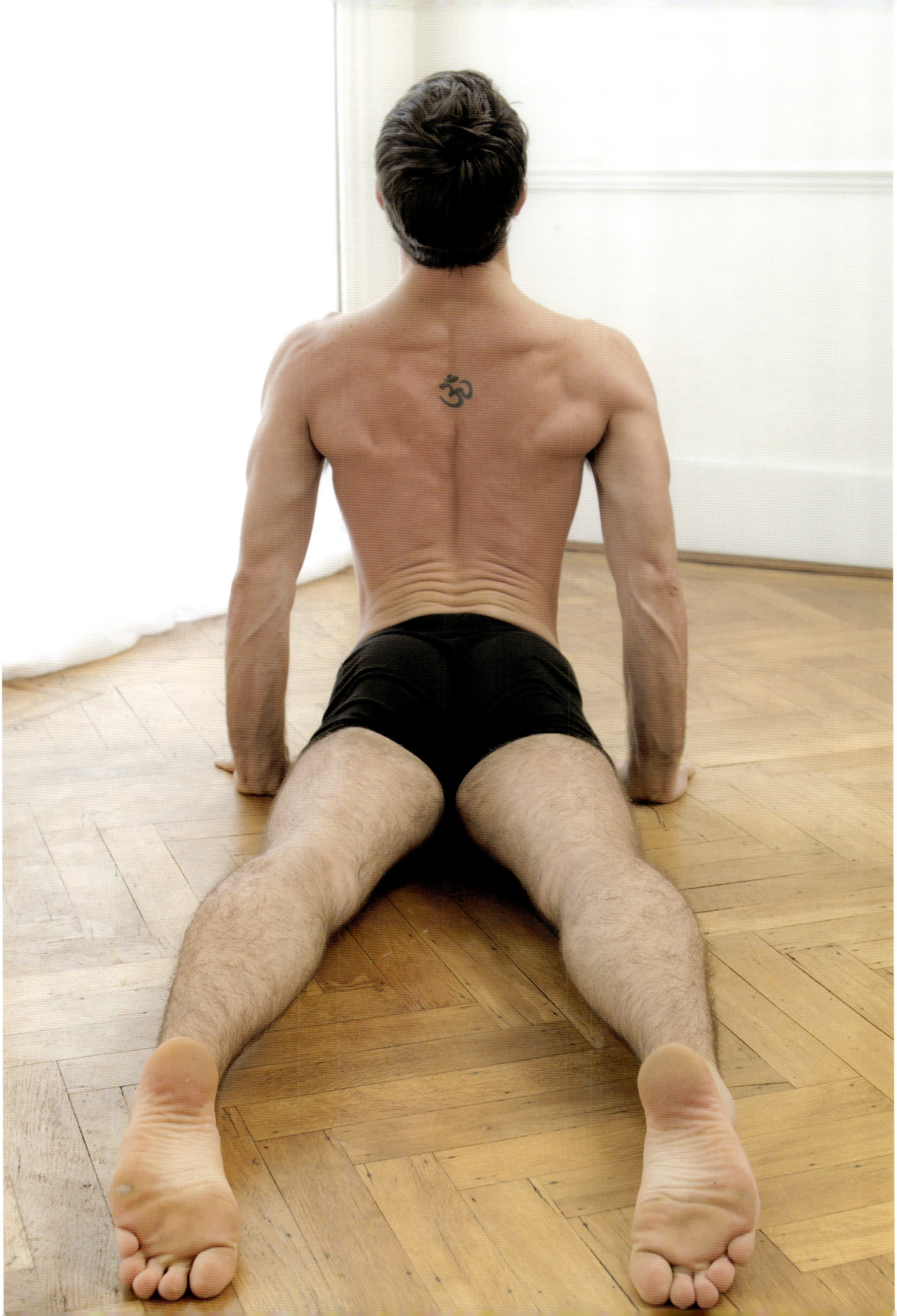

Down Dog

I would prefer to call this posture Bottom Up, for when the sitting bones come up, the lower spine extends and the abdomen lifts up to support the spine. Another name for this pose is Inverted V, and this picture shows the significance of the name.

◀ **1** Down Dog is not easy, as we have a tendency to narrow everything, especially when our legs complain at our bodies being at such a strange angle to them. To flow from Up Dog to here, just pull up the tummy, roll over the toes and push from the wrists to the bottom. Here, the heels do not yet reach the floor, since the Achilles tendons and calves are still rather tight. However, the shoulder blades are wide and away from the head. Keep an eye on your ankles. Is there a line from big toe to hip bones? Are the arches in your feet active?

▶ **2** See how little tension there is inside the back and shoulders. The neck can dangle free and the distance between the shoulders is as wide as possible. This means that any stretch in the chest is not felt at the expense of space and freedom inside the back. Broaden your back, open your shoulder blades and get your shoulders away from your ears. Don't be scared of taking your hands wider than your shoulders, as this will make these actions easier. Use the breadth in the back to open your chest.

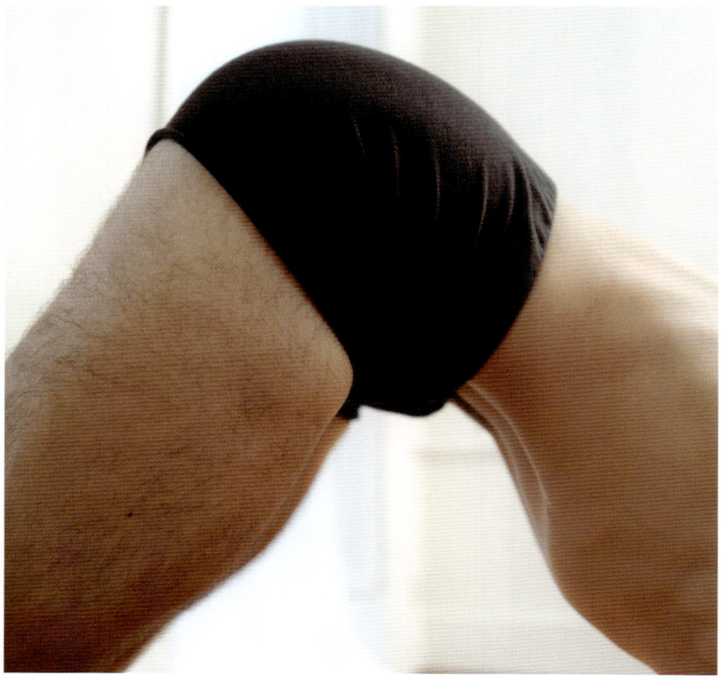

close-up Try really spiking your bottom up while pushing your heels down and keeping your stomach muscles lifted. Imagine the sitting bones up near the ceiling. This will keep you light on your hands, long in your spine and free in your hamstrings.

incorrect This demonstrates how not to do this posture. Look at the big curve in the back. This shows that this is more like an inverted "U" than a "V". The neck is long and dangling, but look at the tension in the shoulders. In this position you will find more weight in the wrists, whereas if you look at the close-up, left, you can see that most of the weight in the body should actually be felt in the hips. Don't worry about your heels. Lift your bottom and lengthen your spine.

incorrect This picture looks strong – look at all the activity around the upper back, neck and shoulders. But see how narrow the shoulder girdle is: the distance between the shoulders is minimal. How can this be considered an open posture? Look beyond the muscular appearance and see the constriction.

Jump

This Jump is the link between Down Dog and the Forward Bend. Any jump is a challenge until you know you can do it, so this is a lot easier to do when you believe your body will let you. Explode, fly, bounce your bottom in the air – gravity will help with the landing.

1 From Down Dog, bend your knees and push your bottom back and up. This should enable you to feel the leg muscles begin to work. Coil your body up as far away from your hands as possible. Pull in the tummy to hold the spine long and lift the heels high.

2 Push your legs straight up and see how high you can bounce. Lift your heels so your stomach pulls right in. Look at your tummy to see where it's gone. As silly as this may seem, it will help you pull higher off the floor, which in turn introduces you to feeling the lift.

3 Extend right through your hands and arms, since these are the struts that hold up the body when you spring forwards. You are less likely to collapse if you keep your arms strong. From the coiled back position, push your legs straight up, bouncing as high as you can.

incorrect This position says, "I'm scared". Notice the way the back is rounded, the shoulders are rolled in and the body is already heading towards the hands. How can you expect to bounce high from here if the spine is not long, the arms not strong and the thighs not curled to pounce? Try bouncing on the spot before bouncing forwards.

▶ **4** Here is how the feet should meet the floor – as though you have been folded in the middle. Stretch your legs all the way to your toes, so you feel you open up as you jump up. Suck your tummy in so hard that you feel you can stay up there. Aim to land with your feet in between the hands, ready for the Forward Bend on the following page. This position requires strength, balance and flexibility, and when you find them, your body can move and jump just as you imagine it can.

Forward Bend

On landing from your Jump, you are almost there. Find the hinge in the hips, and then allow both the backs of the legs and the lower back to lengthen from the top point. All you need to do is push your heels down and lift your bottom. It's that simple.

1 A Forward Bend does not require straight legs. Always keep your chest against your thighs to maintain the maximum length in your lower spine. Pull your tummy off your thighs to help you lengthen the lower spine. Then simply push your heels down and push your bottom up. Do not push your knees straight, unless they go easily, as all this will do is take the work away from your upper thighs.

2 Aim for a perfect hinge from your hips no matter how straight you can press your legs. All that pushing your legs backwards will achieve is taking your knee joint beyond the position where it functions most efficiently. Learn to carry the weight of your body in your hips, not in the backs of your knees. Allow your head to relax while you keep lifting your bottom.

incorrect This picture is just to remind you to keep your shoulders away from your head. Allow the back to broaden. It is so easy in your eagerness to bend down low to use the wrong muscles and take the effort and attention away from where it should be – in your hips. Use your legs to go forwards; they are a lot bigger and closer to the hip hinge than your arms.

▶ **3** If you find the Forward Bend easy, take your upper body out of the equation and lift your arms. Can you keep your back broad, your legs long and your chest on your thighs without the aid of your arms? Pull your stomach off your thighs, yet push your head and chest on to your legs. Feel the work in the thighs and abdomen, as this will strengthen the hips and, in turn, deepen the stretch.

incorrect This looks quite flexible and the hands are touching the floor, but look how the spine is bowing to achieve this. Here the hip hinge is wide open. This means the stress is carried in the back and knees, both a little more fragile than the hips and thighs. A Forward Bend does not require straight legs, it requires a movement of the hips towards the thighs.

Twisted
postures

These are positions to challenge the inside of your body as well as the outside. If you practise them regularly you will feel the benefits in your digestive system and also in your waistline, proving that true beauty starts from within.

Seated Twist and Prayer

It may take some time to become familiar with the sensation of space in your back, but keep searching for it because when you can apply it to a twist, you'll feel a freedom in your spine that you will want to keep.

◀ 1 Begin by standing upright and place your palms together at shoulder height, but as you do, keep as much distance between your elbows as possible. Keep this space as you bend your knees, sit down and twist, for it will help you to maintain some space between your thighs and tummy and also inside your back.

▶ 2 Think of taking your chest forwards and slightly up and your bottom backwards. Check that there is space between your hands and chest. Breathe into your back, breathe out and twist with your tummy. Keep the back of your neck long and remember that your neck is part of your spine, so that if it droops or twists away from that central line of the twist, you are more likely to injure it. Note how the heels, shins and toes are all kept together as a guide to help keep the hips in line. There should be no constrictions. The back is not designed entirely for the purpose of twisting, and twisting it when it is compressed is just silly.

close-up This angle shows the line of the spine. Take a look at where the twist comes from. The lower spine is long and flat, held safe by the tummy. Follow the line up and just underneath the tattoo where the smaller vertebrae of the thorax begin, the twist begins. Let your chest roll round. Use your breastbone as a guide if you cannot feel the twist. Can you keep the top shoulder blade open and the neck long?

incorrect Here we see a twist and droop. The spine is not extended, there is no twist to be seen and the middle of the back will feel the weight of this position. If you find yourself doing this, drop your bottom down and extend your chest. Remember, you have a long spine, so use its full length, otherwise you will begin to feel the strain.

advanced If you are able to do this Pelican pose, it is a good link into the next posture. Gaze at your foot (the one under your elbow) and curl the heel of your other foot towards your bottom. Keep your knees together, as this will help to maintain some stability in the hips and point that foot before getting ready to drive it back.

Revolved Lunge

Keep this posture simple and do not try to twist too far as you may end up losing all stability. Instead, concentrate on keeping your hips balanced and your back open and when this feels natural, begin to twist around by trying to move your belly button to face your thigh.

1 Having lifted the leg in the Pelican, drive it back as long as is comfortable while keeping that angle in the front knee. Holding your bottom will help you feel this strange sensation of pushing the knee forwards while pulling the hip backwards.

2 This angle shows you the space between the shoulder blades, which are free of constriction. It also shows the wrist under the shoulder and the bicep rolled forwards, since this helps to open the back and roll the shoulders down away from the ears.

close-up This close-up draws attention to the centre of this posture, because in the hurry to extend one leg back and one forwards, lift an arm and feel the floor with the opposite hand, it is easy to forget that you are revolving and that to do so you need your tummy to hold your centre still. Notice that the chest is open and yet the top arm follows the curl of the shoulder forward and is not just pushing up to the ceiling. Think from the centre out. Don't get distracted by your extremities.

incorrect There is a lovely line down the back but look at that top arm. Note how the back has constricted with the desire to find the ceiling. Follow the line of the top arm into the body and you will see that it passes straight out of the shoulder into thin air. It is not securely in the shoulder joint.

▶ **3** As you begin to twist around, be aware of the space beneath you and don't be tempted to droop and crush it. Just remember that when you pull the opposite ends of a twisted towel, it deepens the twist, so keep your chest up and forwards and your back leg driving backwards to create the effect in your body. Follow the line of the top arm and you will see it is carried directly through the shoulder joint. There is no constriction within the top shoulder blade and both the back and the chest are open. The back leg is extended as long as possible and yet all parts of the body are revolved around the middle. Pay attention to your core strength.

Side Triangle

When you balance on your side, you naturally think that your arm is supporting you. However, the arm does not need to do much work since its bones provide a solid staff. The side of your body is not so solid, so put your attention to using all the muscles down that side to make it stiff.

1 From the Revolved Lunge, put (or keep) your hand on your bottom, push down hard and lean back a little. Your leg will whip itself back in its desire to straighten. Pushing your legs, and keeping them long, and the stomach strong, will help to hold you up.

2 As a prelude to the advanced posture, try this version. Look at the twist in the middle. It requires all your core muscles – tummy, back and hips – to pull together so that you can push and lift at the same time.

alternative Any pain in the wrist, elbow or shoulder will warrant this amendment. However, just because you are using two hands to balance does not mean you can collapse through your middle. In fact, it means you should work your middle even harder.

incorrect You can lower yourself from the first posture to this and back up again, which is a nice exercise, but to hold this position will do little except help you to strain something. There is no space between head and neck and no sign of a lift against gravity. When people first try this version it is such hard work for them. Then, when they find their middle, they feel so much lighter.

▸ **advanced** This looks tough, but is really quite easy. In Side Triangle, make a big tunnel underneath you by pushing off the floor and sucking the side of your tummy up off the floor. Bend the knee so you can lift your top leg to grab hold of the big toe of the top foot. Then simply push the top leg straight while holding on to it. It may take a little time, but it's not that hard.

Triangle

With both feet back on the floor, turn to face the side, and you are in Triangle. This is also a twist which starts in the abdomen and ends in the neck, so practise rolling your body behind you, twisting away from the floor and looking up to the ceiling.

1 Holding the buttock of the front leg with the opposite hand, lift it to begin your descent into Triangle pose. Pay plenty of attention to the length in both sides of your waist. Use the same activation of your side tummy muscles as in the last posture.

2 Keep lifting your bottom up, hinging through your hip, until your hand reaches your shin, ankle or foot. Extend both sides of your body. Pull your tummy in and roll your chest back over your thighs. If you are really tight in the legs, place the hand higher.

incorrect Spot the mistakes. The hand is on the wrong buttock, meaning there is no biofeedback in the hamstring of the other leg, no matter how high she lifts. A curvy spine and tilt forwards means the effect of this posture is handed to the middle and lower back, instead of to the muscles of the hip. Lengthen, don't droop.

the correct alignment This shows you how your body ideally sits in line and over your leg. You may have no one to assist you but you still have the ability to close your front ribs and roll your chest backwards over your leg. This will keep your spine long.

▶ **3** How many triangles can you see? There are only two, but the importance of them explains the posture. The underside of the body is a straight line and both sides of the waist are even, which means the spine is kept long. Thus the flexibility for this posture comes from the muscles in the hips rather than from a bend in the back, as curves do not appear in a triangle. The other triangle – of the legs – shows how great this posture is for opening the hips. The hand is on the opposite sitting bone to help pull the bottom up and keep the hamstring of that front leg as long as possible. Don't be boxed in by this posture. Be a triangle.

Revolved Triangle

This is a difficult posture and should be approached intelligently. It demands great awareness and stability from your hips, while your core strength maintains a length to your lumbar spine and provides a twist above it. Take it slowly until all the parts work together.

◀ **1** From the Triangle, reverse the hands so the buttock is still being lifted, this time by the arm of the same side. The other arm goes to the shin, the ankle or maybe even the floor. Pull in your tummy well and be prepared to really feel the back of your front leg. Push your heel down and lift your bottom up to extend the front leg long. Keep your front long, as this will mean that the spine is more likely to remain long.

▶ **2** Now try placing the hand further down the leg, aiming for the floor by the little toe of the front foot. Look at the triangles in the posture and at the spine. The strength in the legs means that the hips are more likely to open to allow you deeper over your front leg. Really hold and lift your buttock, as this will help you to lengthen your lower spine and extend your chest forwards. Try to keep your back broad as you roll your chest backwards. Try pushing your sitting bone back into your hand while taking your chest forwards. What happens to your leg?

close-up The revolution of the twist is in the tummy. You can see the proof before you. Keep both sides of your waist long and twist. Then maintain this length by pushing your hand backwards. Give your sitting bone a tug up as you do so.

incorrect The wrong buttock is being held, so when you push your hand backwards the result is a twist in the back rather than more length. Also, how can you extend the front leg when you are lifting the back one? Look at the spine on its gentle curve down to the floor, resulting in a floppy head. The hand on the floor is not important. Take your hand higher if you are inflexible, but keep your spine long and keep your body open.

alternative A helping hand is useful with this tricky posture. The reason for this angle is that it shows how the shoulders and hips should align. When they are aligned, the spine will be in a long line as opposed to bending up or curving down. Watch those front ribs as you twist, as they have a tendency to stick out. Closing them will allow you to feel that the back is long, and eliminate any hollow that may appear in the middle.

Balanced
postures

So what are the advantages of balancing on one leg? We are bipeds, with two legs and two hips providing our main means of movement, and any imbalance between them affects the whole body. By learning to balance on one foot, feeling your weight evenly on the foot through the ankle, both the knee and the hip are strengthened on that side. If both hips are kept even, then not only can hip imbalances be righted but all the torso and core muscles become involved.

Triangle Forward Bend

After all the work so far, you should really be feeling this in the legs. A Forward Bend is found in the hips, and the more they hinge forwards, the farther you will go forwards. Although not strictly a balance, this is a good neutral posture, linking naturally from twists to balances.

1 You have come up from the Revolved Triangle, so bend your knees in line with your toes, maintaining a lift in your tummy. Try not to stick your bottom out or to tuck it under. Use your thighs to hold you there and wait until they begin to burn.

2 Hinge forwards until your hands meet the floor and your chest is parallel to it. Your thighs should still be working. It is from these muscles that you slowly lift your bottom, lengthening the back of your legs. Keep your back long and your tummy pulled in.

3 Allow your upper body to relax. Feel the weight of the chest and head pull the lower spine long from the hips. The essence of a Forward Bend is to feel it within the backs of the legs. Let your head hang, while you push your seat bones up towards the ceiling.

incorrect The ability to touch the floor is worthy of praise, but not if it is achieved through back tension like this. Keep your back long by bending your knees and lifting your seat bones, or you will stretch the muscles of the back. (They are much smaller and tend to give way in the battle with the muscles in the backs of the legs.) Unlock your shoulders and use your thighs.

▶ **4** You can think of the head as a pendulum, hung from the hips via the spine, and here the picture gives a perfect example. Let the action of your heels pushing down and your buttocks going up leave your spine flowing down from your hips. Create as much space as you can between your legs and crotch for the hips to fold through as you bend over. Maintain the space in all your joints and enjoy letting your spine and hamstrings lengthen.

Flying Crow

Everyone falls over when they first try this posture, so you might as well resign yourself to the likelihood. If you are feeling brave but want some sort of soft landing, then practise in front of a cushion. Make sure you try it, for it is balance and not strength that is the key to the Flying Crow.

◀ **1** From the Triangle Forward Bend, bend the knees and start to raise the feet off the ground. If you feel that you have weak arms or are scared that you might fall flat on your face, then stay here. Lift up your heels and lift up your tummy. Your thighs will work hard but ignore them and concentrate on lifting your tummy so high that the legs begin to feel light. The more you lean forwards, the more you will find that the tummy pulls in.

▶ **2** A combination of leaning forwards to engage the stabilizing muscles of the back and a lot of tummy strength means that you can hang around in this posture for a while. The effort is felt in the tummy, but if the strength is not there you won't find yourself here. This is an example of balance through strength. It also shows you the lightness you should feel when performing the Flying Crow.

alternative 1 This picture shows a lower position in which more body weight is felt in the back of the arms. This will enable you to lift one foot tentatively off the floor. Make sure that you are looking forwards. This allows you to focus on the floor and reminds you of your balance. Pull your tummy in very tight as though it would lift straight through you. This will counter your impulse to collapse.

2 Once you find the balance point, the legs actually become quite light. This enables you to lift both legs up off the floor. Keep the shoulder blades open to make sure that both chest and back remain open. Lift your torso with your core strength at the same time – note the height of the tummy in this picture – rather than simply resting on your arms.

advanced If you keep lifting your tummy and the legs continue to be light, then you will find yourself in this position, the Handstand. Being upside down is so much fun and also very good for you. There are many reasons why inverting yourself may be good for you, but the best one is that it makes you feel like a child and reminds you of how much fun life can be. So even if you cannot suck yourself up to here by your tummy and back, then find a wall and play. If you do, remind yourself of how to keep your back open.

One-legged Biceps Curl

Balances are not easy, especially when you begin, because you feel as though something has been taken away from you. However, the mental and physical benefits you gain from their practice are far beyond the initial effort you may expend on learning them.

1 Having slowly rolled up to standing from Flying Crow, lift a leg and grab hold of the knee. Both hips and shoulders are even, although there is a great tendency to raise the hip and shoulder on the lifted side. Try and get the lovely long line in your collar bones.

► **2** One of the great things about yoga is the way it uses the body as its own personal gym machine. Here, you pull the knee high by using the biceps of the arms. As you do this, keep your shoulder blade wide and the elbow close to your side, as this will keep your shoulder blade flat to your ribs. This also has the effect of opening your chest. Notice that the head is right over the neck so that gravity goes straight through the body with the lowest possible resistance in the body.

incorrect Look how the leg is lifted by the top of the shoulder. This is intended to be a biceps curl, not a shrug and lift. Look how the hips are now uneven. If this happens to you, simply sit the raised sitting bone down and your hips will even out. Remember, balance is not just about remaining upright.

close-up This back view shows you how the action of curling your knee up can also teach you how to stabilize your shoulder blade. Keep your back broad and drop your shoulder blade so it feels as though that flat bone is curling under your armpit.

alternative If you really cannot balance in this posture, use a wall to steady yourself. Also, if you find that your hip is tight, then satisfy your need for knee height by stopping at parallel and concentrating on keeping your back long and upright. Pull your tummy in to help.

Karate Kid

This posture is a combination of strength and elegance, but at first it may feel ungainly and difficult. Try the easy version until you discover that your tummy and supporting hip take the strain, not the hip flexor of the lifted leg.

▶ **1** From One-legged Biceps Curl, lift your pubic bone up and lower your chest down to contract your tummy. Let go of the leg and pull your knee higher by pulling your tummy in harder. The effort should be in your tummy, not in your hip flexor. If you can find your balance here, drop your shoulder blades and lift your arms. You should feel the effort in the side of your waist and tummy. Let your supporting leg bend because that will help you to contact your middle. For the easy option stop at this point.

◀ **2** Look at the tummy – it is working hard to keep the leg up and straigtened. The more you pull your tummy in, lift your pubic bone and lengthen your leg, the longer and higher the extension will be. If you lower your arms as here, it will give you a chance to engage your back. This will help you to stabilize yourself and also give you a feeling of pushing up and off something as you find a lift.

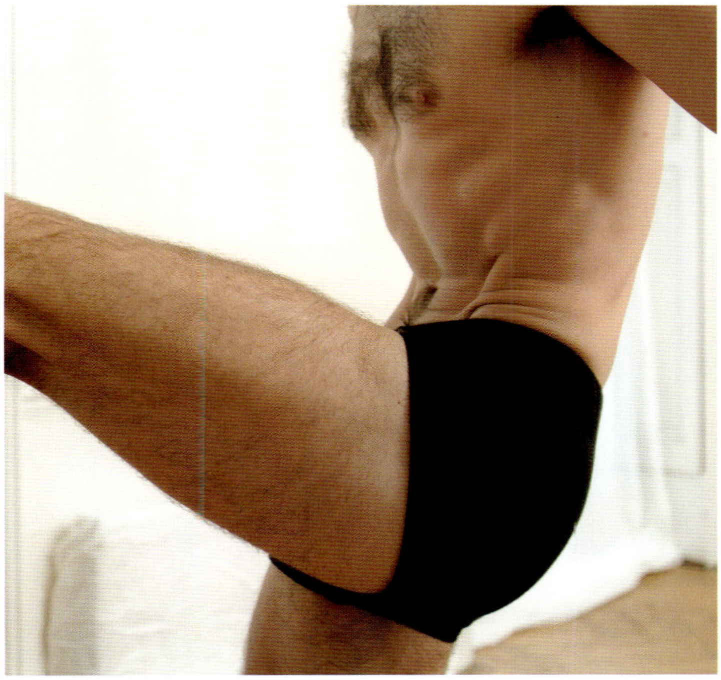

close-up This close-up explains the emphasis on the tummy in this posture. Look at the groove on the side of the waist. That's where you will find the core or support muscles you need as opposed to using the hip flexors, which have the tendency to tighten your hips when you rely on them too much. It also means that you are more likely to extend your leg higher, which will make you feel even more graceful.

incorrect This method of Karate Kid is guaranteed to have your hip flexors flexing, since the entire weight of your leg is being held by them. Notice how the tummy is bulging. As a result of that bulge, the lower spine is once again called upon to hold up the body all by itself. Notice also how the lean backwards is preventing the tummy from being pulled in.

alternative As with the One-legged Biceps Curl, if you feel your balance is something to be worked on, use a wall to steady yourself. As you do so, use your other hand to feel how hard the hip flexor of the lifted leg is working (it will pop up like a cable). With your best endeavour, make your tummy pull in even harder. You may find that your leg will lift even higher as a result.

Seated Eagle

This posture is excellent for your insides, since they are flushed with blood in the action of squeezing your thighs together. After you have finished this posture, let yourself unwrap into the Tree, as you will now find it quite easy to balance and it helps to strengthen the hip further.

◀ **1** Bend the right knee, and cross the left leg over and tuck the toes behind. Cross the right arm over the left at the elbows, aiming the palms together. Push your elbows away from you and up to keep some space between your arms and your chest if you can. Keep the hips level and balanced.

▶ **2** To release the body, pull your tummy up and in, balancing on the straight leg. Unwrap your arms and drop your shoulder blades to lift them up. Place the previously crossing leg into a right angle to form a classic yoga shape, the Tree.

close-up It is not clear where the name Seated Eagle originated, but it does makes sense. You are "sitting" cross-legged, and the pretzel-like action of the arms opens your back and flares your shoulder blades – to spread your wings. The body should sit directly over your hips. Notice the light between the arms – try to keep the elbows up and the hands away from the body.

incorrect This is almost a "Seated Buzzard", with the curve in the middle and the hump in the back! If you collapse your middle and lean forwards, the head will still try to give you the impression that you are upright. Copy this and you will not feel the work of the posture in your thigh but feel as though you resemble a clumsy knot. Spread your wings and sit up. Don't slump.

alternative If you feel unsteady, then place your hands on your thighs and use your arms to help hold your spine long. Use the simplicity of this posture to keep your hips even and feel the work in your thigh.

Rocket Man

Practise this posture, taking time to repeat each leg, as through regular practice you will attain a good awareness of your hips, tummy and back. Also, through learning the feelings you gain in your body and replicating them into other postures, you will gain stability and understanding.

1 Balancing on one leg, use your arms to help stabilize your body on your bent supporting knee. Keep your shoulders down away from your ears and really extend backwards with your back leg. Think about lengthening your hip and thigh, as this will help you to feel the stretch from your stomach to your toes.

2 Notice that the chest is slightly above the hips. This allows the back to pull together, making it solid. The tummy is also pulled up to help stabilize the lower back. This also helps to steady the hip of the supporting leg. Really extend through your back leg as though you are pushing off to rocket forwards.

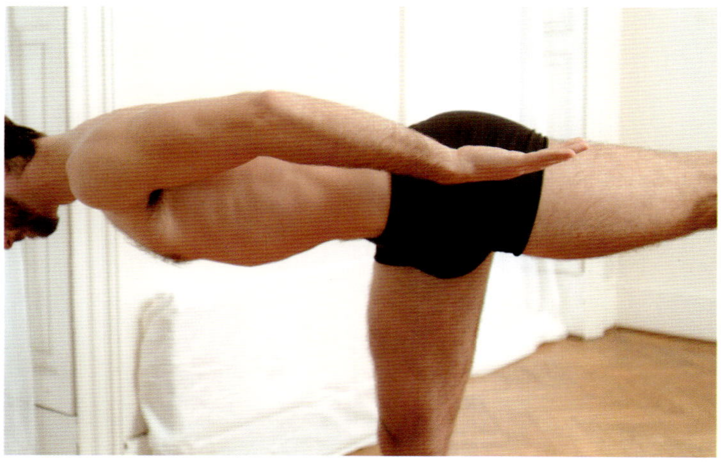

close-up You could call this posture "T", because ideally that is what it should look like. Keep your shoulders open away from your head and you should feel the muscles in the back engage to give you the lift you are looking for. Notice how the front ribs are closed to allow the spine to stretch its full length. The tummy is drawn in tight to support the lower spine and to help extend the back leg and open the hip. Try it, keeping your hips even.

incorrect More "Droopy" than Rocket, this is a common error. The mushroom back means the hips are the highest point, so the disengaged muscles lining the spine are working too hard. Push your back leg straight and lift your chest.

▶ **3** This is an enjoyable posture and this picture explains why. In Rocket Man you feel as though you are flying, with so much lightness in the hips that the supporting leg almost disappears. The body feels very long because of the simultaneous extension of the back leg backwards and the chest forwards. All the time the tummy is lifting up to let you feel a lightness, and the entire body begins to open. From here anything seems possible. Find your lightness and fly, even if you cheat by keeping one foot on the floor.

Seated postures

When you get to the floor postures you will need to remember not to collapse. Although a greater proportion of you rests on the floor, the increase in sensory response provided can give you even more of an idea of where your core is and how you lift. Always come to the floor exercises fresh. Feel your seat bones on the floor and lift your body up from them. Allow the hips to hinge; do not collapse them and bend from the spine. Most of all, remember that any Forward Bend comes from the hips, regardless of the length of the legs.

Seated Forward Bend

You either love this posture or the back of your body complains so loudly that you don't. Be patient. Remember that the body must hinge in the middle, with both sides of the hinge as long as possible. To lie flat, the entire back of the body must be open.

▶ **1** Let your head relax so that your neck is long, and make your tummy as long as possible. After all, the longer the tummy, the longer your lower spine, and that means the deeper you hinge forwards. Think of lengthening your lower spine out of your hips, as opposed to dragging yourself forwards with your arms, and you'll find that any injury is very unlikely. You will also begin to understand more this feeling of a hinge. If you get the chance, ask someone to give you a push there. It's quite safe and feels lovely.

◀ **2** When you can, let the head bow and relax, as you did in the standing Forward Bend. Once again, you should feel that your spine is lengthening up, out and away from your hips. Extend your arms, relax and take time to breathe.

incorrect When people madly grab at their feet to show that they can touch their toes, it sometimes seems that if they let go, they would ping backwards owing to all the tension in their bowed spines. This posture is great as a back stretch, but as a Forward Bend not much of the body is going forwards and there is a big bend in the back. Since we spend so much time slouching over work, dinner or watching television, take this time to extend your spine and lengthen the backs of your legs.

alternative If you are not flexible, try this version and lift your chest as high up your thighs as possible. You will find a stretch in the back of your legs, even if your knees are as bent as you see here. Note how the length of the spine is mirrored by the length in the back of the thighs. Stay here, feeling the freedom of your spine and the stretch in your hips and hamstrings. Only when these lifting muscles are strong enough to counter the tightness in your legs will your hamstrings truly soften.

Table

Have you ever seen a deck chair on a windy day, when its seat is blown through the frame? The Table should eventually have a similar feel, where the back muscles are "blowing" the front muscles open and up. Use your hands and feet to feel the floor and find the "lift".

◀ **1** The Table feels like a natural progression from a Seated Forward Bend, since all that opening needs consolidating. So sit up. Place your hands behind your bottom, slightly wider than shoulder width, which makes it easier to find your back strength until the flexibility of your shoulders appears. As you push up, keep your elbows soft and try to get your chest higher than your shoulders. Try to lengthen the front of your body, and you should find this helps to provide some more strength to stay up. If you find that dropping your head back all the way is difficult, either open your jaw wide or lengthen the back of your neck.

▶ **2** The Table is similar to the Side Triangle, in that you should feel as if you are making a tunnel underneath you. This means really having to find the muscles of your back, especially those that draw the shoulder blades down the back. When you find these, you will feel that they are responsible for lifting the chest higher and higher, opening the front of the shoulders and chest. So find the floor, push up and make a tunnel.

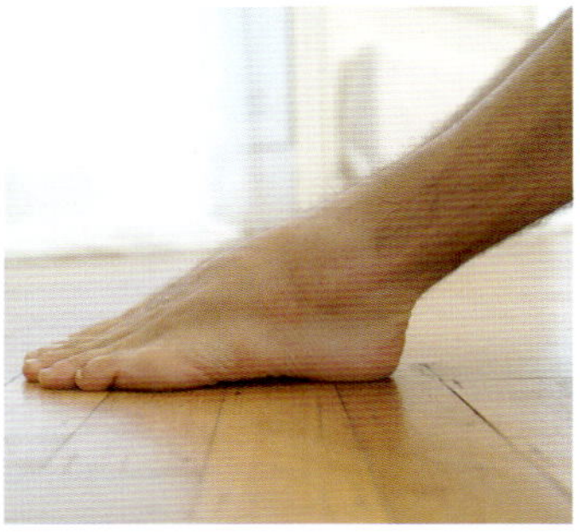

close-up The feet are the forgotten part of this posture – use them and they will help. If you have inflexible ankles, then really extend your toes to the floor, and not only will your ankles open but your arches will also improve. The more you can push down with your feet, the more you can engage the backs of the legs to help you lift. After all, they've been lengthened in the previous posture and now it is their chance to be strengthened in this one. Use your feet and feel the floor.

incorrect People execute this style of Table when they are unaware of their backs and of the fact that they have legs they can stretch. How many times when you've been slouched over your work do you push your chest up to release the tension you feel in it? Well this posture is exactly the same feeling. Get a neck, stop slouching, and you will understand how refreshed you can feel when you come down from the Table.

close-up Try not to lock your elbows, since this hyperextends them and takes the weight out of the muscles in the back and into your joints. If you can, keep working on getting your shoulder blades flat to your ribs, as this will really help to open your shoulders.

Cobbler

This posture is also known as the Butterfly Hinge. Look at how the legs have opened right up, like wings. There is a lightness within the hips that allows this. Open the hips and revisit these postures as many times as necessary, to enable you to find this lightness in their separation.

1 Sit down from the Table and bring your heels towards your bottom as far as is comfortable. Holding your feet or ankles for support, lift your pubic bone up and try not to lean backwards. The higher you lift, the more your knees will spread apart.

2 From rolling back, pull your tummy up and in to lift you upright. As you do this, keep the feeling of separating the knees within your hips. These are separate and distinct sensations that do not seem to fit together, but practice will show that they do.

3 If your inner thighs will not give in, use your arms to help maintain the length of your spine. Pulling the tummy up and in helps in two ways. It stops the lower spine collapsing and, second, the more you lift up, the more likely you will be able to release your inner thighs.

▶ **4** It may take a very long time for your hips to open sufficiently to allow your head to reach the floor, but wherever you get to in leaning forwards, remember that the more open your hips, the more space you have to roll forwards and through. Spend time getting your knees towards the floor before worrying yourself over how far you are from the floor. Spread your knees and hinge from the hips and your spine will look after itself.

incorrect Look at the tension within the upper back during the struggle to get over the hips. As a result of this battle the inner thighs join in, resulting in the knees going up not down. This posture will only push tightness to where tightness already exists. Be alive and be intelligent. Feel the lift and begin to experience the opening of your body.

Bridge

Think of the arc beneath a bridge – the smoother the arc, the stronger the structure. So when you attempt this posture, remember to keep as long an arc as possible in your back. This will prevent you from putting the bend on one part of the back, which always leads to discomfort.

1 From the Cobbler, lift your pubic bone up between your legs, and you'll find you begin to roll backwards. As your lower spine begins to near the floor, your legs will feel light enough to bring them into parallel lines with a nice bend in the knees. Keep lifting your pubic bone up to roll you down, and, as your spine unrolls on the floor, bring your heels as close to your bottom as is comfortable.

2 Once on the floor, lay your hands on either side of your body, pushing your forearms and hands down. This will help you to feel the muscles between your shoulder blades. Then press your heels down to feel the floor and keep rolling your pubic bone up between your legs. The thighs will feel the major work. If they don't, the lack of pubic lift will mean your lower back will begin to constrict.

3 If the posture in step 2 is very comfortable, then continue to lift your shoulder blades up off the floor and lift your pubic bone up between your legs. If in this higher posture you feel light, then take your right hand under your right shoulder and your left under your left. Stay here. Do not push with your arms. Keep lifting your middle, with the power in your thighs and the lift in your hips.

close-up This angle is visually how you should feel. Just as in a standing Forward Bend, your hips are highest. Your thighs and hips are your strength. If you lift from them, you will find far less constriction in your back than if you struggle to lift with your arms. This entire sequence of photographs is one long roll of the pubic bone up between the legs.

▶**4** The Bridge or the Big Back Bend has a status much the same as the Forward Bend or Handstand within a yoga class, for it shows everyone you have a flexible back. Try to think about being upside down, as if you have been walking on your hands and feet and a giant has turned you the wrong way up. This will make you feel as though you are pushing up not just with your arms but your legs and tummy as well. If you can play in this posture, move and sway. Try picking limbs up from the floor to reaffirm where your lift comes from. You are upside down, so be light-hearted and play.

Double Pigeon

The mechanics of this pose make it quite hard to strain and push, so in order to understand why this posture is so important, stay in it, rest in it and work intelligently within it. Be gentle with your body as, even though this posture feels lovely, going into it can elicit some strong feelings.

1 The action of placing one shin upon the other will, for some, be beyond the accommodation of their hips but if the shin does lie almost flat, then trust in your tummy strength and the hip will open up. As you sit there, sit as tall out of your hips as is possible.

2 Push your top knee down (in the Assembly position, both knees) and lift your pubic bone between your legs. You will feel the tummy pull in and the knees spread. Do not lean backwards, just roll your hips up and back. Stay here and feel the spread in the legs.

advanced If your hips do not feel the desired deep stretch with your shins lying on each other, then pull your knees so that they are inside your ankles and you will find the depth of sensation you have been looking for. Breathe slowly and deeply, emphasizing the exhale to help you let go of the tension in those deep muscles.

alternative If when you try and place your shin on top of the other, your body prevents your leg from moving or the knee sticks up high in the air, or your ankle and foot feel as though they are going to snap, then move into the Assembly position sitting with simple crossed-legs.

▶ **3** Keep sucking your tummy in and up until you feel your hips begin to roll forwards. Keep rolling them forwards, up and over your legs, until you find yourself over your legs. Push your bottom down and back, pull your tummy in and up and lift your chest up by using the muscles of your upper back. This will extend your spine and allow you to find space within your hips and lower spine.

Batfink

In this posture you wrap your arms around your legs as though you were cloaking them in bat wings. This will keep your back open and broad while you curl your pubic bone up and draw your knees to your chest by pulling your tummy away from your thighs.

▶ **1** Start by balancing on your bottom and, while maintaining your balance, learn to curl your pubic bone up and your tail between your legs, as this is the beginning of extending your spine into a long, smooth "C" shape. You have to hold this "C" shape in order to have a smooth roll from bottom to shoulders and back up again. Let your arms go forwards and your chest backwards since this will help you round and open your upper spine. You do not want to throw yourself up and down with the momentum from your legs, so spend some time here until you feel that you have the smoothest "C" back you can possibly get.

◀ **2** Rolling back and up is fun. You get a lovely feeling of massaging the muscles along your back and the impression that you are a child's toy. The art of rolling back and up lies in your pubic lift, as this will keep any gaps or holes in your spine from appearing, in other words, any part of your back that does not wish to roll with the rest of your back on the floor. Notice how the body is still in exactly the same position even though it has been turned on to the space between the shoulder blades.

advanced If you have rolled back and forth quite happily and fancy a challenge, try recreating a Forward Bend while balancing on your bottom. Enter Batfink as in step 1, then slowly pull your bent knees as close to your shoulders as you can. Lift the arms and straighten your legs by using the muscles in the front of your thighs. Try it out. Play one leg at a time.

alternative If there is no way your spine will allow you to roll back and forth, assume this position. Keep lifting your pubic bone into your tummy, while keeping the knees relaxed above your hips. This will strengthen your abdomen and allow you eventually to roll through the hips.

incorrect Look here at how the chest is lifted and the tummy is forced to bulge out, leaving more weight to be carried in the lower back. Also, the hip flexors are the main muscle holding the knees high. When these tighten they pull the hip girdle forwards with them and, since your hips are attached to your spine, this means a more pronounced hollow in your lower back. Don't allow feeling tall in the posture to come at the expense of being tight. Besides, straight lines don't roll.

Tortoise

Achieving this posture takes patience and time. When inside it at your limit, slow down and take time. Come out as if coming out of hibernation, for if you move quickly, you will miss great subtleties and sensations. The Tortoise can unlock the deep places where we store our tension.

▶ **1** The Tortoise posture is all about coming forwards. Just as a tortoise extends its head out of its protective shell, you have to figure out how to pull your body up and forwards out of your hips. Put your arms under your bent legs and extend forwards. The posture demonstrated here is more than deep enough for most people, since it requires you not only to roll your hips forwards between your legs but also to extend your spine forwards and up from your rolled hips. The result is an intense sensation in the hips and lower spine.

◀ **2** This is a real challenge since both your legs and your body have to go forwards away from your hips. The arms extend backwards, away from the head. This is going beyond the Forward Bend you are used to, since you have to take your body beneath your legs. However, remember that the bend originates inside the hips, not through dragging your spine between your legs. Whatever you do, keep your back long and take time to feel the groin open up to give the hips space to move through.

incorrect A classic posture of the head bound student, this method of performing the Tortoise will inevitably end with you on your back. The body is collapsing forwards, beginning with the shoulders and moving all the way down the back. Although the hips may feel the stretch, they will not stretch far because of the distinct lack of support from the rest of the body. Be patient and you will win in the end.

alternative If your hips allow for very little play, follow this example. Use your arms as struts to help lengthen and lift your spine up and out of your hips. Not only will this feel more comfortable, but it will also put you in touch with the tummy lift. This lift, when strong enough, will allow your muscles around the hip joint to soften so that the hips can then hinge closer to the thighs. If you find yourself here, then you need to pay more attention to all the Forward Bend exercises.

advanced If your hips and spine allow, proceed forwards and down, rolling your palms up to the ceiling (thumbs facing in) so you can try to grab hold of your bottom or clasp hands. The idea is that through slotting your shoulder blades under your knees, the knees can act as a weight to push your body lower. Clasping the hands on the lower spine then provides some sensations you can respond to and lift away from. Extend your body as long as you can along the floor and you will feel all the tension release from your tail

Shoulder Stand

There are many benefits to practising inverted postures, primarily because it flushes the head and neck with a large supply of blood. This not only helps to relax you and release tension from your head and neck, but may also leave you feeling clearer and fresher than when you began.

1 Lift your pubic bone up into your tummy until your legs are rolling over your head. Lift your shoulder blades up off the floor. Any neck pain should disappear when you work the back muscles hard to lift the shoulder blades up off the floor.

2 If resting your knees on your head strains your back, try this version, as it demands a long spine. Basic rules: if your neck hurts, then lift your shoulder blades up off the floor. If your spine or lower back hurts, then take your hips backwards away from your head.

alternative Roll backwards into an "L". Bend the knees as you need to. Pull the abdomen in, brace the floor with your arms and draw your shoulder blades down your body away from your ears. Menstruating women will benefit from staying in this posture. If you really want to relax then put your legs up against a wall.

advanced Attempt this posture only if you are fully aware of your tummy and back core muscles. If you are, then you will find it. If not, don't try it. It is fun and the key is found between your shoulder blades.

►**3** Follow the same two rules. If your neck hurts and feels tight, lift your shoulder blades up and away from the floor. (Persistent pain means don't be silly, stop doing it and seek advice.) Second, if your lower spine aches, then take your hips back away from your head. Then warm your kidneys with your hands and stay there, constantly feeling the lift, for as long as you feel comfortable. There are many benefits, so practise and learn to feel them. Please note that women are not advised to practise inverted postures during the first three days of menstruation.

Fish to Corpse

These three postures flow into each other and lead you into a deeper state of relaxation. The Fish helps you extend and open the front of your body. The Baby pose helps you be aware of the expansion of your spine and the freedom of your hips. Corpse lets you become aware of this space.

◀ **1 fish** This a classic counter pose to end with after a Shoulder Stand. The reason why can be seen in the neck. Having compressed the front of the neck and lengthened the back, the pushing of the elbows down and the arching of the upper back can allow you to drop your head right back until the top of your head rests on the floor. Remember to stretch your legs and lengthen your tummy, so that you feel as though the arch in the top of your body is grounded in the rest of it. As you do this, try not to make the arch come solely from your lower spine, as this may make your back ache when you slowly lower yourself down. Most of all, open your chest. Breathe into the space between your shoulder blades and, as you breathe out, lengthen your waist.

▶ **close-up** This angle shows the positioning of the hands and that the emphasis is most certainly found in lifting and opening the chest. See if you can find out how to arch your upper back without having to overarch your lower back. Breathe deeply into the top of your chest and open the space between your shoulders.

2 baby If you find your lower back aches at any point at the end, come into the Baby pose. Use this posture to find out just how long your spine can get. Ground your sacrum and coccyx on the floor while pulling your knees down into your armpits, as this will open your hips and flatten your lower spine. Make sure that your ribs do not stick up, as this will leave you with a hollow under your ribs, and keep your shoulders away from your head.

3 From the Baby you know it is time to relax, so lower both heels to the floor with a bend in the knees. This should make sure that your spine feels long and flat on the floor.

4 Let one leg go straight, but as you do so, notice how much of your spine pulls up and off the floor. This is owing to tension in the front of your hip. Allow your leg to let go and the spine to remain soft.

5 corpse When you feel ready, allow your other leg to go straight and, once again, watch how the spine lifts. If your lower spine hurts with both legs down, then return to both legs bent and heels on the floor. Let go and be prepared to spend some time here.

Chilling Out

There is no question that when you're tired you want to rest and that after resting you'll feel better. Another simple fact is that when your muscles are relaxed, you tend to feel relaxed in your head too. When you have finished your practice, you may well find that you feel tired.

◀ **1** Try lying on your front with the soft parts of your body on the floor. You'll discover that it is very easy to find this sinking feeling when there are no bony parts of you causing discomfort. We come back to the scientific law that states that for each action, there is an equal and opposite reaction. So, the harder you work, the better you'll rest. When you know just where the tired muscles are, it is easier to relax them. Equally, the harder they work, the easier it is to get them to relax. What you end up with is a body ready and willing to relax. If you repeat this regularly, you will learn to know the feeling of letting go. Eventually this awareness will be with you all the time, not just after exercise.

▶ **2** Roll on to your back and keep that feeling of sinking that you found on your tummy and let your body go "splat", including your bony parts. Check your hips are open and your shoulder blades are broad and allow your chest to open. Let go, it's the end.

3 As you lie there, you will want to think and be active in your head. So get as far away from your head as you can by finding and mentally feeling your feet with your consciousness. Physically do nothing and mentally take a holiday to your toes. Your mind will want you to fidget, move, think or imagine. It will cling madly on to any source of entertainment, even down to counting your breathing or heart rate.

4 Against the wandering mind, you have an advantage. You have your body beneath you, with its many thousands of impulses and sensations. If your mind wants to be busy, entertain it by watching, living, the sensations of you. This is true relaxation, meditation, chilling out – whatever you want to call it. But most of all, the beauty is that everything you've been wanting – release, a source of wellbeing – is you. Let go and feel.

Sequences

There are three warm-up sequences here, and four routines. You do not need to copy everything you see, but practise what you can. If you like, refer back to the main page for each posture for more details. Spend time in each of the postures to see how your breathing affects them, or flow between them with only one breath held in each. Try spending at least ten breaths in each posture in one practice and then only one in another, as this will build endurance and cardiovascular fitness respectively. At the end of each sequence, make time for five minutes of stillness.

Putting It Together

Look at a river and you will see that in the middle its current runs fast, taking all the sediment it carries far down towards the sea. Look now at the sides or the banks of the river and you will see the current moving slower, eddying and playing with the sediment it carries and laying it down on the banks. This build-up of deposits will eventually lead to a change in the shape of the river as it begins to push the fast-flowing centre farther and farther away from it.

Fat, the river and you

Your body is one big river of energy. Wherever there is poor circulation, sediment (or fat) will build up, and when it does, not only the inside but also the outside will show this. If you sit down, remaining static and inactive, it is common sense that you will not feel or look in prime physical condition. After all, your muscles, which act as pumps, are not active to help your river keep flowing freely inside you, and build-up will occur.

To help you find your river and help activate these natural pumps, put together all that you've learnt so far: hinging through your hips from ape to man to find the "pumps" in your buttocks and thighs, using your back and tummy to keep your spine long and free.

Think of all you learn and read in here as a map. But make sure that at every stage you ask yourself "Does this map make sense to me?" If it doesn't, don't hesitate to discard it and start again. If it does make sense, then follow and feel so you find these words, actions, postures and descriptions making sense in your body. Listen and feel until they become a physical sensation.

Warming up

On the following pages are some simple warm-up sequences. All of them are flowing, which means no postures are held for long; they simply flow as the breath does, from inhale to exhale, standing to bending, looking up to stepping back. All the time you are doing them, make sure that your spine is long, your tummy is engaged and your neck is soft from the shoulder blades going down and out, not up and in.

If you can't do this, return to the beginning of this section and relearn where your core strength is. Remember, too, that you don't move just during the 10 or 15 minutes of this routine, so why apply these rules only for the duration of your practice? When you drive a car, are your shoulder blades up around your ears because of stress? If so, get them down. When you are standing at the sink or cooking, is your spine long and your tummy pulled in to support your lower spine? When you sit at your office desk, can you find the lift up and off the chair? If you become more aware, you will find that all movement will begin to feel easier.

left and right The exercises here can teach you to find your core strength and the lunges and standing postures will help increase your stamina. However, you need to put this information to good use in the rest of your life as well, not just when you are being "fit", and then you will really feel it.

Relaxing Sequence – Warm-up 1

This is a relaxing warm-up to try before moving on to the later postures. This way, the muscles will be primed and know what to expect, lessening the chance of injury. These movements are intended to flow, one into the other, so don't hold each one for long, maybe 30 seconds or two

1 lying down Begin by lying on your back with your arms at your sides. Use your senses to discover how much of you rests flat on the floor, and every time you exhale see if you can release down a little more.

2 upper back arch As you breathe in, direct your breath to the top part of your chest and see if through contracting your upper back – the muscles that line the spine in between your shoulder blades – you are able to lift up your breastbone.

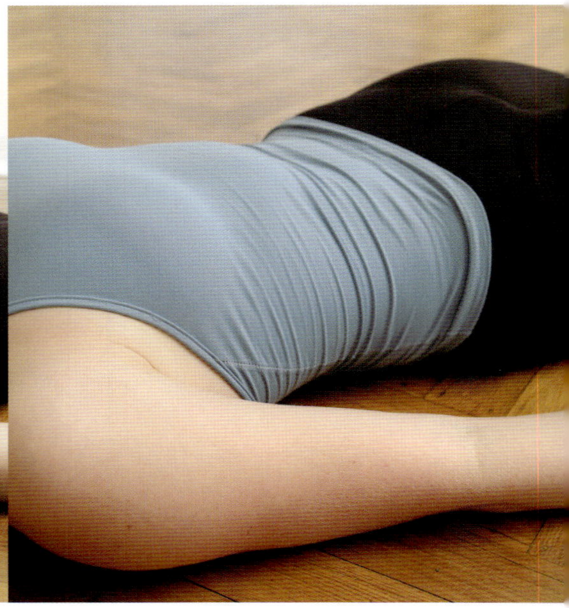

3 softened chest As you breathe out, soften your chest so that the upper back arch is allowed to soften. Repeat these actions so that your upper back begins to be more mobile. See if you can feel just your upper back moving.

7 both knees to chest Slowly pull both knees to your chest. Drag your heels to your bottom before you lift your legs, as this will allow you to maintain a stable core, as opposed to your back having to arch or your abdomen bulge.

8 letter "L" The straightness of your legs is secondary to the feeling of work in your core and stability in your hips. It doesn't matter whether your legs are straight; keep your back long along the floor. Feel as though you are stretching the back of your body. Breathe and lengthen your body.

9 lowering the legs Begin lowering both legs by bending and separating your knees, while simultaneously lifting your pubic bone. This will mean that you are using primarily your core strength to lower your legs.

deep breaths. The whole sequence will take only a few minutes, but the benefits of doing it regularly will soon show in the way that your core strength is improved, and all kinds of movements, not just the ones in this book, will become easier.

4 knee up to chest After resting for a few moments, exhale deeply. Lift one leg up into your chest, clasping your hands just below your knee. Keep both sides of your waist long and see if you can lengthen your buttocks and lower spine.

5 submarine Let go of the knee and extend your leg. If your leg cannot straighten, then keep your knee bent and push your heel high. The key here is not to let your tummy bulge up and your lower back arch off the floor. Keep pulling your ribs and stomach away from the upright leg.

6 lowering the leg Lower the leg with a bend in the knee and the leg slightly turned out, or straight. Maintain the strength in your tummy so that neither your back arches nor your tummy bulges up. Repeat with the other leg.

10 roll up Once your feet have reached the floor, allow your legs to roll away from each other fully and pull your tummy up and in so hard that you end up looking through your legs. Follow this pull and roll up to sitting.

11 roll over Be aware of the movement of your hips as you roll up. As you roll over your legs, do so with your hips and not simply by leaning forwards from your lower spine. Learn to hinge forwards, so repeat rolling back and forth until you can really feel the movement of your hips.

12 corpse Finally, roll back, doing so along your entire spine. When on the floor, slowly extend one leg, then the other, and rest. Use your senses to see if any more of your body is resting on the floor than when you began.

Resting Rocket Man – Warm-up 2

This sequence is all based upon activity and release, so when being active, really use your muscles to make you feel as though you are flying through the poses. Then, when you enter the Child poses they will feel like home since your muscles will be crying out for some rest and this will help

1 lying on front Lie down on your front and concentrate on the soft parts of your body on the floor (tummy, thighs and chest). Try to relax until you feel as though as much as possible of the front of you is touching the floor.

2 chest lift Pull your tummy as far up and off the floor as possible to keep your lower spine in place and lengthen the front of your body from your chest to your forehead. Keep your shoulder blades open and arms relaxed, as they were in the previous posture.

3 grounded rocket man Keeping the back of your neck long, your tummy up and your legs relaxed, lift your elbows up until your thumbs meet the creases under your buttocks. Make sure you leave your shoulder blades open.

7 double leg lift To lift both legs is tricky without drooping your lower spine or collapsing your chest, so pay attention to those details as opposed to the height of your legs off the floor.

8 big-belly child Again, use your abdomen to stop your back collapsing as you push yourself back. The wider your knees, the more open your hips will feel, but if your lower back feels tight, try belly gazing which will help to free any tension.

9 elbows Resting your head on your thumbs, keep your navel the highest point underneath you. Make a long, smooth arc from head to toe to let the strength of your front open your back.

you let your muscles relax further into the pose. Since it does not take long, try repeating it until your body seems to flow through the sequence with your muscles smoothly taking you from one pose to the next. Repeated regularly, you will really start to feel the benefits in your core strength.

4 child Place your hands under your shoulders and pull your tummy firmly up and in. This will brace your back as you push your bottom towards your heels. If your shoulders are very tight, take your arms into a wide "Y".

5 belly gazing Return to the starting position before finding this pose and see if you are any more relaxed than before. Then, placing your hands beneath your forehead, push your elbows down and gaze down at your abdomen, feeling it pull up and in.

6 leg lift Keep your posture the same: open back, long and lifted front, long lower spine. Lift one leg by lengthening your thigh back and away from you. Remember to try squeezing the top of that leg's buttock. Change legs.

10 naughty child This encourages you to push your bottom in the air. Think of a long arch from your bottom to your fingertips – let the length in the back reflect the length of your front.

11 press up Ideally your shoulders are directly over your wrists, with a big space beneath you. Push your chest up off the floor to open the space between your shoulder blades and once again find the arc from your forehead to your toes.

12 lying on front See how far you can let go into the floor; how much more of your front touches the floor than when you began. Consciously contract a group of muscles, then release and relax them.

Standing Sequence – Warm-up 3

This warm-up allows you to take all that you have learnt about your body so far and apply it to a standing stance. We spend most of our waking life in an upright posture, so it makes sense that we practise something that mimics the patterns of our everyday life or we stand little chance of

1 standing Stand tall with your chest lifted, hands by the sides, and as you stand, feel the connection from the heels to the back of your head. Draw the shoulder blades out and down. Soften the chest as you exhale.

2 lifting arms Inhale. Feel the connection between your arms and your back and lift the arms as you drop the shoulder blades, so the shoulders are relaxed and down. Take the arms forward, so you can feel the movement of the shoulder blades, then bring both arms above your head.

3 forward bend Exhale. Soften your knees and lift the bottom so you can lengthen the abdomen and spine. This will ensure that you hinge forwards from the hips, rather than collapse through the lower spine.

7 single leg stretch Exhale. Use your hips as a hinge to simultaneously push the front leg long and lower the torso over the front leg. Enjoy the stretch but keep some softness in your front knee. Do not hyperextend your knee.

8 looking up forward bend Inhale. Step forwards, placing your feet together. Try to do this by bending your back leg. As you step you will really feel the hip of the straight leg. See if you can keep some lightness in your body as you make this move. You may have to make two smaller steps.

9 forward bend Exhale. Push your heels down, keeping the knees soft, lift the bottom, pull the tummy up and in and let the head relax and drop down to the feet. Place your palms flat on the floor either side of your feet.

changing our habitual patterns of movement. Perform this warm-up until it makes sense, and you can really let your breath take you from one posture to the next. When you have achieved this, try to discover a feeling of light-footedness, so that when you move you are in full control.

4 looking up forward bend Inhale. Using your upper back rather than the neck, look up and open the ribs so that you will have more room to inhale. Lengthen the stomach and keep lifting your bottom to the ceiling.

5 lunge Exhale. Keeping your front leg bent at 90 degrees, lunge the other leg backwards, really concentrating on lengthening your leg right up through the abdomen. Keep the hips above the level of the knees, meanwhile keeping the muscles of the stomach strong.

6 lunge Inhale. Raise your hands over the head. Lift up through the hips and keep the lower spine long by lifting your pubic bone. Keep the back leg long and straight, and feel the sensations happening in your hips.

10 flat back to lifting arms Inhale. Look up and extend your spine. Soften the knees and pull the tummy in, so you can hinge up to standing through your hips while maintaining a long spine. Drop the shoulders to lift the arms.

11 standing Exhale. Relax your chest as you breath out, so you feel the weight of your arms between the shoulder blades. Remember to take your arms in front of the body to keep the shoulder blades flat to the ribs. Repeat on the other side to make one round of this sequence.

Earthing Sequence

When you are tired, stressed or anxious, getting close to the floor and truly feeling it can allow your breath and emotions to calm down. Use this sequence to learn where the floor is and how you tense muscles unnecessarily while performing the simplest of postures.

1 sleeping superman Lie on the floor and try to feel yourself free-falling through the floor. Play with the upper back and shoulder blades. This will help you to feel the back open up.

2 child Breathe and take your time. Use the tummy and back to help you move between this and the posture in the previous picture.

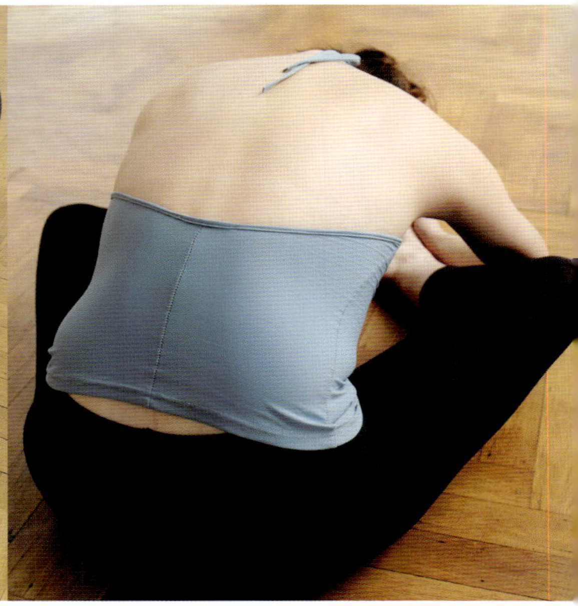

3 cobbler Push yourself all the way back on to your bottom. Keep the hips low and feel the buttocks stretch. Use these muscles to help to separate your knees.

7 knee hug Lower your hips slowly so that you know where the weight of the body is. Keep your awareness in the hips as you hug the knees. Lengthen the lower spine.

8 single leg "L" Lay one leg flat, really stretching through the hip as you lengthen the other leg towards the ceiling. Keep the weight inside the hips. Relax the chest and keep the tummy in.

9 single knee hug As you bend the knee in the air, feel the buttocks and your lower spine lengthen. Do not lose this sensation, but really savour it. Repeat on the other side from single leg "L".

4 letter "L" Squeeze your buttocks to open the legs, then lift the pubic bone to help you roll along the spine to form the shape of the letter "L". If you are inflexible, you may find it necessary to bend your knees.

5 batfink Hold on to the back of the knees to help you begin rolling and make sure you roll through all of the spine, without holes or bumps.

6 bridge Roll up to Cobbler and then, with your feet ready, roll the spine down and lift the hips up in the air. Keep the work in the hips so the spine stays long.

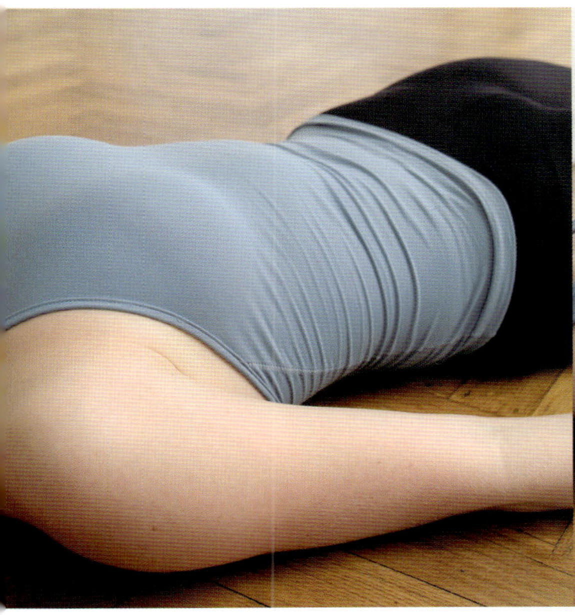

10 upper back bow Lower both legs to the floor, keeping the weight of them inside the hips and abdomen so that the lower back stays long. Separate the shoulders and lengthen the upper spine along the floor.

11 upper back arch Soften your chest and contract the shoulders down and out to feel the neck lengthen and the middle and upper back arch.

12 corpse Release and relax the muscles you have just worked. Feel them soften into the floor and, once again, try to free-fall through the floor. Let the earth hold you up.

Energizing Sequence

To energize, you have to get everything moving, so this sequence is composed of big postures requiring large movements to flow between them. Within the space of these movements you can really begin to feel the body beneath you. Take your time getting from one posture to the next.

1 lunge After performing up to five single leg lunges, stay in the Lunge and really push the back leg straight. Keep the work in the hips by lifting the tummy.

2 pert buttocked warrior Roll the hip of the back leg around, while keeping the front knee still. Let the arms drop to shoulder height, but keep their weight in between the shoulder blades.

3 triangle Push the front leg straight and use that hip as a hinge to rotate the torso towards the ground. Use the tummy to keep the chest and hips rolled at an angle of 90 degrees to the floor.

7 forward bend When you have completed the postures on both sides, jump forwards and, with soft knees, push the heels down while at the same time lifting the bottom.

8 karate kid Roll up to standing and bring your beginning lunge leg with you. Contract the tummy backwards, so that you feel the weight of the leg in the stomach muscles.

9 rocket man Take that leg backwards in line with your body and really stretch that leg through the sensations you felt in Rocket Man.

4 dog split Use the tummy and back hip to roll the chest parallel to the floor. Pushing your hands flat, kick the back leg straight behind you so it makes a line with the wrist.

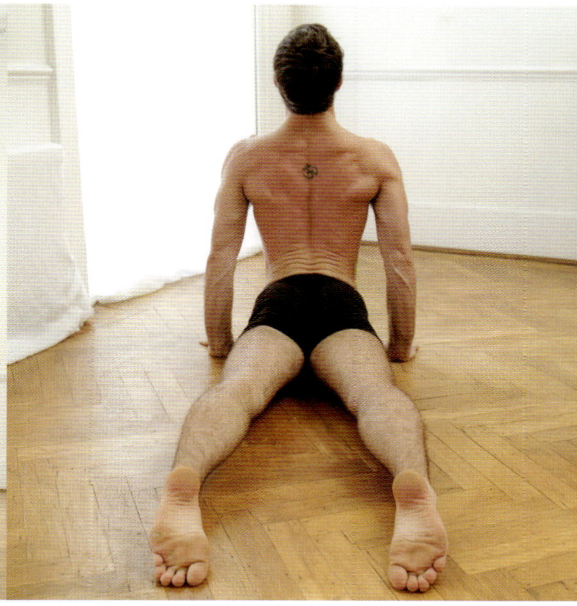

5 up dog Slowly lower yourself into the Press Up position and, with both feet on the floor, drop the hips and lift the chest. Use the back, keep it open and draw the shoulders down.

6 down dog Lift back into Press Up position from your tummy. Continue to lift the tummy as you separate the shoulders while pushing the bottom back and up. Lunge the other leg forwards and repeat.

10 thigh lunge Bend the supporting knee and stretch your back, lowering yourself into this knee trembling pose. Make sure you keep the abdomen high, off the front thigh.

11 revolved triangle Take the opposite hand alongside the front foot and lift the bottom up with the other hand. This will twist you towards the leg, but use the tummy to help twist you around. Via Press Up, Up Dog, Down Dog and a Jump, go back to Rocket Man on the other leg.

12 triangle forward bend Finish with another Press Up, Up Dog and Down Dog sequence, and then jump straight into this posture. Keep the knees soft and lift the bottom. Finish with some relaxing postures and stillness.

Strength Sequence

Although this sequence seems to rely on arm strength, the strength you need is in fact to be found in your core. When you begin the first posture, try to feel the weight of your body being carried within your back and stomach, rather than in your shoulders and arms.

1 press up Keep the navel high underneath you and draw the shoulder blades down the back. Then bend the elbows (do not collapse) and, as you exhale, relax the chest so that your full weight is felt in the back.

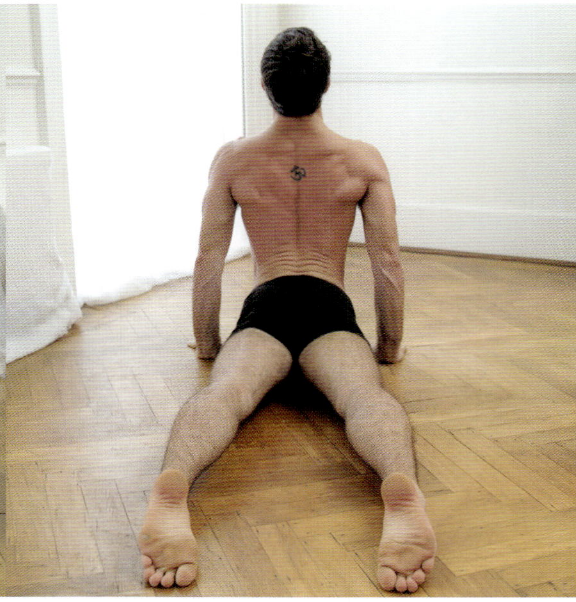

2 up dog Drop your hips and lift the chest with the muscles you used in the Press Up. Stretch the legs through the tummy back to the toes.

3 down dog Using your tummy and stopping briefly in top Press Up, lift the hips into Down Dog. Pay careful attention to the feelings in the wrists, shoulders and tummy.

7 side triangle Roll on to the outside of the back foot and roll on to your side, so the top leg remains in the air. See if you can grab hold of that top big toe without crushing the space underneath you.

8 jump Jump into Lunge on the other side and repeat from the Lunge to the Dog Split and Side Triangle on the other side. Then, after completing both sides, jump both feet to behind the wrists, drop your head and lift your bottom. Release any tension from your lower spine.

9 triangle forward bend Feel the tummy pull up and in as you lift your bottom. Pay attention to this lift.

4 jump Having felt the strength through your wrists, shoulders and tummy, keep it strong as you jump up. At the top of the jump, take one foot forward, ready for the Lunge.

5 lunge Keep light in this posture, as if you are still in the top of the Jump. Use the back to hold the arms up and the tummy to hold you buoyant from the hips.

6 dog split In one smooth move, push the front leg all the way back in a Dog Split, but keep the shoulders and hips even to maintain the strength of the posture in your core.

10 flying crow Place your knees on the back of the arms, lift the heels and find that lift. It feels as though a rope around your waist is holding you up.

11 handstand (advanced flying crow) Press your hands down, contract the back and let the lift straighten you out. Practise this posture separately, against a wall if you wish, but continue to feel the lift from your middle.

12 press up Using the shoulder girdle as a hinge, and keeping the arms strong, let yourself drop back into a Press Up. Omit this posture if you are not sure of your ability. Relaxation and stillness must follow this sequence.

Relaxing Sequence

The postures are all designed to get your hips level – or above your head. Inversion takes a great strain from your heart and provides your head with an amount of blood that gravity denies you. With the release of tension from your shoulders and neck, this will leave you feeling lighter.

1 seated forward bend Remember that a forward bend does not automatically require straight legs. Hinge from the hips and lengthen the tummy up and out of the hips.

2 table Take your hands back behind you and, keeping the back open, use your bottom and back to lift you into the Table. Soften the chest to feel the stretch in the chest and the shoulders.

3 cobbler Lower your bottom down and draw the heels towards the crotch. Use your bottom to open the knees towards the floor and hinge forwards through the hips.

7 tortoise Roll up and separate the legs, so that you can hinge through them. Remember, the object is to open the hips and lower spine, not to straighten the legs.

8 shoulder stand Roll down and make the letter "L" with your legs in the air. Pull your knees and shins towards your face to help you engage the abdomen.

9 batfink Roll down to an "L" again and pause momentarily before rolling any residual tension from the back and spine. Take your time and roll as slowly as you can.

4 bridge Roll the spine back on to the floor and continue rolling the hips up into this back bend. Keep the hips long and learn how you can lengthen the lower spine in this pose.

5 double pigeon Come down slowly, choose a leg to cross on top or in front and hinge forwards to open up the hip and lower spine. Change legs.

6 batfink Draw both knees towards the shoulders, while curling the lower spine so you engage the tummy and roll fluently down and up along the spine.

10 fish Having felt your spine open and bow, lie down to remind yourself of the muscles of the upper back. Arch the upper spine by drawing the shoulder blades wide and then down the back.

11 baby Bend your knees to bring the legs up to the chest. Bend the knees so you can push your bottom away from you along the floor. Once again, you feel the hips and lower spine open.

12 corpse Take the heels down to the floor and rest with the knees still up before relaxing fully with the legs down. Give the back plenty of time to adjust to its new length.

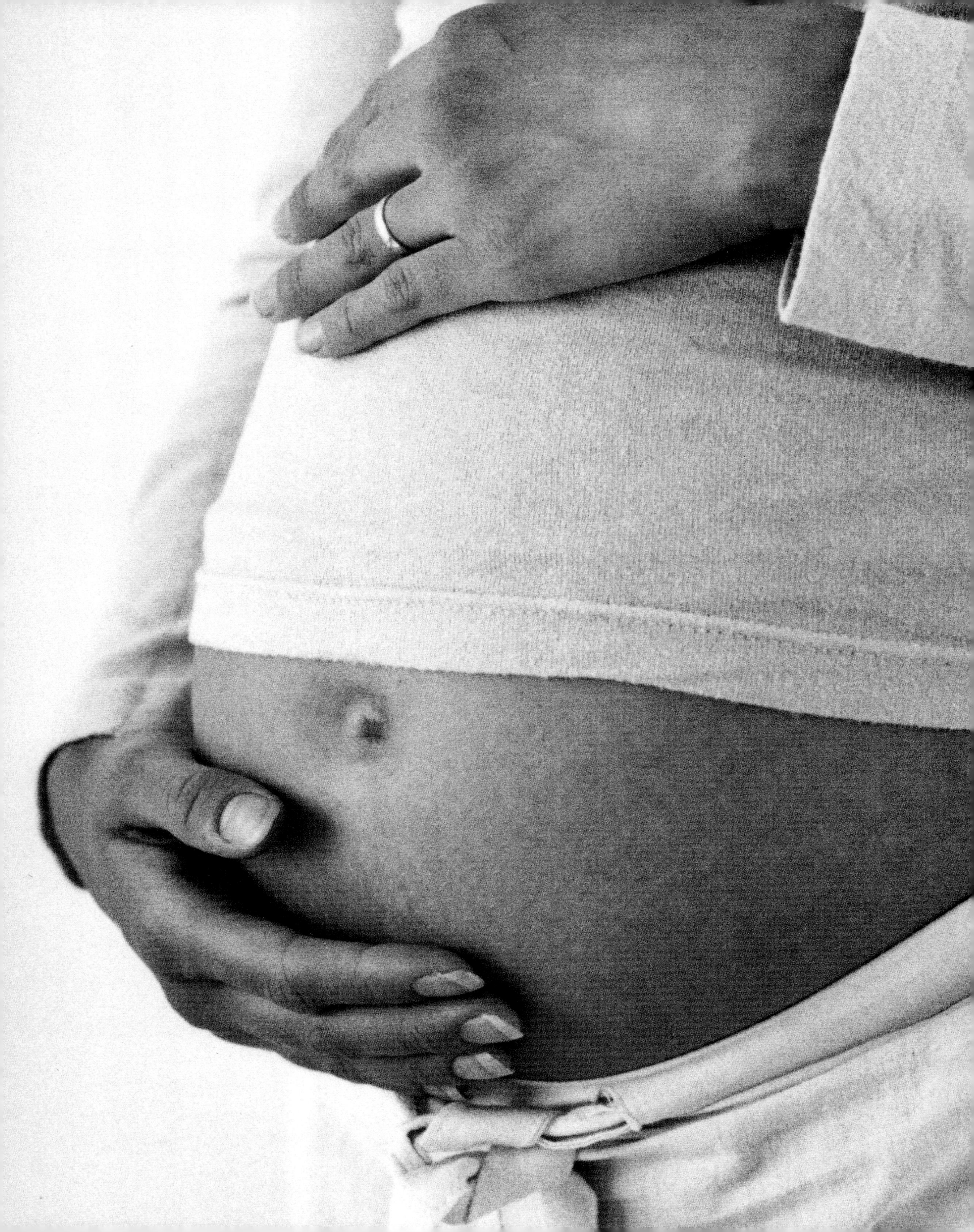

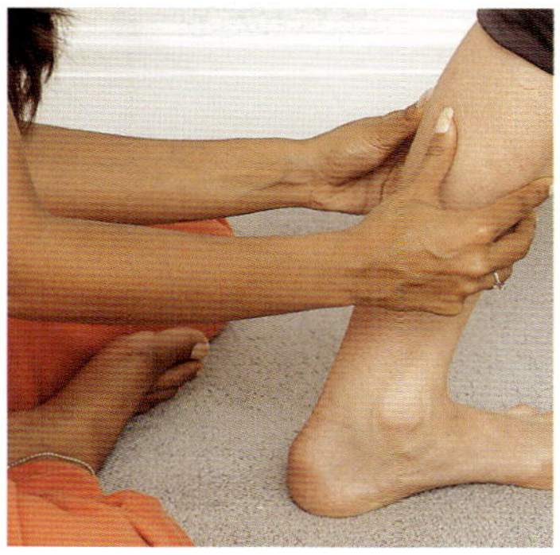

Yoga for Pregnancy and After

Here, a range of specially devised yoga poses take mothers-to-be from conception and pregnancy to early babyhood, helping them stay toned and flexible, have an easier birth and regain their figure afterwards.

Françoise Barbira Freedman and Doriel Hall

Yoga for the Mother-to-be

Regular yoga practice can help enormously at all stages of pregnancy, birth and parenthood, bringing you to a physical, emotional and mental peak. Strong, supple, focused, relaxed and happy, a woman will be well placed both to conceive and to carry her baby joyfully right through to the birth – provided this is what she wants and there are no major medical obstacles.

The yogic routines in this section are specially adapted to suit your needs, both before and after the birth of your baby. They are easy to follow, and have been designed with your safety, and that of your baby, as the first priority. If you feel uncomfortable with any exercise, don't persevere. Trust your instincts: deep self-awareness is the essence of yoga. There is plenty of choice and the exercises are designed to make you feel great – at work, at home, anywhere.

opening yourself up

Whether you are trying to conceive or are already pregnant, it is vital to remain open at all levels. A woman is probably at her most welcoming at this time, offering her love, her body, her womb, her breasts, her nurturing ability and her whole self as a safe haven. Yoga for conception and pregnancy focuses on staying open and creating more space: more space in the lower abdomen for your baby; for the digestive organs to process the food needed by mother and baby; and for the lungs to provide oxygen for mother and baby.

letting energy flow freely

Openness is a yielding, welcoming quality, but it is not a shapeless "giving in", nor a collapse, for it is literally backed up by the strength and support of the spine. A key focus in yoga for both conception and pregnancy is to increase and maintain the alignment of the spinal and pelvic bones in order to provide free flow of vital energies and to protect the growing baby. This is vital for several reasons:

above In many poses, cushions placed under the knees protect your ligaments from undue strain.

- To enable all of the systems of the body to perform their functions with the minimum amount of pressure or congestion. This is especially important when you are planning to conceive.
- To hold the baby in place, to create space for movement as he or she develops, and to make room for vital nourishment to pass through the placenta to the baby without any hindrance.
- To allow free passage through the spine of energies that activate the Chakras, as well as the mechanisms that are vital for the smooth running of the nervous system.

Our bones are held in place by muscles and ligaments. Muscles need exercise to remain strong and flexible enough to do their job properly. Without it, they stiffen and then atrophy, which can lead to greater fat deposits. The muscles that support our body's weight are the largest, strongest ones. In classical yoga, we exercise them a great deal by doing standing poses where the weight of the trunk is taken by gravity through the legs and feet, which are firmly planted on the floor. In

THE THREE MAIN STAGES OF PREGNANCY

Here you can see how the spine changes shape and the organs get increasingly squashed. Yoga helps to keep the organs working well and strengthens the all-important, supportive spine.

At 8 weeks

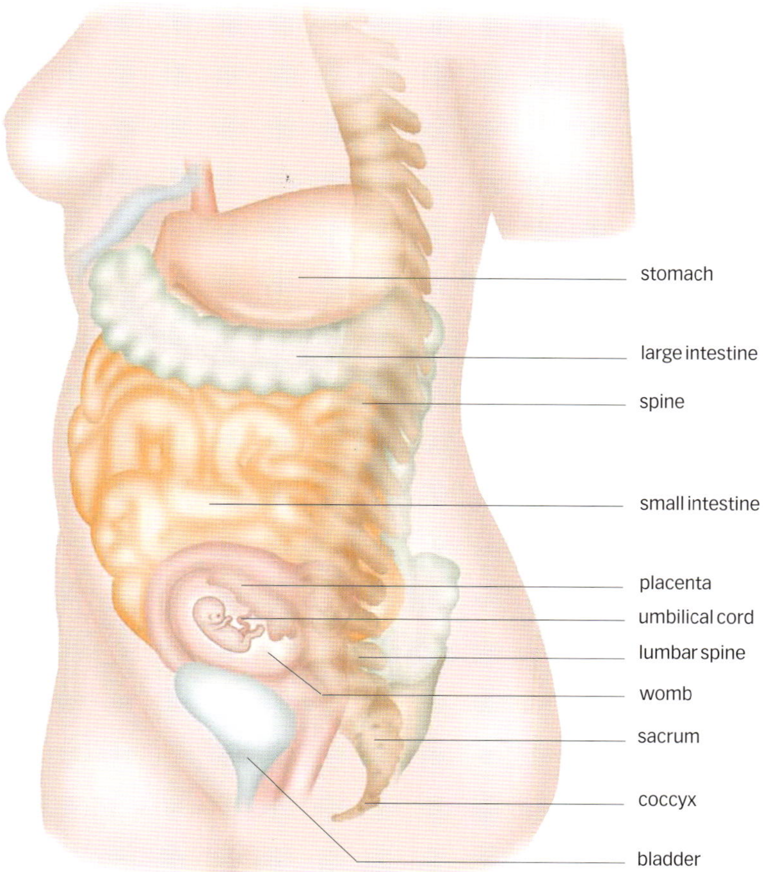

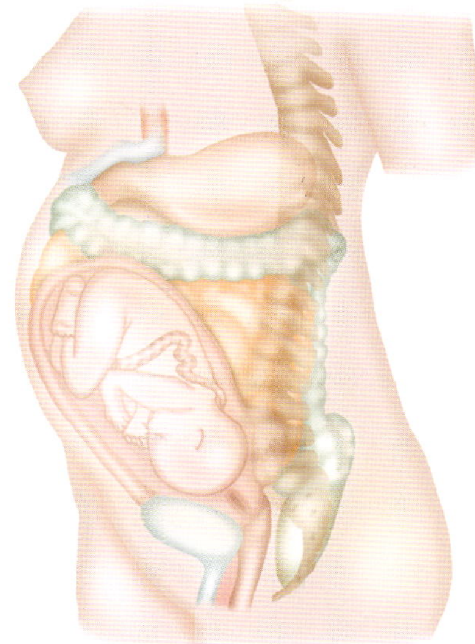

At 24 weeks

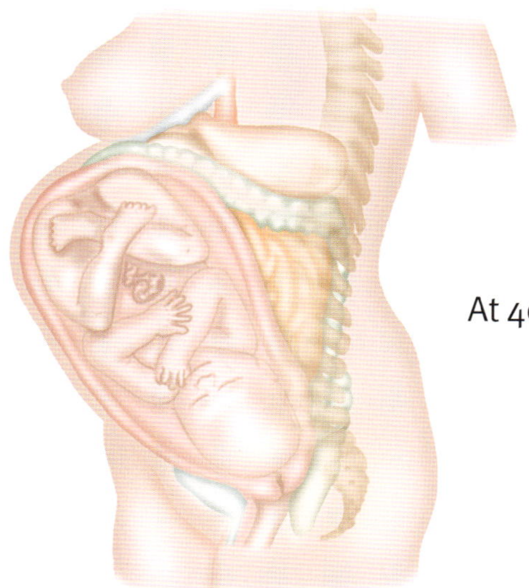

At 40 weeks

pregnancy, however, movement and rhythm are introduced to avoid the strain of holding the classical positions. Various supports may also be used, to avoid tiring or straining while standing. Many poses are performed either sitting down (less tiring than standing) or lying down (where gravity works with you and the ground supports you).

posture and breathing

Yoga creates a virtuous circle: the more aware you are of good posture and spinal alignment, the more you will pull yourself up when you notice you are drooping. The more you stand tall, the better you will breathe and the more vitality you will have. The more vitality you have, the less you will droop and the more you will naturally stand and move lightly and well. Yoga is a holistic discipline, so improving any area affects all other areas for the better.

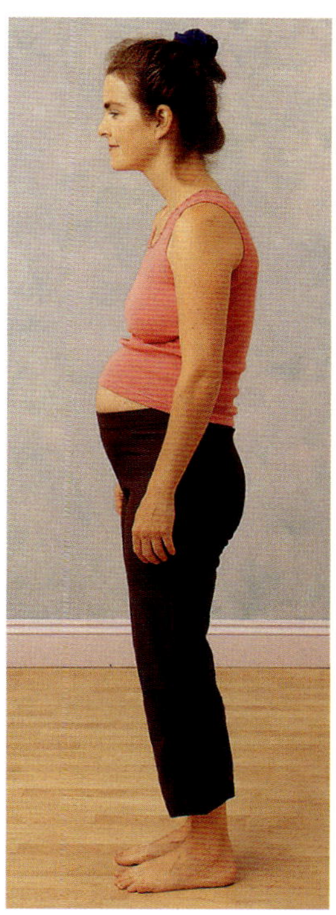

left Poor posture can spark all kinds of problems. Compression of the spine leads to pain in the neck and upper back as well as the lower back, while poor breathing from congestion of the lung space inevitably contributes to tiredness and low vitality. Slack abdominal and pelvic muscles lead to congestion in the abdomen and possibly lower back pain and swollen ankles.

right Good posture means that your head and neck are erect and balanced between the shoulders, and your spine and pelvis are properly aligned. Your abdominal and pelvic muscles are strong enough to support the baby and your chest is open so that the breathing muscles perform fully and fill the body with a positive vitality. Finally, your legs are strong, springy and balanced.

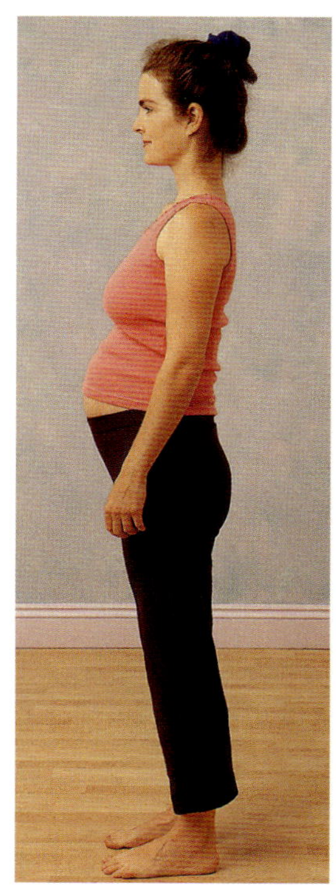

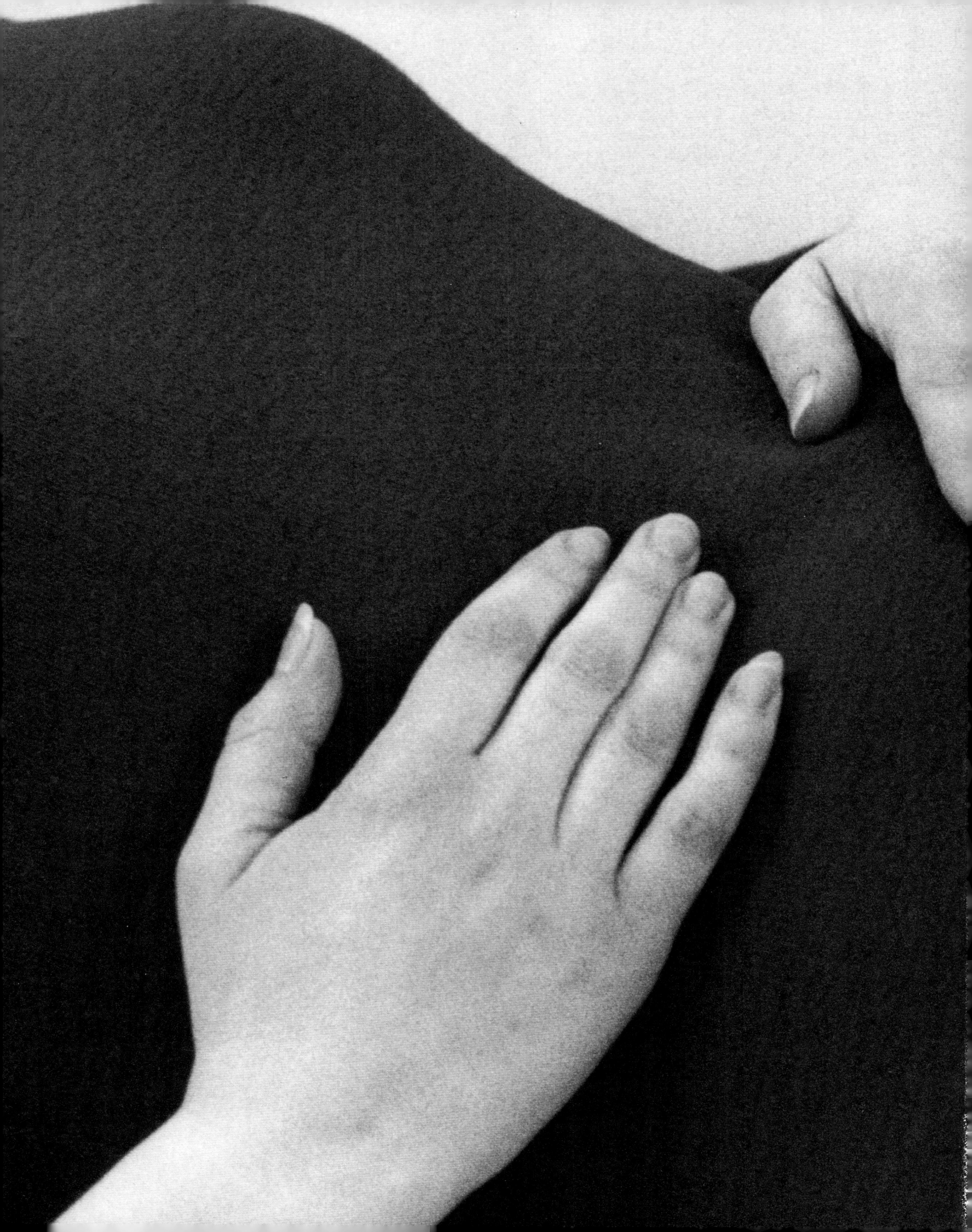

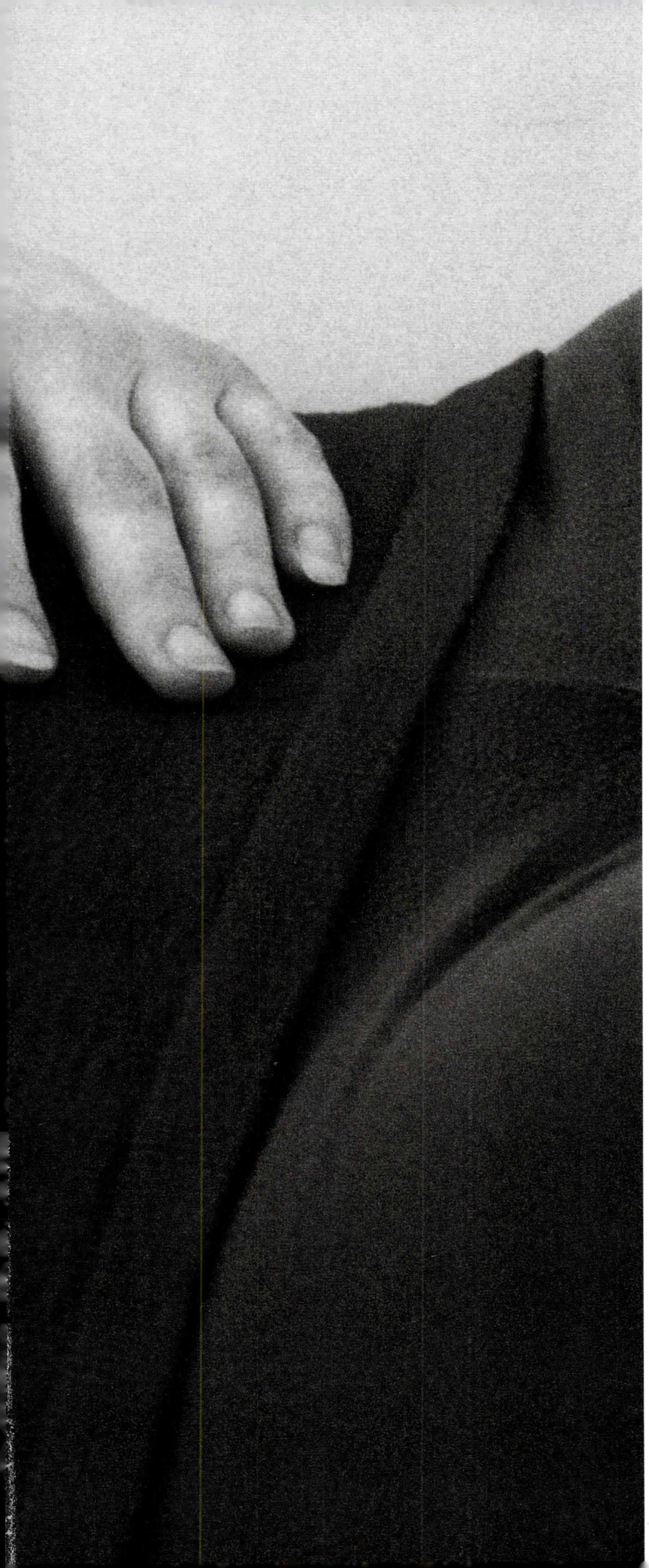

yoga for Conception and Early Pregnancy

Conception is a miracle of energy, timing and receptivity – qualities that are enhanced through regular yoga practice. From the moment of conception, Nature's priority is the welfare of your growing baby, and your own needs take second place. Conserve your energy, respond to your body's needs, and perform gentle yoga poses to stretch and tone your muscles.

How Yoga Can Help You Conceive

Stress can impede conception because it ties up so much of our vital energy – and this is detrimental. If stress is claiming energy for keeping our muscles uptight, our minds on overload and our emotions all churned up, the other systems of the body have to manage on the energy that is left over. If conception is eluding you, stress is the most likely culprit. Indeed, long-term stress can even cause medical problems that require medical solutions. Regular yoga practice is a simple preventative measure and can also be a cure. It increases your energy supply and channels it to all the body's systems to keep them in balance so that you become fit and relaxed, living each moment to the full.

what your body language tells you

The way you sit, stand and move can reveal a lot about your state of mind, health and emotional well-being at any time. If most of your energy is tied up either in your mind (your work, for example), in your emotions (say, problems that may be weighing on your mind) or in your hectic lifestyle, your body becomes depleted. There just may not be enough energy left over to work your reproductive system properly. It can be as simple as that. This stress can be reflected in your body language – legs tightly crossed, upper spine hunched over, or arms crossed over your chest.

"This state, in which the senses are steady and at rest, is known as yoga, the state of union."

Katha Upanishad VI 9

The yogic answer to stress is to rebalance your nervous and endocrine systems so that all functions are enhanced. Use yoga to stretch, strengthen, open and relax. This releases locked-up energy, and so eases conception, pregnancy and birth.

above The "uptight" body language here says it all. This posture displays feelings of fear and vulnerability. The arms and legs form a shield across the trunk, blocking the flow of energy. The chest and abdomen are closed, so that breathing is restricted and energy to the pelvic area is blocked.

above The body language here shows a relaxed mind, peaceful emotions and an erect, vibrant spine. The shoulders, neck, hips and pelvis are relaxed so that energy can flow freely throughout the body.

breath is the key

The respiratory and cardiovascular systems bring oxygen (the prime source of energy) into the body from the outside air and circulate it to every cell. Good breathing habits, therefore, increase the total supply of energy available for the body's systems to use. The diaphragm is the large muscle that separates the abdomen from the chest cavity. It is the chief breathing muscle. If its movement is restricted through poor posture it cannot pump enough air into the lungs and so not enough oxygen is available to the body. Shallow breathing, which does not draw in enough oxygen, is one of the main causes of feeling below par. Deep breathing (using the diaphragm fully) is instantly energizing.

As you breathe in, the diaphragm contracts strongly downwards, massaging and energizing the abdominal organs and increasing lung capacity so that air rushes in, through the nose, from outside. The diaphragm springs back up again as you breathe out, releasing the abdominal pressure and decreasing the lung capacity so that air is forced out through the nose. This contraction and release reflects the whole momentum of yoga – activity followed by rest, followed by activity, in a continuous, balanced cycle. Practised with awareness, deep breathing reconnects us with this rhythm of life and helps us to learn how to relax deeply between all bouts of activity. It also helps to create a calm strength.

Tuning in to your breath

A deep breath in recharges both body and mind. A deep breath out releases muscular tension, chemical waste products and tired, strained feelings. Mentally, take your breath in to the very base of your spine. Taking time to practise breathing slowly, deeply and fully induces calm, positive feelings.

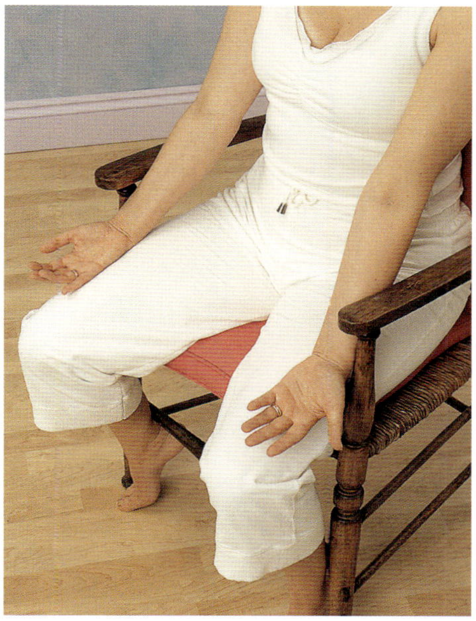

1 Sit at the back of a firm chair with spine erect, knees apart and feet on the floor. Rest your hands with palms up in an open, receptive gesture. This position opens the trunk, so the diaphragm can move freely. Take several deep breaths with awareness of what is happening to your body as you breathe. Repeat the exercise frequently.

CAUTION

Deep breathing is strenuous, especially if it is new to you. Stop at once if you feel tired, breathless or light-headed. Rest for a while before starting again. Very gradually build up the number of deep breaths you take at any one time.

Flexibility in the pelvis

The reproductive system lies within the lower part of the abdomen and is protected by the bony pelvic girdle. This area needs to be open and relaxed so that energy can circulate freely through the reproductive system and conception is unhindered. Regular movement of the pelvis brings energy, flexibility and strength to this area.

1 left Sit on the edge of a sturdy chair with feet apart and set firmly on the floor. Place your hands on your thighs above your knees, with fingers turned in and elbows turned out. Lean forward, bend your elbows and take your upper body weight on your thighs. This frees the pelvis – think of it as a bowl and tip it forward at the front "rim" (the pubic bone) and up at the back "rim" (where the sacrum joins the spine).

2 right Open the front of the body by spreading your arms with palms up, lifting your chest and tucking your pelvis under so that the front pelvic "rim" rises and the back "rim" is lowered. This movement stretches the spine and releases tension. It also tightens the lower abdominal muscles that hold the pelvis in place. Repeat these two movements several times and practise frequently in order to increase mobility in the pelvic area.

Yoga Poses to Release Tension

For many people, tension settles in the pelvic region, causing stiffness in the hips, pain in the lower back, and general congestion and an uptight feeling in the lower abdominal area. Yoga stretches relieve all these conditions and allow energy to circulate freely. They also work on the whole body, so remember to keep the spine extended and the chest open in all these exercises.

CAUTION
Make haste slowly. Locked-in tension impedes movement. As you release the tension through yoga movements, you will find it easier to move much further. All yoga stretching should be performed with active relaxation and not force.

Pelvic movements with focused awareness

These relaxing movements encourage increased awareness, blood flow and flexibility in the pelvic area. Feel that you are opening up to new healing energy and letting go of any tension there.

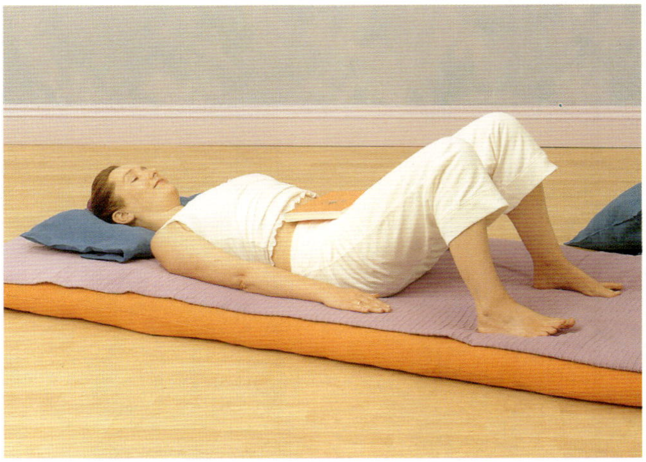

1 Lie on your back, with a large book and three cushions beside you. Place one cushion under your head and tuck your chin in to lengthen the back of your neck. Bend your knees and plant your feet hip-width apart on the floor. Place the book on your lower abdomen, so that it is evenly balanced upon the hip bones and the pubic bone, then stretch your arms alongside your body with the palms down to support you.

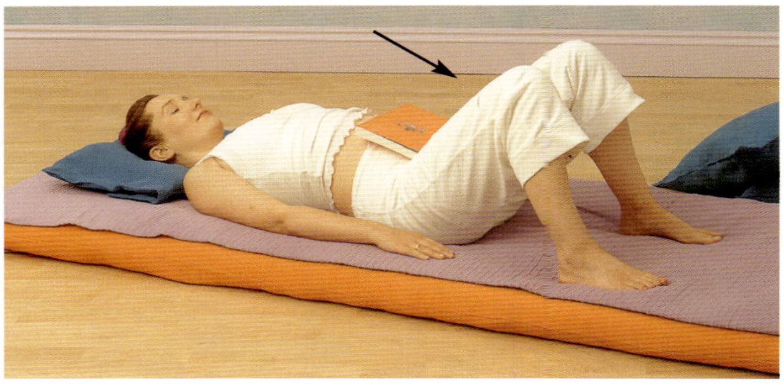

2 As you breathe in press on your hands and arch your lower back as much as you can, so that the navel and hip bones rise and the front "rim" of your pelvis (and the book) is tipped towards your feet.

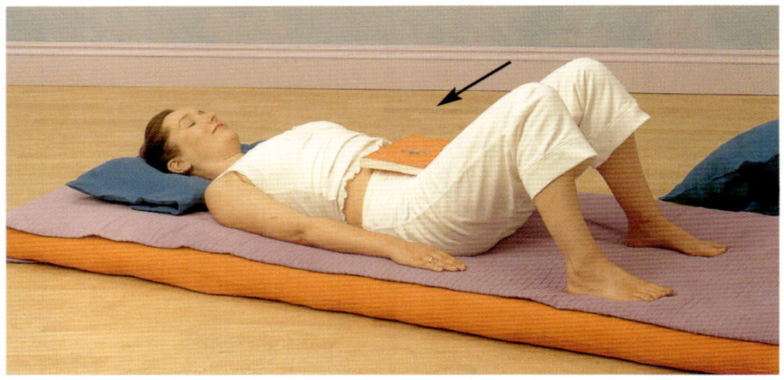

3 As you breathe out pull the navel against the spine and press on your hands to lift the coccyx just off the floor, so that the pelvic front "rim" (and the book) is now tipped backward, towards your head. Keep your waist against the floor and move the lower spine only. Repeat steps 1–3 several times.

4 Now place your hands, in a relaxed pose, on top of the book and breathe deeply. Feel the movements of the book over the pelvic area as you breathe in and out slowly for several minutes.

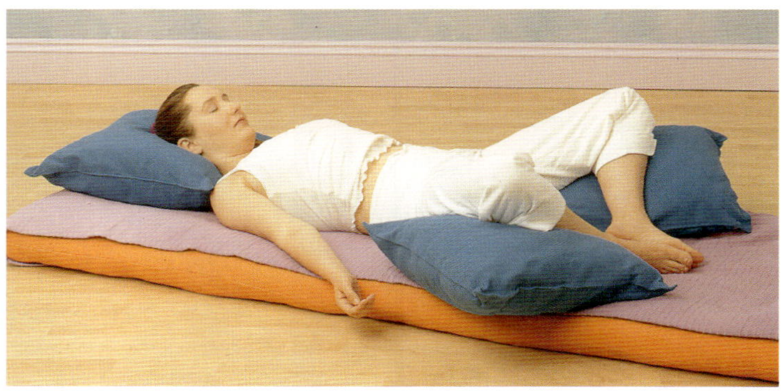

5 Remove the book and bring the soles of your feet together so that your knees fall outward. Support them with the remaining two cushions. Place your hands, palms up, beside you in a gesture of openness and complete surrender. Relax for several minutes.

Seated looseners

Let your partner encourage and help you. It is fun and relaxing for both of you. The closeness of trying to conceive can permeate all aspects of your life together.

1 Sit on the floor with legs extended and feet apart. Bend your right knee and bring your foot to rest against your left inner thigh, with your heel close to the pubic bone. Flex your left ankle and straighten your left knee. Raise your right arm overhead and stretch up through your right side, breathing in.

2 Breathe out as you lean to the left over your left leg, with your left arm sliding gently along your leg and your right arm stretching up. Breathe in as you sit up, lowering your right arm. Breathe out as you bend to the right, walking your hands along the floor each side of your bent right leg.

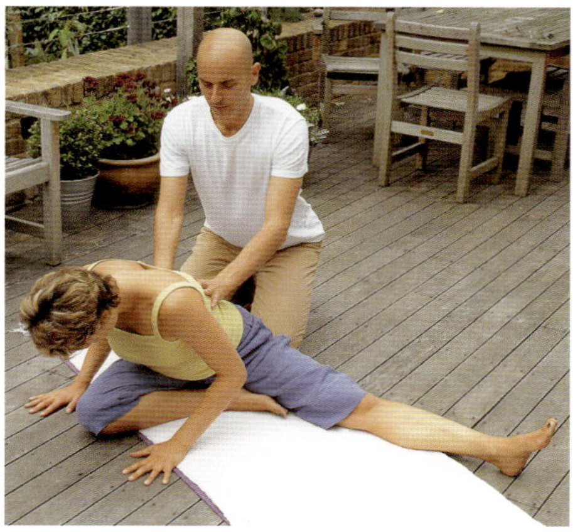

3 Keep the left ankle flexed and stretch right through your left side as you bend over your right leg. Breathe in as you sit up straight. Repeat these movements a few times on the same side. Then breathe naturally as you change legs and repeat the movements with the left knee bent.

Happy womb poses

It is important to focus your attention in the lower abdomen and to create space there in order to bring more energy to the reproductive system. Sit on the floor or a chair and open your hips, with your knees wide apart, as often as possible. You can sit comfortably on the floor to read, talk on the phone, watch TV and do most of those things you normally do sitting in a chair – except that in a chair the pelvic area is apt to be constricted, especially if you cross your legs.

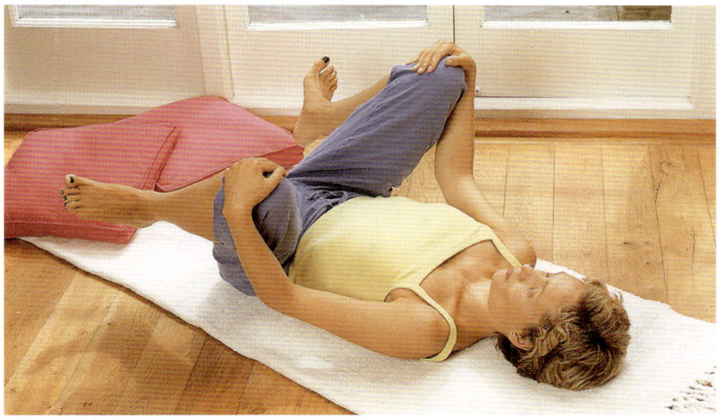

1 Lie on your back, bend your knees and hold one knee in each hand. Keeping your chin tucked down and your waist against the floor (using the abdominal muscles), rotate your knees outwards with your hands, relaxing and opening the hip joints. Circle the knees out and in again for a few moments, several times a day.

2 Sit upright with your legs loosely crossed and a scarf around your middle, crossed over at the abdomen. As you breathe out pull the scarf ends loosely to create pressure. Breathe in deeply against this pressure to open the scarf and bring the breathing movements down into the lower abdomen and pelvic floor. Continue for several minutes.

3 Sit with your knees bent and your feet apart and flat on the floor. Now bring your palms together with bent elbows. Keeping your chest open, gently press your elbows against your inner thighs for a few moments to open the hip joints. Breathe slowly and deeply.

4 Remaining seated, lean forward and place your hands on the floor with palms upwards. Gently press your knees apart with your upper arms. Breathe deeply, lengthening the out breath for as long as you can.

Make Space in Your Life for Your Pregnancy

No doubt you already realize that you will have to re-arrange your priorities once your baby is born. However, the best time to start is right now. Making a baby requires a lot of energy, but our energy is limited, especially if we lead busy lives. That energy must come from somewhere and therefore, since Nature ensures that your baby comes first and gets all it needs to develop, it is vital that you conserve and boost your own energy levels. Yoga conserves energy by reducing stress through deep relaxation and boosts it by increasing your oxygen uptake through yogic deep breathing and movement.

get the yoga habit now

Yoga will stand you in good stead right through your pregnancy, after your baby is born and for the rest of your life. You will soon be hooked on the sense of well-being that it brings. Your daily session can be quite short, as long as it is regular, and many yoga techniques can be incorporated into daily life. As you become more aware of your posture, emotions, thoughts and attitudes, you will want to adjust them, whatever you happen to be doing and wherever you are.

learn to nurture yourself

Many women feel that they should hide their feelings, ignore their needs, always appear strong and independent and keep going, no matter what. But you must learn to stop, relax and nurture yourself. Only when you know what it feels like to be loved will you have the capacity to nurture the life in your womb and care for a tiny baby. Practise being vulnerable and learn to ask for help and support from your loved ones.

CAUTION
Whether or not you have practised yoga before, keep it very easy and simple for the first 14 weeks of your pregnancy. Focus on breathing and relaxation rather than movement.

Feet up the wall sequence

This relaxing sequence rests tired legs and lower back, while stretching the muscles in the groin and preparing the muscles of the pelvic floor. Meanwhile, practise slow, deep breathing with awareness.

1 Sit with the legs along a wall. It is best to bend the inner knee, lean back on the hands and then forearms, and swivel your bottom round before raising the legs.

2 Swivel your upper body round and straighten your legs against the wall – buttocks and legs should touch the wall. Place a cushion under your head.

3 Place your hands under your head with elbows on the floor, to open up your chest. Breathe deeply for a few moments.

4 Take your legs comfortably apart to release tightness in the pelvis and groin. Gently massage the inner thighs while breathing deeply.

5 Bend your knees and slide the soles of your feet down the wall, a comfortable width apart. Place your hands over your lower abdomen and become aware of your pelvic floor muscles. Draw in the muscles as you breathe in, and release the tension gently as you breathe out. Repeat several times.

Lying down stretches

A similar exercise helps to relax the pelvic region for conception but it is just as effective here, where the point of focus is the lower back. The lumbar region of the spine, the sacrum and the coccyx should all relax against the floor – quite easy when the knees are bent and pulled gently toward the chest. If muscular tension prevents the lower spine from softening in this position, take long deep breaths out to relax more fully. The gentle movements will further ease your lower back and remove any stiffness or soreness.

1 Lie on your back with your spine long and chin down. Keeping your coccyx on the floor, take one bent knee in each hand. Bring your knees toward your chest then gently circle them out to the sides to massage your lower back against the floor. This is a great way to release backache. Repeat several times.

2 Gently bring one knee toward the floor. As far as possible, make sure that both shoulders remain relaxed and your back stays flat against the floor. Keep your neck relaxed and breathe deeply.

3 Breathe out as you roll on to one side, bringing your knees together. Relax in this position and breathe deeply. Breathe in to roll on to your back, raising first one knee and then the other, or both together if you can. Repeat on the other side.

The bridge pose

This pose strengthens the leg muscles, especially the inner thighs, which helps you to support the extra weight of your baby as the pregnancy progresses. The Bridge Pose also stretches the muscles around the groin area, opens the chest and frees the diaphragm for deeper breathing. Alternate this exercise with the previous one so that you both relax and strengthen the lower spine and abdominal muscles. This will bring awareness and energy to the whole area.

1 Place your feet flat on the floor near your buttocks, about hip-width apart. Stretch your arms alongside your body, palms down, for support. Breathe in and raise your pelvis off the floor. Breathe deeply a few times in this position. Slowly lower your buttocks to the floor on a long breath out. Repeat several times.

Deep relaxation with focused breathing

Leave enough time so that you can end every yoga session with deep relaxation. It quickly dissolves any stress that may have built up, removing muscular tension and congestion and bringing new energy to all the body's systems.

1 Lie on your back with your spine long and chin down. Drape your legs over a beanbag or a pile of cushions, with knees bent out to the sides. Bring your heels close together and relax your feet.

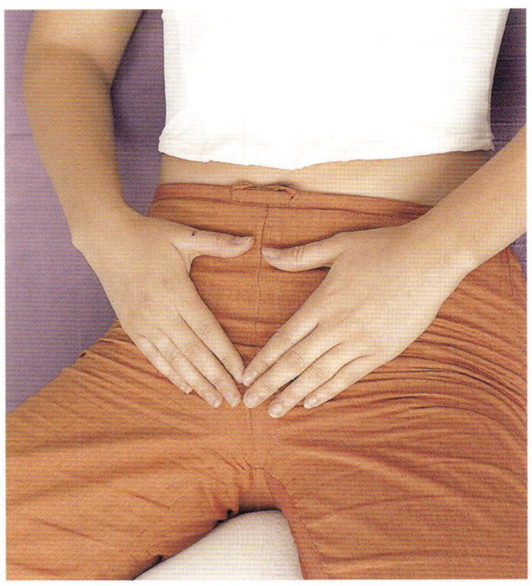

2 Place your palms over your lower abdomen, thumbs touching. Breathe deeply, and feel which is the best hand position to soothe you and bring nourishment to your baby. Close your eyes and relax.

A Strong, Supple Spine Supports Your Baby

Good posture is especially important during pregnancy for the following reasons.

- It holds your womb, in which your baby lies, in its correct position in the lower abdomen. This makes your pregnancy a far more comfortable experience for both of you.
- It relieves backache and can avoid its onset.
- It creates more space in the chest and abdominal areas, which become increasingly crowded by the presence of the growing baby.
- It improves breathing, and therefore your energy levels, because it gives the diaphragm more room to move.
- It improves digestion, which cannot function properly if there is compression in the abdomen.
- It prevents congestion in the circulatory system to the womb, upon which your baby depends for all its nourishment.
- It streamlines your figure, however large or small the bump.
- It makes you feel great. Standing and walking tall express a positive outlook, whereas the general compression and congestion that result from poor posture can make your energy stagnate and your mood depressed.

Although changes to your figure may be hard to detect in the early days, especially in your first pregnancy, it is important to concentrate on your posture from the start, before any bad habits are established.

Dog pose

This pose lengthens the spine and increases spinal awareness, as well as strengthening the muscles in the upper back, arms and hands. It also improves circulation and releases tension across the shoulders, and in the neck and face. Below are three variations on the Dog Pose. Try them all out and see which one suits you best.

Pose 1 Hold on to a table, stool or radiator and step away from it until your spine and arms are stretched and horizontal to the floor, and your feet are hip-width apart. It helps initially if someone checks that your back is flat. Keep your head and neck horizontal, so that your ears are in line with your arms. Breathe deeply and bend your knees slightly if this helps you stretch further.

Pose 2 Make a right angle by walking your hands forward (shoulder-width apart) with knees bent. Straighten your legs (feet hip-width apart) on a breath out, bringing your heels to the floor if you can. As you breathe in, stretch through the spine and arms. Hold the pose for a few breaths, breathing deeply.

Pose 3 From the position shown in Pose 2, balance on one leg and raise the other. Keep the knee of the leg that is on the floor bent. Push down into your arms and hands. Now change legs to repeat on the other side.

Alignment of the spine

Your posture can be improved simply by becoming aware and straightening up whenever you notice that you are drooping. The back of the body, being bonier than the front, has less sensation (fewer nerve endings), so it is quite difficult to be aware of the position of your spine. It helps to stand or sit against a surface such as a wall, so you can feel whether your muscles are holding your spine firmly upright or are slack. With practice, both awareness and posture will improve as you locate and strengthen the relevant muscles.

1 Stand with feet a short distance from the wall and hands behind your waist. Press against the wall with head, shoulders, waist and buttocks. Lengthen your neck, lowering your chin. Breathe in and stand as tall as you can. Hold this stretch and contact with the wall as you breathe out. Repeat a few times.

2 Now bring your heels and calves against the wall and repeat the same stretch up as you breathe in, maintaining contact with the wall as you breathe out. Repeat.

3 Bring your hands to your sides and press your waist against the wall as you stretch up, breathing in. Maintain contact with the wall as you breathe out. Repeat.

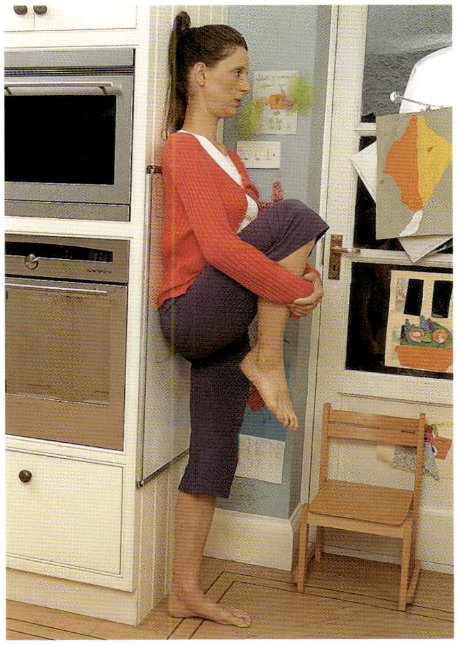

4 Bend one knee and clasp both hands around your shin. Draw your thigh close to your chest as you breathe out, balancing on your straight leg. Release the pull on your shin as you breathe in and stretch up, maintaining contact with the wall. Repeat.

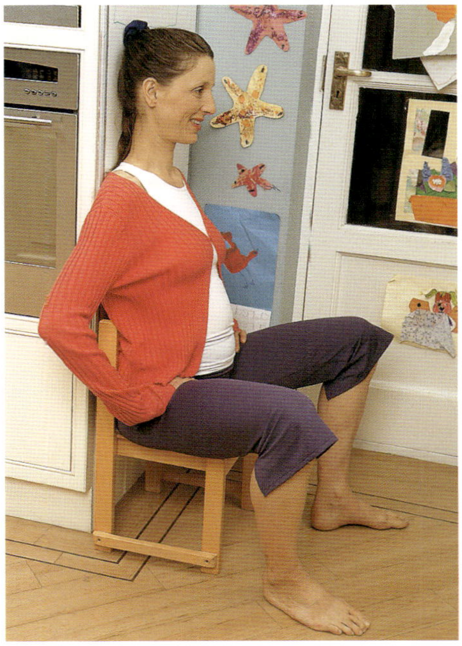

5 Sit on a low stool with knees apart and feet firmly planted on the floor. Maintain contact with the wall with your head, shoulders, waist and buttocks as you breathe in and stretch up, then breathe out and hold the upward stretch.

6 Once you have found and strengthened your spinal muscles, practise lifting up through your spine whenever you are standing or sitting.

Easy Standing Poses

Now that you have learnt how to keep your spine aligned, and know how good that feels, you can maintain the alignment as you move gracefully through these sequences. They develop strength and suppleness, helping you to protect and nourish your growing baby as well as yourself. They also help to keep your feet firmly on the ground and remain steady as your body changes.

Grounding

The joints and muscles around your hips, legs and feet take the weight of your whole body, and the muscles of the pelvis and pelvic floor carry the weight of your upper body and trunk. These important muscle groups can be strengthened and toned by the following grounding exercise, which allows your weight to pass smoothly through your legs and feet into the ground beneath you. It becomes ever more important to work with gravity rather than against it as your baby becomes heavier.

1 Stand with your feet apart and loosely bend your knees, making sure you maintain your upright posture through the spine.

2 Bring your hands into Namaste, the prayer position, and press your palms firmly together with elbows out to the sides.

3 Spread your hands wide, so that you keep your elbows bent and open up your chest area, all the time breathing in deeply.

4 Stretch your arms out to the sides and lower them, breathing out. Repeat steps 1 to 4 several times.

5 For a stronger version of this exercise, place one foot on a low chair and bend the other knee. Change legs after a few breaths and repeat with the other foot on the chair.

Standing stretches

By stretching up from the hips and through the waist, these stretches create space for the diaphragm to contract downwards to a greater extent, so that you breathe more deeply. Twist and sway rhythmically as if you are dancing.

1 left Stand with knees loosely bent and stretch your arms overhead, first one side and then the other. Feel your ribs and waist opening and releasing.

2 right Bring your arms out at shoulder level and swing round from the waist, first to one side and then the other, without changing your leg or arm position. Now repeat both movements.

Adapted easy triangle sequence

This sequence works out your oblique abdominal muscles and your lumbar spine. Strong obliques help to prevent backache, hold your developing baby firmly and trim your figure.

1 Stand tall with feet wide and knees well bent. Place your hands on your hips and sway from side to side, tipping your pelvis up to the right as you sway to the right and up to the left as you sway to the left in a rhythmical movement. Keep your spine erect, coccyx tucked under and chest lifted. Repeat the sequence several times to loosen the hips and pelvis.

2 Bend to your right side without tipping forward. Place your right hand along your leg and bring your left elbow back to open the left side of the waist and chest as you look upwards.

3 Now stretch your left arm right up and back to open the left side of your body. Repeat the movement while bending to your left side. Repeat several times on each side.

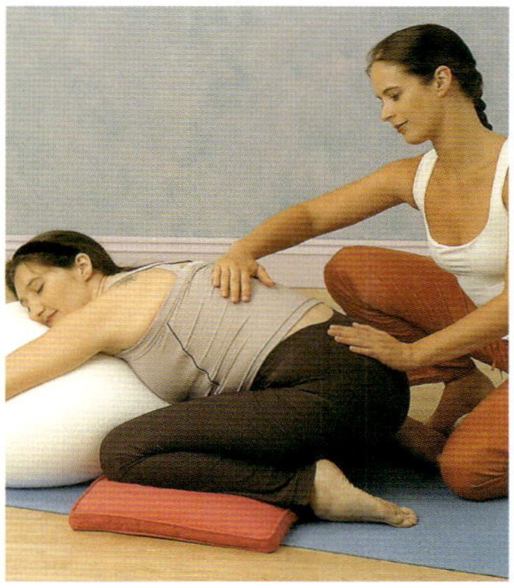

yoga for Mid-term Pregnancy

Your pregnancy is now firmly established and you should be feeling full of vigour and joy, especially if you have been practising yoga regularly. It is time to focus on building up strength and stamina, on making space to "breathe for two" and on creating and maintaining the best possible alignment of the spine at all times. Most of all – time to enjoy your pregnancy to the full.

Breathing for Two

You are likely to be feeling much more energetic during this middle stage, so enjoy your vitality – many of the yoga routines designed for these months are lively, invigorating, almost dance-like. They get your breathing and circulation working optimally and the vigorous arm movements and upward stretches, plus deep breathing, help blood circulate through the abdominal organs and bring fresh, nourishing blood to your baby via the placenta.

You will find at this stage that your balance changes as your abdomen enlarges, so it is important to take your centre of gravity downward, while keeping your spine stretched up and your chest open. This upright, graceful stance will make you feel elegant and confident and also allows more space to be created around the diaphragm, which needs to find room to contract downward so that you are able to breathe really deeply and fully.

"Oneness of breath and mind... this is called Yoga, integration."

Maitri Upanishad 25

Sunwheel stretch

This exercise really focuses on upper body stretches to open the chest and loosen the shoulders. The movements wake up the whole of the upper spine and dissolve tightness in the neck, shoulders and arms – this is particularly helpful if you spend a lot of time sitting at a desk or driving a car. These movements also create more space in the abdomen, so that your digestive system has room to function and your baby has room to grow.

1 Sit with knees a comfortable width apart and feet firmly planted on the floor. Tuck your coccyx under so that your pelvis is level – imagine that the pelvis is a bowl of water and you don't want to spill any of it. Stretch up through your spine from the base to the crown, with your neck long and shoulders relaxed and down. Breathe in deeply to open and lift the chest. Hold the lift as you breathe out, drawing your shoulder blades together with arms relaxed and then pushing the palms down toward the floor with fingers spread wide, to end with straight arms. Repeat, pushing down against imaginary resistance with each breath out and relaxing your hands as you breathe in.

2 Repeat, but this time start with your elbows bent and hands pointing up as you breathe in – this is so that you create a greater push downward as you breathe out. Make your movements graceful and rhythmical, rather like a seated dance.

3 Then, on each breath out, push strongly away from you to the sides, with your palms at shoulder level (the picture shows mid-push; you finish the push with straight arms). Engage the muscles around your spine and the back of your waist as you push. Relax as you breathe in. Repeat rhythmically.

4 On an out breath, stretch your palms to the sides with arms raised as high as you can, engaging your upper arms and back muscles. Finally, repeat the arm movements in reverse order, moving down until your arms are beside you. Repeat the whole sequence several times.

Swing high, swing low

This movement should be done rhythmically and with enthusiasm. It loosens up all the joints from your heels to your fingertips and blows away the cobwebs from your mind.

1 Stand with feet comfortably apart and knees well bent, and rotate your upper body from side to side, making sure your arms are loose and relaxed. Keep your spine upright, your hips and legs steady and your centre of gravity low.

2 Now stretch your arms right up to the right and clap your hands. Then sink into the previous position before stretching up to the left to clap your hands. Keep breathing deeply and vigorously as you alternately sink and relax then stretch to each side in turn.

Centring down

Getting your legs, rather than your lower back, to support your increasing weight and bulk is probably the most important postural adjustment that you can make during your pregnancy because it will save you from backache. Your womb is situated in the lower abdomen, which is held in place by the spine at the back, the pelvic girdle below and the hips on each side, so it has nowhere to expand as your baby grows except upward and forward. Any upward growth is constrained by your digestive organs and diaphragm, so most of the bulk has to move forward. This extra weight should flow downward through strong and well-toned legs, restoring your vital balance and centre of gravity.

1 Stand with legs a comfortable width apart, feet firmly planted and knees loose. Stretch your spine upwards, taking your weight downwards through your legs. Press your palms together at throat height with elbows out to the sides. Breathe in and expand the lungs at the back by opening your back ribs more.

2 As you breathe out stretch your arms forward and bend deeply at the knees. Hold a moment, then breathe in again. Repeat often.

Kneeling Stretches

Some kneeling positions enable you to build up strength and stamina (to help you carry your baby without getting tired), and kneeling stretches can prevent and ease low back pain. At the same time, kneeling exercises focus upon the birthing muscles, especially important if this is your first baby, as these muscles will not have been used before. Getting used to a kneeling position for your stretches is an important part of preparing for labour, since many women prefer this position in childbirth.

Cat pose

The Cat Pose is traditionally used to loosen all the joints before going into classical yogic seated poses. A simpler version, called the "kitten roll" here, is included as a warm-up. Avoid sagging at the waist by holding your middle spine firmly in line, like a table top, as you move through the rolls.

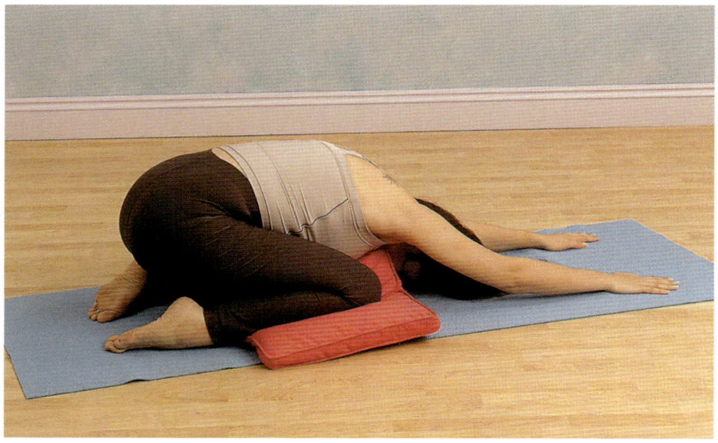

1 Kneel on your yoga mat with knees about hip-width apart, so that there is plenty of room for your baby. Place cushions under your knees, if you like. Sit back on your heels and, without lifting your buttocks, stretch your arms out in front, about shoulder-width apart. Crawl forward with your fingers while anchoring your buttocks on to your heels. Feel the stretch through your spine and breathe slowly into this stretch to loosen any tension in your back, hips or shoulders.

2 For the "kitten roll", sit back on your heels before breathing in to bring your weight forward on to your elbows. Lift your shoulders as you breathe out to arch your spine and tuck your coccyx under before rolling back on to your heels. Repeat the roll several times, and as you do so, focus your attention on feeling the stretch at the back of your waist.

3 For the "cat roll", bring your weight forward on to spread palms as you breathe in, so that your shoulders are directly above your wrists, your arms are straight but not locked at the elbow and your back is flat like a table top. This is the classic Cat Pose. Breathe out to arch and stretch your spine before sitting back on your heels, again, trying not to move your hands. Breathe in to repeat the rolling movement.

Hip and knee circles

These circles are practised while in the Cat Pose. They loosen tightness in the hip joints, can relieve cramps in the groin and increase the circulation of blood around the abdomen and pelvis.

1 Place yourself in the Cat Pose, with your weight evenly distributed and your back and head held firmly in line. Raise your right knee from the floor, keeping it bent at a right angle, and move it around in small circles parallel to the floor so that you are rotating the hip joint. After circling clockwise and anti-clockwise, repeat this sequence of movements on the left side.

Shoulder and elbow circles

These circles are great for relieving tension in the neck and shoulders, stretching the pectoral muscles and opening the chest for deeper breathing. Both Hip and Knee Circles and this exercise provide the same benefits as swimming movements.

1 Place yourself in the Cat Pose and then sit back on your heels. Keeping your weight evenly balanced, and your spine and head firmly in line, stretch your right arm out in front of you.

2 Bend your right elbow and bring your arm up and back in a circle, turning your head and opening the right side of your chest and your right shoulder. Lift the elbow as high as you can before stretching the arm to the front again. Repeat on the left.

Tiger stretch and relax

This is one of the best ways to relieve lower backache and sciatica. This can sometimes become a problem as your pregnancy advances and the weight of your baby presses on the sciatic nerve as it emerges from the lower spine and carries on down your leg. You will need to balance firmly on strong wrists and hands as you raise your leg parallel to the floor.

1 Place yourself in the Cat Pose with spine stretched and firm, especially at the waist. Slowly raise your right leg behind you until it is parallel to the floor, neither higher nor lower. Stretch right through your leg and into your toes, and kick away any tension or pressure.

2 Let your leg sink limply to the floor and relax it completely. Maintain your balance and the strength in your spine, but drop your right hip. Shake your leg loosely from hip to toes to release cramps or pressure on the sciatic nerve. Then readjust your position and do the same movements with the left leg.

Manual back stretch

As your baby grows it becomes ever more important to relax frequently and to ease away tiredness and tension. A partner or friend can work wonders, simply by gently helping your spine to stretch as you lie comfortably draped over a beanbag or pillows, either on your bed or on the floor. Your helper does not need to be an expert, just intuitive and happy to be guided by you to discover the position where you can relax and breathe most deeply.

1 Your helper needs to be in a firm, comfortable position, where they do not strain their own back. He or she extends their hands so their fingers trace light pressure either side of your spine as you breathe out. They release pressure on each in breath. Your partner should avoid direct pressure on the spine and check what feels best for you. The aim is to reduce compression and create space and comfort through a gradual deepening of the breath.

Your Birthing Muscles

A sphincter is a ring-shaped muscle that acts like a valve by squeezing tightly around the bottom of a tube to keep the contents in. If you want to release the contents, you simply relax the sphincter muscle, or you can get it to push the contents out by controlling the flow with rhythmic pulses. Women have three "tubes" that are either sphincters or are sphincter-like. These open at the base of the body – an area often called the pelvic floor – through the perineum (a mass of muscle that stretches right across the base of the body and holds the abdomen's contents in place.) Each of these openings is controlled by strong muscles, which are:

- The anal tube at the end of the digestive system, which opens to release waste matter. It is found near the base of the spine, at the back of the pelvic floor.
- The urethra – the tube leading from the bladder. This is found close to the pubic bone, at the front of the pelvic floor.
- The muscles each side of the vagina, which can contract and release around the cervix. The cervix thins out during labour to become the birth canal and let your baby descend through the vagina. Squeezing the vaginal muscles – "pulling up inside" – helps you locate and feel your cervix.

With regular practice, you can learn to contract or relax these muscles at will. This will help you throughout pregnancy (when your baby is pressing down against the pelvic floor), during the birth (to help control the baby's movement down through the birth canal), and after the birth (to restore perineal muscle tone as quickly as possible, thus avoiding many common postnatal problems).

THE BIRTHING MUSCLES

The pelvic area at around mid-term

Note how the baby presses against the internal organs shown

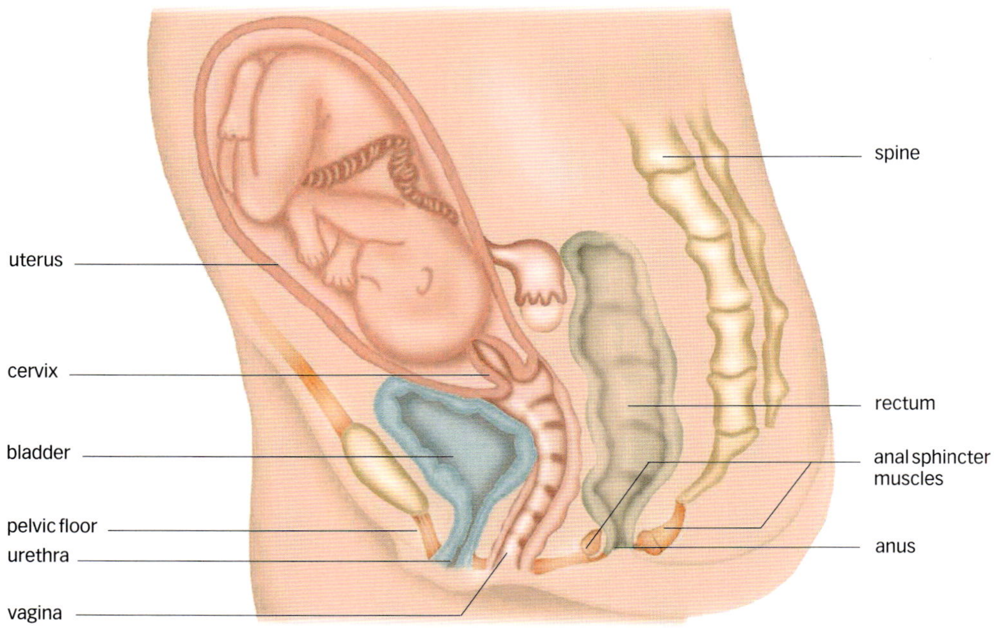

The perineum

(seen from below)

The red, striated areas are muscle

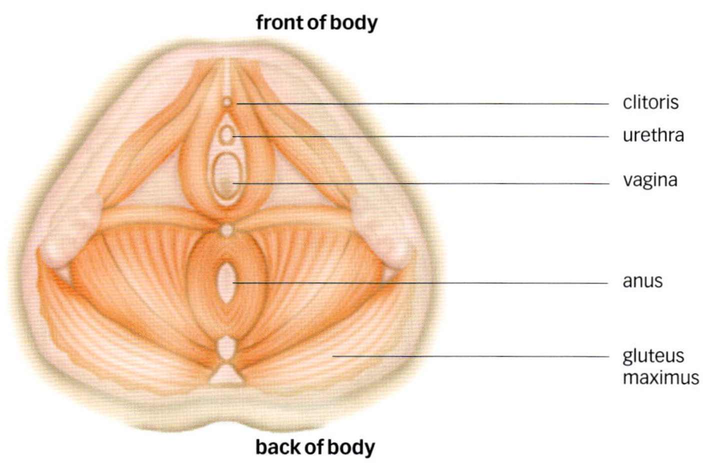

exercising the birthing muscles

Yogic philosophy maintains that energy follows thought. So focusing on muscle groups that we usually ignore helps to bring movement to the area and encourages awareness, which leads in turn to control of those muscles. Using the breath intensifies the muscular action. Yogic actions are never mechanical because you are using your breath and awareness simultaneously with the contraction and relaxation of the muscles. By connecting breath with muscular action you are toning, in a unique way, the muscles of the perineum, including those that attach it to the pelvis at the front and the lower spine at the back.

Begin your birthing muscle workout with the anal sphincter, contracting and releasing it in turn. Focus on how this feels, so that you learn to draw in the anus on a breath in and slowly release it on a breath out. Now focus on the sphincter of the urethra, squeezing it in and relaxing it in small, rapid movements. Finally, focus on the vaginal muscles, squeezing them tightly to draw your pelvic floor up and in. You will find that the lower abdomen is also drawn up and inward. These are the "birthing muscles" that you want to strengthen.

Pelvic floor stretches

In this modification of the Cat Pose your weight is distributed through your knees and elbows, leaving your lower back and pelvis weightless, released from the constraints of gravity that usually restrict flexibility in this area.

1 Kneel in the Cat Pose, with your knees spread wide enough to accommodate your baby as you lean forward on to your elbows. Place your head on a cushion if it is more comfortable. Distribute your weight evenly between your elbows and your knees, so that your head and neck are comfortable and your coccyx is raised as high as possible. Focus upon your pelvic floor, then exercise the three main birthing "sphincters" one by one, as explained on the opposite page.

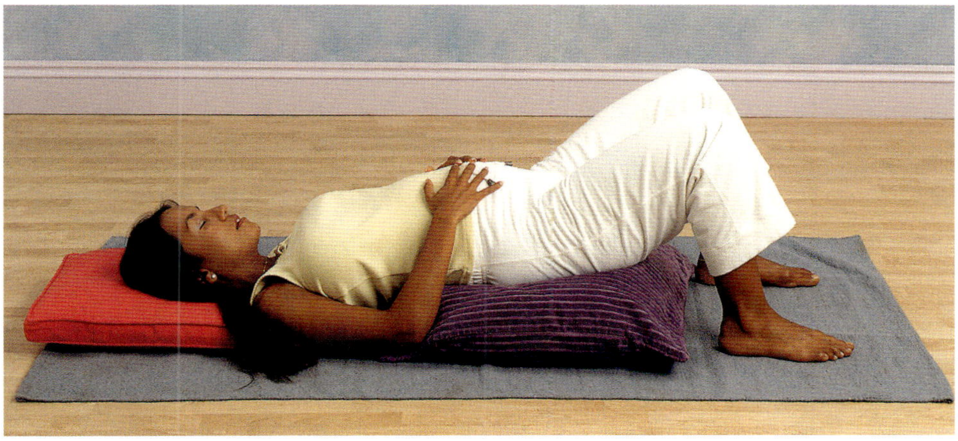

2 Alternate the kneeling position with this pelvic lift, which uses different sets of inner muscles. Lie on your back with your buttocks on a cushion to raise the pelvis. Keep your knees bent, with feet apart and firmly planted on the floor. Place your hands over your baby to feel the movement as you squeeze the whole pelvic floor in and up. Hold the squeeze for a few breaths to strengthen these muscles, then let go and relax completely. Repeat several times.

Supported pelvic floor lift

Your baby needs space to pass down through the vagina. This space is created naturally, as hormones are released during pregnancy to loosen the ligaments that hold your bones in place. This allows your pelvic opening to widen naturally. You can help by relaxing your hip and leg muscles in a wide-legged seated position, reclining comfortably against a beanbag or other support. Do not force yourself, just breathe gently in this position. Once the muscles around the groin have gently relaxed, the ligaments can stretch. In addition, the more relaxed you are the easier it is to practise strengthening the inner muscles of the perineum and vagina.

1 Sit with your legs as wide apart as is comfortable for you. Make sure that your spine is well supported, especially at the base. Flex your ankles and stretch through your legs. Lean back and relax in this position. The muscles around the groin area should be especially relaxed, to allow the ligaments to stretch.

2 Now clasp your hands in front of you at chest height, breathing in as you press your palms firmly together, and at the same time contract the muscles of the perineum and vagina. Hold this contraction for a breath or two, and then relax completely before repeating.

Some Subtle Yoga Movements

You have discovered just how effectively yoga can help you to strengthen your body and increase your awareness, and how you can use these benefits in all aspects of your everyday life. Well, in yoga there are also certain positions that look – and are – extremely simple to do, yet they create very subtle internal adjustments and strengthen groups of muscles that we are not usually aware of. These can bring huge benefits once you have explored, practised and become thoroughly familiar with them. These exercises require a calm, focused approach; in turn, they foster inner strength and self-confidence.

Gentle perineal stretch

This simple exercise should be done as often as possible from mid-pregnancy onwards, as it stretches all the muscles that make up the pelvic floor. It also strengthens, relaxes and brings awareness to the whole perineal area, which is the area through which your baby passes to be born. If the perineum is flexible, strong and lively, it helps you to give birth actively and with greater ease. You will be able to take your foot further out to the side as you gradually loosen up with practice.

1 From the Cat Pose, bring your left foot forward, placing it as far to the left of your hands as you can comfortably manage. Lean forward and breathe in deeply, keeping your spine stretched.

2 Breathe out as you sit back on your right heel without moving your left foot. This stretches the perineal muscles. Repeat several times, then change sides and repeat.

Rib stretch with Namaste hand mudra

This powerful exercise helps you to open your lungs more fully and to breathe more deeply by stretching between the ribs, especially at the back where your ribs are attached to your spine. It brings increased awareness to your back and is also an isometric exercise that strengthens your arms and upper spinal muscles. A mudra is a gesture with a spiritual as well as a physical expression. Adding the Namaste Hand Mudra focuses your scattered thoughts and centres your vital energies. It should be practised frequently for greater posture awareness, increased vitality and a focused mind. In late pregnancy, this exercise helps to create more space in the chest for your lungs to expand as your baby develops below the diaphragm.

1 Stand with your feet hip-width apart and knees loosely bent. Stretch the spine and drop the shoulders. Raise your elbows to the sides at shoulder height and press your palms hard together as you breathe in slowly and deeply. Feel your sternum rise and your ribs open at the back.

2 Now, breathe out slowly as you bring your hands down, with palms still joined. Relax your chest completely. Pause and rest with the breath out, then repeat the sequence twice more. When you have finished, rest for a moment and observe how you feel deep inside.

Sectional breathing with mudras

You will probably be surprised to discover that your breathing changes according to the position of your hands in these subtle hand mudras. Ensure that the first three types of breathing come easily to you before you join them together in the complete yogic breath. Allow a minute or two of rest before and after this practice to gain maximum benefit.

1 Sit up straight with your chest lifted to make room for your breathing muscles to move freely. Place your hands at your lower abdomen with fingers pointing toward each other. Join the tips of your index fingers and thumbs together to create a closed circuit of energy. Breathe in deeply and feel your abdomen expand as your diaphragm contracts downward. This is called "lower breathing" and gives you energy. Breathe out and repeat.

2 Now change your hand position, so that your fingers are curled into your palms and your thumbs are free. Breathe in deeply and feel your sternum lift and your ribs move out to the sides. This is called "middle breathing" and it also gives you energy. It comes to your rescue when your growing baby makes it difficult for your diaphragm to contract downward fully. Breathe out and repeat.

3 Change your hand position again, so that your thumbs are enclosed within your curled fingers. Breathe in deeply and feel how your upper chest is now moving much more freely. This is called "upper breathing" and is very useful if you have indigestion. Breathe out and repeat. You may also need this during labour, so start practising now.

4 With your thumbs and fingers curled into your palms, press your knuckles together with the fingers of each hand back to back. Turn your palms upward, with your hands in front of you. Open your chest and breathe in fully, from the bottom of your lungs to the top. Breathe out fully and repeat several times. This is full yogic breathing, excellent for recharging your energy and integrating mind, body and spirit in the here and now.

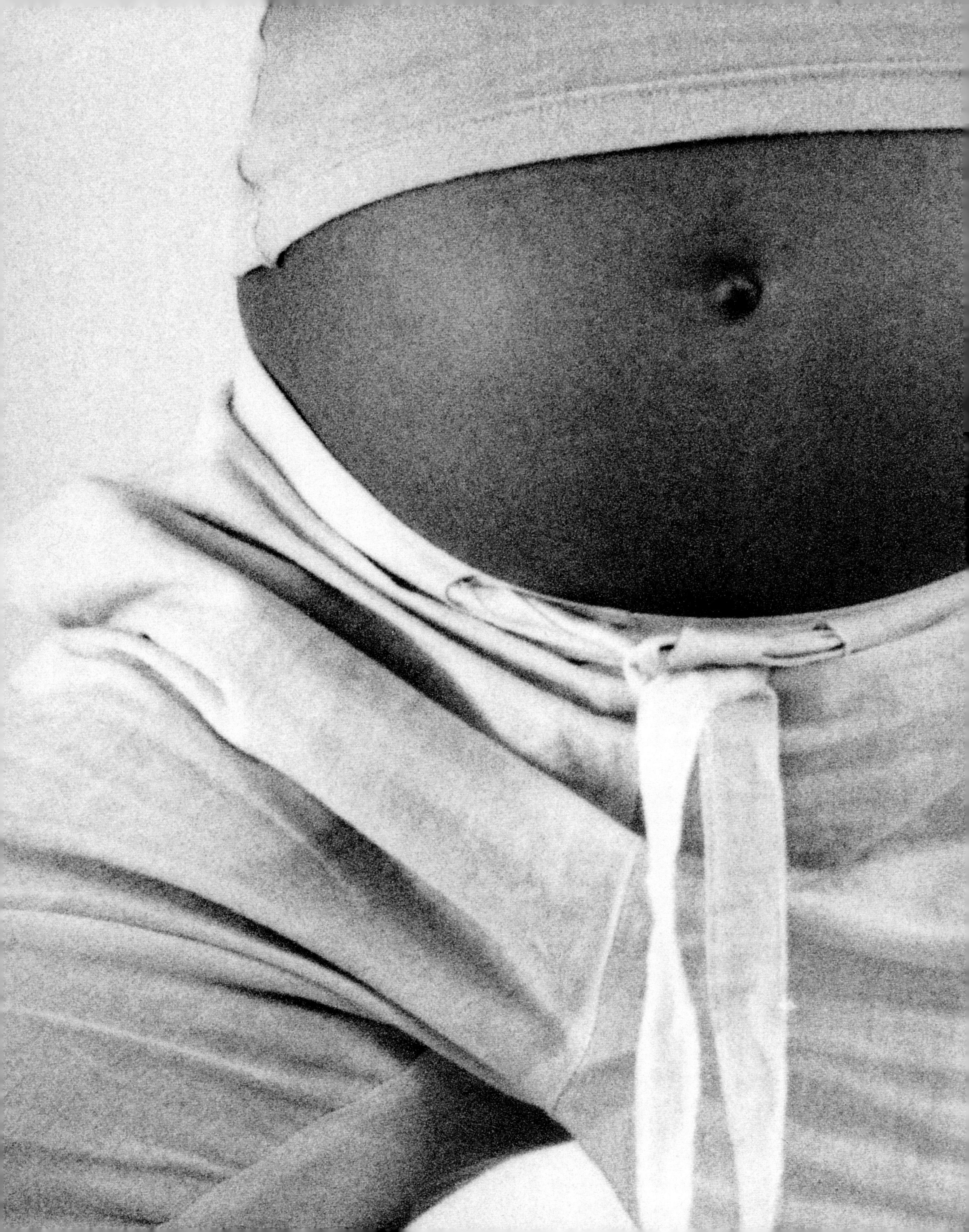

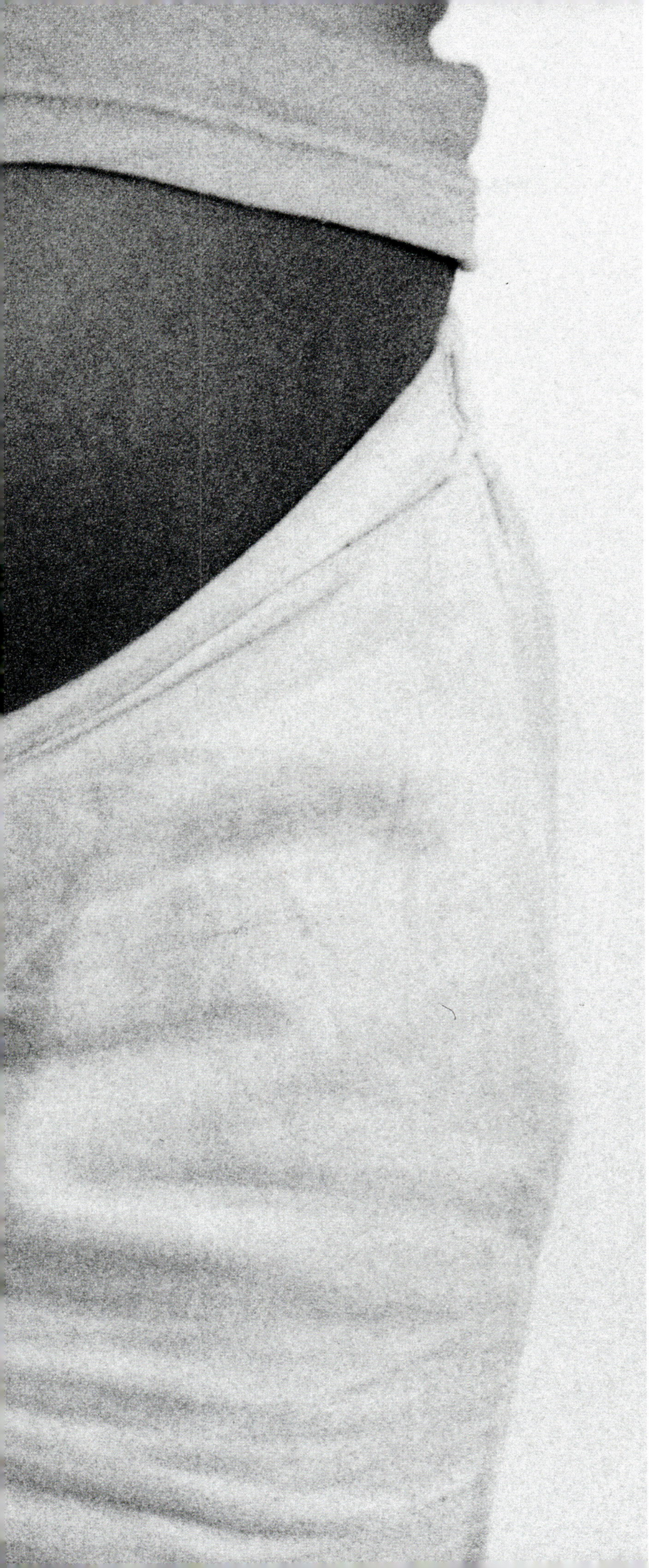

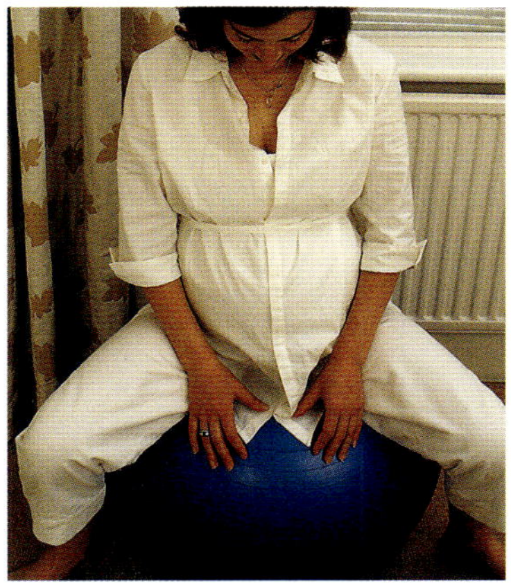

yoga for Late Pregnancy and Birth

During the last few weeks of your pregnancy your priorities will be to keep yourself as fit and comfortable as possible, and to practise yoga techniques that can help you during the birthing process. These prepare you physically, mentally and spiritually for labour. However your birthing may unfold, yoga will help you to feel centred and empowered.

Yoga in Late Pregnancy

Your baby will be growing rapidly by now, so your yogic priorities need to change. First, you will need to protect your back much more by ensuring that your pelvic and leg muscles are able to carry the extra weight properly. Your focus will be on building power in these supporting muscles. This means paying more attention to centring and grounding exercises, and always remembering to keep your knees well bent in any of the standing poses and movements. Cushions and beanbags should be used to support your back at all times, to enable you to rest more deeply during relaxation. Second, you will need to make more space for your baby, your breathing and your digestive organs. Finally, you will be focusing specifically on increasing the tone in your birthing muscles – in other words, the muscles of your lower back, abdominal area and pelvic floor.

Centring into the earth

This exercise combines both power and release. Imagine that you are hauling yourself up a ladder, one arm at a time, and then climbing down again as you support your weight with your arms. Your legs should be well bent to support your weight. Feel a line of strength developing along a vertical axis between earth and sky, passing through your body.

1 You are going to climb up your metaphorical ladder. Stand with knees bent and spine loose. Now, stretch first one arm overhead and then the other, as though you were climbing a rope ladder without using your feet. Squeeze your fingers tightly to hold on to the ropes. When you get to the top, spend a few moments just hanging from both arms, alternately squeezing and releasing your hands.

2 To climb down again, imagine you are going down a fireman's pole. All the strength is in your arms as you lower your weight one hand over the other down the pole. Slide down several times, bending your knees and grounding strongly along the vertical axis. These exercises can be done anytime, anywhere.

Supported side stretches

You need to practise side bending while sitting and resting your spine against a soft but firm support – here we show a beanbag placed against a wall, which is ideal.

1 Sit, leaning against a beanbag or a pile of cushions, with your legs stretched out in front of you and comfortably apart. Bring your hands behind your head with your elbows wide and pressed back to open your chest and stretch the sides of your body – you can breathe much more deeply in this position. Relax as you breathe and lengthen the breath out.

2 Still leaning against the beanbag, tilt your upper trunk to one side as you breathe out. Breathe in to straighten up and then tilt to the other side as you breathe out again. Repeat a few times.

3 Now, open your arms wide and stretch overhead, breathing deeply. This stretch really eases pressure in the lower body.

4 Keep one arm overhead and take the other forearm on to your thigh for support, then tilt to the side on a breath out. Breathe in to straighten up and out to bend to the other side.

Hugging rest

This resting pose is ideal for late pregnancy. You may also find it comfortable for deep relaxation. The beanbag (or pile of cushions) supports your abdomen, spine and head. Spread your arms wide to lift and create more space in your chest.

1 Kneel down, facing the beanbag, with your knees spread wide to accommodate your baby. Rest the front of your body and the side of your face against the softness of the beanbag and give it a big hug. Breathe deeply and relax completely.

Stretches for a Strong Lower Back and Abdominal Muscles

Think of yourself as an athlete in training who needs to build up power in specific groups of muscles for the task in hand, in this case giving birth. The muscles you will be using for childbirth are those in your lower back (for support and pushing against), your abdomen (to push the baby down the birth canal), your perineum and pelvic floor (for elasticity and control) and your breathing muscles (to make sure you stay energized throughout). You do not need complicated or expensive equipment in order to strengthen these particular muscle groups – you can find the props you need around your own home.

Kitchen yoga

Isometric exercises help to strengthen muscle groups, and a good way to do this is to push or pull against an immovable object to create resistance. For these exercises, do make sure that what you are pushing and pulling against really is immovable.

1 Stand in front of a wall unit (or a wall). Place one foot well in front of the other, with the front knee well bent. Lean forward and place your palms on the unit at head height. Adjust your position so that you are the right distance away to push hard. Breathe in deeply and push, taking the force down through your back leg. Involve all your abdominal muscles on the breath out as you maintain the push. Swap legs and repeat.

2 Bring your feet in line as you stand facing a ledge or shelf. Get a good grip with your fingers and, as you breathe out, pull down hard, bending your knees and sinking into a half squat. Hang there, breathing deeply and stretching through your trunk and arms as you work the muscles in your legs.

3 Stand in front of a counter top with one leg forward and the other back. Lean forward, bending your knees, and place your forearms on the edge of the counter with your forehead on top. Now, push down to open your chest and upper trunk, taking the push through your back heel as you lengthen your lower back. Hold, then repeat with the other leg back.

Stretch and squat with chair

Use a steady, upright chair to both stretch and squat down, as both positions will help to open up in the groin and stretch the pelvic floor. Keep your spine horizontal and your heels on the floor. To make the chair even steadier, push it against a wall.

1 Stand in front of the chair with feet apart and toes turning outward, so that your knees will bend over your feet at the same angle. Bend forward and hold the sides of the chair seat, keeping your back stretched and horizontal.

2 Squat down, bending your elbows to keep your back as flat as possible. Focus on stretching the inner thighs, the groin and the pelvic floor in preparation for giving birth. Breathe through this stretch, exhaling as you go down. Repeat frequently.

Perineal stretch with chair

Use a chair to help you when practising the Gentle Perineal Stretch at this stage. For comfort, place a cushion under the shin and foot that you are going to sit on. This exercise will really help you to prepare your body for birthing. Finding the position in which your perineum is most relaxed and you can move your pelvic floor muscles easily is most important for this exercise – you might even get some kicks from your baby.

1 Move from the Stretch and Squat with Chair posture to a wide kneeling position, resting one knee on a cushion. Place the other foot out to the side of the chair. Now, holding on to the chair, press down and stretch through the whole perineal area on an out breath. Change legs and repeat the stretch. Practise frequently.

Relaxation throughout the day

Never miss an opportunity to relax, alone or in company. If you can relax the muscles that are carrying your baby at every opportunity, it will greatly enhance your feeling of fitness and well-being. Keep a beanbag handy for those blissful moments.

above Kneel in front of a beanbag and flop over it to conduct weighty conversations with your toddler.

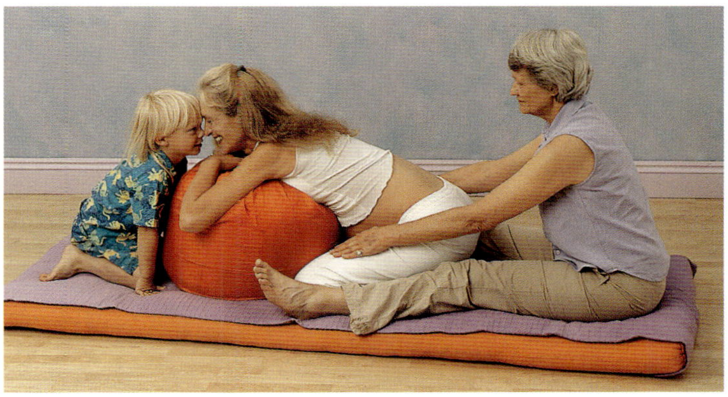

above If someone can be gently massaging your thighs meanwhile, then so much the better. Relaxed enjoyment is the key.

Massage, Breathing and Relaxation

The last few weeks are the time to take full advantage of all the help and support that family and friends can give you.You need to build up your reserves of physical and emotional strength in preparation for the birth, and the changes in your life once your baby is born. So rest and rest again, at odd moments and in whatever position you find comfortable.While relaxing, breathe deeply in order to nourish both your baby and yourself, and to let go of aches and tensions. Massage can be a great help, and the person doing it does not need to be an expert, as long as they are happy to do what you ask.

right Cuddles and closeness are especially soothing and sustaining during this final period of waiting. Let the whole family join in.

Back massage for deep breathing

This is one of the most soothing things that one friend or partner can do for another. It can be heaven for the recipient and also very soothing and relaxing for the person doing the massage. The recipient kneels with her knees wide and toes touching, and stretches over a beanbag in a relaxed and comfortable position. The beanbag will yield to fit the baby comfortably. The helper can kneel comfortably to one side, leaning forward slightly to massage her friend's back in soothing, circular movements. Both of you should make sure you are relaxed and comfortable before starting the massage. If pregnant herself, the helper should not lean forward too far, as this could cause backache.

left The helper places both hands gently on the recipient's back for a few moments, to establish gentle contact while she co-ordinates her breathing with that of the recipient. The helper then moves her hands as the recipient is breathing out (and thus relaxing), lifting them slightly to give the recipient room to breathe right into her lungs. The helper traces light finger pressure either side of the spine as the recipient breathes out, releasing pressure on in-breaths. Avoid all direct pressure on the spine.

Ankle massage in supported Warrior Pose

The purpose of this exercise is to relax the thigh and calf muscles passively while a friend supports your stance and massages your lower leg. Leaning against a wall with your head on your hands lifts your upper torso and creates more space for you to breathe deeply into your abdominal, pelvic floor and buttock muscles. You will find that this brings blissful relief generally, and relieves tight calves and lower backache in particular. Cramping in the calf muscles is common in late pregnancy as your legs cope with the extra weight and your blood circulation slows down.

1 Stand tall and lean your head against a wall with your forearms at head height. Take one foot forward. Bend the front knee and stretch through the back leg, as you take your weight into your back heel. Your helper should now get into a stable position where it is easy and comfortable for them to massage your leg.

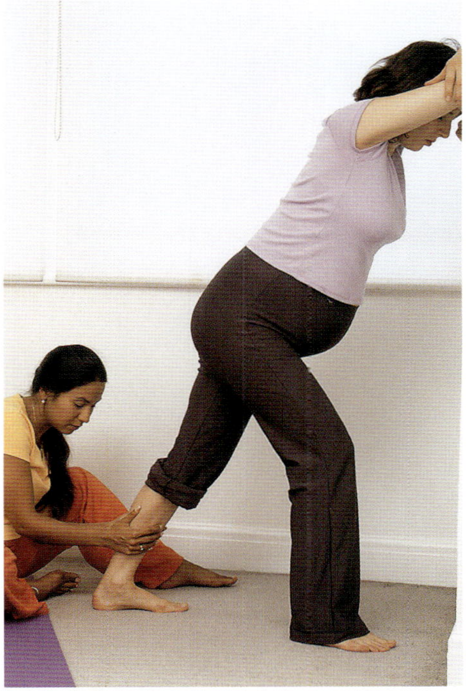

2 The helper should hold the ankle of your back leg to ensure that it doesn't lift from the floor as you lean forward. This increases the stretch in the calf. Lean into the stretch as you breathe deeply.

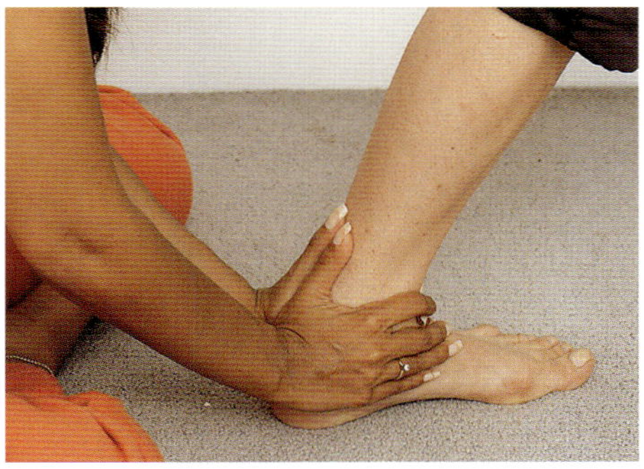

3 The helper can now slowly massage your lower leg, breathing in time with your own breathing, to release stiffness and tension and improve blood circulation.

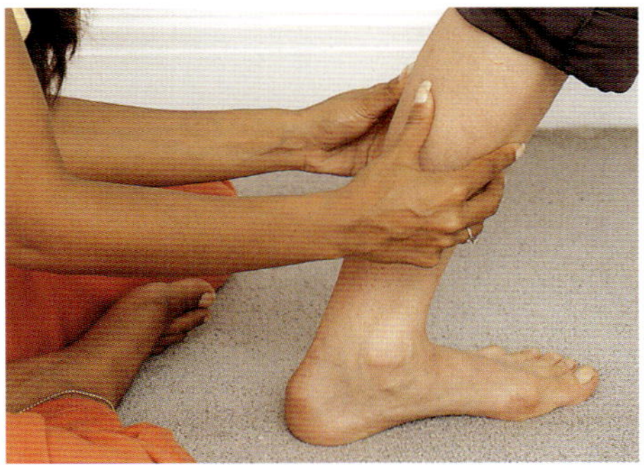

Supported reclining

Lying on your back after about 31 weeks is neither comfortable nor recommended, as the weight of your baby can put pressure on the vena cava, which carries blood from the uterus to your heart. Instead, recline at a comfortable angle on a nest of cushions, on your bed, a sofa or the floor. Have your "nest" ready and waiting for you, so that whenever you get the chance you can crawl in, lie back, close your eyes and relax.

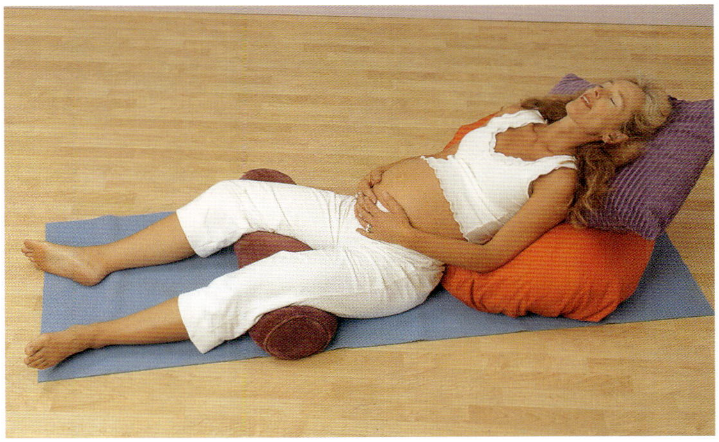

1 Lean back against a beanbag or a pile of cushions. Make sure that your trunk is raised and your head is at a comfortable angle. Add cushions under your bent knees to lessen the pressure in your lumbar area.

2 You can place your hands over your baby to increase your loving connection to him or her – or them.

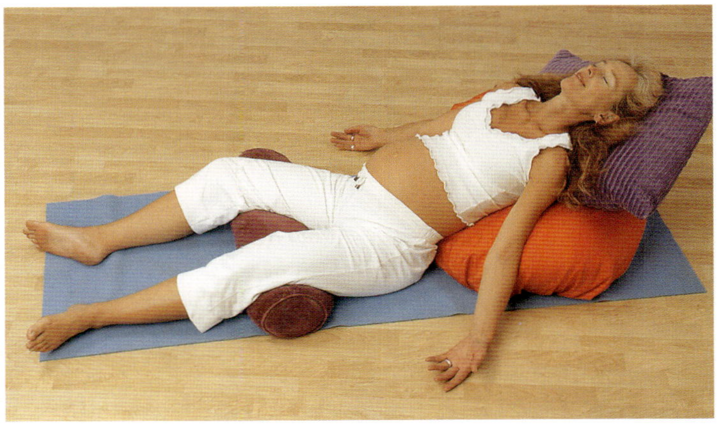

3 If you prefer, let your hands simply flop to the sides. Breathe deeply and feel yourself letting go of any strains or tension.

Yoga Breathing for Labour

Many of the complications of labour arise from physical exhaustion, often made worse by lack of sleep, so you need plenty of deep rest as the birth approaches. Conserving your energy is also a priority from the moment you discover that labour is starting, and the best way to achieve this is through deep breathing that follows the rhythm of your contractions. Taking a sip of water after each contraction is helpful too. When you are fully dilated, the breath takes on another role by helping you to give birth with minimal strain.

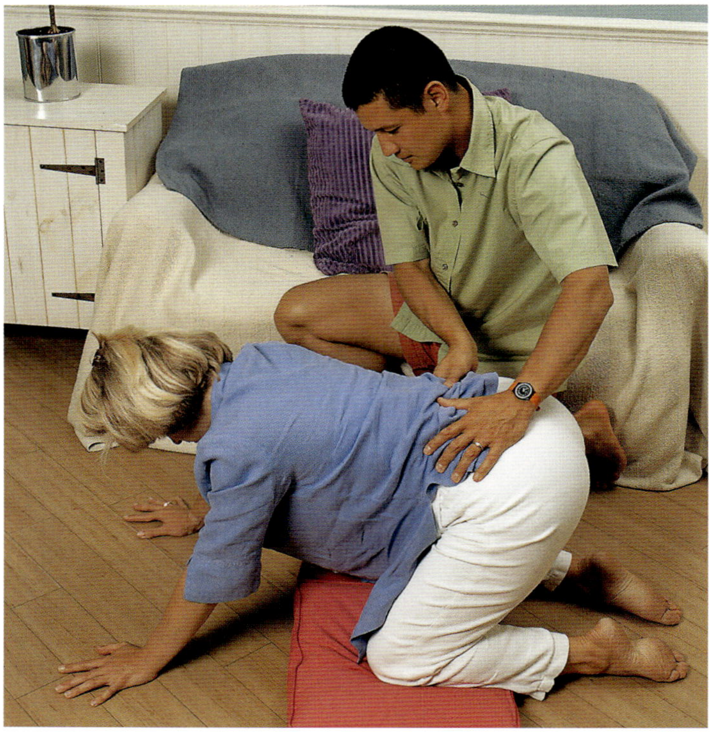

left Kneeling on all fours, keeping your head relaxed, can be a very effective position for grounding you and helping you to cope with backache during labour.

breathe out to welcome the contractions, then let them go

In the first stage of labour, most women have contractions at intervals that gradually become shorter as the labour progresses. From the very beginning, your most important task is to relax as much as possible between the contractions and to avoid dissipating your energy, particularly by talking. Your breath out needs to be used for getting rid of tension as the contractions come and go. During each contraction, focus on breathing as deeply as you can, depending on its strength. Then start to relax again, even if only for a minute.

centring with breath during labour

Your labour circuit positions may involve your partner, who can be holding you or massaging you, or you may prefer to labour on your own, drawing deeply upon your inner resources. Whichever way is best for you, the ebb and flow of your breath can help you to remain centred through awareness of the flow of breath – both during and between your contractions. You will find that breathing is your most powerful tool for surfing the contractions rather than attempting to resist them. After any conversations or medical procedures, use your breath to re-centre yourself.

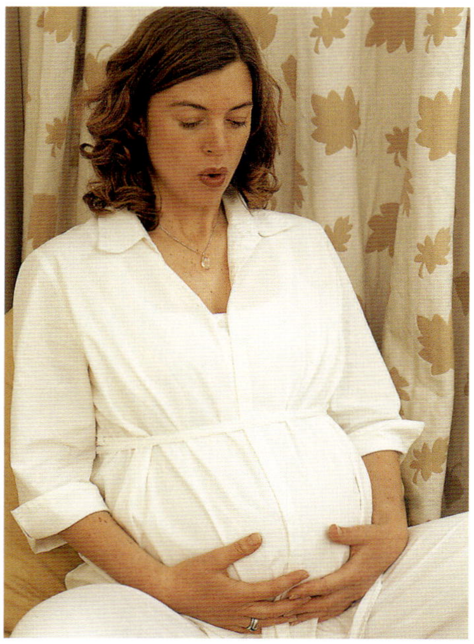

left Each time you feel a contraction on its way, breathe out deeply. This allows you to welcome it with relaxed muscles, and this, in turn, helps the contraction to work more effectively to open your cervix. Breathe throughout the contraction in whatever way feels best for you. When the contraction peaks, it is time to breathe out again deeply, to send it on its way and to dispel as quickly as possible the inevitable tension that results from pain.

right Sitting astride a gym ball allows you to use gentle pelvic rocking, in time with your breath, to relax between contractions and to centre yourself once more.

breathing for birthing

The second stage of labour begins when your midwife confirms that the birth passage is fully open and ready for your baby to pass through. You may already be feeling a strong urge to push your baby out, or you may feel nothing at all. Every woman is different. The two priorities in all cases, however, are to relax as deeply as possible to make space for the baby, and to relax all the muscles of the pelvis, particularly those in the buttocks, for birthing.

When it comes to breathing, voicing your breath out, on any note that feels good to you at the time, helps the abdominal muscles to work together with the powerful bearing down contractions. The longer that you can extend the breath out, the farther your baby is able to move down the birth passage during one contraction. Engage your inner pelvic muscles on your out breath, pushing from within. Try to keep your facial muscles, and the rest of your body, as relaxed as possible as you do this, to lessen the strain.

Your midwife will guide you as to when, or if, you should breathe lightly – as if you were blowing on hot soup. This need arises if you have to hold back and wait for your perineum to stretch as the baby's head crowns. By blowing lightly, you are disengaging your abdominal muscles from your breathing and so weakening the impact of the uterine contractions.

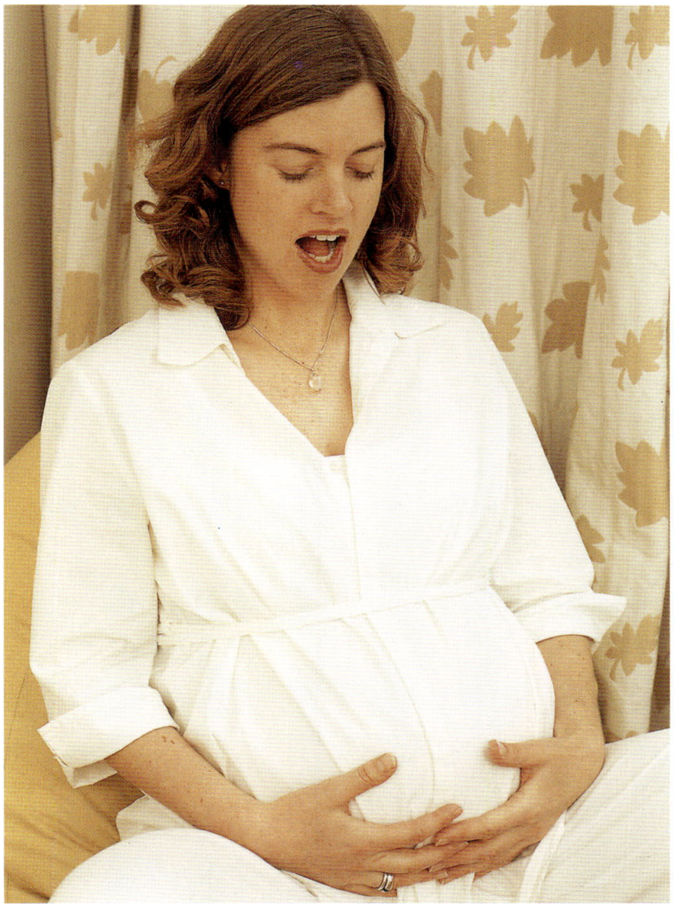

left Voice your breath out with a "Haaah" sound deep into your lower abdomen. Extend it for as long as you can to increase the pressure of your contracting uterus on your baby's body as he or she moves down the birth canal.

Gravity, centring and a voiced breath out can be combined in a powerful yet light action to push your baby out. Let awareness of your baby guide your breathing. Breathing your baby out into the world is a loving action that is open to most women and brings many possible long-term benefits to both mothers and babies. Even if medical intervention is necessary during your labour, breathing and relaxing with yoga will facilitate any birth process.

breathing to deliver the placenta

To deliver the placenta after the baby is born, use the same breathing that you employed for the birthing.

Zoë's story

Mine was a highly positive birthing experience – due to my husband's very vocal encouragement and essential breathing advice from Françoise [Barbira Freedman]. Having attended a yoga class throughout my pregnancy, I felt well-prepared, but when contractions suddenly started on my due date, I was taken by surprise by the strong back discomfort. I stayed at home for as long as possible with my husband and friend, timing contractions and pushing on my back to relieve the pain.

When I arrived at the hospital, my friend and husband arranged my pillows, sat me on my birthing ball and set up my specially chosen music. I started to meditate, breathing through the contractions. After a long labour, where the contractions hit me hard, and I became rather frustrated by watching the head bob back and forth for a couple of hours, I heard the word "episiotomy" from my midwife and with one contraction focused on my breathing and pushed five times to deliver my wonderful daughter, Kira.

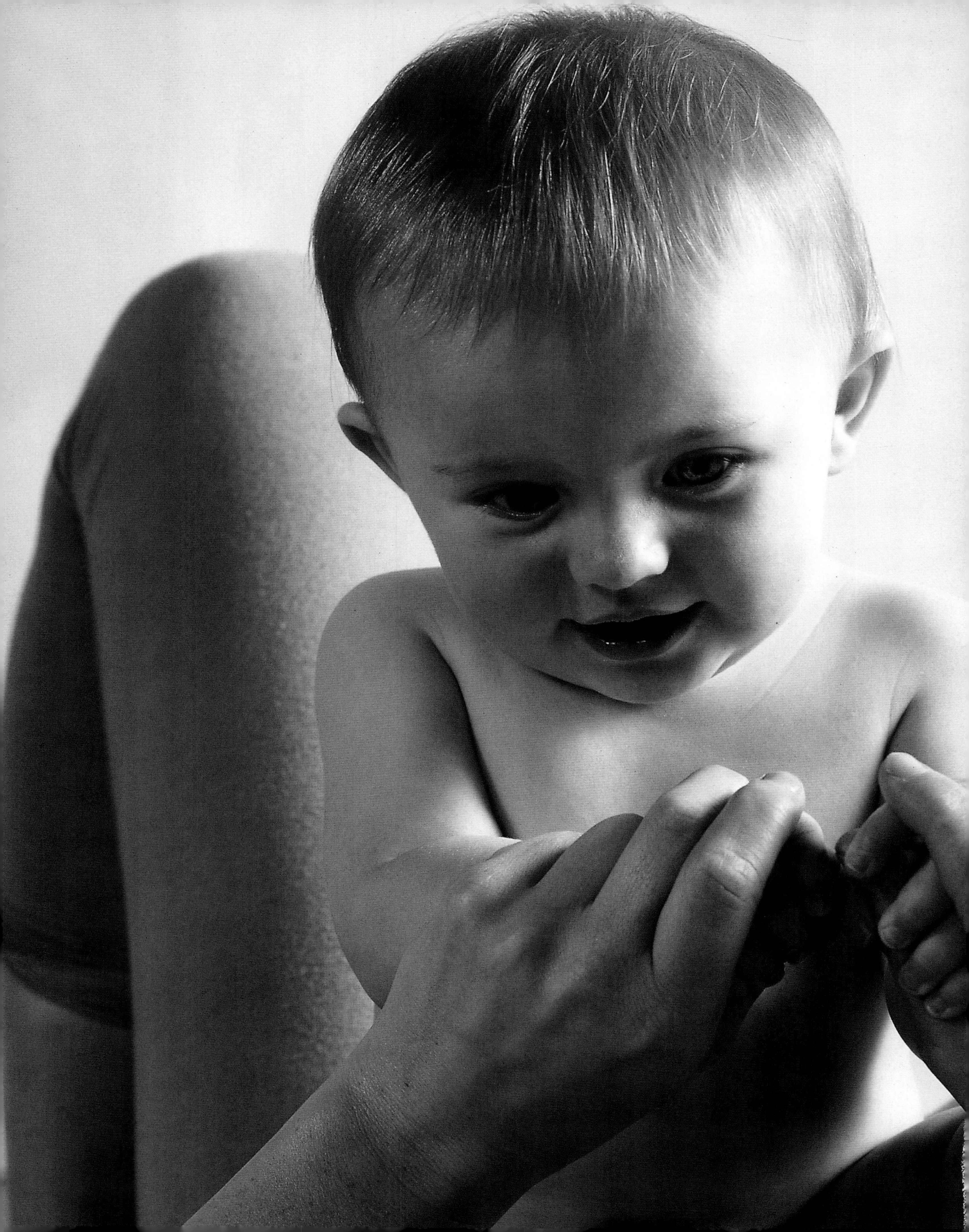

Postnatal
yoga

The feel-good factor of gentle yoga is expanded by the regular practice of movements and postures that increase new mothers' energy and enjoyment of life day by day. This is the time to replenish or renew your vitality, gaining stamina while remaining centred in mindfulness.

Six to Twelve Weeks: Standing Sequence

For the first few weeks after giving birth, stick to very simple and easy stretches and relaxation routines. By six weeks after birth, once you have more of your strength back, you can try the kind of sequences shown below. Do not push yourself or attempt anything you find uncomfortable or too difficult, and remember that many standing poses can also be practised more easily with your back against a wall. If you stand a half-foot away from the wall, you can then use it as a support for your back by leaning against it while in the pose.

As ever with yoga, you must work with the breath. Movement that flows with the breath is relaxing, effective and more "yogic" than a stretch in which you try and conform to a pre-set notion of how you should look in a posture. Before you feel comfortable holding "asanas" (the word for classical yoga poses), you can practise at least some of them by using movement and rhythm. When you do hold a pose, the dynamic is created inside your body with breathing, which is what makes yoga poses enjoyable. Whenever you feel tension, come out of it and relax.

Dynamic archer pose

As you become stronger day by day, stand tall in Tadasana, which is also known as the Mountain Pose, and feel the strong vertical axis between earth and sky.

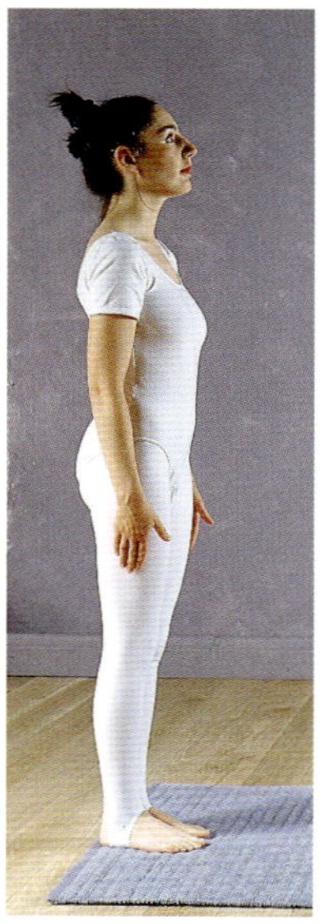

1 Stand in Tadasana, as shown. This is the starting pose for standing postures in yoga.

2 Jump or walk your feet about 1m/3ft apart. Turn your right foot out, your left foot in. Inhale, raising your arms open to shoulder level without tensing them. Exhale bending your right knee and turning your head right, extending both arms as much as you can. Inhale, straighten your legs, centre your head and turn the left foot out, right foot in. Exhale, stretching to the left. Continue alternating sides in an easy rhythm.

"Easy" triangle pose (Trikonasana)

Find an easy rhythm, stretching only as far as you can go without disturbing your relaxed breathing. This sequence combines a stretch, the Archer Pose, and an open twist in the Triangle Pose.

1 Begin in the Archer Pose, above. With your feet still apart and your arms extended, tilt your trunk to the right. Breathe naturally, letting your right hand slide down your right leg to the point where you feel you cannot go any further down without bending forward. Lift the inner arch of your right foot.

2 Keeping your weight on the left leg, inhale and stretch from your left heel all the way to the fingertips of your left hand. Look at your left hand and stretch more as you exhale. Come back to centre and repeat on the left side.

"Easy" forward bend

It is pleasant to let gravity stretch your spine while your shoulders, neck and head can relax completely in this forward bend, which also stretches the back of your legs.

1 When you have stretched both sides a couple of times, come back to the centre and lower your arms to flop into a gentle forward bend. Relax your neck. You may like to swing your head and shoulders gently from side to side, to ease your lower back. Bend your knees as you breathe in to come up from this pose.

"Easy" tree pose (Vrkasana)

Start with a low chair or stool for this pose and graduate to a higher one as you become more confident and flexible. You may prefer to have your back against a wall to do this pose, if your balance is unsteady.

1 Stand in Tadasana, facing the chair. Place one foot on the chair and bring your hands into the prayer position ("Namaste"), as shown. Use deep breathing to stretch and align your spine and centre your energies. Hold the pose with your body, breath and mind remaining steady.

2 When you feel ready, bring your knee up toward your chest, with both hands clasped below your knee. Keep steady and balanced, with your spine in line. As you breathe out squeeze your bent leg towards your body and release as you breathe in. Breathing deeply, hold the position for a moment. Release, regain your balance and steadiness, then bend the other knee and repeat.

Six to Twelve Weeks: Kneeling Sequence

Sitting on your knees enables you to lift your lower spine and stretch without straining your lower back and abdominal muscles. Yoga "asanas" in this position straighten your back and make your spine strong and supple. They also tone your thigh muscles in a way that may surprise you at first. They remove fatigue and refresh your whole body with little effort.

Vajrasana

This is a classic sitting pose in which you can develop the awareness of your vertical axis – from the pelvic floor to the crown.

1 Sit up erect on your heels with your feet flat. Use a cushion as shown if this is more comfortable. Now practise "Reverse Breathing": inhale deeply, imagining the breath being drawn up through the base of your body into the abdomen. As you exhale (longer than the in breath), pull in your waist, draw your navel up and back, and feel the breath flow up into your chest.

Kneel tall

In this dynamic version of Vajrasana, left, the flow of breath assists the lift of the diaphragm in a rhythmical stretch up and down.

1 Bring your hands together in front of you. As you breathe in, raise your buttocks, keeping your spine vertical and tailbone tucked under, and lift your arms above your head. Breathe out as you sit back. Breathe in and rise again and, if you can, hold for a few breaths before sitting back.

Chest expansion

This exercise is both a stretch and a forward bend. The challenge is to find the position in which your arms can stretch the most while your chest can open the widest. Make sure your neck remains relaxed throughout.

1 Clasp your hands behind your back, sitting tall. Bring your arms up behind you, keeping them as straight as possible and squeezing your shoulder blades together.

2 Next time you breathe out fold forward from the hips, keeping your arms raised. Breathe in, sitting tall. On the out breath, fold forward from the hips and lift your clasped hands, opening your chest as wide as possible. Keep expanding forward, breathing as deeply as possible.

3 Aim to place your head on the floor (or cushion) in front of you, while still sitting on your heels. Breathe deeply and work to bring your arms higher with each breath out. Release your hands and come up on an in breath, sitting quietly in Vajrasana and observing the effects of the last exercise.

Kneeling twist

Twisting in Vajrasana is slightly more difficult than the sitting twists on a chair presented earlier. Make sure you can kneel comfortably, with a straight spine, before you practise this kneeling twist. It allows further rotation and therefore is stimulating and enjoyable, even more so when you add a circling movement of the shoulder.

1 Place the back of one hand against the outside of the opposite knee and the other hand on the floor behind you. These are your levers. Sit up extremely straight as you breathe in and turn as you breathe out. Improve your twist with successive breaths out. Keep your neck relaxed and turn your head only to the extent that your spine twists. Eventually, you find yourself looking back without strain.

2 When you are ready, bend your back elbow and put your fingertips on your shoulder. Circle your elbow, loosening your shoulder and upper back. Repeat on the other side.

"Look at today for it is life.

The very life of life."

Three to Six Months: Elongating the Spine

As you go through successive stages of feeling aligned and stronger after giving birth, it is a pleasure to recover, or perhaps discover, the joy of stretching your spine. These deceptively simple adapted yoga poses make use of a support – a chair here – to help you enjoy the benefits of a fully stretched back. Feel the downward pull of gravity and the uplift in your lower back.

Leg-up sequence

This is harder than it looks! Find a support for your leg at a height that suits your physique and level of fitness – from low to high chair, to table top.

1 To begin, stand in Tadasana and circle your straight arms in wide backward sweeps, lifting in the waist, breathing freely.

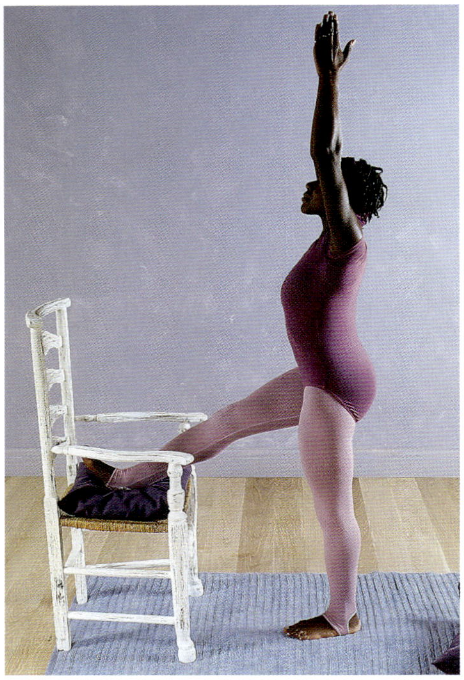

2 When you feel loosened up and stretched, place one leg on the chair with the knee straight and the foot flexed. Regain a balanced and upright posture and bring your palms to face each other overhead. Stretch up more on each breath out, squeezing in at the waist. Hold the position for three to five breaths. Relax your leg. Then change legs and repeat.

Open twist

While opening the chest wide, this pose allows a stretch from the standing leg to the extended hand.

1 With your right leg resting on the chair, as shown, place the corresponding hand on the inner side of your thigh as a lever and twist, circling your straight arm. Make sure you feel grounded and safely balanced before you start to twist.

Closed twist

In this twisting stretch, the pressure of the hand on the outer side of the raised leg allows a rotation of the hips.

1 When you twist to the left this time, your leg is on the chair and the back of your right hand is the lever against the outside of your left thigh. Circle your left arm several times in wide upward and backward sweeps, lifting at the waist. Twist both sides equally.

Forward bend

The raised leg helps you find more extension in the back as you bend forward, breathing as deeply in your lower abdomen as possible. Open the backs of the knees and enjoy aligning your hips for further stretch.

1 Rest one straight leg on the chair with the foot flexed. Pull your spine up tall and raise both arms slowly overhead, palms facing each other. Stretch with the breath, then, on an out-breath, hinge forward from the hips with a straight and stretched spine. Hold on to the back of the chair and breathe freely.

2 Alternatively, hold your foot. Keep your legs straight and make sure that your neck and head remain relaxed as you extend in the forward bend. Keep the hip of the raised leg pulled back.

3 To rest after these stretches, kneel down in front of the chair, with a cushion between your heels and your buttocks if you wish, and rest your folded arms on the chair seat. Breathe deeply into your back to relax.

Upper back strengthener

This exercise continues toning your central, vertical abdominal muscles as well as strengthening the upper back.

1 Sit in an upright chair and raise your baby high above your head as you inhale. Lower the baby slowly into your lap as you exhale, remembering to use your abdominal muscles as you breathe. Repeat whenever you have a spare moment.

Six Months and Beyond: Yoga for Energy

As you follow the rise and fall of the flow of your breath while you extend into the postures, you will enjoy the special energy that yoga brings. Rather than pushing your body to the limit in a workout, breathing in the postures as you can do them today – there is always more to come – stimulates all the systems of your physiology and increases your vital energy. Ups are not followed by downs after yoga. On the contrary, inner strength and enjoyment of life are constantly expanded.

Triangle pose (Trikonasana)

In this pose, the straight legs make a triangle. The back foot, firm on the floor, is your base as you stretch your spine vertebra by vertebra from the coccyx to the head, while you reach for the sky with a relaxed but straight arm.

1 In the classical pose try to place your feet wider apart than for the "easy" version – about the length of your leg – so there is more stretch. Practise first with your back to a wall, so that your head, shoulders and top hip brush against the wall as you stretch to the side and down. The point is to keep your spine elongating from the side, not to reach down. When you have a good "feel" for the position, practise away from the wall. Hold the position for several deep breaths, then repeat on the other side.

Downward-facing dog pose (Svanasana)

This is an inverted position, excellent for stretching and strengthening the whole body. The base of your spine is the apex of the pose, as you extend from the hands up your back and from your feet up your legs.

1 Start in this "Swan" Pose, sitting on your heels and stretching your fingers forward. Prepare to turn your toes under.

2 Breathing in, raise your buttocks into the air, coming on to your toes, and extending the back. Push your buttocks back and up, bending your knees.

3 Progressively extend your heels toward the floor, straightening your legs. Make sure you release your neck and shoulders. With each exhalation, let your back grow longer and the top of your thighs stretch. When you are ready, breathe out and place your heels on the floor and your head between your arms, so that you are looking at your navel.

Upward-facing dog

This phase is an upward-facing stretch with the spine bending backwards while the weight is on the wrists and feet.

1 From the Downward-facing Dog Pose, bring your hips down without moving your toes but lifting your heels, so that your body is suspended between your hands and your toes. Your head will come up. Gaze steadily forward and breathe deeply. When you feel strong enough, and only then, lift your hips up into the Downward-facing Dog Pose. You can use the breath in these stretches: breathe out to face down and in to face up, in an easy swinging rhythm.

Equestrian pose

This pose continues the two phases of the Dog Pose as part of the classic Sun Salute. It is an intense toner of the legs and the hips as well as an energetic spinal stretch.

1 From the Downward-facing Dog Pose breathe in, as you swing your right foot forward between your hands. Lean hard to the side opposite your swinging leg, in order to get your chest out of the way.

2 With your left knee on the floor, inhale and raise your arms above your head while dropping your hips.

3 For a stronger pose, keep your back knee a short distance off the floor. Breathe deeply, then return to the Downward-facing Dog Pose on an out breath and swing the other foot forward, breathing in. Change sides, then relax.

Yoga for Children

Making yoga a fun activity for children is easy. Here are exercises designed to develop an understanding of yoga practice, and there are plenty of fun ideas too.

Bel Gibbs

How is Yoga Suitable for Children?

Adults have been practising yoga for many centuries, and while many people complain that children today are growing up too fast, they're never too young to start enjoying yoga. Introducing the concept and practice of yoga and a yogic lifestyle to your children means that you are giving them the very best start in life.

left Yoga encourages us to find quiet time and to enjoy being rather than doing.

Yoga for children

Childhood is a vibrant time when natural energy and creativity are high, also when eyes and minds are open and learning is fun. This makes it the perfect time for children to explore and enjoy their bodies, while putting them in touch with how their minds work and introducing them to the idea of an inner self, or soul.

We all have the potential to develop our inner self, and yoga can show us how. Yoga is expressive, and this is what makes it so appealing to children. There are countless benefits of yoga for children, but the principal focus is to nurture a strong, healthy body, a calm, contented mind and, with commitment, a sense of inner peace.

What's in it for parents?

This section is primarily aimed at children between the ages of 3 and 11 years, but in a sense it is for children of all ages. As you demonstrate the yoga postures to your children, you will be rekindling your own sense of fun, putting you in touch with your inner child. You will also be increasing your motivation as a parent by taking an active role in the well-being of your child, physically, emotionally and spiritually. By practising yoga as a family, you will be spending valuable time together, learning new skills and having fun, and all without having to go near a television or the car!

What's in this section?

This section is written with a sense of fun and adventure. It is bursting with animals and objects from the natural

left Enjoying spending time with family and friends is an important part of growing up and will help us to build lasting relationships later on in life.

world, all of which will appeal instinctively to a child's imagination. So this is where we start. Encourage your children to "become" an animal from the colourful, easy-to-follow Animal Parade chapter. As they become adept at the animal postures, try some of the other fun poses and encourage your children to make up their own, or link them together in the themed story sequences in the Putting It All Together chapter. Try some of the yoga games, and even act out a yoga play.

In addition, learn how yoga breathing exercises can alter your children's moods and how peaceful postures, chanting and meditating can soothe away tension and nurture quiet time and contemplation.

below Yoga postures can help you to view things from a different perspective.

left The thought of imitating the behaviour and movements of their favourite animals is most children's idea of a lot of fun!

below Crow walking helps to physically strengthen our legs, and teaches us not to take everything too seriously.

what's it all About?

The following pages will inspire you to put yoga firmly on your family agenda. A brief "history lesson" explains how yoga began and why it is still relevant to our busy lives today. We all have a special place inside us that holds the key to our inner potential, like a treasure chest of precious jewels, and here we show children how to unlock their own inner powers.

Where Does Yoga Come From?

Yoga evolved several thousand years ago, in India, as a system of self-enlightenment. Today, in spite of all the benefits of 21st-century living, more and more people are turning to yoga for inspiration, confirming its timeless appeal.

The meaning of yoga

Originally, yoga evolved as a way of feeling closer to a higher, divine presence, and the focus of yoga practice was spiritual rather than physical. Today, yoga can be enjoyed as a physical discipline, known as hatha yoga, as well as a spiritual one. Many people still find that practising yoga can help to deepen their faith.

The Indian sages, or gurus, who first developed the idea of yoga believed that to attain spiritual enlightenment required a systematic approach. They devised a code of practice to follow in order to achieve all-round health, and believed that by training the physical body – the first step in yoga – they could tame the mind, improve the concentration, and find their inner self, or soul.

left Put down strong roots and you will be able to breeze more easily through life's ups and downs.

Nature knows best

The gurus sought their initial inspiration from the natural world around them. They watched and studied the patterns of nature and the behaviour of animals with a scientific passion. They marvelled at the power and focus of predatory creatures and birds as they hunted, at their ability to conserve energy and to sleep soundly when the opportunity arose.

left and below Some animals inspire us with their quick agility, while others show it pays to take things slow.

Admiring this balanced, instinctive way of living, the yogis – the gurus who developed and practised the yoga philosophy – began to imitate the way the animals moved and behaved, and soon they found themselves empowered with special qualities. And so the classical asanas, or animal postures, were born.

above Just like the yogis of ancient times, you can learn from the natural world around you. Simply open your eyes and strive to see the good in everything.

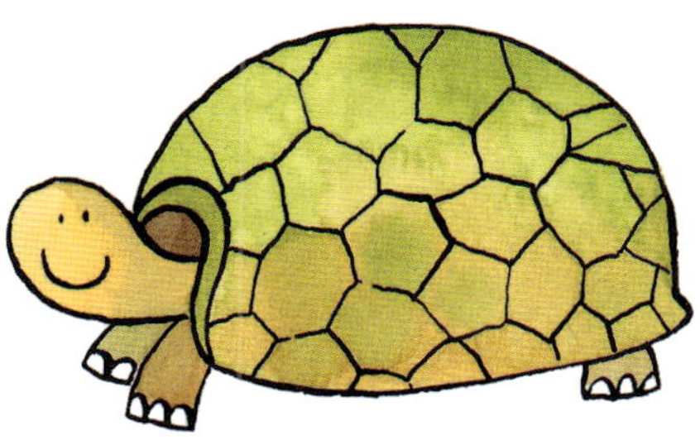

What the yogis learned

The gurus observed the breathing patterns of animals, and noted that animals with slow heart rates, like the elephant and the tortoise, lived much longer than agile and nervous animals with quick heart rates, such as mice and rabbits.

They saw the sun as the centre of their energy universe after watching how plants and flowers grow upwards to bask in its warmth and energy. They admired the huge trees because they were at the same time strong and flexible, rooted firmly in the ground but with branches moving freely in the wind. Seeing these attributes as metaphors for a human code of living, they saw that people could be happier and healthier if they, too, could be both grounded and flexible.

Yoga and Your Body

According to yoga philosophy, a human being is made up of different layers, a bit like all the layers you can see when you cut an onion in half. These are known as koshas.

You are an onion!

The outermost layer is our physical body, called the *anna maya kosha*. This is the layer we are most familiar with because it is visible and we use it for all our everyday activities. At a deeper level is our mind or mental layer, or *mano maya kosha*. This is where our thoughts, feelings and emotions take place. The deepest layer of all is our spiritual layer, or *ananda maya kosha*, the home of our inner self or soul.

The mental and spiritual layers are more difficult to relate to because they are invisible, but the aim of yoga is to use the physical body as a way of reaching first the mental and then the spiritual layer. It is here that yogis believe true happiness resides, and if we can reach our inner self we can enjoy a whole new side of our personality. Regular yoga practice can help to connect us with the inner self and develop our spiritual nature. The sooner we start on this wonderful inward journey the better.

above Think of all the parts that go into the layering of an onion. The more parts you unravel, the more there seems to be. This is the wonder of you too!

Getting physical

The human body is made up of a brain, a heart, two lungs, trillions of tiny cells, 206 bones, 600 muscles and lots of blood. More than half our body weight is made up of water.

The brain is the body's central computer, delivering instructions and messages to the limbs and internal organs, while the heart is a powerful pump pushing blood around the body. The blood is our body's "river of life", transporting its precious cargo of oxygen and nutrients to where they are needed, and relaying waste and carbon dioxide back to our lungs to be breathed away. Our lungs are like two big sponges that soak up oxygen from the air we breathe to keep us alive. As for all that water inside us, this is vital as every bodily function, from swallowing and blinking to breathing and moving – including reading this book – needs water.

Our bones are like scaffolding bound together by bandage-like muscles that literally stop us from falling apart. If our muscles are too tight, we feel stiff and our movements are limited. If left for long periods of time, tight muscles can affect our physical posture and how we carry ourselves, locking our bodies into uncomfortable positions and leading to rounded shoulders, stiff necks and knock knees. The good news is that muscles can be retrained through gentle, regular stretching, which helps them to regain their elasticity. This allows us to straighten our shoulders and open up our chests, stand tall with our heads up, touch our toes with ease, avoid injuries and generally feel in good physical shape.

Why it is wise to exercise

The benefits of physical exercise are enormous. Exercise strengthens the heart, and this promotes good circulation, which increases the flow of oxygen- and nutrient-rich blood to all parts of the body. Boosting the circulation speeds up the elimination of waste products, improves digestion, and helps to relax tense muscles, releasing mental stress and negative emotions. Exercise also strengthens bones, and tones muscles and ligaments, keeping us trim and fit. It increases energy levels and leads to the production of endorphins, the body's natural feel-good hormones, which enhance mood and well-being.

All types of exercise are good in moderation, but a variety of activities will work a wider range of muscles. Introducing yoga as a complement to regular exercise is manageable because it can be done at home and it doesn't cost anything. Because yoga can involve all members of the family, it offers valuable bonding time while teaching important new life skills.

Hatha yoga

Physical or hatha yoga relates to the practice of special postures called asanas. These asanas have evolved to work all parts of the body. They fall into families of postures, including forward bends, backward bends, standing poses, seated poses, twists, side-bending postures, balances and inverted postures. As you work through this section you will see that the groups of postures have different physical and emotional effects. Some are calming and grounding, while others are energizing and uplifting.

above We can use our bodies in so many ways. This assisted Sandwich pose quietens the mind as you fold your upper body forwards, and it gives your partner a nice back stretch at the same time.

right The body is your temple and physical activity makes your body an exhilarating place to live in.

What's on Your Mind?

According to yoga philosophy, the mind is the force that both drives the physical body and feeds our inner world or soul, where the yogis believe our true nature is to be found. The mind plays an essential role in determining whether our journey through life will be smooth or bumpy, or whether we will see our glass as half full or half empty.

The guru Patanjali defined yoga as "the mastery of the stilling of the mind". He believed in training the mind to focus completely on one thing at a time and therefore become as useful as possible.

above Give it a rest! A mind that is always busy can become physically exhausting.

left Thinking before you speak or act helps you to behave appropriately.

Five ways of thinking

The gurus who developed yoga philosophy believed that our thought processes functioned at five different levels, from muddled and irrational to clear and focused. The latter, superior level of thinking is attainable by all of us, but we first have to conquer the lower thought processes that govern our irrational or base behaviour.

Our least refined level of thinking is likened to a drunken monkey swinging from branch to branch, where thoughts are random and jumpy with no common thread. Moving up, the second level resembles a lethargic water buffalo standing in the mud, inactive and uninspired. The third level – which is the most common mental state – is a mobile mind that flits endlessly between doubt and conviction, knowing and not knowing. The fourth level reveals a relatively clear mind that has direction but lacks attention. The fifth and highest level is where the mind is linked exclusively with the object of its attention. Here, mind and object merge to become one.

Minding the mind

Learning to refine our thinking processes is one of the rewards of regular yoga practice. The yoga techniques outlined in this section concentrate on yoga postures, breath awareness and learning to enjoy stillness and silence. Getting to grips with these essential techniques will help you to improve your ability to concentrate. This is the first stage in learning to control the endless fluctuations of the mind.

Why concentrate?

The art of concentration is being lost. It is being undermined by the desire to be permanently busy and a notion that we must always be achieving, producing and progressing. So involved are we in multi-tasking that we risk becoming a jack of all trades but master of none. The absence of concentration makes it difficult for us to sit still, or think before we speak, or plan before we act. Those unruly monkeys take over our mind and our physical body responds with restless behaviour and hyperactivity.

above Left to its own devices the mind can become as unruly as these monkeys.

Present and correct

Concentration helps us to enjoy the "bloom" of the present moment and to think about tomorrow only when tomorrow comes; this is how it feels to be absorbed in a good book or enjoy an interesting conversation with a friend. Concentration makes for attentiveness in school and the ability to understand and retain information. It lets us fully engage with the people around us, and helps to cement relationships. It allows us to put 100 per cent of ourselves into everything we do, and means we will always do our best. In the same way that the sun's rays can be intensified through a magnifying glass, our fragmented thoughts can be harnessed together to make a powerful tool.

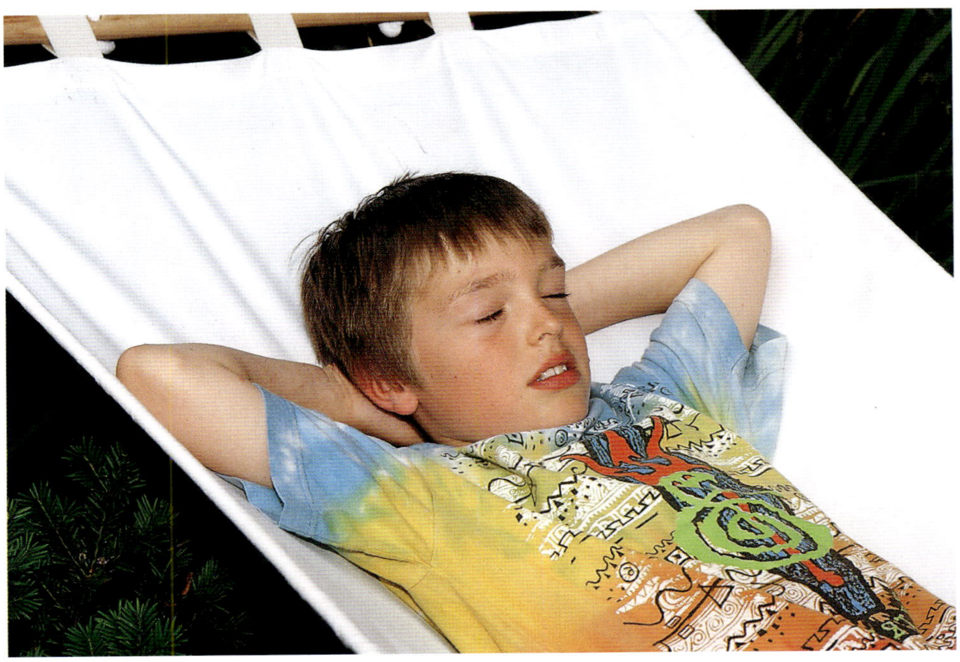

Meditation

Once we have learned how to concentrate and focus our mind and energies on one thing at a time, we can begin to talk about meditation. Meditation is simply concentration in a more *concentrated* form. Think of concentration as a flow of water that stops and starts. Meditation is simply a flow of water that continues unbroken in an endless stream.

One way or another, we are all looking for the peace of mind that this deeper level of concentration brings. When our attention is fully engaged, our mind becomes silent, worries are temporarily forgotten and an inner contentment replaces all else.

left The inner contentment that a quiet mind brings is available to all of us.

Your Invisible Friend the Breath

Breathing is our most important daily activity and, alongside eating, it is one of the two ways in which we provide our body with the energy it needs to live. That said, we can live for a few days without eating but only a few moments without breathing. Learning to be aware of, and improve, our habitual breathing patterns can dynamically enhance our physical, mental and emotional well-being.

above Finding the breath. All children will enjoy the challenge of trying to find something they cannot see.

left Look, no hands! Blowing a feather demonstrates the power of the breath – something we all take for granted.

Regular breathing encourages the exchange of old air for new. Breathing in and out through the nose involves complete in and out breaths, which encourage the diaphragm to contract and relax, massaging the heart and all of the abdominal organs respectively.

Shallow breathing, on the other hand, robs the lungs of oxygen and the diaphragm of its potential range of movement. With the lungs unable to function properly, stale air can become trapped and the body is deprived of oxygen. This is when our resistance to illness drops.

Posture

Diaphragmatic breathing, or tummy breathing, opens up the chest and allows the lungs to expand. We all have to stand tall or sit upright to breathe in this way. This means that our chest opens, our shoulders drop and overall posture is modified for the better. All in all, good breathing habits produce a stronger respiratory system, improved posture and a happier frame of mind.

Prana

In yoga philosophy, the other function of breathing is to increase our vital life energy, known as *prana*. The yogis believed that this in turn would lead to control of the mind.

Prana is controlled by special breathing exercises or *pranayama* (*ayama* meaning to lengthen or add a new dimension to). These exercises are designed to enhance our life energy and help us connect to our quiet inner self.

The breath as a bridge

The breath acts as a bridge between the mind and the body. You can see this in action by synchronizing simple stretches with your breathing patterns. Notice how the ebb and flow of your breath soothes your mind and helps your body to stretch.

Your invisible friend

Who has seen the wind?
Neither you nor I,
But when the trees bow down
their heads
The wind is passing by.

This poem illustrates that by seeing what the wind touches, we know it is there, even though we cannot see the wind itself. The same goes for our breath. If you blow a feather into the air, puff out a candle or watch your breath condense on a frosty day, you will see your breath at work. You can find "where" your breath is by using your hands. To do this, lie on your back, with your feet flat on the floor and your knees bent. Place both your hands, palms down, on your tummy. Position your hands so that they are covering your tummy button. Now feel the rise and fall of your breath.

above Breathing slowly and deeply through your nose as you stretch your arms is a wonderfully empowering gesture that says "I am me!"

left The taller and straighter you stand, the better you breathe and the better you feel.

above Tummy breathing is simply breathing with your hands on your tummy. Notice how your fingers gently separate as you breathe in and come together again as you breathe out.

Getting Into the Spirit

Yoga teaches us that we are more than just a collection of muscles and bones, and that we possess an inner spirit or soul. In many developed cultures, it is the appearance of the physical body that is championed and not what we are like on the inside. Not surprisingly, many people question whether the body does have a soul. However, the committed yogi would not only confirm its presence but would add that the soul is *the* essential element of our make-up.

Our secret self

In yoga philosophy, the physical body is considered to be a vehicle for the soul on its journey towards truth and enlightenment. The soul represents our true nature and identity. It is an inner world that lies not in the body's external casing but in the deeper ananda maya kosha, also known as the bliss sheath. Like a hidden jewel, the soul is always there for us to discover. It is always with us, just as the sun is always in the sky even though it may be hidden behind a bank of rain cloud.

Reaching the soul

The regular practice of yoga can take us to this special internal place, so that we can experience the real us. Beginning to practise yoga asanas for physical reasons, to improve agility and strength or to ease a specific complaint such as backache, is the logical place to start. This gives us visible results and begins to break down our physical shell. As our awareness of our physical body grows, so too does our emotional sensitivity. We begin to experience things differently, and very soon it dawns on us that not only does yoga meet our initial expectations, but it gives us an extra something too.

"A man travels the world in search of the answers and comes home to find them."

Showing your true colours

Yoga is a process of self-discovery, an unpeeling and unravelling, a working down through the layers until we reach our core. To begin with we may only glimpse the tranquillity of this inner sanctum, but over time, we may notice a subtle change in our approach to life. We feel more content with what we have got, rather than dissatisfied that we don't have more. We find that we have become more philosophical, more accepting of life's ups and downs, and less bothered by the little problems. This subtle, gradual evolution helps us to marvel at the spectacle of life rather than be overawed by its complexity.

Less is more

For children, getting spiritual is about learning to tap into this inner joy. Yoga encourages us to use our natural, inner resources. With guidance you will see that you have all you need to be happy within yourself.

left Home is where the heart is. The security of a happy home environment makes for sweet dreams.

right Yoga philosophy states that we are all naturally sunny by nature. Simply blow away the clouds and see that the sun is still there, shining away as brightly as ever.

left Get your heads together! Group bonding helps you to enjoy the people you are close to, and to appreciate that life is all about giving and receiving love.

below Nothing beats the familiar feeling of a big hug from your favourite bear.

Finding the Wizard Within

All children can be encouraged to believe in themselves and to locate their inner strengths or powers. They only need to be shown how.

above All of us have magical powers within ourselves, and with a bit of help from yoga we can learn how to unleash them.

Positive atttitudes

One aspect of yoga has to do with our actions. It means acting so that all of our attention is directed towards the activity to which we are engaged. This starts at home as we practise the physical aspects of yoga, and can then be applied to daily life.

Patanjali, author of the classic text the Yoga Sutras, outlined a set of guidelines for living. These comprise *yamas*, which help us to check our behaviour, and *niyamas*, which help to refine our attitudes. Together they teach us to act in a conscientious and attentive manner in all that we do, making the very best of ourselves.

Yamas

Non-aggression, or *ahimsa*, is one of the principal yamas. This encourages us to avoid injury in yoga asanas by underlining the importance of being nice to our bodies.

Developing compassion for others and protecting the environment are also aspects of the non-aggression principle. Always try to help others who are less fortunate than yourself, and take your litter home with you.

The honesty yama, known as *satya*, is about not trying to be what you are not. It asks us to know our strengths and weaknesses and to be proud of who and what we are.

Openness, known as *asteya*, teaches us to be flexible and open to change, allowing time for postures, like everyday situations, to evolve rather than trying to control them. *Asteya* literally means "not stealing", and it teaches us not to take advantage of others or to be jealous of what they have. It tells us to think about what we *have* got instead, and to nurture contentment within ourselves.

Niyamas

Cleanliness, or *sauca*, is about living healthily and taking pride in our appearance. One way you could do this is to keep your bedroom tidy.

Contentment, known as *samtosa*, is about doing what we do because we enjoy it and not because other people are doing it.

Enthusiasm, known as *tapas*, which literally means "heat", is about keeping our passion for life alive: making the best of ourselves, putting in the effort and really going for it.

Energy chakras

In yoga philosophy the chakras are invisible centres of spiritual and physical energy located in the body. They reflect our emotional state, and can affect our behaviour and attitudes. There are seven main chakras:

- Root or base (1) Feeling grounded and safe; the survival instinct
- Sacrum (2) Feelings about friends and family, social skills, and the ability to enjoy ourselves
- Solar plexus (3) Self-belief and enthusiasm for life
- Heart (4) Being open-hearted and joyful
- Throat (5) Communication
- Third eye (6) Clear thinking
- Crown (7) Wisdom and spirituality

Many yogis believe that learning to balance our chakras can help to restore harmony to our lives. Think about these energy centres and use visual imagery to bring them alive. A traditional image is the lotus flower. The idea is that when the petals of the lotus flower are closed, the chakra is closed too. Encouraging the petals to open and to be filled with a warm light is the way to bring back life and energy to the chakra. Try making up your own positive images that are relevant to you and your feelings.

Using visual imagery in this way can give all children a sense of the power of awareness. Don't be afraid to talk about your emotions. Ask yourself "where" in your body you feel sad or hurt. Describe and direct a visual image at the relevant chakra to help soothe emotional problems. Remember that a physical problem is often a sign of an underlying emotional imbalance.

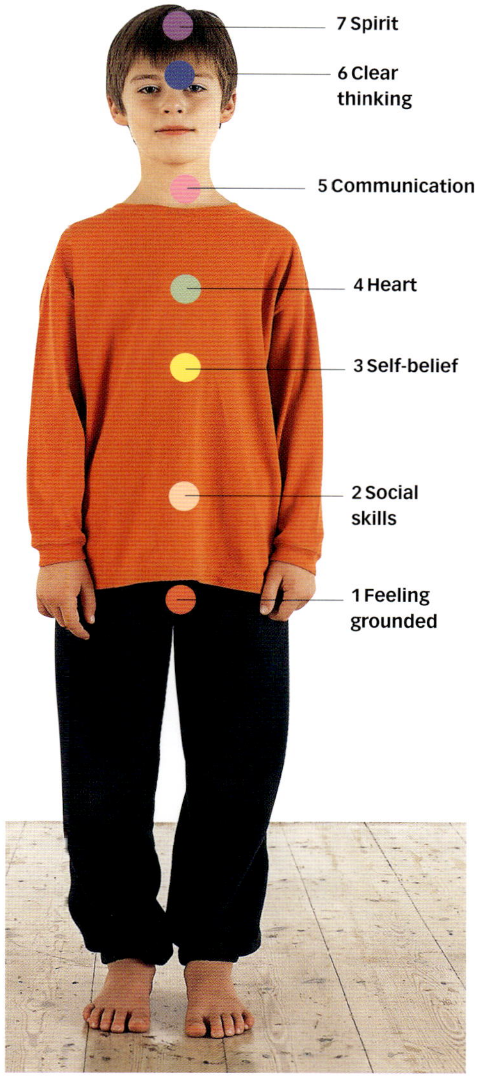

left The seven chakras are located along the spine. Awareness of these special energy centres can enhance emotional well-being.

Open your heart

Rounded shoulders may mean that the heart chakra is closed. The heart chakra represents love for ourselves, for others and for life in general. Encourage open-heartedness and boost self-esteem by using upper body stretches that emphasize the meridians to the heart. Finger, arm and shoulder stretches are all good for this. Suitable stretches are found in the Lion, Fish and Camel poses.

You could also visualize rays of warm sunlight flooding into the body in Little Buddha pose.

Standing strong and still

The inability to concentrate or sit still can suggest a lack of grounding. Feeling able to stand on our own feet relates to our root chakra. Strong poses such as Warrior or Tree develop conviction, and make us feel anchored to life. Visualize a strong, majestic tree and feel its roots anchored deep in the earth. Try Little Buddha pose to feel grounded but still.

Shout it out!

Shyness and the fear of speaking up relates to the throat chakra. Use sound to encourage self-expression and build confidence. Try Lion roar and Humming Bee Breath. Stretches that open up the chest, such as Cobra and Camel, may help too.

right Sitting in Little Buddha pose keeps you grounded but helps your mind to think clearly.

Let's Warm Up!

Warming up with gentle limbering exercises is essential preparation for your yoga practice. Spending just 5 or 10 minutes on these fun and simple exercises before you start your session will help to warm up cold muscles, focus your mind and get you in the mood. Preparing your body in this way is important as it will help you to avoid injury.

Keep the movements small to start with, working up from your feet and legs to your hands, wrists and arms, neck and head. Then move on to the body warm-ups and partner work.

Getting started

- Choose a warm, light room in a quiet part of the house. Make sure the television is switched off!
- Wait a good hour or two after a meal before you start your yoga session.
- Practise on a rug or carpet, or on your own yoga mat if you have one.
- Wear loose, comfortable clothes.
- Have some soft cushions handy and, for younger children, a few soft toys as props.
- Light some candles or mild incense to set the mood.
- Play some relaxing music for the quiet time session.
- Plan for a 15 minute session and build it up gradually to 30 minutes as you become used to it. Use your body language and energy levels as your guide, and learn to recognize when enough is enough.
- Aim to make your yoga positive not perfect. Have fun!

Planning a yoga session

- Do some of the warm-up exercises before you start.
- Practise nasal breathing.
- Come in and out of postures gently and thoughtfully – asana means "comfortable seat", and you should always feel at ease in the poses you do.
- Encourage self-expression by accompanying animal poses with sound: roar like a lion! bark like a dog!
- Balance the body by doing postures on both sides of the body.
- Erase the last posture by following it with a counter pose. For example, follow a forward bend with a backward bend, and lie down to rest after a series of strong standing poses.
- Poses that twist the spine are best done after you have stretched the back forwards, as in the Rag Doll pose (standing forward bend).
- Think about linking breath to movement and, as a general rule, breathe in when you stretch up or back and out when you fold forwards or down (the Sunshine Stretch is a good example of this).
- Sequence your session with asanas, games, breathing exercises and quiet time, and always end a session with at least 5–10 minutes in relaxation, or longer if you like.
- Keep a yoga diary using stick men to show the postures you have done. Record feelings and sensations and talk about which parts of the session you enjoyed the most.

left Spinning top Make a pointy hat by holding your hands together above your head. Now draw an invisible circle with your pointy hat to wake up your waist.

right Draw circles Use your feet, your hands and your hips to draw circles in the air. Make circles of different sizes; the slower you can make them the better. If there are a few of you, you may want to hold hands to stop yourselves falling over!

left Windmill arms Gently circle your arms like the sails of a windmill. Breathe in as you stretch up your arms, and breathe out as your arms come back down to your lap.

right Shoulder shrugs Squeeze your shoulders up to your ears as you breathe in, and round behind you and down again as you breathe out. Notice how long your neck feels now.

▷

Rocking the Baby

This warm-up gives a strong stretch to your hips and buttocks. Imagine your lower leg is a little baby that you are gently rocking to sleep in your arms. Cradle your lower leg as you would a sleeping child and rock from side to side, breathing deeply. Lift your foot to kiss the baby's forehead.

1 Sitting on your bottom, lift up your right leg and gently bend your knee. Draw your right foot in towards your tummy button, cradling your ankle in your hand.

2 Hug your knee and lower leg with your arms and gently rock your baby from side to side. Finish off with a little kiss on your baby's forehead as you lift your foot towards your face.

Cat, Dog, Snake and Mouse

Do as many rounds of this flowing animal warm-up sequence as you like. It wakes up your back, stretches your legs and strengthens your arms, wrists and hands. You can do the sequence on your own but it is much more fun to do it in pairs. Let each part merge into the next and don't forget to breathe!

1 Kneel on the floor in Cat pose, with your shoulders over your hands and your claws (your fingers) spread wide. Rub noses with your cat friend and breathe in deeply.

2 As you breathe out, curl your toes under and lift your knees and bottom upwards, letting your head hang forwards and down. Let your heels sink into the floor as you imagine you are a dog doing his morning stretch. Take a few more breaths.

3 As you take your next breath in, roll over your toes and let your hips and tummy drop to the floor. Point your toes behind you, stick out your tongue and hiss like a snake. Keep breathing steadily.

4 Lift your bottom up as you breathe out and sit back on your heels with your forehead on the floor. Rest like a quiet little mouse. Then lift your bottom up to come back to Cat pose, and start all over again.

▷

Partner Work

Doing limbering exercises and yoga postures in twos gives you double the fun. You can make your stretches deeper when you have someone to help you. Working together makes you more considerate and helps you to develop responsibility for your partner. Talk to each other as you do these exercises to help each other get the most out of each movement.

At a spiritual level, partner work builds connectedness and reinforces the concept of yoga – to unite. It is a wonderful way to bond relationships and to promote the idea of sharing.

left Table top Stand facing each other and place your palms on each other's shoulders. Hold on gently but firmly and then step away from each other until the crowns of your heads come together. Keep hold of your partner's shoulders and stretch your bottom back, so that your back flattens. Breathe deeply then walk your feet in towards each other and relax.

right Rainbow In this pose the sides of your bodies create the arc of a beautiful rainbow. Kneel down about 1m/3ft away from each other, with your bottoms lifted off your heels. Extend your outside legs, and rest your inside hands on the floor between you for support. Breathe in and, as you breathe out, bring your outside arms up and put your hands together to give a lovely stretch to the upper side of your body. Picture a rainbow filling you with its vibrant light. Release and change sides.

left Seesaw Sit opposite each other with your legs outstretched. One of you needs to place the balls of your feet against the inside of your partner's shins. Reach forwards and take her hands. Gently pull her forwards towards you so that she gets a lovely stretch in her back and the backs of her legs. Release and swap.

above Figure of eight Sit opposite your partner with crossed legs and your knees touching. Reach your right arm forward and down towards your partner's right arm. Fold your left arm behind you and reach round to grasp your partner's right hand. Breathe steadily and deeply and on each out-breath, gently pull your partner's left hand towards you. Hold for a few long breaths, then change arms.

above Washing windows Kneel opposite each other, raise your arms and press your palms together. Imagine you have a sheet of glass between you. One of you will guide the other's hands as you wash the window, and one of you will let yourself be guided. Draw big circles, reaching as high up and as far to the sides and down towards your knees as you can. Keep the hands together as you make the circles.

above The fountain Sit cross-legged on the floor. Hold each other's lower arms. Breathe in and, as you breathe out, lean back and allow your partner to support your body. Do this one at a time to begin with, then do it both together.

left Chair Stand with your backs to each other, feet apart. Squat down until your bottoms touch, and put your hands on your hips. Breathe deeply. When your legs begin to ache, imagine energy flowing between you so that you can hold the pose for a few more breaths. Release and relax.

Did you know that...
Ligaments and muscles need to be stretched gradually and naturally without hurry or forcing. This is especially true during childhood, when the muscles are still growing. This is what makes warm-up exercises so important.

Sunshine Stretch

This sequence was designed as a greeting to the sun god, who in Hindu mythology is worshipped as a symbol of health and immortality.

The Sunshine Stretch limbers up and energizes the whole body, particularly the back, making it flexible and strong. It also clears your mind, puts a smile on your face and makes you ready for the day ahead.

Stand in front of a window for this sequence, particularly if the sun is shining, or stand opposite a friend. Breathing deeply will help each part of the sequence flow into the next. As a general rule, you breathe in as you stretch up or backwards and breathe out when you bend forwards.

"Truly, a flexible back makes for a long life." CHINESE PROVERB

1 Stand in Mountain pose (Tadasana), looking straight in front of you – facing your partner or a window – with your legs straight and your feet together. Hold your hands in Prayer position (Namaste). Breathe deeply and imagine a cord from the crown of your head, gently drawing you upwards while your feet remain firmly grounded.

2 Stretch your arms up high above your head as you breathe in. Bring your palms together and hold for a few seconds.

3 Now exhale and fold forwards, bending your knees, and bring your hands to the ground in front of you, keeping your palms flat.

4 Step one leg back as far as you can, and then the other. Push back through your heels, keeping your legs straight. Imagine that your whole body feels like a stiff, strong plank of wood.

A summary of the movements

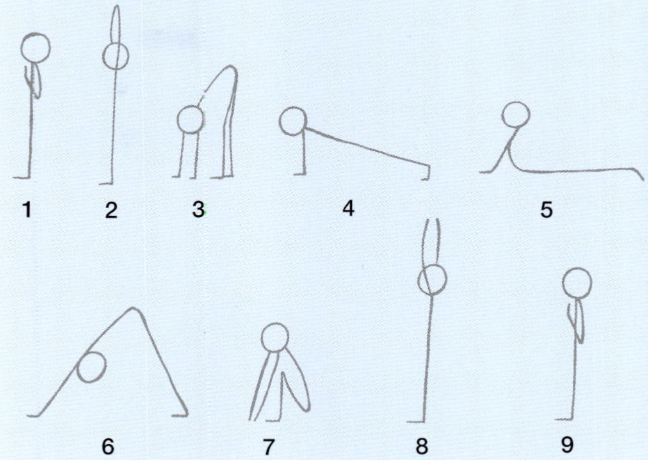

5 Lower your legs to the floor, drop your hips forwards and arch your back as you breathe out. Keep your head up. This is Cobra pose.

6 Breathe in and, as you breathe out, tuck your toes under and lift your bottom up into Dog pose. Hold here for a few breaths. Try to sink your heels into the floor and straighten your legs.

7 As you breathe out, bend your knees and look forwards so that you are facing each other. Then jump both feet forwards towards your hands and squat down.

8 Now straighten your legs and lift your arms up high above your head with palms together. Breathe in deeply. Stretch upwards to make yourself grow as tall as you can. Hold for a few breaths.

9 Breathe out and bring your hands into Namaste, or prayer position, in front of you. This completes the Sunshine Stretch. Repeat as many times as you like until your whole body feels warm and alive.

animal Parade

This section allows you to have some fun as you come face to face with a parade of animals of all shapes and sizes. These expressive poses show you how to imitate the instinctive behaviour and movements of your favourite creatures, birds and insects, so that you can assume the characteristics of each. Feel the power and pride of the roaring lion or soaring eagle, the quiet serenity of a fluttering butterfly, the suppleness of a slithering snake and the joyful agility of a leaping frog.

Lion Pose
SIMHASANA

Roaring Lion
SIMHAGARJANASANA

The lion is known as the king of beasts. He sleeps in the heat of the day and hunts by night, when it is cooler and his energy levels are at their highest. This is a very simple pose that all children love, and it is easy enough for even the very young or those who are new to yoga. It is lots of fun, and things can get quite noisy when everybody starts to roar!

Benefits

Lion pose energizes the body and mind. It builds self-confidence and improves communication skills. In addition, it dispels nerves and physical tension in the face, and helps to allay sore throats and problems with the eyes, ears, nose and mouth. It also clears your mind, makes you smile and gets you ready to start the day.

When to do the pose

This is a good pose for when energy levels need a boost. It can also be very helpful before an important event that may be making you feel anxious and a little apprehensive. Because it is so easy to do, it is suitable for children of all ages. It is a fun way to start a yoga session, especially if you can make a nice loud roar.

A summary of the movements

1 First, bend your knees and sit on your heels with your hands on the floor in front of you. Then rest your hands – which are now your paws – gently on your lap. Sit quietly, breathing gently.

2 Breathe in steadily and sit forwards on your knees, with your hands and arms out in front of you. Roarrrrr! Look upwards and stick out your tongue. Now sit back on your heels and roar in this way twice more to make yourself feel powerful but calm.

Dog
ADHO MUKHA SVANASANA

Domestic dogs have been man's best friend for thousands of years. The Downward Facing Dog is a classic pose that imitates the stretch that dogs do when they wake up. It combines an instinctive grace with a lovely elongation of the whole back.

Benefits
This pose will give you energy. It also stretches the back from the tailbone to the top of the neck, and strengthens wrists, hands, arms and shoulders. It brings fresh blood to the head and helps to release stiffness in the neck.

When to do the pose
Do this gentle stretching pose when you get out of bed in the morning, or as part of your warm-up sequence before a yoga session. It is particularly good as preparation for the Sunshine Stretch.

below Downward Facing Dog at full stretch.

1 Rest in cat pose on all fours. Your knees should be under your hips and your hands under your shoulders. Spread your fingers wide and spread your body weight evenly into each hand. Curl your toes under.

2 Breathe in, and as you breathe out, lift your knees off the floor and push your bottom upwards. Keep the legs a little bent to begin with and push your chest gently back towards your thighs. Walk your heels up and down a few times. Then try to release both heels to the floor, straightening your legs as much as you can. Imagine someone lifting you up by your tailbone so that your body resembles the two sides of a capital "A". Look back towards your tailbone, allowing your head to feel really heavy. Breathe deeply. To come out of the pose, drop to your knees and sit back on your heels, with your forehead on the floor. Relax.

A summary of the movements

Variation

Now try the Upward Facing Dog, which turns the pose into a back bend. From Downward Facing Dog, bend your knees and rest them on the floor. Push your hips forwards, but keep them off the floor. Push into your hands, lift your chest and look up as you gently arch your back.

Cobra
BHUJANGASANA

In this strong, energizing back bend, let your legs feel really heavy and keep them still so that the top half of your body can rear up strongly, like a cobra poised to strike. Feel free to hiss as loudly as you like.

Benefits
Cobra pose keeps the spine supple and healthy, and tones the nerves, improving communication between the brain and the body. It also helps to stimulate the appetite.

When to do the pose
Practise Cobra when you are feeling floppy and in need of an energy boost. It is also good for when you want to feel strong and powerful.

1 Lie on the floor with your forehead touching the ground. Tuck your elbows in at your sides and place the palms of your hands under your shoulders. Concentrate on keeping your legs and hips heavy. Push your feet into the floor.

2 Breathe in deeply and, as you do so, slowly lift your head off the ground. Begin to look upwards as you push your hands into the floor. Keep your legs out straight behind you, with your toes pointed and your feet pushed into the floor.

3 Keep breathing deeply and gently try to straighten the arms, arching your back a little more. Lift your chest each time you take a breath. Stick out your tongue and hiss like a snake. Say "Ssssss!"

4 If you fancy scratching your head with your tail, simply widen your knees and arch your back a little more as you raise your feet towards your head. Gently lie down again and curl yourself up in Child's pose, sitting on your heels and resting your forehead on the floor in front of you, with your arms lying relaxed by your sides. This is a counter pose to "unsnake" your back.

A summary of the movements

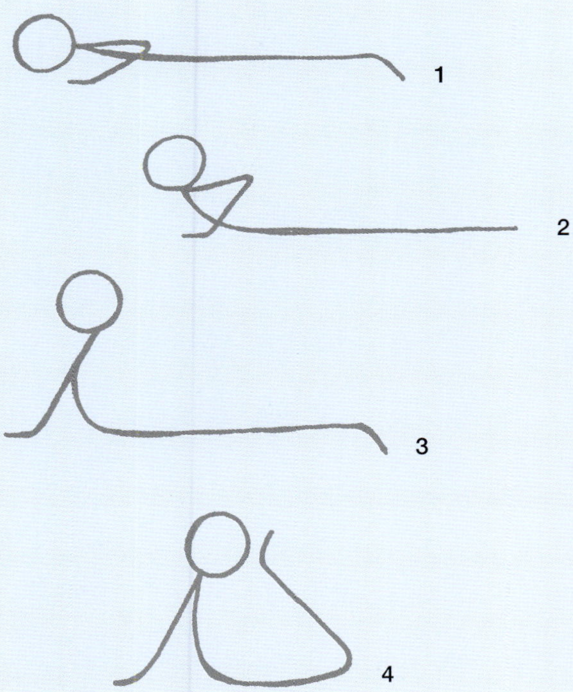

below Slither like a snake in Cobra pose.

Eagle
GARUDASANA

One minute the golden eagle can be standing motionless, high on a mountain top, scanning the landscape. The next minute he can summon all his energy, stretch out his enormous wings and plunge through the air at speed in the search for prey. Eagle pose is a standing balance that mimics the poise and strength of the golden eagle.

Benefits
Eagle pose is very good for nurturing determination and inner conviction. It also helps you to concentrate and makes your legs feel really strong.

When to do the pose
This is a good movement for when you are feeling uptight or unsure, and need to find some inner strength.

1 Stand in Mountain pose (Tadasana), looking straight in front of you with your legs straight and your feet together. Put your hands in Prayer position (Namaste). Visualize a beautiful golden eagle perched high on the peak of a mountain, looking down majestically on to the valley below. Steady your breath.

2 As you breathe out, bend your knees and spread your arms out to your sides like a pair of wings. Feel yourself firmly rooted in the floor. You are the eagle high on the mountain peak.

A summary of the movements

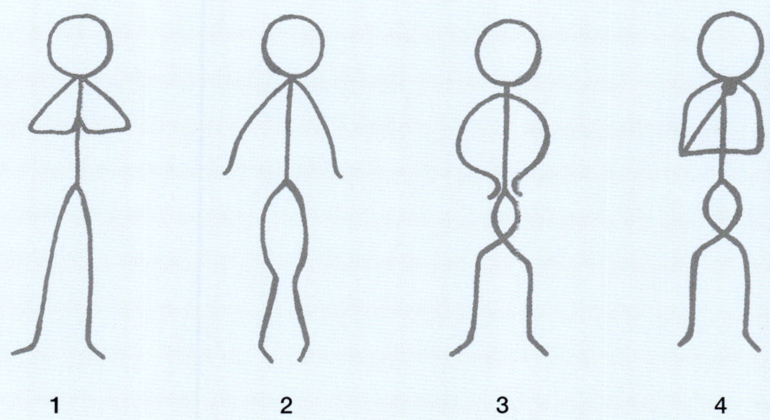

4 Make a soft fist with your right hand and place it under your chin. Support your elbow with your left palm. Breathe steadily for a few moments. Release the pose, shake out your arms and legs, and repeat on the other side.

3 Keeping both of your knees bent, cross your left leg over your right so that the ball of your left foot makes contact with the floor just to the side of your right foot.

Fish

MATSYASANA

In Hindu mythology the God Vishnu turned himself into a fish, or *matsya*, to save the world from the flood. Fish pose is a gentle yet powerful back bend in which the raised chest mimics the rounded back of a fish. In the pose you lie on the floor with your knees bent and your back arched.

Benefits

Fish encourages deep breathing and can give relief to mild symptoms of asthma and bronchitis. The graceful arching of the back opens up the chest, keeping the heart chakra open and releasing positive feelings of love and well-being.

When to do the pose

Use Fish to improve posture and chase away negative feelings. You can do it after Shoulder Stand, Candle or Dragonfly pose too. The very young may find this pose a bit too much for them. They can try Crocodile instead, which has many of the same benefits.

1 Lie on the floor with your knees bent, legs together and feet flat on the floor. Your arms should lie straight by your sides.

2 Breathe in and, keeping your knees bent, lift your bottom off the floor and slide your hands underneath. Bring your hands close together so that the fingers touch.

3 Lie down on your hands. Extend your legs and allow them to feel heavy. Let your breath become steady.

A summary of the movements

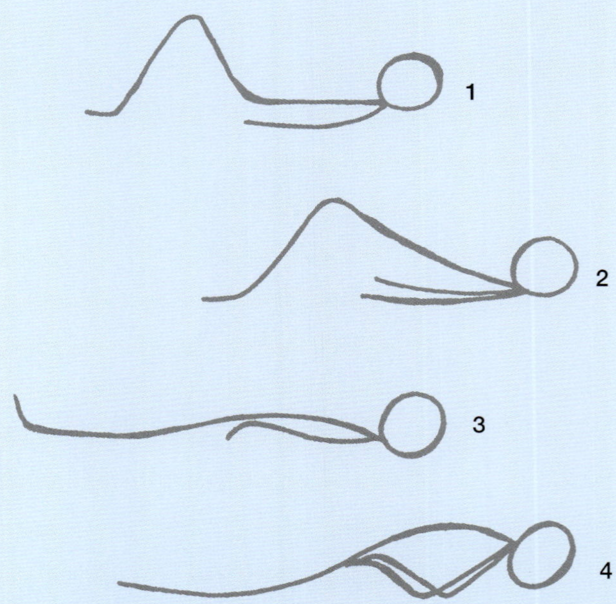

4 On a breath in, push up your chest, letting your back arch and the top of your head roll on to the floor. Push your elbows down. Take five deep breaths, then release to the floor, slide out your hands and hug your knees.

Frog
MALASANA

Frogs are cold-blooded amphibians that start life without any limbs at all. They develop arms and legs as they grow older, and by the time they are adult frogs their legs are strong and very springy. This is a fun action pose that grows from a quiet squat into an explosive leap upwards into the air.

Benefits

Frog is good for strengthening the upper and lower legs and making them more flexible. It also helps to tone the ankles and feet. It is a fantastic way to raise energy levels quickly if you are feeling tired but still have lots of things to get done.

When to do the pose

Leap like a frog when you feel tired and lethargic and want a quick boost of energy, or if you feel over-excited and need to let off some steam. Because this is quite a sudden, jerky movement, it should only be done after the warm-up exercises.

A summary of the movements

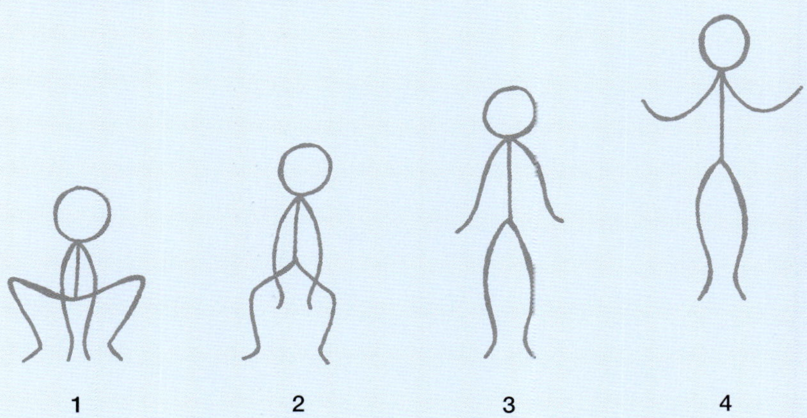

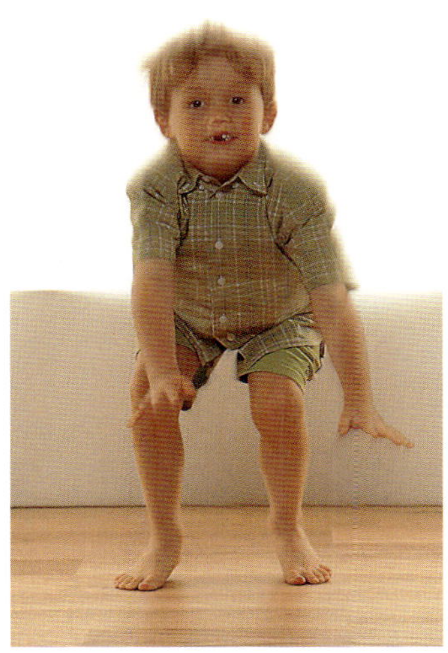

1 Crouch down on the floor with your knees wide and the palms of your hands flat on the floor in front of you. Breathe steadily and visualize your legs becoming strong like a frog's.

2 When you feel ready, push down into your hands and feet and spring upwards.

3 Stretch out your body and jump as high as you can. Make frog noises as loud as you can – "Grribbiid!"

4 Try to land on both feet as you come down from the jump. Crouch down again, ready to repeat the jump. Sit quietly for a few seconds when you have had enough jumping.

Crocodile
MAKARASANA

This playful posture will encourage self-expression and is fun to practise in a group. Look out for it later on in this section in the children's game called Snap and Snack.

Benefits
Crocodile pose strengthens the back and gives you energy. If you find yourself in a bad mood, Crocodile can help release anger and aggression.

When to do the pose
When you feel low or cross, Crocodile helps you to get rid of negative feelings and will brighten your mood.

below The crocodile is a fierce fighter.

1 Kneel on the floor in Cat pose, with your shoulders over your hands and your fingers spread wide. Stretch out your legs behind you.

A summary of the movements

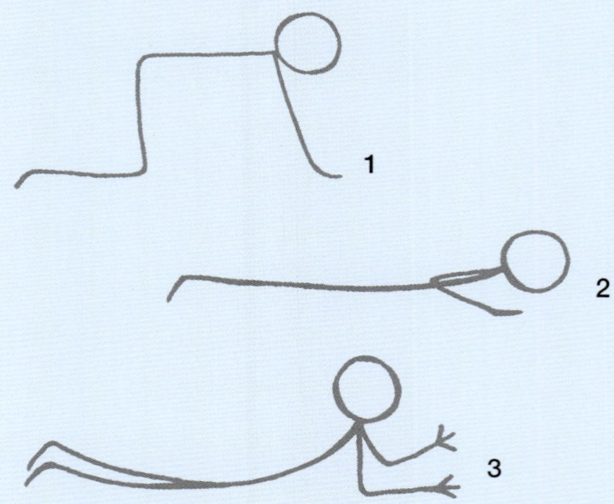

2 Lie down on the floor and bring your hands underneath your shoulders with your elbows tucked into your sides. Spread your fingers like claws. Make a heavy tail by bringing your legs together. Rest your forehead on the floor and visualize yourself as a crocodile.

3 As you breathe in, lift your legs and rear up your head. Keep swishing your tail from side to side to help you slither forwards and sideways. When you have had enough, curl up in Child's pose to release your back.

Crow
KAKASANA

The black crow is the largest of the songbirds. He has strong feet and legs to enable him to move swiftly and purposefully on land, and broad wings that help him to soar powerfully in the air. In this pose your hands turn into the crow's feet and your back becomes his body. This pose requires strength, confidence and concentration. Imagine the beady eye of a crow to help you concentrate on the position.

Benefits
Crow pose focuses the mind. It also strengthens the wrists, arms and upper body, and helps to develop physical balance and co-ordination.

When to do the pose
Do Crow when you feel apprehensive about something and your mind is jumpy. It will help you feel in control and will strengthen inner conviction.

below Rising to the challenge in Crow pose.

1 Place a cushion on the floor, and then squat down with your feet hip-width apart and the cushion in front of you. Place your palms on the floor with your fingers spread out and turned slightly inwards.

A summary of the movements

1

2 and 3

2 Press your upper arms against the inside of your knees. Start to rock forwards until you feel your body weight spreading on to your hands. Rock back to transfer the weight to your feet. Use the cushion for support and don't worry if you lose your balance, just keep trying.

3 With practice you will be able to balance on your hands for longer and longer. Then bring your feet together to make your crow's tail. Hold for as long as you can and then lower your feet and release.

Blue whale
SETU BANDHASANA

The yogis called this Bridge pose because it makes your tummy look like a bridge. But being a big blue whale is more fun!

The blue whale is the largest living animal and even though it weighs as much as 15 elephants, it still manages to be graceful. Blue Whale pose is an energizing back bend. The lower part of the body makes the back of a big blue whale – imagine your navel is its blowhole. Start off from Dead Man pose, lying on the floor with the feet hip-width apart, the arms away from the body and the eyes closed.

Benefits
Blue Whale pose is very good for strengthening the back and leg muscles, and it gives a nice stretch to the back of the neck. It helps to keep the spine supple and opens up the heart, chest and lungs.

When to do the pose
Practise Blue Whale pose when you need a little lift after something has upset you. Not only can this help to calm you down, it will also help to relieve backache.

1 Lie down on your back in Dead Man pose (Savasana). Rest your arms by your sides and steady your breathing.

2 Bend your knees so that your feet are flat on the floor, hip-width apart and a little away from your bottom. Keep your arms at your sides.

3 Breathe in and slowly peel your back off the ground. Breathe out and imagine you are spurting water out of your tummy button – just like the whale's blowhole.

A summary of the movements

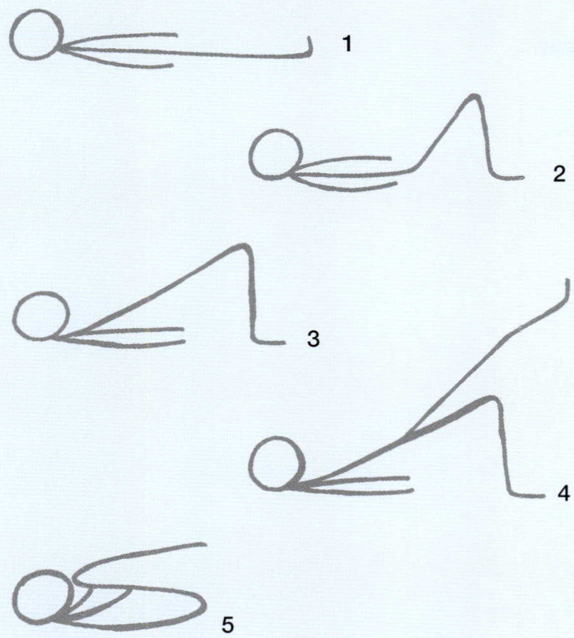

4 Keep breathing steadily. With your back still off the ground, lift your right leg and straighten it. Look at your toes and pretend they are the tip of the whale's tail. Lower your right leg and repeat with your left leg.

5 As you breathe out, roll slowly back down to the floor again and hug your knees to your chest like an upturned beetle. This is a counter pose to release your back.

Butterfly
BADDHA KONASANA

The butterfly is a wonderful example of transformation. It starts its life as a humble caterpillar and evolves into a beautiful, winged creature. This simple seated pose will help your hips to become more flexible, allowing your spine to elongate. Try sitting on a cushion if you find it hard to sit up directly on the floor.

Benefits
This will give your inner thighs a lovely gentle stretch, and will help to improve your posture when seated. It will also help you to feel grounded.

When to do the pose
Practise Butterfly in preparation for Little Buddha pose and to relax your legs after Rocking the Baby, as part of your warm-up sequence.

1 Sit on the floor with both legs outstretched in front of you and your feet together. Hold your hands in Prayer position (Namaste). Look straight ahead.

2 Bend your right leg and bring the sole of the foot into the inside of your left thigh. Hold the position.

below Learning Butterfly pose will help you to sit up straight.

3 Then bring the left leg in so that the soles of your feet are together. You will be able to feel a gentle stretch of your inner thighs. Try opening your feet with your hands like the covers of a book. This will help your knees to drop open a little more.

4 Then interlace your fingers and place them under the outer edges of your feet. Sit up tall, with your back nice and straight.

A summary of the movements

5 Gently lift and lower your knees as if you are a butterfly flapping its delicate, colourful wings. Relax.

Pigeon
KAPOTASANA

Homing pigeons have an in-built compass that allows them to navigate their way home, no matter how far they have flown.

Benefits
Pigeon pose will give a deep, long stretch to your buttock muscles. The forward bending stage of this pose is particularly good at helping to calm an agitated mind.

When to do the pose
Pigeon energizes the body after a busy day or after a series of strong standing poses, such as Warrior and Triangle.

1 Get down on your hands and knees in Cat pose.

2 Now tuck under your toes, lift your knees and come into Dog pose. Take a moment to stretch out your legs.

3 Then lift your left leg upwards, bend the knee and lunge it through your hands.

A summary of the movements

4 above Place the knee on the floor and bring the heel to the right. Sit to the outside of your left knee. Let the back of your left thigh release on to the floor. Stretch out your right leg and prop yourself up with your hands.

5 below Breathe steadily and, as you exhale, lean your chest forwards over your knee. Make a pillow with your hands and relax. Close your eyes for a few minutes. Release and rest in Child's pose, then change sides.

Tortoise
KOORMASANA

This gentle seated pose will help you to feel the quiet and calmness of a tortoise who knows he is protected by his strong shell. A famous Indian fable called the Bhagavad Gita states that if you can stay safe and calm inside your body, without reacting to danger or difficulty, then, like the tortoise safely inside his protective shell, you will become mighty and wise. This is a useful piece of advice!

Benefits

Tortoise pose will make you feel calm and secure because you will imagine yourself protected by a strong shell. This pose will also provide your back and legs with a long stretch.

When to do the pose

Practise Tortoise when you want to feel safe and quiet. It will also help to release your back after a bending pose.

1 Sit on the floor, legs wide apart and bent at the knees. The soles of your feet should be flat on the floor. Your hands can be held in Prayer position (Namaste). Breathe steadily.

2 As you breathe in, reach up with your right arm, keeping your fingers stretched. Breathe out and feed your right arm underneath your right knee. Hold it there.

A summary of the movements

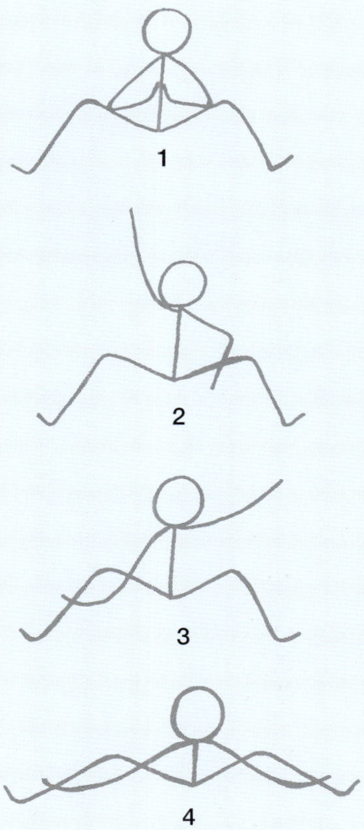

3 Now do the same with your left arm, reaching up and feeding it under your left knee. Breathe steadily.

4 Gradually lower your chest towards the floor as you walk your fingers and hands in the opposite direction to your feet. With practice you may be able to place your chin and chest on the floor in front of you, and straighten your legs on the floor. Slowly release yourself from the position and relax. Have a friend or parent close by to help you unravel yourself from the position.

Locust
SHALABHASANA

A locust is a tropical grasshopper, with long, strong legs with special springy knees that launch its body into flight. It can jump the equivalent of you jumping over your house! This is a very strong back bend and it may prove too difficult for younger children to hold both legs off the floor. With regular practice it will get easier, but begin by lifting one leg at a time. If you find it too uncomfortable lying on your arms, rest your arms by your sides and rest your forehead on the floor. You can lift your legs in this position too.

Benefits
Locust is a challenging pose that strengthens the back muscles. Like other back bends it will also boost your natural energy.

When to do the pose
Practise Locust after you have got the hang of Cobra pose – this will make it easier for you. Follow Locust with a relaxing forward bend such as Child's pose or Sandwich.

below A hungry locust snatching at a fly. Try to lift those legs a little higher!

A summary of the movements

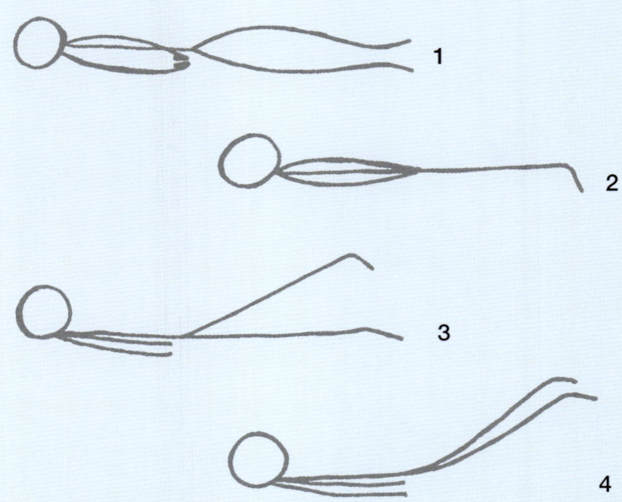

1 Lie on your side in a straight line with your arms extended in front of you. Wrap your fingers round the thumb of each hand to make a fist. Bring both of your fists side by side.

2 Roll gently on to your front so that you are lying on your arms. Wriggle them down as far as you can towards your feet. Let your chin rest on the floor, close your eyes and breathe steadily and deeply to prepare yourself.

3 Breathe in and lift your right leg off the floor. Push your fists into the ground to help lever the leg upwards. Lower the right leg and, on another breath in, repeat with the left leg. Breathe and hold. Lower the left leg and give yourself a rest.

4 When you are ready, take a big breath in and try to lift both legs off the ground. Hold for as long as you can. Gently lower your legs, and come into Child's pose on your knees to relax your back. Well done!

Dragonfly
SARVANGASANA

This is a wonderful variation of the classic Shoulder Stand pose. It is known as the queen of yoga postures because of its many physical and holistic qualities. It may look quite hard but when you get into it and have practised a few times you will find that it isn't all that difficult. Resting your knee on your forehead will help you to keep your balance.

Benefits of the pose

The Dragonfly pose helps to develop patience and emotional stability. It gives the heart a temporary rest from the effects of gravity, and it feels really wonderful if your legs are heavy and tired. The increased blood flow to your face helps to refresh your brain, and you will find it gives you a big burst of energy.

When to do the pose

Dragonfly is just the thing to do when you come home from a tiring day at school and you feel physically and mentally exhausted and a little bit sluggish. It is good to practise Dragonfly before a dream time sequence, and it can help you to feel emotionally calm and quiet before you go to bed at night.

1 Lie flat on your back in Dead Man pose (Savasana), with the feet hip-width apart, the arms away from the body and the eyes closed. Breathe steadily.

2 Slowly bring your knees in towards your chest, keeping your arms in position at your sides. Continue to breathe steadily.

3 Then slowly draw your knees in towards your forehead by pushing your hips and lower back towards you. Use your hands to guide you, then support your back with your flat palms.

4 Still supporting your lower back, extend your legs upwards so that your toes are directly above you. Hold here and breathe while you get your balance and get used to being upside down.

A summary of the movements

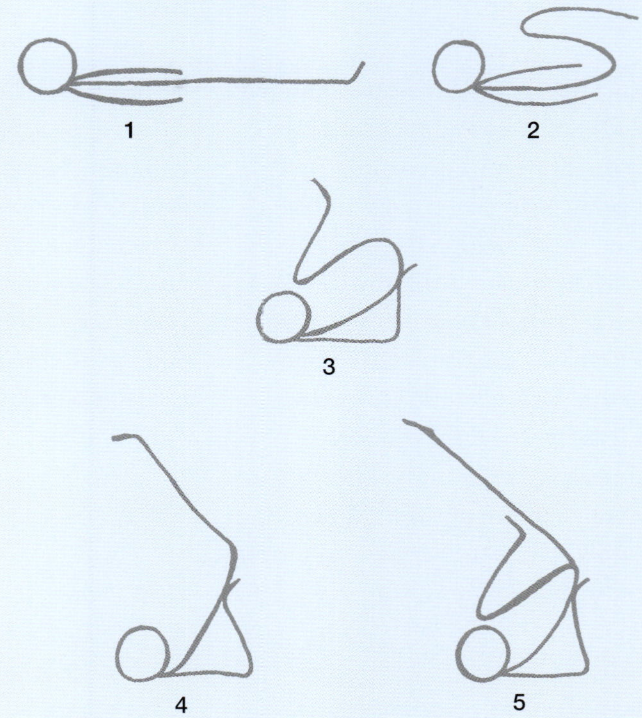

5 Bend your right knee and rest it in the middle of your forehead. Let the front of your left leg rest on the sole of the right foot. Close your eyes and rest in the pose, keeping your breathing quiet and steady. Change legs when you are ready. Then bring both knees in towards your chest and roll back down on to the floor. Extend your legs and rest on your back.

Cow
GOMUKASANA

In India the cow is considered a sacred animal, and is allowed to wander the roads on its own. In this seated pose, your body is supposed to resemble the face of this beloved creature. Your stacked knees form the lips of its face and your raised elbow is one of its ears. Practise the pose in stages, if you like. Begin by sitting with just your legs crossed until you feel comfortable, then practise kneeling with your arms in position. When you are happy to sit like this you can move on to the full Cow position.

Benefits
Cow pose will release tight muscles in the area around your hips and bottom. It opens up the chest, which will improve your posture, and can also help to release and realign tight or rounded shoulders.

When to do the pose
This is a great pose to do when your hips and shoulders feel stiff from tiredness, too much sitting or too much exercise. It is a good pose to do when you want to challenge yourself. Because you end up looking like a cow's face, it will also make you laugh.

right Don't tie yourself in knots over Cow pose. Take it easy and build up the positions in stages.

1 Sit down on the floor with your legs folded to the left of you. Hold one hand over the other and rest them on your top knee. Steady your breathing.

2 Lift up your left leg and cross it over your right knee, so that your knees are now on top of each other. Wriggle your bottom a little so that it is sitting flat on the floor.

below You can give yourself an additional stretch by bending your body forwards over your knees. Breathe deeply and hold for a moment.

A summary of the movements

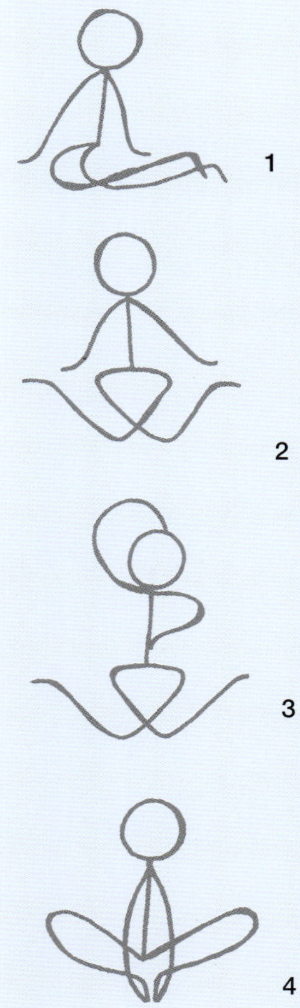

3 Reach up with your right arm and rest your fingers at the base of your neck. Place your left arm behind your back and wriggle it up to meet your other hand. Try to interlink your fingers without rounding your back. Catch hold of your T-shirt if you can't reach. Breathe deeply.

4 Slowly unravel your legs and arms and come into Butterfly pose to relax the muscles. Have a short rest, and change sides whenever you are ready.

Camel
USHTRASANA

This pose is performed on the knees and involves arching carefully backwards so that you make the rounded hump of the camel with your upper body. The arch of the back is particularly important for Camel, so practise getting this part right.

Benefits
Camel pose opens up the chest and the heart, and this helps to correct poor or lazy posture. It can help all children to stand tall and feel proud of who they are. Camel encourages good use of the lungs and aids digestion.

When to do the pose
Camel pose is good when you have been working hard, bent over your desk all day at school. It is also good when you want to wake up your back muscles, and when your energy levels are low and need a boost.

1 Kneel on the floor with your knees hip-width apart. Breathe steadily and deeply for a few minutes.

2 Then sit up and look straight ahead of you, bringing your hands on to your hips.

3 Tuck under your toes so that your heels lift up off the floor, then breathe in and lift your left arm upwards. Look up at your hand.

A summary of the movements

4 left Circle your left arm round and rest your fingertips on your left heel. Keep pushing your heart and chest forwards. Lift your right arm in the same way.

5 right Circle your right arm round behind you and bring your fingertips on to your right heel. Breathe in and out steadily, pushing your chest proudly forwards to make the camel's hump.

6 Release and lean forwards in Child's pose to rest your back. Sit down on your heels and rest your forehead on the floor in front of you, with your arms by your sides.

putting it all Together

Here we show you how to build the stand-alone poses you have learnt into flowing themed sequences, to help you discover new and more challenging poses. There are three of these for you to try, as well as a yoga play, and all are lovely ways of show-casing your new skills to friends and family. As your confidence grows, try making up and naming your own poses. Simply remember to practise them slowly and mindfully, breathing deeply and steadily at all times.

Your Postures: Make Them Up

Just as the first yogis created postures from studying the world around them, you too can get creative and make up some of your own. Inventing postures is a wonderful way to stimulate your imagination. It will also help to keep you interested by showing you how much you can adapt yoga to suit your mood.

Think about creatures or objects that inspire you. It could be magical creatures from story books, such as fairies and unicorns, gremlins and ghosts, or favourite animals, birds or insects seen in the garden, on holiday or studied at school. Think about how these animals move, sleep and hunt. Are they big or small, fast or slow, gentle or dangerous?

In addition to the animal kingdom, use the modern world as a source of inspiration. Try the Aeroplane pose below, or think about other modes of transport and how you could imitate them. How would you translate a silent, slow-moving submarine into a yoga pose? What about a sailing boat?

Remember to do the poses slowly and to keep breathing while you do them. If you are feeling really creative, think about what type of pose should come after the one you have made up. These are the counter poses that help your body erase the last posture and move it in the opposite way, allowing it to rebalance itself.

above Seagulls Kneel on one knee with one leg outstretched and your arms spread to your sides. Imagine warm sea air rising up under your wings, helping you to glide in the air.

below Aeroplanes This is a strong pose and is very good for your legs. Stand up tall with your hands in prayer position. Breathe in and, as you breathe out, lunge one leg forwards. Spread your arms (or wings) out to the sides and drop your chest towards your front knee. Enjoy the flight, then change legs.

left Beetle and sparrow The upturned beetle, here on the left, must roll out of the way of the hungry chirping sparrow.

below Rag dolls Stand up straight with your feet hip-width apart. Hang your head and let your body and arms fall gently forwards like a drooping flower or a floppy rag doll as it is lifted from the toy box.

above Animal antics See if you can squat down low like a spider. Which one of you will be the first to collapse?

right Cactus plants Stand up straight and lift one knee so that you are balancing on one leg. Angle your arms and legs to make the eerie shapes of prickly cactus plants…but don't touch or it could hurt!

▷

left Geckos Use your body to imitate the nimble movements of a gecko – which is a type of lizard – as he clings to a wall. Stretch out your arms and legs, spread your fingers and toes and hang on.

Dragon

This is a pose for two people. As it involves one person carrying the other on their back, it helps if the supporter is an adult. Roaring and fire-breathing are optional!

1 The supporter sits on her knees with her forehead on the floor and both her arms stretched out in front. The ch ld lies across her back, and stretches out his arms and legs. It may take a few attempts for you both to find your balance and hold the position.

2 The child on top takes hold of his partner's arms and holds on tight. The supporter tucks her toes under anc lifts her back. The dragon then stretches out his legs and gets a wonderful ride, while the supporter strengthens her arms, wrists and legs. Hold still, or lower and lift as many times as you can while the dragon roars. Relax.

Elephant walk

The more of you the merrier for this one as you imitate the lumbering, trunk-swinging swagger of a herd of elephants.

1 Stand in line, one behind the other. All of you now reach forwards. Put one arm between your legs to make a tail and grasp the hand of the elephant behind you. Hold out your other arm in front of you to make a trunk and grasp the hand of the elephant in front.

2 Make sure you are all connected in this way, then amble slowly forwards, with your feet stomping and trunks trumpeting.

3 Continue stomping and trumpeting your way around and around the room or the garden. Release your hands and and relax, straightening up your back and stretching your arms up above your head.

I Am Strong

Developing stamina and strength helps us to feel the amazing power of our physical body. We have all felt the sense of elation that follows physical activity. These poses are empowering, and are designed to build confidence.

Give it some muscle!

It is through our musculoskeletal system that we experience the physical potential of our bodies. It also gives us the sense of how strong we judge ourselves to be. This system of muscles and bones works as a team to give us an extraordinary range of movement and a sense of inner power.

Strong yoga poses – particularly those that support our body weight on either our feet or hands – keep muscles and bones in peak condition. Bones renew themselves and continue to grow only in response to such weight-bearing activity. Muscles like to be stretched gently and smoothly and supplied with as much oxygen as possible. Coming into these poses slowly, and breathing deeply and steadily as you hold them, allows the body to move in a natural way. This gives your muscles a lovely slow, non-violent stretch, and builds solidity and strength in your bones.

Emotional strength

It's important to have emotional strength too. It means that we can stand on our own two feet and deal with the knocks of life and still come up smiling. The drive to succeed and persevere is rooted in a natural instinct for survival deep inside us. These strong poses can help children to access this instinct and deepen their inner conviction and drive.

above Chair or fierce pose Stand with your legs together, feet firm. Exhale and bend your knees as if you were sitting on an invisible chair, arms down by your side. Breathe in and lift your arms out in front of you at shoulder height. Hold the position and breathe. To release, roll your body forwards into the Rag Doll pose.

Woodchopper

This pose is fun and will quickly fill you with energy. You can also do it when you are in need of some inspiration. Repeat three or four times until you feel full of energy.

1 Stand with feet hip-width apart, and your knees gently bent. Make a strong fist with both of your hands together, and as you breathe in, lift the fist over your head.

2 Swing the axe through your legs, keeping your knees bent, and exhale through your mouth with a loud "Haaa!". Breathe in and lift your hands over your head again. Repeat.

above Warrior Step your feet wide apart and bend your front knee over your ankle, with the front foot facing forwards and the back foot turned away by 30 degrees. Breathe in and lift both arms to the sides. Breathe out and bend your front knee a little more. Look at your front hand. Feel strength growing in your legs. Release and change sides.

right Triangle Position your feet in the same way as for Warrior and stand sideways, this time with both legs straight. Lift your arms to the side as you breathe in and, as you breathe out, reach as far over your front foot as you can. Inhale, then drop your hand down to touch your lower leg as you breathe out. Look up at your other hand and hold for a few deep breaths. Release and change sides. It may be easier for little children to think of this pose as a teapot.

above Crescent moon Kneel on the floor with your bottom off your heels and your back straight. Step your right foot forwards at a right angle to your left leg. Inhale and, as you exhale, push your right knee upright over your right foot. Inhale again and lift your arms over your head into Prayer position. As you breathe out, arch your back to make a lovely curved C-shape from your fingers to your toes. Push your back foot into the floor to keep you steady, and hold. Slowly release and change sides. Rest for a few minutes in Child's pose to rebalance your body, bending forwards over your knees.

left Wheel Lie on your back with your knees bent and your feet hip-width apart. Raise your arms behind your head, bend them and place your palms flat on the floor with your fingertips tucking in below your shoulders. Take a deep breath and exhale with an "Aahh!" sound as you push into your hands and lift your bottom off the floor. Take a few deep breaths. Lower your back to the floor. Relax and hug your knees.

Jungle Walk

Setting your yoga session in an imaginary location such as the jungle gives you plenty of scope for having fun, as everyone can become the wild creatures and characters they might find there.

First you need to prepare for your jungle journey, shrugging and rolling your shoulders as if to put on imaginary rucksacks, and flexing and pointing your toes to put on your big, strong jungle boots.

Walk through the trees, scanning the horizon for wild animals. Walk on tiptoe to look over the tall grass, and stomp through muddy swamps. Introduce an array of animals and spend some time imitating each one.

1 Lunge forwards as you set off and look all around you. Who knows what creatures may be hiding in the trees!

2 Tiptoe quietly through the tall grass. Keep a hand on the shoulder of the person in front of you to make sure no one gets left behind.

3 left Look over there, there's an elephant! See his long trunk! Where is the rest of his herd?

4 right Now strike a pose as a fierce jungle warrior to make yourself feel more brave.

5 Watch out everyone! Over there in the trees are a couple of lions. Let's hope they aren't hungry!

6 Once the group is safely back at the camp you can make a fire to warn away the wild animals. All sit in a circle on the floor and lie on your backs. Raise your legs and bring your feet together to make the flames of a fire in Candle pose.

Yoga Games

Yoga postures can be very easily incorporated into many traditional children's games. All that is called for is a little imagination and modification. Using games in this way is a clever way of keeping enthusiasm for yoga practice alive.

Games are also an ideal activity for when friends come round to play, and in fact, the more children the better.

You may recognize the classic games that have been adapted in this section. Copy Me is a version of Simon Says and the idea for Wise Man Walk has come from Grandmother's Footsteps.

Copy me

Appoint a leader to call out the yoga poses. The group must perform the posture only when the leader says "Copy me!" followed by the name of the pose. Anyone who makes three mistakes is out of the game.

1 Copy me and squat like a rabbit! Everyone squat on the floor and hop up and down.

2 left Copy me and be as tall as a mountain! Everyone put your arms in the air and stretch out your fingers to make yourself tall.

3 below Copy me and hoot like an owl! Form "O" shapes with your fingers to make big, wide owl eyes.

4 Copy me and be a seal! Everyone sit down on the floor and stretch out your legs, lifting them slightly off the floor to make your tail. Extend your arms in front of you to make your flippers.

5 Copy me and be a tall ship! Now all lean back, and hold your legs out wide to make the sails of your ship. Feel the wind in your sails as you try to keep your balance.

6 Copy me and be a Little Buddha! Everyone sit with their legs crossed and their hands in prayer position, with palms flat together. Try to keep those backs straight!

7 Copy me and be a slippery slide! Now everyone stretch out your legs and point your toes. Push up with your hands to lift your bottoms off the floor.

8 left Copy me and stand in Mountain pose. Then squat down slowly to the floor. Uh-oh, out you go!

9 left Copy me and be a snake! Lie on your front with your legs stretched behind you. Push down into your hands and lift your chest and head strongly upwards.

10 Copy me and jump up into squatting! Squat down on the balls of your feet and lift your hands up above your head, with your palms together in prayer position. Oh no, you're out!

▷

Snap and snack

This group game involves a cluster of crocodiles lying side by side. Choose an intrepid explorer to step gingerly over the sleepy crocodiles without touching them. If he or she fails, the crocodiles arch up with tails swishing and teeth snapping and the explorer is out. Try this game as seals too, lying on your backs.

left Crocodiles Come into Crocodile pose by lying on your front and bringing your legs together to make the heavy tail. Bring your hands underneath your shoulders and place your palms flat on the floor. These are your clawed feet. Look out for that unwanted visitor. SNAP!

right Seals These lazy snoozing seals will soon let you know if you've woken them up. Watch out for their noisy barking and flapping fins if you touch them.

Wise man walk

This involves a group of wise men and a watcher, who stands with his back to the group. The wise men can move only when they are not being watched, and must freeze in a posture when the watcher turns round. If anyone moves when the watcher turns, the whole group goes back to the start.

1 Offer a choice of postures before the game starts. When the group is ready, the watcher shouts out, "Everybody become an eagle!" The group of wise men now have to take up the posture. From a standing position, bend your knees and cross one leg over the other. Make a fist and place it under your chin. Support your elbow with the palm of your other hand, and try to balance.

2 When the watcher shouts "Everybody become an aeroplane!", stand up tall and breathe in. As you breathe out, balance on one leg and lift one leg behind you. Spread your arms out to the sides (for the aeroplane's wings) and drop your chest towards your front knee.

3 When the watcher shouts "Everybody become a wise old owl!", point your elbows in the air, make circles with your middle finger and thumb, and place over your eyes. The first wise man to touch the watcher is the winner and becomes the watcher for the next round.

Bunny hopping

This relay race is great fun. Organize your guests into two teams (a minimum of three in each). Each child holds a balloon between their legs and must hop with a carrot baton in their mouth to the next child in the team. The baton is handed over and the next child sets off at full hop.

1 Take your positions with the two teams side by side. One bunny from each team stands facing their team at the other end of the garden. Make sure everyone has an inflated balloon between their knees. The first bunny in the line-up has the carrot baton in their mouth. On your marks, get set and GO! The first bunny sets off, hopping over to their opposite bunny team member.

2 The first bunny of each team hops right across the garden towards the opposite bunny and makes the first exchange of the carrot baton. Take care not to let the balloons slip!

3 The first bunnies now stay where they are while the second bunnies set off hopping back across the garden to the rest of the team line-up, keeping the carrot batons in their mouths.

4 Keep those legs springy and hold your hands up like rabbit paws as you hop across the garden.

5 As the second bunnies reach the rest of their team they hand over the carrot baton for the final lap of the race.

6 After exchanging batons, the third bunnies in the line-up now hop over to their opposite team members. The first team to hand over the carrot baton is the winner!

7 Wave your balloons in the air as the winning bunnies celebrate!

Party poppers

If your guests are still full of energy, get them to be party poppers, crouching down small to begin with, and preparing to spring up into the air with a high-energy burst. This should help to build up an appetite ready for the party food.

1 All crouch down small together and imagine you are a party popper filled with streamers and confetti and ready to explode. On a count of "1, 2, 3!" leap up into the air, stretching your arms as high as you can. If you like, you could let off party streamers as you jump up.

2 Come back down and repeat your leap all over again. Keep stretching your arms up high. Repeat as many times as you like until you can explode no more. Then all of you flop down together and rest.

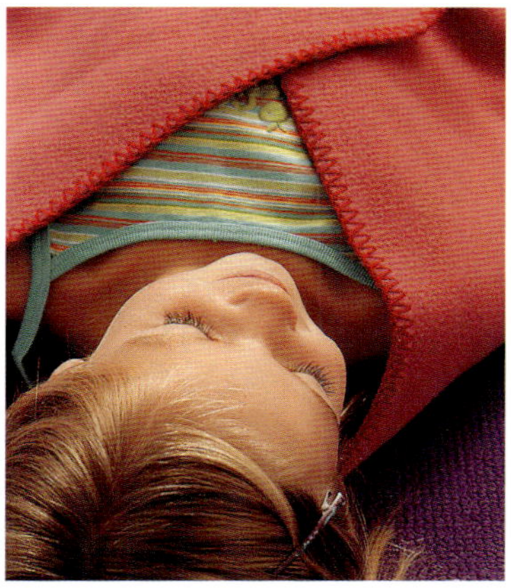

quiet Time

The appreciation of peace and quiet, the notion of being rather than doing, and the ability to jump off the merry-go-round of life and take time out are valuable life skills that we all find beneficial. You can enjoy these tranquil yoga postures when energy levels are low and you are in need of emotional nourishment. Learn how to appease everyday problems with simple, specially chosen postures.

Being Quiet

Cultivating quiet time in our busy lives should be a weekly if not daily priority. Yoga teaches children to rediscover the joy of stillness and silence, and to see that being able to relax is just as important to health and well-being as exercise and activity.

These are a few simple exercises that can reconnect us with our breathing and encourage us to explore our senses. Being able to spend time in this contemplative state is a very important life skill, making us less reliant on external distractions, such as the television, and helping us to keep calm when life becomes frenetic.

above Re-acquainting yourself with special objects or treasures helps to rekindle happy memories and encourages contemplation.

Tummy breathing

Lie down in a quiet room in Dead Man pose (Savasana). Place your hands or a soft toy on your tummy so that you can feel where your breath is and how it moves. Breathe deeply so that your tummy rises as you breathe in and falls as you breathe out. After about 5 minutes, roll to one side and slowly come up to a sitting position.

Touchy feely

Our skin is a powerful sense organ. Simply touching objects with a pleasant surface can engender feelings of well-being. Stroking a pet, cuddling a soft teddy bear or exploring the surface of a pebble or sea shell encourages sensory awareness and a calm, contended state of mind.

Mala beads are used in traditional yoga practice to encourage inner contentment and mindfulness. The beads are held in the right hand and each bead is rolled between thumb and middle finger while a mantra (a special phrase or syllable) is repeated. You can use any string of beads instead of mala beads. Choose two words that are relevant to you. Sitting cross-legged with eyes closed, the beads can be rolled through the fingers while you repeat the word "Peace" on the in breath and "Calm" on the outward breath.

left Letting your mind rest on the ebb and flow of your natural breath is soothing and encourages physical stillness, which to a child can be the most challenging of all activities. Using a toy as a prop makes relaxation more fun.

"Concentrate on silence. When it comes, dwell on what it sounds like. Then strive to carry that quiet wherever you go."

Simple sounds

Relaxing music is used instead of medication in the treatment of some stress-related illnesses and problems, and often with tremendous success. This testifies to the power of sound and its effects on our well-being. On the other hand, the wrong type of sound can be damaging to our health. The rumble of traffic in our cities, constant background music piped into shopping centres and the ringing of phones both inside and outside the home, can wear us down.

A breaking glass can shatter nerves whereas bird song or the chiming of bells can elicit positive feelings of peace and joy. Everyday sounds, such as the simple ticking of a clock, engage our minds and, in turn, can improve our ability to concentrate. As our mind tunes in, our body gets a chance to "chill out" for a while. Try writing a list of the sounds you like, along with another list of the sounds that make you feel edgy or cross.

above The gentle repetition of a pleasant and familiar sound, such as a ticking wall clock, can help to still a busy mind.

below Spend time encouraging connectedness. Caring for special things at a young age can develop a child's ability to care for others later on in life, as well as showing her the pleasures to be found in modest possessions.

Peaceful Postures

Poses that bring calm and tranquillity are restorative and rejuvenating to mind, body and soul. They are lovely to practise after a busy day or when you just feel like being quiet. You can practise them to wind yourself down after the energizing animal poses in the Animal Parade chapter, and done before bedtime they will ensure you get a sound and restful night's sleep.

Peaceful postures help to conserve your energy, rather than drain it out of your system. Even though you may feel you are doing very little as you practise them, you are actually doing something extremely powerful. You are recharging your internal batteries, rekindling your life force or prana, and this is what will keep you feeling full of energy, alive and well.

Many of the poses that bring a sense of peace to the body are done lying or sitting down with the eyes closed. The exceptions are the standing poses such as Tree pose, Mountain pose and Dancer. Concentration is needed to stand completely still. In doing so, we encourage our mind's internal chattering to fade away softly into the background.

below Tree Stand on one foot and lift the other up, placing the sole of your foot against your inner thigh. Bring your hands into Prayer position (Namaste) in front of you and steady yourself. Begin to feel your supporting foot spreading into the floor like imaginary roots growing down deep into the earth. Focus on a stationary point in front of you. Gently lift your arms above your head to form the branches of your tree. Feel strong and silent like a magnificent oak. Hold for a few deep breaths, then slowly release and change sides.

above Child's pose Rest on your knees with your forehead on the floor or a cushion in front of you, arms by your sides. Picture a mouse curled up small and still, or a pebble on the beach, made smooth by the sea and warmed by the sun.

left Sleeping snake This is a lovely exercise for a group of friends. Lie down, one by one, with your head on the stomach of the person beneath you, forming a herringbone pattern. When assembled, close your eyes and feel your head gently lifting and dropping as the person you are resting on breathes in and out.

above Mountain and Dancer Feel as motionless as a mountain (left), with feet firm and an imaginary cord from the crown of your head helping you stand tall and proud. Face straight ahead to hold the position correctly. Dancer pose (right) requires a firm foot and an elegant grace.

above Candle Lying flat on your back with your legs up the wall, like a tall candle, gives legs a rest from the effects of gravity. Stretch your arms above your head, close your eyes and breathe deeply. Imagine a cool waterfall refreshing your legs and whole body.

above Little Buddha Sitting with the legs crossed ensures your spine is anchored and that you are able to sit tall and straight. With your hands in your lap or resting on the knees you can feel strength and wisdom growing inside you. This is a classic pose for meditation.

Dream Time

Dream time is simply deep relaxation for children. This is a time when you lie completely still, allowing your body to relax and switch off for a while. With regular practice and encouragement, you will come to look forward to this part of your yoga session, particularly if you aim to make it special.

Preparation

To make the dream time session more fun, put some thought into getting ready. Think about the music you would like to listen to and allow yourself one special toy that can lie down with you while you dream. Select a favourite cushion or blanket and make yourself feel as warm and comfortable as possible. The best time for dream time is towards the end of the day, when your energy levels are naturally low, and fading light and the prospect of bedtime makes you want to feel cosy and snug. You can either practise dream time after your active yoga poses or on its own as an extra special dream session, especially if you are feeling tired.

The rewards of stillness

Children can be offered a simple reward for stillness if they are unable to concentrate on being quiet – for example, a pretty pebble, shell, wild flower, feather or crystal. Younger children can be told that a visiting fairy or elf will place something nice in their hands but only when they are completely still and quiet. This small incentive can work wonders.

Dead Man pose

The classic yoga relaxation pose is Savasana, also known as Corpse pose or Dead Man pose. The body lies still, with the feet hip-width apart, the arms away from the body and the eyes closed. Resting in Savasana allows the body to rest and recharge depleted energy stores.

Sweet dreams

- Choose a quiet room, turn off the lights and light a few candles (but do not leave these burning unattended). Make the children comfortable with cushions, pillows, blankets and any toys or props.
- Put on some soothing music – natural sounds such as bird song, waves or rainfall, soft drums or pipes usually work best.
- As they lie on their backs, ask the children to feel really heavy. As gravity gently draws them down into the ground, let them feel their body melting like ice cream.
- Do the "spaghetti" test. Gently go round to each child and lift one leg or arm at a time and tell them to make it feel really heavy. This will show that they are starting to relax. Rock the limb gently from side to side, then place it carefully back on the floor.
- Ask the child to think about their breathing and whereabouts in their bodies their breath is. Ask them to feel their tummies moving up and down as they breathe in and out. They could try to imagine a tiny boat at sea, bobbing up and down gently on the ocean waves.
- Tell them to relax their feet, repeating, "Relax my feet, my feet are heavy and r-e-l-a-x-e-d", and continue for each part of the body right up to their head.
- Tell them how difficult it is to be still and how clever they are to resist moving. Remind them that their ability to relax is a special gift.
- Visually guide them on a special journey. Let their yoga mat become a flying carpet gliding over a tropical rainforest or a soft cloud passing through a rainbow. Or take them to a golden beach where they can feel the warm yellow sand underneath their feet, and hear the playful call of dolphins inviting them to come and swim. Choose a theme, using your imagination, and keep the language simple. Allow time for them to explore their "dream".
- When the children look relaxed and still, introduce a simple affirmation or resolve, such as "I feel free and happy!". Ask them to repeat it to themselves three times. Pause for a moment and then gently guide them back to reality. Tell them they are waking up in bed and ask them to gently stretch and yawn.
- When they are ready, ask them to talk about their dream and share it with you.

above Savasana Praise your child for lying motionless and resisting the urge to move. Tell her that in doing so her mind is being taken on a wonderful holiday.

left The magical image of a dolphin is an old favourite with young children and it is easy for them to relate to.

Special time

Many important physiological changes take place in Savasana. Respiration levels are lowered, strain on the heart is reduced and the vital life energy, or prana, that has been created in posture work can be assimilated into the body. As the breath quietens and softens, the mind becomes clear and detached. It is then receptive to any positive images or sounds you may hear.

Making an affirmation

Relaxation encourages the mind to be open and receptive. It is therefore a wonderful time to be introduced to positive ideas and images in the form of affirmations or *sankalpa*. These little seeds of hope will embed themselves in your consciousness over time, and can help you to feel good about yourself. Affirmations should only ever be simple, even for older children and adults, and negative words and images should be avoided as these can be counterproductive. Choose one affirmation for the session, and repeat it in your head three times.

below If you are talking a child through their dream, keep the images and words that you use light, sunny and positive.

Sounding It Out

Sound is an invisible yet powerful form of energy created by the vibration of molecules. Adding sound to your practice encourages self-expression and develops good communications skills. Sighing, humming or chanting also helps to put us in touch with the quiet place inside us, where new sensations and emotions can be experienced.

left Imitating animals and the sounds they make is a fun and creative part of your yoga practice.

Animal antics

Everyone will enjoy panting like a dog, sniffing like a rabbit, hissing like a snake or roaring like a lion as they practise the animal poses in the Animal Parade chapter. Get really involved and make sounds and movements to elaborate on the pose.

Humming bee breath

This breath helps to open up the throat chakra, which is the centre of communication. It can help to dissolve the fear of speaking up at school to teachers, and will help when speaking to new friends. To do the Humming Bee Breath, sit in Little Buddha pose with your eyes closed. Breathe in and as you breathe out through your mouth, gently hum at the same time. Feel the sound gently vibrating in your throat.

Try putting your fingers in your ears as you hum to really help you concentrate and feel the sound resonating deep within you.

above and below Removing the distractions of external noises by putting fingers in your ears can help to put you in touch with your inner world.

Sighing breath

This breath helps you to let go of stresses and strains at the end of a busy day. First breathe in deeply, then sigh the breath out of your mouth with a lovely strong "Aaaahh!" sound. Repeat a few times and now visualize anything that has made you cross or sad floating out with your breath and up and away into space.

Chanting

Yogic chanting is a form of singing or humming and produces special vibrations that soothe body, mind and soul. A mantra is a special word that can be hummed as you chant.

"Om" is the classic yoga mantra – meaning absolute peace. The wise yogis believed that we should "live in Om". In other words, we should live our lives in total peace and harmony.

Begin by repeating Om in your head, breaking it down into three sections. Start with an "Ah" sound, then an "Oh" sound then "Mmmm". Then breathe in and, as you breathe out, hum the Om out nice and loudly, visualizing each syllable as a little bubble of energy growing inside you and floating up into the sky. Try lifting your arms up slowly as you hum it to help your energy bubbles float upwards. Pause after each repetition and see if you can hear or feel the echo of Om in your mind, and maybe in your body, too, as the sound waves keep on vibrating through you.

above Chanting "Om" with your friends bonds you together. It makes you feel good about yourselves and makes friendships stronger.

You can also make up your own mantras, choosing a word relevant to how you are feeling. Evocative words such as "Peace", "Calm" or "Love" work very well. Let their soothing tones suffuse every molecule of your body.

right Sighing out through the mouth brings a sense of relief and helps you let go of unwanted feelings.

The Wise Yogi

Yoga is often referred to as "skill in action". This defines not just the physical skills that yoga provides us with, but also the mental skills that teach us control of our mind and our emotions.

Establishing these skills helps us to understand our true nature, and this gives us more control over our lives. Getting to know and accept our strengths and weaknesses gives us a sort of inner power and equips us with a code for living. This helps us to manage the up and downs of daily life more easily and with confidence.

Being able to help yourself and the rest of your family overcome everyday ailments and upsets is a wonderful example of how yoga gives us better control over our lives. In addition to the physical advantages of yoga practice, you can learn how to use the postures therapeutically and holistically to make yourself feel better.

below Wheel Prepare your back by doing Blue Whale pose a few times. Then lie in the same starting position tuck your flat palms under your shoulders. Breathe deeply and on a breath out, push strongly into your hands and lift your bottom and head off the floor. Hold for a few breaths, then release and hug your knees.

Headaches

Forward bends can help to relieve everyday headaches. The act of leaning forwards also helps to still the mind and lessen the load on the heart. In a darkened room, try Child's pose with your head on a cushion, or a Forward Bend supporting your head and arms with a chair. Close your eyes and breathe calmly for 5–10 minutes.

Low energy

Back bends are energizing as they open the heart and lungs, allowing us to breathe deeply. They also strengthen the nervous system and stimulate the digestive organs, improving the elimination of waste products. Try Cobra, Fish or Locust poses, or simply lie over a bean bag, arching your back. Take long breaths. For a really strong back bend, try doing Wheel pose.

Stiffness and tension

Aches in the lower back can be caused by many things from slouching to carrying heavy loads, or strenuous physical activity. You can find relief by lying on your back and hugging your knees tightly to your chest. Rocking forwards and backwards helps massage the back muscles, "ironing" away strain and tension. Child's pose, Beetle and Blue Whale are also very effective. To maintain spinal mobility and strength, practise Sunshine Stretch and Cat, Dog, Snake and Mouse.

> "Yoga helps to cure what need not be endured and to endure what cannot be cured"

Tummy ache

Lie on your front allowing the floor to gently cushion your tummy. Breathe deep breaths to let your tummy relax.

Sore throat

Roaring Lion is good for keeping sore throats at bay. It is also guaranteed to bring a smile to the face of anyone in a bad mood. Practised in a group, it encourages teamwork.

Nerves

Woodchopper pose or Roaring Lion help to release pent up energy and nervousness, particularly before an important event.

Asthma

With commitment, yoga can help you to manage and even control the symptoms of bronchial asthma. Regular practice strengthens the respiratory system, drains mucus from the lungs, promotes breath awareness and control, and relaxes tense chest muscles. Gentle movements, which encourage rhythmic breathing, are good for asthma sufferers; aggressive movements may over-stimulate the lungs. Try Sunshine Stretch to get the whole body moving, and gentle back bends to relax the chest.

A breathing exercise such as Sniffing Breath can be useful. Sit quietly with crossed legs. Bring your mind to your breath and breathe naturally for a few moments. Then begin to sniff as you breathe in, taking two or three short sniffing breaths until the lungs are full, then a long breath out. Repeat until your chest feels open and relaxed. This also helps if you have been upset or crying.

Hyperactivity

Strong poses and animal postures with accompanying noises will use up excess energy and disperse physical tension. Follow with some of the breathing techniques, such as Sighing Breath or Humming Bee Breath, to soothe and relax you.

below Supported back bend Arching your body backwards over an exercise ball or bean bag makes you feel wide awake. Not having to support your own weight means you can relax and hold the pose for longer.

Shoulder stand

This calming pose revives you after a busy day and reverses the effects of gravity on the legs and heart. Close your eyes and visualize a refreshing mountain waterfall pouring energy back into your legs. For a milder version, lie sideways against a wall, and extend your legs so that they rest against the wall. Take your arms to the floor behind your head and relax completely for 5 minutes.

1 Lie on your back on the floor and lift your legs upwards, with your knees bent. Keep your chin tucked in towards your chest to protect your neck.

2 With your hands on your lower back, drop your knees down towards your face. This will allow your back to peel off the floor. You can support your back with your hands.

3 Lift your legs upwards as you push your lower back towards your face with your hands. Close your eyes and breathe. Roll your back down on to the floor. Hug your knees.

▷

above Forward bend with chair This lovely relaxing pose requires no effort and helps to quieten a busy mind or an aching head.

below Canny cat Cat pose is a very versatile pose and it is fun and easy to do. Get down on your hands and knees and roar like a big cat or tuck your toes under, lift up your bottom and become a dog. Become a cat again, then sit on your heels and be quiet again in Child's pose.

above Easy twist To ease a strained or aching back, lie on your back, knees bent and feet flat on the floor. Interlace your fingers under your head and, as you breathe out, let your knees drop to one side. Hold for five deep breaths and change sides. Feel your back waking up.

left Seated twist Twisting poses help to unravel knots or tight bits in your back and, according to yoga therapists, any knots or problems in your head too. Sit cross-legged with your left leg on the top. Slide this leg over so that your knees are almost on top of one another and your left heel is by your right thigh. Breathe in and lift your chest. Then breathe out and turn your body to the left. Let your spine spiral round, from the bottom upwards. Place your right arm on your left thigh and try to catch your left toes with your left hand. Change sides after a few deep breaths.

right Sweet dreams The yogis believed that stilling the eyes and focusing the gaze, or *drushti*, would help to focus the mind. Learn to relax with a prop. A soothing, lavender eye bag or silk scarf will help you to keep inquisitive, seaching eyes closed.

above Savasana "I closed my eyes so I could see". Just a few quiet moments lying down wrapped in a cosy blanket can help you to feel calm and good about yourself again.

Meditation

Taking time to meditate either on your own, or with a group, is a beneficial and uplifting experience. Meditation helps us focus on the present, quieters the mind and creates serenity.

Doriel Hall

What is Meditation?

Human beings have many levels: our physical bodies, energy flow, instinctive responses, thinking processes and wisdom each play a vital part in our overall functioning, and all need to be in balance to ensure health and well-being. All too often, however, a hectic modern lifestyle can unbalance these levels, making us feel jaded in body, mind and spirit. The regular practice of meditation helps us to rebalance ourselves so that all the levels are able to work together in harmony.

Meditation has three aspects: the regular practice of techniques that enable us to reach the meditative state, the experience of the state of meditation, and recreating this state in daily life. There are traditional meditation techniques appropriate to all temperaments and levels of attainment. They all involve symbolically "going up into the solitude of the mountains" so that we can then "return to the bustle of the marketplace" and live a changed life as a result of our experience.

We practise meditation because we believe (with Robert Browning) that:

There is an inmost centre in us all,
Where Truth abides in fullness...and to know
Rather consists in opening out a way
Whence the imprisoned splendour may escape.

Meditation allows us to experience that splendour for ourselves and live our lives in the glow of our own inner radiance.

above Meditation is practised with the spine erect and the body motionless. The mind is still but alert, vibrant and focused inward.

"Only the present moment exists."

Removing inner obstructions

The path to and from our "inmost centre" may be obstructed by lack of awareness, self-obsession, the stress of an unbalanced lifestyle, or by negative attitudes and thought patterns.

Most of us try to crowd too much activity into our lives, and lack the stillness and silence that are necessary to rebalance the nervous system. Regular meditation practice establishes a healthy rhythm of activity and rest for both mind and body. Our minds are constantly active, mulling over current problems, planning anxiously for a future we cannot control, regretting past actions or creating personal doctrines

above Symbolically compared with the solitude of the mountains, meditation involves a withdrawal from the bustle of human activity.

right These traditional clay figures in a circle of friendship represent the unity nurtured by the meditative way of life.

and dogmas, opinions and prejudices. These mental "games" draw us, like magnets, away from the present moment. Meditation teaches us to live in the moment, and grow through the experiences of here and now. When we are inclined to wallow in negative emotions such as anger or resentment, and to see insults and dangers where none exist, meditation helps us to replace defensive energy-sapping reactions with open and trusting responses that enable us to build loving relationships.

Reducing stress

If you practise the meditation techniques outlined in this section regularly and with enthusiasm, you will soon start to feel the benefits, as both the causes and the effects of stress diminish.

Stress is a normal part of life, and a certain amount is essential to motivate and develop humans, but the pace and complexity of life in modern Western society can overburden our systems and block our natural ability to manage stress. Human beings are (as far as we know) the only animals with brains that are constantly thinking – but the result may be that we allow ourselves to remain stuck in negative thought patterns, squandering our precious energy and unbalancing the nervous system.

Like that of any other animal, the human nervous system operates instinctively and is programmed to deal physically with threats to survival. Stress is a natural reaction that enables us to respond to danger, either by fighting or running away. Once the threatening episode is over the nervous system should rebalance itself as we return peacefully to our normal activities. Unlike other animals, however, humans are apt to remain in a state of arousal, because we go on feeling anxious about past and future events, as well as preferring to be continually active and stimulated in the present.

Because stress hormones make us feel excited, it is easy to become addicted to activities and challenges that trigger their release. This is why we want to watch exciting programmes on television and take part in testing activities. But if we remain in a constant state of arousal, we deny our bodily systems the chance to rest and renew themselves. Stress accumulates until the system reaches breaking point – and the result is illness and malfunctioning of the body or mind. By practising the techniques of meditation, we can reverse this build-up of stress by learning to stop and consciously clear the mind and emotions of negative attitudes the moment we become aware of them.

Stress and your health

Meditation practice can help to reduce the unpleasant effects of prolonged stress, protecting you from symptoms such as:

- muscle tension and pain in the joints
- tension and migraine headaches
- the inability to concentrate or think clearly
- digestive problems, which may include diabetes
- interrupted sleep patterns
- breathing difficulties
- cardiovascular problems
- allergic reactions
- physical fatigue
- nervous exhaustion
- weakness of the immune system
- other auto-immune problems

below Regular meditation gives you the energy and clarity you need to deal with the multiple demands of daily life.

the practice of Meditation

There are many routes to the meditative state: it can be reached in stillness or movement, with sound or in silence. The sage Patanjali saw hatha, or physical, yoga as a preparation for this transformation of consciousness. His teachings on yoga as the path to meditation still form the basis of most of the yoga practised today.

Universal Meditation Techniques

left The postures traditionally used for meditation allow the body to stay motionless while keeping the spine erect.

below Wrap a shawl or blanket around your shoulders so that you stay comfortably warm while sitting still to meditate.

Most classical meditation techniques are common to all the great spiritual traditions, although their forms may vary. Whatever the methods used, the meditation will follow a similar pattern.

For meditation practice to bear fruit in daily life there are four essential elements: detaching the attention from competing distractions outside and within; returning the mind to a single focus in order to enter a state of expanded awareness (the state of meditation); recalling and reflecting on the insights gained while in the meditative state; learning to apply these insights to daily life. The final stage of mastery is to live constantly in the meditative state, "enlightened while still embodied". It is said that the effects of meditation are cumulative and that "no effort is ever wasted".

Stilling the body

Settling into a position that can be held without effort means that the body can cease to occupy our attention. Hindus, Buddhists, Zen Buddhists and yogis usually sit on their heels or cross-legged on the floor. Christians may kneel and many Westerners prefer to sit upright on a firm chair. Classical yoga postures are designed to hold the body upright and still for long periods. The eyes may be closed to avoid outside distractions or open to gaze upon a specific object.

Breathing and chanting

Slowing and deepening the breath induces relaxation of the nervous system. Chanting aloud is a traditional way to lengthen each breath and the repetition of a mantra or prayer is soothing and uplifting. Buddhists, Christians, Hindus and yogis all practise chanting and repetition, either aloud or silently. A string of beads – such as the *mala* used by yogis or the Christian rosary – is often used for counting the repetitions of a mantra or prayer.

Focusing on a single object

When the attention is focused, the incessant chattering of the mind quietens naturally, and we become oblivious to outer or inner distractions. Sound is a universal focus, and may take the form of music, the note of a Tibetan singing bowl, a mantra or *nada* (the mystical sounds of our inner vibration).

Gazing – often upon a flower or lighted candle – is another universal practice. Christians may choose to focus on a picture of Christ or a saint, Hindus and Buddhists on an image of a divine being or incarnation of God. If you prefer an impersonal image, you might choose the Sanskrit symbol of OM, the *shri yantra* or a *mandala* (both of which are pictorial

left You may wish to sit for meditation before a low table holding natural or symbolic objects on which to concentrate your gaze.

below One of the most basic focusing techniques involves gazing at a single object: focusing on a flower helps you to feel at one with creation.

representations of universal energies). The focus may be something touched or felt, such as mala beads or the breath within the body. Even the senses of smell and taste may serve as focal points for meditation.

Observation and acceptance

"Witnessing impartially" consists of relaxed observation and acceptance of what is, without any reaction of liking, disliking, criticism or judgment. After watching the contents of the mind in this way we can record them truthfully in a diary. Once we stop reacting instinctively we can start to respond from the heart and open ourselves to life as it is. This is the aim of both Western and Eastern psychotherapies.

Mental visualization

Visualization is the intentional creation of a mental image or series of images, which may be of objects, feelings or symbols, as a focus for meditation practice. Informal visualizations are often used by Western psychotherapists and might, for instance, involve experiencing a walk by the sea or in the countryside using all five senses. Skill in visualization enhances the ability to create and maintain healthy and happy attitudes, thoughts and emotions, replacing former negative feelings.

Healing through love

"Placing the mind in the heart" is an essential step, for love is an attribute of the heart – or feeling nature – and not of the mind. Love should serve our highest aspirations. When loving feelings and thoughts radiate out from the heart like light from a lighthouse, both the meditator and those meditated upon receive healing.

Living in loving kindness

When we live consciously from the highest we can glimpse in meditation, we are living from the heart. We feel strong, relaxed, focused, accepting, creative and joyful.

People in all ages and traditions have achieved this goal. The Hindu tradition has always perceived the divinity in everyone – hence the Indian greeting of "*Namaste*", meaning "The divine in me greets the divine in you". Both Buddhists and yogis practise the meditation of loving kindness, in which love is beamed from the heart to all sentient beings, including those who cause pain and distress. Jesus said, "You shall love the Lord your God with all your heart and soul and mind and strength, and your neighbour as yourself." St Francis of Assisi included all of nature in his love, and the English monk who wrote *The Cloud of Unknowing* declared that "God can be known by thought never – only by love can he be known." This wisdom is available to us all: we can find it for ourselves through the practice of meditation.

right The Buddha is represented in contemplation of a lotus, the symbol of enlightenment, with his right hand raised in a gesture of reassurance.

Peeling Away the Layers

left The concept of the five koshas gives us a mental map to help us on the spiritual journey inwards during meditation.

The line of command through the Koshas

Through meditation we can influence the levels above, as well as the levels below, the one that is the focus of our meditation.

- At soul level (called *ananda maya kosha*, or sheath full of bliss) we form our life's purpose and express this through our attitudes
- which influence our conscious choices (in *vijnana maya kosha*, or sheath full of intellectual understanding)
- which influence our unconscious mental programming (in *mano maya kosha*, or sheath full of mental activity)
- which directs our flow of vital energies (in *prana maya kosha*, or sheath full of life force)
- which move our physical bodies (*anna maya kosha*, or sheath full of food) to perform our actions and behaviour, such as thinking and communicating.

According to the ancient Hindu philosophy of Vedanta, a human being consists of five bodies, each contained within the next, which hide the immortal spirit as if with a series of veils of varying density. These bodies are known as the *koshas*, or "sheaths".

Our progress towards self-realization through meditation can be seen as a journey inwards, through each of these five sheaths, from the outermost layer – the physical body – to the deepest "soul body" of unchanging consciousness, where we are in loving touch with all souls.

left The koshas can be visualized as the layers of an onion, forming a series of sheaths around the centre.

The five koshas

The further from the physical body they are, the finer the veils become. The most dense of the koshas is perceived by the senses as the structure of the physical body, which can be weighed and measured by scientific instruments.

The next is the energy body, perceptible to clairvoyants, which can be detected by Kirlian photography (a technique that uses a high-voltage, low-current electric charge to represent the body's energy in visual form). This is the level at which we are aware of the presence of someone entering our "space" before we see them. It contains a web of energy channels meeting at the *chakra* points, or energy centres, that correspond to the concentrations of nerves, or plexuses, of the brain and spinal cord. All physiological processes interact through these channels.

Next comes the "lower" or instinctive mental body. This contains the "mental computer" that is programmed to react

right Learning to understand your own nature and shedding negative feelings of fear through the practice of meditation puts you at ease with yourself and makes for trusting, open relationships with others.

according to the input keyed in by our temperament and previous conditioning. The nervous system operates this computer, mostly at instinctive and tribal levels below conscious awareness.

The next level is the veil of the intellect, involved in thinking, discrimination and choice. It can choose to override mental programming, and to respond consciously rather than reacting instinctively.

The finest veil of all, often called the soul body, is linked with the spiritual dimension and survives death. If we can reach this level in meditation, we can change our whole attitude to life and the way we live. This is conscious evolution, opening up the dormant areas of the brain.

Instinct, interaction and reasoning

It often seems that different forces co-exist within us, pulling us in opposing directions. This is because we have three distinct brains governing how we behave, feel and think. Our ancient reptilian brain is tiny but very powerful. Situated at the top of the spinal cord, it controls the primitive instincts and urges that ensure physical survival in animal bodies. It drives the basic needs that ensure our physical and species survival – food, safety, shelter, sleep and procreation. The mammalian brain, above the reptilian brain at the back of the skull, evolved later and processes herd, tribal and social instincts. The rest of the skull contains the most recent development, the neo-cortex. This uniquely human brain enables us to think, reason and evolve spiritually.

The neo-cortex is so new that we use less than ten per cent of it, and it cannot easily override our older brains. However altruistic our intentions, we feel frightened and angry, and may indulge in self-centred behaviour, whenever we consider our basic needs are not being met. We actually need very little to survive, but modern society depends on inflaming our instinctive fear and addictive greed, so that we keep buying the products that keep the wheel turning – unsustainably in the long term.

Trusting more, needing less

The practices of meditation help us to balance our evolved and primitive natures. The tradition of Vedanta claims that all creation arises from the desire of the one absolute reality to experience itself as life (nature) and light (consciousness or spirit) in relationship (love) with each other. This relationship is continuously enacted within us, and is seen as the purpose of human existence. The attributes of life, light and love (*sat-chit-ananda*) are immortal, and therefore so are we, as part of the one indivisible whole. Trusting in the divine process of life-light-love creates joy rather than fear and makes the accumulation of things seem less important than expressing our true nature. It is like being protected from negativity by a shield that beams out goodwill to all, while hiding a glory we cannot yet understand.

above Fear of isolation and exclusion from the crowd can be a result of feeling unhappy with yourself at a fundamental level.

above Reaching a state of inner content means that you can be happy and relaxed whether you are a one or part of a group.

Freeing Vital Energies

"It is just as unbalanced to be held fast by material concerns as to be too heavenly to be any earthly use."

In the Eastern traditions (and also in many modern therapeutic systems) it is assumed that our vital energies – or "life force" – flow through the energy channels (*nadis*) of the second kosha (prana maya kosha), or subtle body. Techniques that operate at this level are aimed at healing, balancing and increasing our energies. Yoga postures can get energies flowing when they are sluggish or blocked, while breathing techniques clear and balance the energy channels.

The chakras and granthis

One of the major energy channels follows the spinal cord and links the seven main chakras. The chakras can be thought of as spinning vortices of energy. Breathing with awareness (pranayama) is practised to influence the energies in the chakras and to weaken the three *granthis* (knots of attachment) that bind us to our negative attitudes and prevent us from experiencing the fullness of life-light-love. Although the granthis are seen as obstacles on the path of spiritual awareness, they also act as safety valves, protecting us from surges of vital energy and misplaced enthusiasm for changes we are not ready for. We need to practise well-tried and tested methods (such as meditation) to open them slowly and naturally, rather than forcing them with drugs or stimulants.

above Yoga postures use movement and stretches to tone the physical body and stimulate the chakras and the connecting energy channels.

right The chakras are often described as lotus flowers; meditation makes them bloom and perfume our lives with their positive attributes.

The energies of all the koshas are expressed in each chakra. We can behave spiritually in practical ways from the base chakra, or serve the divine efficiently from the crown chakra. However we behave, feel or think we cannot help bringing life and

left The granthis are visualized as three knots that bind us to negative attitudes and material concerns, keeping our minds and spirits closed. The granthis constrict the free flow of energy that leads to true understanding and acceptance.

light together in the relationship of love – even if we can perceive only conflict and fear. Awareness is the key to all meditation practice, so we must first "switch on the light" in the brow (mind) chakra before doing anything else, through breathing techniques that quickly "light us up".

Life chakras and the life granthi

The life chakras correspond to the positions of the nerve plexuses attached to the spine behind the abdomen. Their energies are concerned with our survival in the physical human body (the base chakra, connected to the legs and feet), our role in human society (the sacral chakra) and our sense of self-esteem as a human personality (the navel chakra). The life granthi that binds us is our attachment to material well-being, physical comforts and luxuries, and the amassing of things. Patanjali teaches self-discipline for regulating the energy through the life chakras and life granthi.

Love chakras and the love granthi

The love chakras are situated in the chest (the heart chakra, connected to arms and hands) and neck (the throat chakra, connected to voice, mouth and hearing). In this area self-concern gives way to sharing with others. The heart chakra energies are concerned with relationship – especially unconditional love – and the throat chakra with expressing the truth and hearing what others are telling us. The love granthi that binds us is our attachment to emotional excitement and the desire to be the hero of every drama, so that we are not receptive to the needs of others. Patanjali teaches self-surrender for increasing the energy through the love chakras and love granthi.

Light chakras and the light granthi

The light chakras are situated in the skull. They are the brow chakra (connected to the mind) and the crown chakra (connected to the spirit). "Taking the mind into the heart" is an essential element of meditation, bringing the realization that relating, not thinking, is the purpose of life. The light of divinity is received through the crown chakra and is present in us as "the eternal flame burning in the cave of the heart". The light granthi that binds us is our attachment to our own opinions, prejudices and fantasies. It is hard to relinquish treasured opinions and pride in our own intellect, yet it is not our minds but the light and love in our hearts that make us divine. We cannot claim ownership of universal life-light-love. Patanjali teaches self-awareness to dissolve pride and those mental habits that obscure divine light.

left The seven main chakras are represented in a line running up the spinal column. Each is traditionally associated with a colour.

The chakras

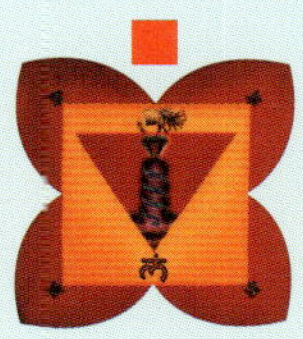

The base chakra (*muladhara*) is concerned with survival.

The sacral chakra (*svadisthana*) is related to our role in human society.

The navel chakra (*manipura*) is related to energy and self-esteem.

The heart chakra (*anahata*) is concerned with relationships.

The throat chakra (*vishuddhi*) is related to communication.

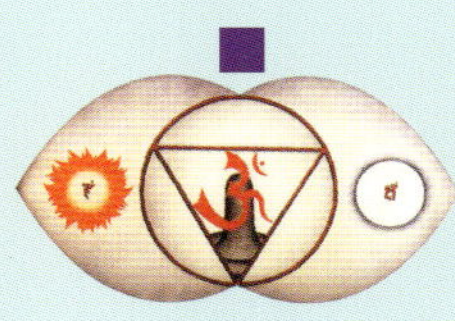

The brow chakra (*ajna*), also known as the third eye, is related to intuition.

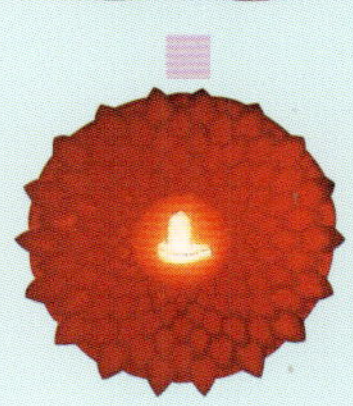

The crown chakra (*sahasrara*) is related to spiritual understanding.

Breathing Techniques

Focusing on the breath is a universal technique for enlightenment and healing, and many traditions use breathing practices either as a way to prepare for meditation or as meditation techniques in themselves. Conscious control of the breath, or pranayama, is the fourth of Patanjali's eight limbs of yoga. The technique of holding the breath – either in or out – is beyond the scope of this book, as accomplishing it safely requires one-to-one teaching, but becoming aware of the breathing process and directing the flow of the breath is within the capacity of everyone.

Slowing down the breathing and lengthening the breath out (which is what happens when we sing or chant) switches the nervous system into its peaceful happy mode, allowing stress to be dissolved and rest, digestion, absorption and healing to take place at every level of the five koshas.

Patanjali's path to enlightenment

This use of the breath fits in perfectly with Patanjali's philosophy. He describes three vital steps (which have been called "preliminary purificatory practices") that encapsulate his path to enlightenment. The steps are as follows (quoted words are from the translation of Patanjali's *Sutras* by Alistair Shearer, Ch 2, v 1/2):

"Purification" [through self-discipline]
"Refinement" [through self-awareness]
"Surrender" [through self-surrender and continual letting-go]
"These are the practical steps on the path of yoga. They nourish the state of samadhi" [absorption/ecstasy/expansion]
"And weaken the causes of suffering."

The whole process of self-development starts with taking conscious control over our own nervous system, so that we experience more "expansion" and joy and less stress and unhappiness. Our circumstances influence the outcome of events far less than our own basic attitudes, and these can be changed from negative to positive by the simple act of changing our breathing pattern.

The breath forms part of the energy system and the physiological processes in the energy kosha, while nervous energy runs the mental computer in the kosha of unconscious programming. All the koshas meet and blend in the chakra system in the energy kosha and all can therefore be consciously influenced through the practices of breathing and meditation.

Although some translations of the *Yoga Sutras* describe Patanjali's three "purificatory steps" as "preliminary", there is really no end to our need of them. We always have to maintain our discipline and keep our attention focused – and we never stop needing to let go of something or other.

"Those who see a glass as half empty feel deprived, whereas those who see it as half full feel blessed."

Viloma: focusing on the breathing muscles

This useful focusing technique can be practised anywhere, sitting with the spine erect and the hands and eyes still.

1 Place your hands on your knees, palms either up or down, with thumb and index fingers touching to close the energy circuits. As you breathe in deeply, feel your ribs expand and your diaphragm contract downwards against your stomach. Notice how these movements cause air to flow into your lungs.

2 As you breathe out, count "One and two and...", then stop your breath in mid-flow for the same count. Repeat until you have slowly and comfortably expelled enough air, then repeat this cycle four times more and rest. Then reverse the cycle, breathing in counting "One and two and..." and out slowly for five breaths. Use the fractional breath in to start your day or whenever you need energy, and the fractional breath out to relax before meditation.

Watchpoints for breathing practice

Regular practice will calm the mind and raise your energy levels. As the lungs strengthen, their capacity will be increased. Practise little and often – a few rounds of the breathing exercises now and then throughout the day will prepare you for longer sessions during meditation practice.

- Avoid any breathing practices after meals – when your stomach is full it presses against your diaphragm, constricting your lungs.
- Keep your spine stretched and as straight as possible (allowing for its natural curves) whether you are standing, sitting, kneeling or lying down to practise breathing. This allows maximum lung expansion and helps the free flow of both air and energy.
- Keep your breastbone lifted to open your chest and give your diaphragm room to move freely. Keep it lifted even when breathing out, letting your diaphragm and rib muscles do all the work.
- Always breathe in through your nose, as it is the filter that protects your lungs from cold, dust and infections from outside. Breathe out through your nose unless you are making sounds.
- Develop your focus on, and conscious awareness of, your breathing patterns, so that you constantly monitor their effects upon you. Develop the habit of watching yourself breathing.
- Slow your breathing down – especially your breath out – whenever you feel agitated or anxious, in order to gain conscious control over your autonomic nervous system.
- Stop your breathing practice and rest for a few natural breaths the instant you feel breathless. Start again when your nervous system has settled down and relaxed. It is not used to being watched and controlled, as breathing is usually an unconscious process.

Alternate nostril breathing

This universally popular exercise quickly balances the nervous system, so that you feel calm and centred after just a few rounds – ready either for meditation practice or to get on with your day refreshed.

1 Sit erect with your left hand placed on your knee or in your lap. Raise your right hand to place it against your face. Your thumb will close your right nostril, your index and middle fingers will rest against your forehead at the brow chakra and your ring finger will close your left nostril.

2 Your eyes may be closed, or open and gazing softly ahead. Keep your eyeballs still, as quiet eyes induce a quiet mind. Close your right nostril with your thumb. Breathe in through the left nostril.

3 Release the right nostril and close the left with your ring finger. Breathe out slowly, and then in again, through your right nostril. Then open the left nostril, close the right and breathe out. This is one round. Do five rounds, breathe naturally to rest, then repeat a few times.

Choosing a Posture

Regular practice is the best teacher, as your body quickly gets used to the new routine and settles into it more and more easily. When you find a position that is comfortable for you, practise sitting in it until you can remain motionless, relaxed yet alert, for half an hour or more. It is helpful to vary your position when you sit at home, or to change purposefully from one position to another without disturbing your inner focus whenever your muscles begin to ache. This is much better than focusing on the complaints coming from your body when you push it to sit too long without moving.

above You may find it helpful to attend a meditation class, where you can be shown different ways to sit and try out the various props available before buying any of them for yourself.

Simple cross legs (Sukhasana)

This involves sitting erect with hips loose and knees wide. Each foot is tucked under the opposite thigh so that the weight of the legs rests on the feet rather than the knees. Place cushions under each thigh and/or under the buttocks if you feel pressure in the lower back. The tailbone (coccyx) should hang freely, letting the "sitting bones" take the weight of the trunk. Place your hands on your knees or rest them in your lap with palms facing up.

left If the hips are not sufficiently flexible for the knees to rest on the floor when sitting cross-legged, support them with a couple of cushions. Resting the hands palms up enables you to hold a mala, or rosary.

right This low chair, which folds for easy carrying, is specially designed for meditation. It supports the back when sitting in the cross-legged pose. The hands are in gyana mudra, with the tips of thumb and forefinger joined to complete the energy circuit.

Buddhist position

The Hero pose (Virasana) is sometimes used as a position for meditation. Buddhists often choose to sit on a very firm cushion that lifts the hips, with the knees resting on the floor on each side of the cushion and the shins and feet pointing back. Lifting the hips in this way helps to keep the spine correctly aligned, and this position can be very comfortable as long as your knees are fairly flexible.

left Using a "kneeling" chair helps to keep the spine straight and gives a good, well-supported position that is similar to the Buddhist kneeling pose.

right While sitting on a firm cushion in Virasana, the knees and feet can also be supported on a larger cushion. The meditator sits between the feet, rather than on the heels. The hands are in the gesture called bhairavi mudra, to focus the energy for meditation.

Early morning meditation

Many people like to meditate first thing every morning, while the mind is quiet and before the events of the day have a chance to distract it. If you meditate in bed, use a V-shaped pillow or ordinary pillows to support your back, so that you can sit erect in a cross-legged position. Wear a shawl round your shoulders and pull up the bedclothes so that you feel warm while you are doing your meditation practice. Choose a practice that energizes rather than relaxes you, such as chanting or repeating a mantra using a mala. You may prefer to keep your eyes open in a soft gaze.

right Your bed can be a haven of peace and warmth if you prefer to meditate on waking in the morning.

below A V-shaped pillow helps you to maintain an erect posture while meditating in bed. A mala, used for counting the repetitions of a mantra, is traditionally kept concealed in its special bag when not in use.

The Time, the Place

left Your "meditation corner" may contain a number of objects on which to focus: any object can act as a trigger to put you in the right frame of mind for your practice.

right A crescent-shaped "moon cushion" is often used as support when sitting for meditation.

It takes determination to establish a new habit and to make room in your life for a new regular activity. It helps if you train your mind to meditate routinely at a specific time and place. You may still be tempted sometimes to skip your meditation slot and do something else instead, but you will begin to feel uncomfortable when you miss your practice. There will be days when you have to forgo your normal routine, but that will be a conscious decision rather than simply forgetting or procrastinating.

Meditating at a regular time

It is helpful to place your meditation practice in the context of long-established habits – such as before showering in the morning, or after cleaning your teeth, or before lunch or supper. Since you do all these things daily you will meditate daily as well. A good time is when you wake up or before a meal – after meals people are apt to feel sleepy – or in the evening after a brisk walk or listening to soothing music. You might read an uplifting book in bed and then meditate before going to sleep. Choose a time when you are normally alone and undisturbed – the fuller your day, the more rewarding and de-stressing your meditation session can be. Couples often meditate together at a mutually convenient time, or get up early before the household is awake. Whatever time you choose, stick to it to establish your meditation habit.

Creating a meditation corner

If you always do your practice in the same place this will also help to establish your meditation habit. Choose a quiet and uncluttered space so that the moment you sit there your mind becomes calm and focused. Make sure you will be warm enough, as body temperature drops when you relax and turn inwards.

Your "meditation corner" might consist of a special chair in a peaceful part of your home, or perhaps you might sit on a

Meditation in bed

If you practise meditation in the early morning your bed (with a warm shawl around you and the covers pulled up) can become your "meditation corner". Have a wash, a drink and a good stretch to really wake you up first – and make sure you sit with your spine erect.

If you regularly meditate in bed in the morning, and this is the place where you are in the habit of turning your mind inwards, it can also be very soothing to perform simple meditation techniques before you go to sleep at night.

above When you wake up, have a relaxed, "releasing" stretch before starting your early morning meditation.

above Last thing at night, relax with your mala and repeat a mantra or simple prayer before you go peacefully to sleep.

above If you choose to meditate sitting on the floor, a low table is useful for holding objects on which you wish to focus your gaze.

favourite cushion, or spread out a lovely rug. The corner might contain a table holding a candle and flowers, or anything you find soothing and inspiring.

Objects of devotion

The things you keep in your meditation corner can be used for the classic technique called *tratak* – or "gazing". This involves sitting erect and motionless while focusing your gaze upon an object.

The point of focus is often a lighted candle. If you practise this form of meditation, check that there are no draughts to move the candle flame, as this can give you a headache. (Epileptics and migraine sufferers should avoid gazing at a flame.) After gazing softly, without staring, for a while, close your eyes and keep the image in your mind's eye. When it fades, gaze at the candle again and repeat the visualization. Your mental image will gradually become firmer and your concentration deeper.

You may like to light a candle before starting meditation practice and blow it out with a "thank you" as a final gesture. A flame is a universal symbol for the presence of the divine, and you may like to develop a greater awareness of this presence dwelling within you and surrounding you.

There are different forms of tratak. A flower can be held and turned around in the hand, as you observe every detail of its beauty and structure. Holding a crystal in your hands and feeling its contours and coolness is another form of tratak – in this case the eyes are closed throughout and the "gazing" is accomplished through the sense of touch. You could equally well choose to gaze at any object that inspires you.

Postural stretch

If you have been sitting all day in a car or at your desk, you may want to regain a strong upright posture before you start an evening meditation session. You could try standing with a weighty object on your head to strengthen the spinal column and improve your sense of balance. Previous generations learned "deportment" by walking around the room balancing piles of books on their heads, and porters the world over have strong straight backs, developed by carrying loads on their heads.

right Stretching your spine up against the weight of gravity makes your meditation pose "firm and comfortable", as Patanjali recommends.

Relaxing horizontal stretch

Stretching out on your back is the perfect preparation for meditation. Ten minutes lying stretched out on the floor on your back, with your mind gently but firmly focused on the movement of your breath while your body relaxes, is an instant restorative.

above Keep alert and warm while you relax on your back. Stretching in this position prepares you for keeping your spine erect – the spine should always be as straight as possible when meditating. While you lie on your back and relax your body, many meditation techniques can be used to keep your mind alert and focused, such as counting your breaths from one to ten and back again, visualizing energy moving through the spine, repeating a mantra, or visualizing a tranquil scene in the country or by the sea. After your relaxation take a few deep breaths, move your fingers and toes, stretch and yawn and sit up very slowly. You are now ready for meditation practice.

The Art of Visualization

Visualization is a technique that brings the senses into full play, and enables us to build up a happy inner world. Relaxed visualization is a tool used in many different types of therapies. Its aim is to help us change our perception of the world by changing the way we feel inside ourselves. It can be done lying down or reclining just as well as sitting in an upright meditation pose. This means that we can help ourselves to feel better when we are tired and depleted, or ill in bed, or needing to create a calm and relaxed state to prepare for a peaceful night's sleep.

Choosing an affirmation

You can use your relaxation time for your own greatest long-term benefit by using affirmations to create lasting change. The first step is to decide on an affirmation or resolve, known as a *sankalpa*, to repeat when you are in a state of deep relaxation.

You need to ask yourself what positive changes in your behaviour (life), perception (light) or attitude (love) would make you more like the person you would wish to be. The answer requires reflection and an honest appraisal of your personal qualities. Having decided on your sankalpa, you can set about creating a suitable visualization by using your imagination and all five senses to become fully present in a place of your choice where you feel naturally safe and relaxed. Once this scene is set you can go deeper and reinforce the changes in attitude, outlook and purpose that you have already decided to adopt. The unconscious mind is happy to respond to the suggestions put to it by the conscious mind, provided your nervous system is in a thoroughly relaxed and trusting state and that you express your intention in the following ways:

- Phrase your affirmation as clearly and as briefly as possible, with no "ifs" and "buts", descriptions or qualifiers.
- Mention just one change. When that change has occurred you can replace your sankalpa because it will have become redundant.
- Describe the change you wish for in the present tense, such as "I am...[happy, healthy, confident, successful at..., or forgiving of...]" or, "I am becoming more and more...day by day." The unconscious mind lives only in the present and ignores the past or future. Tomorrow never comes and is of no interest to it.
- Express your sankalpa in positive terms only, for the unconscious mind becomes confused by negative words such as "not" and "never".
- Avoid any words like "try" or "work at" or "difficult" because they immediately put the nervous system on guard and undo all the good relaxation you have achieved up to now
- Repeat your sankalpa three times slowly and decisively, so that your unconscious mind knows you mean business. In this way you are programming it to carry out your intentions all the time – even when the conscious mind is busy with other things. This is why the sankalpa has such a powerful effect.

above For relaxation adopt a comfortable position lying on your back with your knees raised and feet flat on the floor. A cushion under your head keeps your neck from contracting at the back.

below Once you are deeply relaxed, focus your imagination and all your senses on being present in the place you want to be.

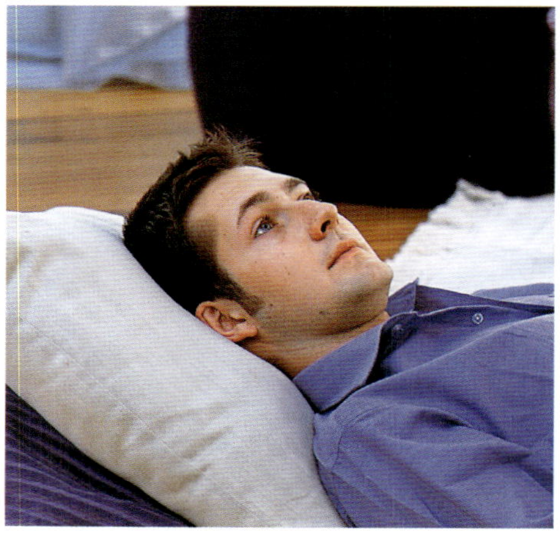

Creative imagining

It has been said that nothing can be imagined that we have not already experienced – either at first or second hand. We have an almost infinite variety of memories to choose from. Our life happens in our heads, so we should create as harmonious an inner world as we possibly can. There is no need to put up with a haphazard and chaotic inner world once you know how to change it. The choice is yours and meditation techniques are the tools.

VISUALIZING A BEACH SCENE

You have become deeply relaxed, perhaps after some stretching and deep breathing exercises. Sit or lie down in a comfortable position and start to imagine yourself reclining on a beautiful beach. You are lying on soft sand near the water's edge on a pleasant sunny day. Use all your senses to appreciate all the details of the scene, so that you experience it fully.

You can feel the texture and dampness of the sand beneath you, dig your toes into it and let it run through your fingers. Look at the scenery around you, the deep blue of the sea and sky, the pale sand, the distant horizon, a few fluffy white clouds, seagulls flying overhead. You can hear the seagulls calling, the wavelets lapping across the sand and the sound of a gentle breeze moving the leaves of the trees behind you. You can smell the salt air and taste it on your lips. What else can you feel, see and hear? Perhaps the air caressing your body, the intricate patterns of individual grains of sand and tiny shells, the sound of children laughing in the distance. Can you smell the sea, taste a half-eaten peach, feel the welcome coolness of the wind lifting your hair?

When you have built up all the details of this lovely scene, stay in it for a while feeling peaceful and contented, grateful and relaxed. The whole purpose of this visualization is to bring you to this inner place where you know that "all is well", now and always. Before you decide to leave the beach repeat your sankalpa (the affirmation or resolve you have already decided upon) slowly and clearly three times. Then gradually let the whole scene dissolve, knowing that it is always there for you to return to, no matter what is going on in the external world.

above The beauty, warmth and peace of a tropical beach make it pleasing to all the senses, so it is an ideal subject for a visualization to help you create your happy inner world.

right The more detailed your visualization the more completely you will be able to experience the scene. Taste and feel the coolness of an iced drink on a hot day.

left Feel the sand between your toes and visualize the soft sheen of seashells.

Meditation in Daily Life

Many people think of the meditative state as being rather "otherworldly", something that they can only achieve if they divorce themselves from daily life. Although regular meditation practice requires that you set time aside to turn the attention inwards, it can also be woven into daily life. You can turn mundane chores into a form of meditation by practising "mindfulness" – focusing all your thoughts on them; you can experience a sense of spiritual enlightenment from appreciating the beauty of everything around you; you can use meditative practices when trying to engage with and understand your emotions; and you can introduce meditative elements into the ways in which you relate to others.

right By focusing all your awareness on everyday activities such as eating, you can turn them into a form of meditation.

Key elements

There are many ways in which you can bring meditation into every aspect of your day-to-day life:

- Focus your mind and body entirely on what you are doing at this moment, letting distractions wash around you.
- Live in the present moment as much as you can.
- Try to perceive the beauty and worth in everything (and everyone) around you, and in everything you do, no matter how mundane the task.
- Learn to use your senses to the full.
- Develop self-awareness, and work with the interplay between your emotional and physical self – noticing how certain breathing practices and positions affect your mental state, for example.

Working with your feelings

The following traditional technique, based on experiencing "opposites", allows you to become impartially aware of your feelings (many of which are usually below consciousness):

- Relax deeply – sitting, reclining or lying on your back.
- Imagine various "pairs of opposites" and notice the physical sensations that arise.
- Start with pairs that have little or no positive/negative emotional associations – such as hot/cold, hard/soft, light/dark – and observe how you feel in your body while remaining deeply relaxed.
- Move on to a more emotionally challenging pair, starting with the positive side, and observe what feelings are evoked: birth/death, spacious/confined, happy/sad, delighted/angry and welcome/excluded are some examples.
- Still deeply relaxed, observe what feelings arise in your body as you contemplate the negative half of the pair – so that you can recognize and identify them from now on and understand what "pushes your buttons" and how you feel out of sorts when your emotions are negative. You can then take appropriate action to make you feel better and defuse tension in and around you.
- Repeat the positive half of the pair before moving on to the next pair of opposites.
- End with your sankalpa and some gentle deep breathing before coming out of relaxation with a grounding ritual.

Relating to others

This Buddhist "loving kindness" meditation helps you to relate better to those around you. Breathe in universal love and kindness to help and support yourself, then breathe it out, directing it to a specific person or group. Repeat this meditation often, until it becomes second nature both to receive and to give loving kindness. Make it part of your daily life: any part of it can be used in any situation to promote peace and harmony.

- Relax deeply in a seated position with your spine erect.
- Breathe in, drawing "loving kindness" from the universe into yourself.
- Breathe out, directing that loving kindness with gratitude towards a particular person, or to all those who have taught you (given you light in many ways). Breathe more loving kindness into yourself.
- Breathe out, directing loving kindness with gratitude towards a particular person or to all those who have nurtured and nourished you (given you life in many forms). Breathe in...
- Breathe out, directing loving kindness with blessings towards a person or people you love dearly. Breathe in...
- Breathe out, directing loving kindness with blessings towards acquaintances, neighbours, people you work with. Breathe in...
- Breathe out, directing loving kindness with forgiveness to people who annoy or obstruct you, who are unkind or dismissive. Breathe in...
- Breathe out, directing loving kindness with forgiveness to anyone who has ever hurt or injured you in any way. Breathe in...
- Breathe out, radiating the prayer, "May all people everywhere be happy." Breathe in and give thanks for all the loving kindness you receive. Pause before coming out of your meditation and grounding yourself with a ritual.

above The traditional Indian greeting "Namaste", spoken with a bow while bringing the hands together at the heart chakra, acknowledges the presence of the divine in the heart of each person, conveying the sense that everyone is part of the unity of creation.

How are you feeling?

As a way of linking the physical and non-physical, it is important to get into the habit of noticing consciously what your senses are telling your mind. This makes it much easier to monitor your emotions as they arise, because you can feel them through your senses. In fact, there is no other way to feel how you are "feeling". For every emotion there is a corresponding physical sensation: we "see red" when angry, our legs "turn to jelly" when we are frightened, sadness makes the heart "ache" or we are "in the dark" when confused.

Once you learn to recognize how you are actually feeling you can avoid reacting negatively to everyday situations. Whenever you notice a negative feeling arising, pause for an instant (the proverbial "counting to ten"), relax and visualize the positive, opposite feeling. You can then respond in a positive manner instead, bringing what you have learned through the regular practice of meditation into your daily life.

right Use the time you spend in the bath or shower each day to relax and enjoy the present moment.

left When you take a walk among plants and trees, focus your whole mind and all your senses on the experience, noticing the beauty of everything you pass along your path. Plants teach us how to "just be".

Meditating on: the OM Mantra

Patanjali begins his list of meditations with: "Complete surrender to the almighty Lord...who is expressed through the sound of the sacred syllable OM. It should be repeated and its essence realized." (From Alistair Shearer's translation of the *Sutras*.) OM, or Aum, is recognized in many cultures as the primordial sound, whose vibration brought the universe into being. Repetition of the OM mantra on a daily basis, chanted aloud, whispered or repeated silently, has a cumulative and profoundly beneficial effect.

When chanted aloud (intoned rather than sung), the OM sound – pronounced as in "home" – should be deep and full, with the vibrations resonating in the life chakras, then moving up into the chest and the love chakras, and finally closing with a long, humming "mmm" in the head and the light chakras – all on one deep steady note. Overtones may sometimes be heard. These are the faint sounds of the same note at higher octaves, as when groups of Buddhist monks chant in a deep resonant rumble, with the overtones wafting above like celestial choirs.

a–u–m

The syllable can also be divided into three sounds – A (the created beginning), U (the sustained now) and M (the dissolution of creation). This trinity corresponds to sat-chit-ananda. A is the beginning of life, time and forms; U is maintained through the relationships of cosmic love; M comes when we experience personally that all is spirit – and the rest is mental illusion.

above The Sanskrit symbol of the sacred syllable OM is often used as an object on which to focus. Place it on a low table so that you can concentrate your gaze on it during your meditation practice.

Chanting with a mala

The mala has 108 beads. It should always be held in the right hand and passed between thumb (representing universal consciousness) and middle finger (representing sattva guna). One bead is passed with each repetition of the mantra. Start from the larger bead (*sumeru*) and, when you come round to it again, do not cross it but turn the mala and go back for another round.

1 Sit in a meditation pose and settle your body and breathing.

2 Hold the mala in a comfortable position (traditional positions are near your heart or on your right knee).

3 As you breathe in chant OM silently. As you breathe out chant OM aloud (or silently), then move to the next bead on the mala and repeat 107 times. If your mind wanders bring it back gently to the mantra.

4 Sit for a few moments and feel the vibrations of the sound within you, before grounding yourself. The sensation of these vibrations creates a trigger for you – recalling them at other times will take you back instantly to the harmonious state you were in while chanting.

"This Self, beyond all words, is the syllable OM.
This syllable, though indivisible, consists of three letters – A–U–M
[representing three states of being]...The fourth [state], the Self,
is OM...the supreme good, the One without a second. Whosoever
knows OM, the self, becomes the Self."

Mandukya Upanishad

Chanting the mantra in a group meditation

This meditation is particularly effective when done in a group. Each person sounds his or her own note, all taking a breath in together (as indicated by the leader) and then chanting A, U, or M on the slow breath out. The meditation ends with everyone chanting OM on their own note and in their own rhythm, so that the sounds mingle together until a natural pause occurs. Silence follows until the meditation ends with a grounding ritual. The more people who join in the OM chanting the more powerful the effects become and the longer the subsequent silence is likely to continue.

1 Sit in a circle in a comfortable meditation pose with spine erect and sternum lifted. Place the hands in front of the body with palms facing the lower abdomen and fingertips just touching. Breathe in together and chant A (aah...) on a deep note on the breath out, to resonate in the life chakras in the abdomen. Repeat this sound at least twice more, to energize and remove blockages.

2 Move the hands up, with palms in front of the heart and fingertips just touching. Breathe in together and chant U (oooh...) on the breath out to resonate in the love chakras. Notice the different quality of the sound and the vibrations. Repeat twice more, feeling your own sound resonating within you.

3 Move the hands overhead, stretching up and out in a joyful expression of complete freedom, palms facing forwards. Look up (without compressing the neck) and breathe in together. Breathe out to chant M (mmm...) into the skull cavity and the light chakras, experiencing the sound within. Repeat twice more, then bring your hands down and remain silent. Finally chant OM, each in your own rhythm and pitch, until the group naturally falls silent. Sit in this silence for a while.

4 Finish by bringing hands and forehead to the floor in a gesture of grounding and complete surrender.

Dharma and Karma

OM is said to be the sound of creation, harmony and order. The eternal being expressed through the sound of OM is not the personal deity of any religion but the super-conscious organizing principle that sustains the divine order (*dharma*) by means of cause and effect (*karma*), and whose wisdom is available to all human beings as "the teacher of even the most ancient tradition of teachers".

right OM is the sound vibration that underlies every part of the universe, down to the smallest detail.

Meditating on: the chakras

left Most of us have a dominant type of chakra energy, and traditional correspondences can help to define the basic character of the chakras. Each of the four lower chakras corresponds to one of the four elements.

The chakras, which exist at the energy level, can be thought of as transformers that process the energy from all the koshas through our bodyminds into the physical world. The body, mind and emotions are all extensions of chakra function. Changes at one level will bring automatic changes at every other level.

The chakras are vortices of energy within our own being that we can become aware of for ourselves and then work with to balance and activate all levels of our being. We can gain a wealth of psychological insight by using meditation to explore the qualities traditionally attributed to each of the major chakras.

Awareness of the chakras

To gain true insight into yourself, you need to understand the current state of your own chakra system – and this means becoming aware of it. To help you do this, work through the series of three meditative breathing routines that follows. You should bring focused awareness and discrimination to your exploration, so that, whatever your meditation may reveal, you can remain an impartial observer and learn from the experience, rather than getting carried away by it – especially if emotional responses catch you unawares.

As you explore your chakras during the meditation, try to feel each one's individual brightness or dullness. All the chakras spin, giving off light, colour, sensation and sound, and it is by picking up these subjective phenomena that you can assess if or when a particular chakra is under- or overactive within the system as a whole.

"Balance comes when we can accept and get along with everyone without compromising what we believe in. The balancing of the chakras and the flowering of each one brings us to Patanjali's "state of unclouded truth" and heaven on earth."

Chakra Correspondences

Each of us has a mix of influences, but one particular influence is usually dominant. Like each sign of the astrological zodiac, each chakra is associated with an element, which can help us to recognize its basic character. The four lower chakras display the following characters:

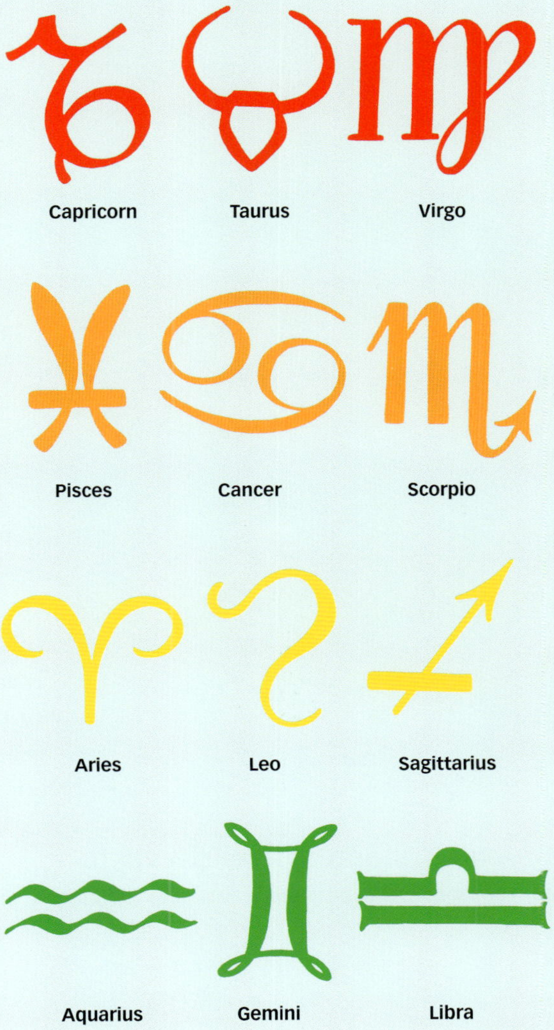

1 The base chakra (muladhara) corresponds with the element of Earth – as do the star signs of Capricorn, Taurus and Virgo. Their characteristics ensure survival, and among them are practicality, reliability, tenacity, logic, and a generally materialistic and no-nonsense approach to life. An Earth weakness can be a rigid and unimaginative outlook, unless it is tempered by other influences. If Earth is blocked we fail to ensure that we have the wherewithal to survive and if it is overactive we are obsessed with protecting ourselves by acquiring possessions.

2 The sacral chakra (svadisthana) corresponds to the element of Water – as do the signs of Pisces, Cancer, and Scorpio, whose characteristics ensure social bonding. Among them are empathy, enjoyment, sensuality, homemaking and caring for others. A Water weakness can be a tendency to tearfulness, emotional sensitivity and slipping into overindulgence to avoid facing facts. If Water is blocked we may become outcasts from society, upon whose acceptance our lives depend, and if it is overactive we may become addicted to substances, pleasures or people.

3 The navel chakra (manipura) corresponds to the element of Fire – as do the signs of Aries, Leo and Sagittarius, whose characteristics enable us to achieve personal success. They include warmth and friendliness, enthusiasm and zeal to inspire others to believe in themselves and their opinions. A Fire weakness is the tendency to burn out through overconfidence and ignoring obstacles. If Fire is blocked we lack the energy to plan or achieve anything and drift helplessly through life, and if it is overactive we develop inflated egos.

4 The heart chakra (anahata) corresponds to the element of Air – as do the signs of Aquarius, Gemini and Libra. Their main characteristic is to reach beyond the ego to other people, beauty and harmony, ideas and ideals. Air is a property shared by all, and Air signs understand that we are all interactive parts of a greater whole. An Air weakness is a tendency to be disorganized and unrealistic, though well-meaning. If Air is blocked we are imprisoned by our ego and if it is overactive we do not recognize boundaries.

Chakras 1–3 are the life chakras that combine to maintain physical life for the individual. Chakras 1–4 can be perceived as forming the base that supports the three "higher" elements: Ether (or communication), Mind (the organ of consciousness) and Spirit (the link with the whole).

1 Chakra awareness: "switching on the light"

First, settle yourself into a suitable position for meditation practice to promote a sattvic state. Awareness is a function of the brow (ajna) chakra, so this meditation begins by "switching on the light".

right A good "switching on" practice is tratak – focused gazing for a few moments upon an object such as a candle flame, flower or crystal. This balances the nervous system and focuses energy in the centre of the head to light up the mind. Alternatively, you could perform a short breathing practice, such as alternate nostril breathing.

continued over page ▷

2 chakra awareness: breathing up and down the spine

This sequence will make you sensitive to the energy pathway upon which the chakras are located, like roundabouts or junctions on the busy highway that lies within the spinal cord.

1 First breathe in and "drive" up the motorway from the tailbone to the top of the head.

right 2 Breathe out and drive back down again. Alternatively, you can imagine drawing light up on the breath in and letting it release back down on the breath out – like mercury rising and falling in a thermometer. You may like to feel the flow of breath with your hands as you practise this exercise.

3 chakra awareness: stopping at each chakra

You should really feel the quality of each major chakra as you practise the following meditation.

1 At the base of the spine breathe in and out of the base chakra. Energy is concentrated at this point on the breath in and radiates outward as it is released on the breath out. Repeat twice more before moving up to the next chakra point, the sacral. Again, breathe in to focus energy in the chakra and breathe out to allow it to radiate outward.

2 Continue up the spine with three breaths to activate each chakra point. After breathing into the crown chakra three times, pause and rest, letting its energies inspire and heal you, then start the downward journey, beginning with the crown chakra. After reaching and breathing in and out of the base chakra three times, pause and rest again – feeling the nurturing support and safe solidity of the physical plane upon which you live. The aim is to restore balance between the chakras by understanding and putting right what is causing imbalances.

3 Repeat the whole process once or twice more in a slow, relaxed and observant manner. Then come out of your meditation gently and ground yourself throroughly.

left 4 Once out of the meditation, you may like to record your experience to help you reinforce your increasing sensitivity to the different "feel" of each chakra.

chanting the chakra bija mantras

Once you have located your chakras and can breathe in and out of them easily, you may like to explore chanting to brighten them up or nourish them. Each chakra has its own sound (see box below). These are bija, or "seed" mantras, which have no literal meaning but are designed to plant the seed of a concept in the mind. They should each be chanted three times on a low, slow note that vibrates in tune with the chakra's own vibratory rate. The Sanskrit sound "AM" is soft – somewhere between "ham", "hum" and "harm".

right 1 Start at the base chakra and chant in each chakra all the way up. Pause after chanting in the crown chakra, then start again at the crown chakra and move down, pausing again after chanting into the base chakra.

2 Repeat the whole cycle twice more before coming out of the meditation. The bija mantras are represented by Sanskrit letters placed within a symbol that you may also like to visualize.

The Sounds of the Chakras

As you chant these sounds, think of the qualities of each chakra, expressed perfectly by their particular symbol.

- **LAM** for the **base chakra (muladhara),** placed within a **yellow square** (the compact quality of earth).

- **VAM** for the **sacral chakra (svadisthana),** placed within a **white crescent moon** (the moon governs the waters).

- **RAM** for the **navel chakra (manipura),** placed within a **red triangle pointing downward** (fire spreads upward and outward from a single point).

- **YAM** for the **heart chakra (anahata),** placed at the centre of **two interlaced triangles** (the colour varies, as does the colour of air, which joins heaven and earth together).

- **HAM** for the **throat chakra (vishuddhi),** placed within a **white circle** (ether or space pervades the entire universe).

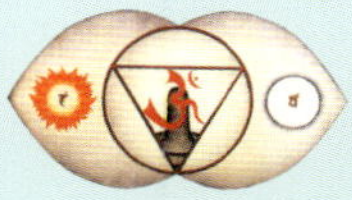

- **AUM** for the **brow chakra (ajna),** placed within a **grey or mauve circle between two petals.** This is the "command centre" where all opposites (the two petals) merge and are transcended through awareness and understanding.

- **OM** for the **crown chakra (sahasrara),** placed at the **centre of a sphere of light** radiating in all directions – spirit pervades all creation.

Societies and Useful Addresses

Australia

BKS Iyengar Yoga Association of Australia
PO Box 199
Bondi Junction
NSW 1355
www.iyengaryoga.asn.au

The Body Control Pilates Association
(for information on qualified Pilates instructors in Australia)
www.bodycontrol.co.uk

Umbrella organization for information about/classes in bodywork for pregnant women and new mothers:
Childbirth Education Association of Australia
PO Box 240
Sutherland
NSW 2232
Australia
tel. (02) 8539 7188
www.cea-nsw.com.au

Canada

Iyengar Yoga Association of Canada
www.iyengaryogacanada.com

For listings of yoga institutes in Canada:
www.yogadirectory.com
www.jivamuktiyoga.com

The Body Control Pilates Association
(for information on qualified Pilates instructors in Canada)
www.bodycontrol.co.uk

India

Ramamani Iyengar Memorial Yoga Institute (RIMYI)
(the home institute)
Mr Pandurang Rao, Secretary
1107 B/1 Hare Krishna Mandir Road
Shivaji Nagar
Pune 411 015
Maharashtra
tel. 91 202565 6134
www.bksiyengar.com

New Zealand

The BKS Iyengar Association of New Zealand (IYANZ)
PO Box 9278
Wellington
tel. 64 9 571 3110
fax 64 9 571 3101
www.iyengar-yoga.org.nz

Body Studio
2/141 Wellesley Street West
Victoria Square
Auckland
New Zealand

Pilates Natural Fitness Studio Ltd
1 Barrys Point Road
Takapuna
Auckland
tel. 64 9 489 1987
email info@pilates.co.nz
www.pilates.co.nz

South Africa

BKS Iyengar Yoga Institute of Southern Africa
PO Box 74
Main Street Post Office
Pearl 2193
tel. 27 021 863 2343
email ddeacon@worldonline.co.za
www.bksiyengar.co.za

For information on Pilates courses and teacher training in South Africa:
www.pilatessa.com
www.pilatesteachers.co.za

United Kingdom
Iyengar Yoga Institute
223a Randolph Avenue, Maida Vale
London W9 1NL
tel. 020 7624 3080
www.iyi.org.uk

Iyengar Yoga Association of the United Kingdom
www.iyengaryoga.org.uk
email admin@iyengaryoga.org.uk

Information on general yoga classes, with trained teachers:
The British Wheel of Yoga
25 Jermyn Street, Sleaford
Lincolnshire NG34 7RU
tel. (01529) 306 851
www.bwy.org.uk
email office@bwy.org.uk

Yoga classes and training courses for conception, pregnancy, birth and beyond:
Birthlight
7 Essex Close
Cambridge CB4 2DW
tel. (01223) 362288
email info@birthlight.com
www.birthlight.com

The Body Control Pilates Association
6 Langley Street
London
WC2H 9JA
tel. 020 7379 3734
fax 020 7379 7551
email info@bodycontrol.co.uk
www.bodycontrol.co.uk

Pilates Institute
3rd Floor
Wimborne House
151–155 New North Road
London
W1 6TA
tel. 020 7253 3177
www.pilates-institute.com

Danceworks (Jonathan Monks)
16 Balderton Street
London W1K 6TN
tel. 020 7629 6183
email info@danceworks.net
www.danceworks.co.uk

United States
For listings of yoga institutes in the US:
www.yogadirectory.com
www.jivamuktiyoga.com

Contact network for all kinds of pregnancy/childbirth information:
Midwifery Today, Inc.
PO Box 2672
Eugene
OR 97402-0223
tel. 541 344 7438
email:
inquiries@midwiferytoday.com
www.midwiferytoday.com

BKS Iyengar Yoga National Association of the United States
1576 Hilton Head Ct., #2288
El Cajon, CA 92019
tel. 800 889 9642
www.iynaus.org

Balanced Body (Pilates)
8220 Ferguson Avenue
Sacramento
CA 95828
tel. 916 388 2838
www.pilates.com

Acknowledgements

Authors' and Publisher's Acknowledgements

Iyengar Yoga (author Judy Smith)

The author: I would like to give heartfelt thanks to my guru, Mr Iyengar, who has not only been a wonderfully patient teacher, but who also constantly inspires his students to delve deeper into the art, practice and science of yoga. His knowledge, intuition, intelligence and humour have motivated thousands of yoga practitioners all over the world, and for this we are eternally grateful. I would also like to express my gratitude to Silvia Prescott and Penny Chaplin, my senior teachers, and to my husband, Rob, and my children, Matthew and Cassy, for their continual support and encouragement.

Pilates (author Emily Kelly)

The author: Without the help of my associates and dear friends, this book [*Commonsense Pilates*, published 2000) would never have been more than an idea. I would like to thank Michael King and Anoushka for being great teachers; Susan Newsom, Malcolm, Tiffany, Nikki, Saban, Jeanette Haslam, and Alex Fugello; and all my wonderful clients. I would also like to thank Valerie Foldvary who acted as an advisor on *Commonsense Pilates*.

Yoga-Pilates (author Jonathan Monks)

The author: Thank you to the space above my mat. Mum and Dad. Julia. Carly. Lesley. Friends, for without you the world seems hard work. Students and all those who continue to show me all that I'm too close to see. The publisher for this opportunity. Play well.

Yoga for Pregnancy and After (authors Françoise Barbira Freedman and Doriel Hall) and Meditation (author Doriel Hall)

Doriel Hall: I would like to thank all our marvellous models, to Alistair Shearer for his inspiring translation of *The Yoga Sutras of Patanjali*, and especial thanks to my colleague Françoise.

Extracts from *The Yoga Sutras of Patanjali* by Alistair Shearer published by Rider. Used by permission of the Random House Group Limited. For editions sold in the USA and Canada: Extracts appear from *The Yoga Sutras of Patanjali* by Patanjali, translated by Alistair Shearer, copyright © 1982 by Alistair Shearer. Used by permission of Bell Tower, a division of Random House, Inc.

Françoise Barbira Freedman: My thanks go first of all to the many yoga teachers and to all the Birthlight mothers who have helped me develop and refine the approach presented in this book over half a lifetime. Thanks to all those people who have supported me in making this yoga more accessible to mothers-to-be. Also to very dear Doriel Hall, with whom friendship has deepened through our collaboration as co-authors. My warmest thanks are to my whole family for their love and inspiration.

Yoga for Children (author Bel Gibbs)

The author and publishers would like to thank all the children who modelled for us and also Oilily and Adore Mail Order for lending us beautiful clothes for the photography.

Photographic Acknowledgements

All photographs are © Anness Publishing Ltd except for the following images: Gerry Clist and Michael Rabe: p19 (both). Gettyone Store: 151R, 215, 216L, 217T, 217B, 218BL, 224TR. Magnum: 149BL. Superstock Ltd: 216R, 218TR.

Index

A
abdomen
Abdomen Tuck 238–9
abdominal exercises 166–7
abdominal muscles 154–5
abdominal stretch 198
drawing in the abdominals 213
locating the transverse abdominis 155
postures 78–91, 94
aerobic exercise 215–21
affirmations 471, 496
alternate nostril breathing 491
animals
inspiration for yoga 400–1
poses 420–47
sounds 472
ankles 256
ankle circles 220
anxiety 118–19, 340
Ape Back 247
Ape Stance 237
arms
arm crosses 160
Arm Lift 249
arm sweeps 161
asanas *see* postures
Assembly Position 244
asthma 124–5, 475

B
back
Ape Back 247
backache 130–1
Basic Bend 250–1
basics 246
deep chest and back stretch 197
exercises 166–7, 474
imbalance 252–3
balanced postures 294–307
Batfink 320–1
bed, place for meditation 494
birthing 383
muscles 370
Blue Whale 432–3

Boat Pose 55
body 12, 19, 402, 254
breathing 18, 107, 152, 355, 406
alternate nostril 491
breath 407
Breathing 90–91
Humming Bee Breath 472
sighing breath 473
techniques 490–1
tummy 466
Bridge 316–17
Bunny hopping game 462
Butterfly 434–5
Butterfly Hinge 314–15

C
calories 222, 225
Camel Pose 88, 446–7
Candle 469
candle, meditation 484, 495
carbohydrates 222–3
cardiovascular programme 215–21
Cat, Dog, Snake and Mouse 415
Cat Pose 476
Catching Arms Behind 68
Chair 417
chakras 411, 488–9, 503
chanting 505
meditating on 502–5
chanting 466, 473, 484, 500–1
chakras 505
chest
deep chest and back stretch 197
stretch 196
Child's Pose 469
children and yoga 9, 395
animal poses 420–47
developing stamina and strength 454–5
dream time session 470–1
games 456–63
inventing postures 450–1
partner work 416–17
quiet time 464–69
suitability 396–7
Chilling Out 328–9
Cleaning the Floor 188
climbing stairs 212
Cobbler 314–15
Cobbler Pose 53
Cobra 424–5
colds 122–3
concentration 19, 153, 404–5
conception 354–5
constipation 128
Copy me game 458–9
core strength 8, 146, 154–5, 232–357
Corpse Pose 89, 470–1
Cow 444–5
Crescent Moon 455
Crocodile 430
Cross Bolsters 81
Crow 431

D
Dancer Pose 469
Dead Man Pose 89, 470–1
deep chest and back stretch 197
depression 121
dharana 19
dhyana 19
Diamond Curl 243

diarrhoea 129
diet 222–5
Dog Pose 85, 423
Dog Pose (head up) 86
Dog Split 270–1
Double Pigeon 318–19
Down Dog 256, 276–7
Downward Facing Dog 423
Dragon 452
Dragonfly 442–3
drawing the shoulder blades
down the spine 214
dream time session for
children 470–1
Drop the Chest and Feel the
Lift 248

E
Eagle Pose 44, 426–7
Earthing Sequence 340–1
Easy Pose Twist 64
Easy Twist 476
Elbow Lift 241
Elephant walk 453
energies 411, 488–9
Energizing Sequence 342–3
equipment 22–3
exercise, benefits of 403
exhaustion 114–15
Extended Lateral Angle
Pose 30–1
Extended Leg Raises 36
Extended Triangle
Pose 28–9

F
fat 223, 225
fatigue 114–15
feelings 499
experiencing "opposites" 498
feet
flat feet 255
Jimmy Choo 256, 257
walking through the feet 162
fibre 225
Fierce Pose 45
Figure of Eight 417
Finger to Toe Pose 43
Fish Pose 80, 428
Fish to Corpse 326–7
Flying Crow 298–9
Forward Bend 280–1
Forward Bend with Chair 476
Forward Bend with One Leg
Bent Back 58
Forward Extension 42
Forward Extension Legs
Wide Apart 41
Fountain, The 417
Frog 429
Full Forward Bend 59

G
games for children 458–9
Garland Pose 60
gazing 484, 495
gluteals stretch 197, 220
granthis 488–9
gurus 400–1

H
Half Boat Pose 56
Half Moon Pose 34–5
Half Plough Pose 76
Hamstring-stretching Poses 98
hand stretches 213
hatha yoga 400, 403, 483
Head of Cow Pose 52
Head to Knee Pose 57
headaches 116–17, 474
Hero Pose 49
Hero Pose Forward Bend 51
Hero Pose Twist 65
Hero Pose with Extended
Arms 50
hips 256
hip flexor stretch 198
hip flexors 242
imbalance 252
stiff 137
Humming Bee Breath 472
Hundred, The 170
hyperactivity 475

I
imbalance 150, 206–7, 252–4
indigestion 126–7
insomnia 120
Intense Side Chest Stretch 40
inverted postures 70–7, 94
Iyengar, B.K.S. 6, 12, 15, 16, 17,
20, 23, 110
Iyengar yoga 6, 7, 11
history and philosophy 16
introduction 12–13
see also postures

J
Jimmy Choo 256, 257
Jump 278–79

K
Karate Kid 302–3
knees 256
knee hinges 219
posture routines 106
problems 136
koshas 402, 486–7

L
labour 382–3
legs
Extended Leg Raises 36
Leg Pull Prone 174

Legs Stretched to 90 Degrees 83
Legs Up the Wall Pose 72
one leg circles 164
One Leg Kick 189
One Leg Stretch 172–3
Prone Leg Stretch 84
lifting a heavy object 212
Lion Pose 422
Little Buddha 469
Locust Pose 87, 440–1
Lotus 61
loving kindness meditation 485, 499
Lower Back Stretch 194
lower body exercises 178–8
Lunge 262–3

M
mala beads 466, 484, 485, 500
mantras 466, 473, 484, 500–1
meditation 9, 19, 405, 479
creating a meditation corner 494–5
in daily life 498–9
introduction 480–1
loving kindness 485, 499
practice and techniques 482–505
menopause 142–3
menstruation 71, 138–9
mental skills 474
migraine 116–17
mind 12, 14, 19, 404
mobility exercises 159, 163–5
Mountain Pose 26, 469
muscles 146, 150, 236, 402, 454
abdominal 154–5
birthing 370
muscular system 150
pelvic floor 157

N
natural world, influence of 400–1
neck
neck stretch 214
tension 134–5
nervousness 474
niyamas 18, 410
nutrition 222–5

O
OM mantra 473, 484, 500–1
one leg circles 164, 219
One Leg Kick 189
One Leg Stretch 172–3
One-legged Biceps Curl 300–1
Open V, The 186–7
origins of yoga 400–1

P
partner work for children 416–17
Party poppers game 463
Patanjali 9, 93, 404, 410, 483, 489, 490, 500
Peaceful Postures 468–9
pelvic floor muscles 157
Pert-buttocked Warrior 264–5
Pigeon 436–7
Pilates 6, 7–8, 145
benefits 150–1
exercises 158–221
history 149
introduction 146–8
key elements 152–3
programme 200–5
questions and answers 226–7
Plough Pose 76
post-natal yoga 384–93
posture 210–11, 212
faults 206–7
improvement 208–9
positions 492–3
postural stretch 495
postures 6, 7, 12, 18, 403
balanced 294–307
equipment 22–3
inverted 70–7, 94
practising 20–1
routine practice 92–109
seated 46–61, 94, 308–29
standing 24–45, 94, 258–81
supine and prone 78–91, 94
twists 62–9, 94, 99, 282–93, 476, 477
warm-up sequences 331–9
pranayama 18, 107, 406, 490
pratyahara 18
pregnancy, yoga for 8, 349–51
early 356–63
labour 382–3
late 374–81
mid-term 364–73
post-natal 384–93
Press Up 272–3
prolapsed uterus 140–1
Prone Leg Stretches 84
protein 222
Pubic Lift 245
Push Ups 180–1

Q
quiet time 464–9

R
Rainbow 416
Reclining Hero Pose 83
relaxation
dream time session for children 470–1

postures routines 98, 100, 103, 105, 107, 109
relaxation position 162
relaxing horizontal stretch 495
Relaxing Sequence 346–7
Reverse Triangle Pose 38
Revolved Lunge 286–7
Revolved Triangle 292–3
Revolving Lateral Angle Pose 39
Roaring Lion 422
Rocket Man 306–7
Rocking the Baby 414
Roll-up, The 169
Rolling Back 168
rolling down the spine 163

S
samadhi 19
Savasana 470–1, 477
sciatica 132–3
Seated Angle Pose 54
Seated Eagle 304–5
Seated Forward Bend 310–11
seated postures 46–61, 94, 308–29
routines 96–99, 100–2, 106, 108
Seated Twist 477
Seated Twist and Prayer 284–5
Seesaw 416
shoulders
Shoulder Balance in Chair 75
shoulder bridge 165
shoulder circles 161
Shoulder Stand 324, 475
Shoulder Stand Bridge Pose 77
tension 134–5
Side Bend, The 177
Side-kick, The 175
Side Lunge 266–7
Side-squeeze, The 176
side stretch 199
Side Triangle 288–9
sighing breath 473
Simple Cross Legs 48
Simple Twist 67
Simple Twist Using a Chair 66
sitting 211
Sitting Twist 69
Sleeping Snake 469
Snap and snack game 460
sore throat 474
soul 408
sounds 467, 472–3, 484, 500–1
spine
drawing the shoulder blades down the spine 214
imbalance 252–3
neutral 156
rolling down the spine 163
Spine Press 195
Spine Stretch 192
Spine Twist 193
standing balance 162
standing postures 24–45, 94, 258–81
routines 96–98, 101–8
Standing Twist 64
stomach ache 474
Stomach Curl 240
Strength Sequence 344–5
stress 19, 114, 118–19, 207, 340, 354, 481
stretches 190–9, 220–1, 418–19, 495
sugar 225
Sun Salutation 109
Sunshine Stretch 418–19
supine and prone postures 78–91, 94, 105, 108
Supine Cobbler Pose 82
Supported Shoulder Stand 73
Supported Shoulder Stand (against wall) 74
Swimming, The 171

T
Table 312–13
Table Top 416
therapeutic yoga 110–43
thighs
inner thigh lift 185
outer thigh blaster 185
Thigh Lunge 268–9
thinking, levels of 404–5
Tortoise 322–23, 438–9
touch 466
tratak 484, 495
Tree Pose 27
Triangle 290–1, 455
Triangle Forward Bend 296–7
Tricep Dips 184
Tricep Push Ups 182–3
tummy breathing 466
twisted postures 62–9, 94, 99, 282–93, 476, 477
routines 99, 102, 104

U
Up Dog 274–75
upper body exercises 178–88

V
visualization 485, 496–7

W
waist lifts 199
walking through the feet 162
warming up exercises 158–62, 331–9, 412–15
Warrior Pose I 33
Warrior Pose II 32
Warrior Pose III 37
Washing Windows 417
weight loss 224–5, 226
Wheel 455, 474
Wise man walk game 461
Woodchopper 454
wrist circles 213

Y
yamas 18, 410
yoga-Pilates 6, 8, 229
introduction 230–1
see also postures
Yoga Sutras 9, 18–19